Announcing for Broadcasting and the Internet

Announcing for Broadcasting and the Internet is the standard text for traditional broadcasters and emerging pioneers. While many still pursue careers in traditional fields such as television and radio news announcing, broadcast performance has expanded to Internet radio, podcasting, home voice-over production, and performance on YouTube and other Internet video venues.

This text is an update of the classic text *Announcing*. The practical guide to mastering the techniques and mechanics of broadcast announcing remains, updated to give readers the ability to produce their own portfolio of performance products and get started in the career they want. It covers audio and video editing programs, new streaming media, and how to develop a powerful, consistent, and noteworthy speaking voice.

Carl Hausman is professor of journalism at Rowan University and has worked in television, radio, and new media. Hausman was one of the team of faculty who developed the university's New Media minor and has developed the department's online course presence. He is currently producing and narrating audiobooks from his home in suburban New Jersey.

Philip Benoit is retired from a career in higher education, most recently as an adjunct professor of journalism at Millersville University. He, too, is an audiobook narrator, and has developed an extensive array of online video instruction.

Fritz Messere is Founding Dean of the School of Communication, Media and the Arts at the State University of New York at Oswego. He is an expert technologist who has also written extensively on the broadcast industry.

Announcing for Broadcasting and the Internet

The Modern Guide to Performing in the Electronic Media

Carl Hausman
Philip Benoit
Fritz Messere

Routledge
Taylor & Francis Group

NEW YORK AND LONDON

First edition published 2019
by Routledge
52 Vanderbilt Avenue, New York, NY 10017

and by Routledge
2 Park Square, Milton Park, Abingdon, Oxon, OX14 4RN

Routledge is an imprint of the Taylor & Francis Group, an informa business

© 2019 Taylor & Francis

The right of Carl Hausman, Philip Benoit, and Fritz Messere to
be identified as authors of this work has been asserted by them in
accordance with sections 77 and 78 of the Copyright, Designs and
Patents Act 1988.

Library of Congress Cataloging-in-Publication Data
A catalog record has been requested for this book

ISBN: 9781138294493 (hbk)
ISBN: 9781138294516 (pbk)
ISBN: 9781315231464 (ebk)

Typeset in Sabon and Helvetica
by Apex CoVantage, LLC

Contents

Foreword by Al Roker

I just may have the best job ever. As the weatherman for NBC's *Today Show* I tell millions of people what the weather will be like each morning, but in my job I've been able to travel all over, meet people from every part of the United States, cover news events near and far, interview interesting people and lead the Macy's Thanksgiving Day Parade. Every day I feel lucky.

What other profession could allow me to do so many different interesting things?

But while announcing is incredibly rewarding and endlessly fascinating, it is also tremendous demanding work. When you're doing live television you need to be able to think on your feet, be ready for last minute changes and the unexpected. Sometimes you need to ask the right question to get the person to open up and talk. Don't let anyone tell you that announcing is a walk in the park. It may look like that on LIVE television, but it is challenging work.

If you want to join in this exciting work, this book, now in its sixth edition and updated to reflect the realities of announcing for broadcast and the Internet, can help you as you learn the ropes. The authors— all experienced communicators—have put together a text that combines a real-world view of the media business today with proven insights into effective communicating.

You'll find a good mix of practical instruction and many thoughtful pieces designed to get you thinking critically about the process of conveying your message to your audience. Whether you're informing about the current political scene or entertaining on the local morning show, this book can help you. As they say in the business, "Practice. Practice. Practice." With help from this book and a lot of hard work, you can go far.

FIGURE 0.1 Al Roker

Preface

While this may seem odd, we'd like to start this book on an historical note.

One of the authors of this book, Carl Hausman, at the very beginning of his career worked with a much older man who was near the end of his career.

The older man, at the beginning of *his* career, had been involved in the earliest days of television, and worked with Edward R. Murrow on some of his earliest TV broadcasts.

Just a couple of years ago, Hausman remarked to the journalist, who was then quite elderly and near death, that he envied how lucky the old man had been to work in the pioneering era of electronic media.

The old man said that was silly. Today, he said, is the most exciting period in the history of media.

Why? Because today a performer has the option of reaching millions of viewers on his or her own terms. You can, of course, still follow the traditional route and work for a TV station, but you can also have a TV station in your home with audience reach and technical capabilities far surpassing anything even conceivable in the early days of broadcasting.

It is in this spirit that we look forward to sharing with you this latest edition of a book that got its start in the 1980s.

We cover what, for lack of a better term, we might call the traditional aspects of announcing, but devote about half the book to the new media frontier: Internet video, podcasting, home-based narration, and the ability for the modern performer to synthesize inexpensive (or in some cases free) media technologies to create a constellation of personal media . . . sort of an individual media empire.

Please take a moment and scan the table of contents and you'll see how this work covers everything you'll need to know to perform on both traditional and non-traditional media (and the considerable overlap among them).

Along the way, you'll learn about the history of announcing, the techniques of communicating a message, the ethics involved, the methods of news announcing, strategies for interviewing for news or a talk show, skills for acting on camera, how to be an independent performer in the new media marketplace, and how to market yourself to employers and audiences.

We know you'll agree with us that this is, indeed, the most exciting of all eras in which to be a broadcast and Internet communicator.

The Communicator in Modern Media

Power and magic attend the electronic media. The mystique was there from the earliest days of broadcast history. Radio waves *could* be explained by science, but people were still fascinated by the idea that voices and music could somehow crystallize out of thin air. A cat whisker moving over a quartz crystal attached to primitive earphones could bring the distant sounds of concert music into the most remote prairie cabin. The simple "crystal set" quickly became a common feature in American homes and a popular pastime for families and individuals to don headsets while they used their imaginations to picture the events they were hearing (see Figure 1.1).

As radio developed and flourished, it became possible for virtually the entire nation to participate—in a weekly drama program, a comedy or variety show, a vivid description of a news event—at exactly the same moment.

Never before had it been possible for the attention of such vast numbers of people to be focused on the same thing at the same time.

THE POWER OF MEDIA

The power of this phenomenon was dramatically demonstrated by the famous Mercury Theater presentation of *War of the Worlds* on October 30, 1938. This dramatized invasion of "Martians" was mistaken for a real news event by millions of frightened listeners. Many people fled in panic from the supposed site of the invasion in New Jersey.

Only a short time later, a young journalist named Edward R. Murrow focused attention on ominous events across the sea (see Figure 1.2).

Murrow's broadcasts from London during World War II brought the sounds of war to millions of Americans. These sounds created deep empathy with the plight of Londoners who lived with the constant threat of destruction as Nazi bombs fell on them night after night.

Video gave us instant access to news events. Live television pictures of the events surrounding the assassination of popular young President John F. Kennedy preceded the shooting of his alleged assassin on live television (see Figures 1.3 and 1.4).

TV coverage let millions of viewers watch as Neil Armstrong made the first human footprint on the moon's dusty surface (see Figure 1.5).

In 1989, dramatic live coverage showed people toppling the Berlin Wall, ending Soviet control of East Germany and challenging it in Eastern Europe. As the attacks on the World Trade Center brought the nation to a standstill, we watched, transfixed in horror by the devastation and human tragedy. For three days, all the major television networks cleared their schedules to provide live coverage of the unfolding events. Since 2000, television and cable networks have given us unprecedented coverage of the ongoing conflict in the Middle East, the rise of ISIS, and the terrorist attacks in Paris, London and elsewhere.

FIGURE 1.1 Console radios like this were common in living rooms in the 1930s and 1940s.

FIGURE 1.2 Pioneering broadcast news reporter Edward R. Murrow.

FIGURE 1.3 The assassination of President Kennedy took place when the afternoon editions of newspapers were already out, so television became the most important medium of the day.

FIGURE 1.4 Television coverage galvanized the nation again as presumed assassin Lee Harvey Oswald was shot to death—live on one television network.

FIGURE 1.5 People around the world gathered in front of their televisions for an historic moment.

The list of events is long. (See Box 1.1.) Nearly everyone can relate personal experiences that were made dramatic and memorable by broadcasting's power.

BOX 1.1 **The Medium is the Message**

The mid-to-late 1990s saw a classic example of what Marshall McLuhan meant by "the medium is the message." Increasingly, television became a live medium, and the on-air performer emerged as an increasingly powerful voice.

What do we mean by "the medium is the message"? The broadcast media became a part of the live, unfolding stories. The trend was firmly established in 1991 when new technology enabled live coverage of the Gulf War, a conflict that played out almost like a video game.

Then came the O. J. Simpson chase and trial (see Figure 1.6), magnetizing the live TV audience with hour after hour of coverage of the investigation and trial. The *coverage* of the case became a story as big as the case itself.

The invention of the smartphone in 2007 helped to revolutionize news coverage as citizens began sharing video clips or live footage of news events. The terrifying power of nature has been dramatically captured as weather-related events are shared by bystanders. Heart-warming acts of kindness and the brutality of some police events have been vividly illustrated as personal videos were picked up for network coverage. Importantly, we need to point out that news reporters and anchors provide narration and context for these images.

Through the early years of the 21st century there has been considerable controversy involving coverage of civil unrest and the role of news media in politics. Charges of "fake news" have been leveled by critics from all points of the political spectrum.

The point? When the medium becomes the message, the obligations of the messenger become more onerous. The broadcast communicator—whose reach is now extended to the

BOX 1.1 *(continued)*

FIGURE 1.6 The trial of O.J. Simpson established the format of legal-discussion shows; after the trial ended, many shows kept the same basic thrust, and in this way, the medium truly became the message.

Web and mobile apps—must balance a sense of the newsworthy, the fair, and the ethical. And this principle applies to all communicators who reach the public in this increasingly media saturated society, not just to newspeople.

Gone today is the "romance" that once stirred the imaginations of people huddled over crystal sets, plucking distant sounds from the "ether." We now take for granted our ability to tune into events anywhere in the world and at any time.

But broadcasting is an even larger part of our daily lives than anyone could have imagined in its earliest days. Media has become our eyes and ears on the world and, with the growth of portable tablets and smartphones, people can access information from anywhere. We stay in touch as we drive, jog, and vacation. Cut off from this link with events, we feel deprived.

According to a 2016 Nielsen study, Americans spend ten hours a day with media,[1] and given the influence of different media on our lives, it's remarkable to realize how recent these developments are. And we do not yet fully understand how these developments have shrunk our globe and changed our prospects.

AN HISTORICAL OVERVIEW

The discovery of electromagnetic waves by 19th-century German physicist Heinrich Hertz forms the basis of radio and television broadcasting. But a number of experimenters turned theory into practice. Guglielmo Marconi perfected the device that would allow radio waves to be put to such use. The Italian inventor and businessman refined the technology, acquired patents, and set up an organizational structure to explore commercial applications for electromagnetic waves. Marconi's development of radio communication in the early 1900s removed the need for wires in telegraphy. So the term *'wireless'* was applied.

One outgrowth of Marconi's work was the development of ship-to-shore communication.

When the ocean liner *Titanic* sank in the Atlantic in 1912, the ship-to-shore wireless allowed the American public to read in their newspapers about the rescue efforts shortly after they occurred. A young wireless operator, David Sarnoff, sat for long hours at his telegraph key and relayed information from rescue ships to eager newspaper reporters. Several years later, Sarnoff predicted that radio would become a "music box" that would bring quality entertainment to people far from cultural centers.

Lee De Forest's invention of the Audion tube, which allowed radio to go beyond its role as a wireless telegraph opened the way for putting voice on radio. Marconi showed us how to impose on radio waves the simple on-off changes necessary to transmit the dots and dashes of telegraphy, but enabling the medium to carry and then reproduce voice and music was much more complex. De Forest's work made the breakthrough.

Extensive application of De Forest's invention began in the era immediately after World War I. The Roaring Twenties were on the horizon. The "jazz age" was dawning, and while many radio sets were the playthings of technically skilled tinkerers in the early 1920s, full radio sets were being manufactured for the home on a large scale by the end of the decade.

Soon nearly every family could tune in to the sounds of this exciting era. Schedules in those days were hit or miss, and programs always originated from a studio. Broadcasters took their roles seriously, and performers commonly wore formal clothes when appearing before the microphone. Guest performers were brought in to fill up the broadcast hours.

All programs were live. So that performers would not be intimidated by the technology, studios were usually richly furnished to look like sitting rooms.

The microphones were often concealed among large houseplants; thus, the term "potted palm era" became a slang designation for this period.

These years gave birth to commercial radio. "Leasing" a radio station's airtime for delivery of a commercial message first took place in New York.

While radio was developing, networks also evolved as distinct entities.

By connecting stations and broadcasting the same programs simultaneously, networks could offer high-quality programming on a regular basis. From the stations' standpoint, networks were needed to fill the long program hours that so quickly drained the resources of local operations.

Networks soon dominated radio programming. The first network, NBC, was developed in 1926 and evolved into two separate arms, known as the Red and Blue networks. Years later NBC Blue split from NBC and became ABC.

CBS started in 1928. The networks occupied much of the attention of the US radio listening audience for many years.

As radio developed through the 1930s and 1940s, its promise as a commercial medium ripened. Early advertising in radio used such devices as naming a performing group after the sponsor's product. Every time an announcer introduced the Cliquot Club Eskimos, the sponsor was mentioned. Trying to capture the male audience Gillette razors began sponsoring sporting events.

This soft-sell tactic was much favored over the less-dignified direct product pitch. But there were sometimes gross advertising excesses. Bizarre items such as Dr. Brinkley's Famous Goat Gland Medicine and other products were extolled in terms reminiscent of snake oil pitches.

Since then, advertising has dominated the broadcast media. Advertisers associated with stars, and products became known through catchy musical jingles. During radio's heyday in the 1940s and early 1950s, the distinction between program production and advertising blurred. Advertising agencies actually *produced* much of the programming, which was then delivered through the facilities of the stations.

And advertising developed the one type of program most closely associated with this era of radio broadcasting—the soap opera still bears the name of its advertising connection. Soap operas efficiently solved a major problem confronting the broadcast media, namely, the need to fill hour after hour of program schedules with entertainment that would attract daytime audiences. The soap opera let writers work with a basic formula for establishing and developing a daily situation. All that was required was to introduce plot changes in the lives of the characters and to write dialogue that told the story. The extraordinary audience appeal of these imaginary everyday people made the soap opera a staple that then expanded to daytime.

Radio programs of the 1930s and 1940s consisted of the various program types that we see today in modern television. Radio plays (Figure 1.7) were popular, with sound effects specialists adding an aural texture that created a fabric of believability.

Comedies like *My Friend Irma*, dramas like *Lights Out* and *The Goldbergs*, crime stories like *Dragnet* and westerns like *Gunsmoke* made up much of the evening programming schedules of the major radio networks.

Many of the most popular programs were sponsored by a single advertiser whose product became associated with the program. Many of the top radio programs were produced by the advertising agencies that handled the advertising of the sponsors. In some instances, the networks had little control over the programming they supplied to their affiliated stations.

The close association of advertiser and program production and the lack of supervision by broadcasters led to a crisis in the 1950s. The public found out that sponsors, producers, and agencies rigged some highly popular TV quiz programs to inject more drama and excitement into the shows. When the quiz scandal was uncovered, the advertising community lost much of its control over the programming function of broadcasting. And the broadcast industry became more involved in the content of its programs.

Radio journalism initially met resistance from newspapers. Publishers feared that if people could listen to news on radio, they would stop buying newspapers. Although that situation never developed, radio news had great impact in the uneasy days before and during World War II. The ability to transport the listener to the scene of an event and to hear the voices of newsmakers "shrank" the globe and led to a growing awareness that *nations cannot live in isolation from one another.* This revolution in thinking led to the development of the modern broadcast media.

FIGURE 1.7 A rehearsal of live radio play being broadcast at NBC Studios, New York.

The First Announcers

The people who filled the airwaves with their talents created a tradition in early broadcasting. They developed a specialty that had roots in show business.

The announcer was part salesperson, part master of ceremony, part sophisticated worldly interpreter. Early radio announcers performed a wide variety of tasks. The announcer had to read commercial and news copy, pronounce foreign names, be conversant with classical music, and be knowledgeable about current performers and musical trends.

The announcer was expected to be witty and sophisticated, and was perceived as performing, rather than talking, when on the air. By the mid-1930s, radio broadcasting had become the era of the golden-voiced announcer. A deep male voice was considered essential for success in radio.

Delivery was stylized and emphatic. Announcers used a distinctive and instantly recognized style of speaking *that was heard nowhere else but on radio*. Anyone who talked like an announcer in normal conversation would have been considered strange, to say the least. Yet this style was expected and demanded on the air. This occurred partly because it was thought that radio announcers were guests in your home and needed to show both the manners and decorum of a guest.

How the Modern Media Evolved

By the end of World War II, broadcasting had begun to change dramatically. The emergence of television led directly to developments that characterize contemporary broadcasting.

Television, which became a major force in the early 1950s, turned out to be much more than radio with pictures. Television revolutionized the lives of Americans everywhere. Radio engaged our imaginations and provided stimulus for the theater of the mind, but television allowed us to react with less involvement. Sporting matches and crime dramas were much more vivid on television.

TV filled empty hours effortlessly. By merely turning a knob, one could be in direct visual contact with arresting activity that occupies the senses. Television spread rapidly and quickly captured the US psyche. And what about radio?

Many observers felt the radio was on its deathbed. They argued that sound alone could not compete with sound and pictures. Those successful program forms that had been the bread and butter of network radio were being usurped by television. Many successful radio stars moved their programs directly to television.

A new application of Sarnoff's music box theory emerged.

By specializing in the new popularity of recorded music, and by making this music available to the public day and night, local radio emerged as a healthy new entity even as network radio faded. At the same time, radio news evolved into a short format. News was given in brief doses at frequent intervals so that listeners could tune in and quickly hear about developments. With the newly developed transistor radio, the public found that radio could go anywhere, and the medium became a constant companion, particularly for teens, keeping the listener company while driving, picnicking, or studying.

As radio flexed its muscles in this new role, it learned to appeal to advertisers more effectively by targeting specific audience segments. The music selected for programming could attract one segment of the mass audience; then advertisers who wanted to reach this group with a specific message could easily do so.

Developments in Announcing

Announcers of this era began to break away from the stilted formality that had characterized the medium in the 1930s and 1940s. The disc jockeys of the 1950s took their lead from radio personalities like Cleveland's Alan Freed and Philadelphia's Dick Clark and New York's Cousin Brucie. The style was fast paced, often mixed with light-hearted quips. The DJ became one of the many elements making up a steady stream of sound that came to be widely known as top-40 radio.

The energy of the style captured the imaginations of American youth and became a focal point of a national youth culture. Rhythm and blues music merged with "hillbilly" music to form rock and roll. Performers like Elvis Presley, Jerry Lee Lewis and Chuck Berry created this new sound and developed new styles of performance that caused sensations at live concerts.

And the role of the radio announcer changed, too. The DJ became an architect of fun. It was his job (the field was very much male dominated) to inject energy. Rather than merely inform listeners about program elements, it became the announcer's task to fill the spaces between records with zany patter and a fast-paced delivery of time, temperature, and weather interspersed with information about the music and performers that dominated the airways of top-40 stations.

The more formal announcer-host remained a fixture of many stations until the early 1970s, but as the youth culture came to dominate broadcasting, the traditional announcer became rare. Today the sophisticated man-about-town style is found at just a few nostalgia sounding "Music of Your Life" stations.

The imprint of the early rock DJs has carried forward into the style heard on modern stations that program the contemporary hit radio (CHR) format.

Meanwhile, television became the mass entertainer, offering something to everyone. At both the local and national levels, news programming developed as an entertaining and moneymaking product appealing to a broad audience. Situation comedy, adventures, sports and other kinds of entertainment rivet vast audiences, and families today gather around an electronic hearth, which one astute social observer has termed "the cool fire."

CURRENT TRENDS

Today's technology is transforming media again. The abundance of dramatic shows offered by cable, satellite and new tech outlets provide an array of choices for any taste while sports plays 24 hours per day on several cable channels. In 2005, a small start-up called *YouTube* began by providing users with the ability to upload media. The service quickly took off and by 2010 *YouTube* claimed it was serving more than two billion videos per day, nearly double the audience of the major TV networks. Other new technologies spurred development of new social media sites, some of which reinforce modern broadcast and cable outlets while others, like Netflix, Hulu and others compete directly. And, while visual programming is vitally important it is easy to overlook very important media segments like podcasting, books-on-tape and other audio outlets where good announcing skills are critical.

It seems safe to predict that modern developments and technology will reinforce certain trends that have emerged:

1. *More program choices, and increased specialization of the programs themselves.* Business reporting, for example, has developed into a distinct specialty, and certain cable and broadcast outlets offer extensive segments devoted to it.
2. *Increased importance of one-to-one contact between announcer and audience, especially in today's segmented radio markets.* With this development comes the continued decline in the use of the stylized "announcer voice."
3. *The ongoing regulatory debate about the range of expression permissible on broadcast media.* The questions of what constitutes indecency and whether or not such regulatory agencies as the Federal Communications Commission (FCC) can establish standards that don't trample on constitutional guarantees of free expression can affect the program content of both radio and television. Today electronic media has two different standards. Broadcasting that pushes the limits of such expression is likely to experience continued pressure from the FCC while cable and mobile apps have many fewer restrictions.
4. *The ever-increasing importance of news, talk radio and cable commentary demonstrate a growing appetite for news and talk of all types.* Technological advances, including using smartphones for

connecting to live events and providing instantaneous commentary are making further inroads into on-the-spot news coverage, placing additional demands on announcers' ad-libbing skills. For example, during the ongoing conflicts in the Middle East, we see network correspondents use a variety of media from satellite picture phones to iPads with Skype to bring on-the-spot coverage.

5. *Consolidation in the media.* Group radio and television station owners have reduced the number of personnel needed to run several stations at once, often sharing resources among several media outlets in the same market. Automation and economies of scale make it possible to do more with fewer hands.

These and other trends have strongly affected all segments of the broadcast industry, but they relate specifically to the on-air performer in a number of ways.

Era of the Communicator

This book focuses on the communicator in the broadcast media. We use the term *announcer* because it remains in common usage and still serves in industry job descriptions. Eventually this outdated term will be replaced. A modern on-air performer does not simply announce. He or she entertains, converses, informs, and provides companionship, but rarely proclaims a program element in the formal, stylized way of the old-era announcer.

The Communicator's Role

Today's on-air broadcaster is a *communicator*, a catalyst for a message. Whether the message is news, commercial copy, an interview segment, or a game show, the communicator's task is to serve as a conduit for communication between the originator of the message and the audience.

Today the successful professional is one who can convey greater intimacy, the image of a real person rather than a disembodied voice or a talking head.

A program director of one major-market station, for example, wants air personalities to come across as "next-door neighbors." Another broadcast executive disdains the type of performer who speaks, as if from a pulpit, "to everyone out there in radio-land." One television news director specifies that staff members must show credibility and generate trust. But most news directors want personnel who show their humanity and concern for their community. Frequently air personalities may be seen doing the nightly news or weather during the week and hosting public service events in the community on weekends.

The communicator in the modern media must use more than good diction and appearance, although these qualities are undeniably important. He or she must also use qualities of personality and physical presence in the job.

In addition to being adept at conveying the facts, a news reporter must show that he or she understands the story and is a trustworthy source of news, while communicating the story in a way that holds audience attention.

While it is true that we can still hear the stylized, rhythmic affectations of the announcers of radio's golden age, these presentations are usually done for effect. Most producers of commercials today ask announcers to sound natural. That means that the delivery, as such, should not be noticeable. The ideas are the most important aspect, and the announcer's job is to *interpret* and *communicate* them, not *announce* them to all those people in radio-land.

On-air jobs today frequently call for specialized knowledge and skills.

In the 1930s and 1940s, the same radio announcer was sometimes expected to host an interview show, do a classical music program, deliver commercials, introduce various types of programs, and read the weather report.

Merely having a good voice and some knowledge of pronunciation is not enough to guarantee success today. Duties of a modern radio announcer do vary widely, especially in smaller stations, but the tasks are confined to a more focused area, such as a specialty in the music the station plays. Technology is creating new opportunities and challenges. In today's competitive media environment, radio and television on-air duties may be only part of the job. Frequently news anchors or station personalities may also host live talks on Facebook or spend time working on longer community pieces that provide meaningful local content to the community.

Jobs may overlap, especially in smaller stations where a radio staff announcer may double as a local TV weather anchor. As you advance in market size, your duties will generally become more specific. Primarily, though, most on-air jobs fall into seven basic categories (see Box 1.2).

BOX 1.2 What Kind of Broadcasting Job Do You Want?

Broadcasting has many different specialties, and you will probably find yourself doing one of these jobs:

1. Radio staff announcers, typically thought of as "disc jockeys" (DJs).
2. Radio or television news reporters: general-assignment reporters who file reports from the field, and anchors who deliver news from a studio.
3. Play-by-play sports announcers and sports commentators or anchors, in television and radio.
4. TV and radio weather reporters and anchors, who are now often certified meteorologists.
5. Talk-show hosts for radio and television.
6. Specialty announcers, such as commercial voice-over announcers.
7. Vocal talent for podcasts, blogs, corporate video and book narration.

Stations do not ordinarily hire announcers only to do commercials.

Instead, these duties are assigned to staff announcers or freelance announcers and actors or they are supplied by an advertising agency for the product. Other specialties include narrators and hosts of movie presentations.

Responsibilities and Ethics

A communicator has a great deal of responsibility, both to the employer and to the audience. Much has been made of broadcasting's potential to manipulate. In fact, during the 2016 presidential election candidates made frequent claims about news accuracy and balance. The term "fake news" continues to be bandied about by various politicians today. However, a variety of industry standards and government regulations address this issue.

Like professionals in most fields, the broadcaster must follow principles and standards that guard against misuse or abuse of the power and influence of the media. Considerations of accuracy, fairness, honesty, and integrity constantly apply to broadcast journalism, where they are paramount. While some cable news outlets have begun to mix news reporting with unsubstantiated commentary we generally perceive the broadcast journalism practitioners as responsible and honest. We discuss these considerations as they apply, throughout the book.

A CAREER SELF-APPRAISAL

Preparing for a career as an on-air performer begins with an honest appraisal of talents, qualities, and abilities. Strengths and weaknesses must be examined honestly; this is no time for rationalization and excuse making. Make a sincere effort to discover whether you have what is needed to succeed as a broadcast communicator.

Do You Have What It Takes?

It is no disgrace to decide early in life, after a candid look at yourself, that on-air work is not for you. A broadcast announcing course, if you are now enrolled in one, will be the first indicator. If your performance is excellent to outstanding, you stand a chance in this highly competitive field. Keep evaluating yourself as you work through the course and through this text.

Physical Requirements

Experience and critique will tell whether you have the physical tools necessary to succeed. For example, although a deep voice with "rounded tones" is no longer essential, and the field is open to women as well as to men, an announcer does need a certain amount of vocal strength and a versatile voice with a pleasing quality. Severe speech impediments, voice problems, or a pronounced foreign or regional accent must be evaluated realistically. If uncorrected or uncorrectable, they will limit your chances of success.

Poor appearance—to which obesity, bad teeth, and skin problems contribute—will certainly interfere with advancement in television. Overall poor health is a detriment on the air because the work is physically taxing and the hours demanding.

Educational Requirements

As soon as possible, evaluate your educational preparation. Most broadcasters who hire talent advise that it is important to be broadly educated. Some people who aspire to broadcasting careers make the mistake of concentrating on narrow, vocational courses. But to be an effective communicator, you need to be able to discuss and recognize concepts from a variety of disciplines. The news reporter who is ignorant of political science and history will sooner or later misunderstand a story element and blunder badly on air. An announcer who doesn't know how to pronounce and use words will often appear foolish. *Both these flaws will hinder careers,* as will any on-air betrayal of a lack of education.

Whether gained through formal training or through reading and life experience, education is the best tool for success in this industry.

Also, the ability to write well—an outgrowth of the total educational process—is essential for almost all broadcasters.

Emotional Requirements

Whether you are meeting a deadline for a news story or coming up with a funny ad-lib during a music program, you're sure to find stress in broadcasting. For one thing, your job will typically be performed before thousands of people, and that creates stress. Second, "time is money" in broadcasting. Tasks must be performed quickly and accurately to avoid retakes. Broadcasting is a constant race against the clock, and the clock never loses. An announcement slated for 5:59:30 p.m. must be made precisely at 5:59:30, and in most cases it had better be finished exactly at 6:00:00 because that is *precisely* when the news is fed from the network.

The ability to handle stress of this magnitude is critical because for some people stress problems can become emotionally crippling.

IS BROADCASTING FOR YOU?

It is also important to look honestly at the broadcast industry as a career field, a field that has been described variously as a golden path of opportunity and as a snake pit.

Nature of the Business

By its very nature, commercial broadcasting is a money-oriented industry. Depending on the level at which you work, you may be paid very well or very poorly. Job security is not particularly good in the industry in general, and it is especially poor for on-air performers in radio. Local television stations have tried to make sure their anchors participate in the community and they frequently become well known for hosting public service and charitable events. You should not be surprised to be expected to do more than the standard 40-hour week.

Except for noncommercial radio and television, ratings are money. (Ratings and market studies are also becoming increasingly important to public broadcasting programmers and fund-raisers.) As an on-air performer, you must produce ratings, and you will be looking for work if those ratings don't materialize.

To add to the problem, consider that the situation is not always fair: a performer with good on-air abilities may be poorly rated because of inept station programming or an unfavorable time slot. You may come to work one day and find that the station has been sold to new owners who plan a new format, or that the station has replaced live announcers with voice-tracking or that budget cuts have eliminated your job. We have talked with several young television newspeople who were ready to get out of broadcasting because of the uncertainty and insecurity of the field. One news producer had just been hired as part of a "new commitment to news" at a medium-market television station. Three weeks after leaving his former job in another part of the country, he was called in by his new employers and told that his job had been eliminated because of budget cuts.

Careers can take off quickly and rise steadily. You may also, however, find yourself waiting for that big break for years, traveling from station to station. Sometimes that big break comes. Sometimes it doesn't.

Benefits and Drawbacks

On the plus side of broadcasting as a career is the sense of importance and the degree of celebrity status that accrue even at lower levels of the business. It is also a job that gives a lot of personal satisfaction, a job that many people do for free.

In the highest levels of broadcasting, the money is excellent, and it is not uncommon to make a good living at the medium-market level. As large corporations increase their involvement in the broadcasting industry, fringe benefits and salaries have been improving at all levels. It is not as common as it once was for radio stations to be staffed entirely by those willing to work at minimum wage, but minimum salaries do exist in small markets nevertheless.

Many who make good salaries have climbed a vast and heartless pyramid. For every announcer in Boston or Chicago, hundreds or thousands of announcers work for poor salaries in small markets while waiting hungrily for an opportunity to move into the big time.

A REALISTIC EVALUATION

Any on-air person knows that there's no greater feeling of accomplishment than that generated by those good days, those magic moments. But there are lows for most of the highs. Hard work may or may not be rewarded. The excitement of the business may make every day a new challenge, but stress may take a serious toll.

So how do you make a choice? There is no pat answer, but we sincerely hope this book will help you decide. When you have finished the chapters and exercises, you should have a realistic picture of what is required and where your particular strengths and weaknesses lie.

If you decide to pursue the profession of on-air broadcasting and performance, you will be entering a field that offers tough standards but wonderful rewards. You, too, will feel the unparalleled excitement of participation in important and significant moments.

Connections

The Broadcaster and Social Sciences

An on-air performer wields a great deal of influence. In general, people take your word seriously and put great faith in information they receive from the media.

Almost every on-air person can tell a story about an off-hand remark, or one made in jest, that was taken literally by at least one listener or viewer.

Social scientists, researchers who study the behavior of people in societies, have only recently (in the last half-century or so) turned their attention to media effects. The reason for this is that media are relatively new additions to the society. But even though researchers cannot give highly specific formulae for how the media affect society, we know that media are enormously powerful.

An interesting sidelight is that one of the milestones of early communication research was undertaken precisely because a broadcast performer said something in a drama that people took seriously—with some disastrous effects.

Here's the story: On October 30, 1938, listeners who tuned in to CBS radio heard an announcer interrupt a music program with a bulletin: An unusual cloud of gas had been observed on the planet Mars (see Figure 1.8).

That was interesting, but not earthshaking, and the announcer returned the audience to the concert.

A little later, another bulletin interrupted the music, and the announcer implored observatories to watch the situation carefully.

FIGURE 1.8 Photo of Orson Welles, actors, and musicians rehearsing for a CBS dramatic broadcast.

Connections *(continued)*

More music . . . and more bulletins. A "meteorite" had landed in New Jersey. But reporters at the scene saw that it was no mere piece of stone.

The top opened up. As a radio newsman reported this, death rays suddenly cut down the observers standing by the impact site.

Martians marched from the spaceship. They devastated the US military sent to stop them. War machines sliced through the cities. Reporters were cut off in mid-sentence by death rays. At last, only the choked and quavering voice of an amateur radio operator remained on air.

"Isn't anybody there? . . . Isn't anybody . . ." As you certainly have surmised, that was fiction, a radio play based on an H. G. Wells story. But here is a true account of what happened next. You might find it stranger than fiction.

RADIO LISTENERS IN PANIC, TAKING WAR DRAMA AS FACT Many Flee Homes to Escape "Gas Raid From Mars"—Phone Calls Swamp Police

A wave of mass hysteria seized thousands of radio listeners throughout the nation between 8:15 and 9:30 o'clock last night when a broadcast of a dramatization of H. G. Wells's fantasy, *"The War of the Worlds,"* led thousands to believe that an interplanetary conflict had started with invading Martians spreading wide death and destruction in New Jersey and New York.

The broadcast, which disrupted households, interrupted religious services, created traffic jams and clogged communications systems, was made by Orson Welles, who as the radio character, "The Shadow," used to give "the creeps" to countless child listeners.

This time at least a score of adults required medical treatment for shock and hysteria.

—*The New York Times*
Monday, October 31, 1938

Why did people believe a radio play recounting, of all things, an invasion of Martians armed with death rays? One fundamental factor was that radio was a relatively new medium, and at the time it had been reliably bringing to a stunned United States reports about the advance of Hitler in Europe. Problems seemed much more distant and less immediate in the days before electronic mass communications. In 1938, the importation of the sounds of war into the living room was improbable, but nevertheless it was real.

So the Martian story came over an unfamiliar conveyance that had, up until this time, provided a quite reliable new view of events in Europe—which, in 1938, seemed about as far away as Mars.

But what truly puzzled observers was that many of the listeners who panicked ignored several explicit announcements by Orson Welles that this was, in fact, a prank and a work of fiction given on Halloween. Nor did they bother to check other radio stations to confirm the incident. What made the incident *particularly* troubling at the time is that the world was on the verge of war, and the power of the media to persuade was a topic heavy on the minds of those who viewed the success of Hitler's propaganda films.

So, why did this happen? What did it say about the effects of media on the populace?

We had been vaguely worried about the effects of media for a couple of decades, beginning shortly after the introduction of motion pictures.

There are many stories about moviegoers who were simply dumbfounded to see events unfold, bigger than life, before their eyes. It was widely reported that when motion pictures were first shown in a rural area, first-time moviegoers shrieked in panic and clambered out of the theater when a stampede of cinematic horses thundered toward them.

Connections *(continued)*

That story is probably apocryphal. And that is a perfect illustration of the need for communications research! First, we needed to know if such events really occurred and, secondly, whether motion pictures really could so profoundly affect people's grasp of reality.

Such investigation began in earnest in 1929, when a series of research efforts called the Payne Fund studies were undertaken. The Payne Fund studies attempted to gauge how powerful movies really were, and that research indicated movies had enormous power.

But there was a flaw in the Payne Fund studies. Investigators simply *asked* teenagers if movies had a powerful impact on their life, and the teenagers, possibly wanting to accommodate the researchers, said yes. In hindsight, we can laugh at such mistakes, but hindsight should also allow us to be a bit charitable in our evaluation of past efforts. Social science measurement techniques were then in their infancy, and the notion that *the way a question was asked could drastically influence the outcome of the response* was not yet clear to investigators.

The Payne Fund studies led researchers to believe that the power of movies figuratively pierced into the psyche of the person watching and listening. This notion became known as the "magic bullet" or the "hypodermic needle" theory of media effects. The "hypodermic needle" phraseology reflected the idea that a media manipulator could "inject" beliefs into unwilling subjects.

But do media really have such targeted and powerful effects? Would anyone be vulnerable to a magic bullet? Those questions were important for a number of reasons, not the least of which is that behavior of the masses—if the theories were true—could be manipulated by Svengali-like media-masters who would overtake the evolving media.

Communications scholar Hadley Cantril set to work studying media effects, to see if the magic bullet theory held true. His subject was not movies, but the Martian "invasion." The *War of the Worlds* radio play used the technique of a "newscaster" interrupting normal programming to report that strange gas clouds had been sighted on Mars. Later, the music was interrupted again to inform listeners that a strange craft had landed in Grovers Mill, New Jersey. (That was a quite a departure from the original British setting of H. G. Wells' story, but Orson Welles—no relation to H. G.—had been driving through New Jersey a day or two before the show and had randomly picked Grovers Mill from a road map.)

Even though there were frequent reminders that this was a dramatization—reminders that carried something of an urgent tone after panicked listeners started calling the radio station—many people still assumed that the events were real. Indeed, a fabric of believability was woven into the narrative; the "newscaster" would conduct a breathless interview with an "expert" and then return the program back to the network . . . only to return moments later, agitated, with reports of Martian war machines on the rampage.

Actually, the vast majority of listeners did not for one second believe that Martians were invading the earth. But why did some people see through the thinly disguised ruse while others disintegrated into a panic?

Cantril found that the *War of the Worlds* scare was a living laboratory for his studies of media effects. After extensive interviews and data collection he theorized that it was *level of education and critical thinking skills* by the audience that separated the believers from the nonbelievers.

Cantril would later theorize that those skills also enabled people to resist propaganda.

Cantril's studies refuted the magic bullet theory (the conclusion of the Payne Fund studies). Whereas earlier it was believed that media could be used to precisely target anyone, Cantril stated that the effects of media were weaker than first thought and that media manipulation was effective primarily on the unsophisticated and unintelligent.

Given that media affected some people some of the time, *how much* did it affect them and *how* did media go about insinuating these effects?

The next major study to examine media effects tackled precisely these questions. Called "The People's Choice," the study was conducted by a team of researchers led by Paul Lazarsfeld.

Connections *(continued)*

In 1940, Lazarsfeld's researchers studied voter behavior in Erie County, Pennsylvania. The goal was to determine how media affected the way people decided which candidate to vote for. Specifically, the researchers tracked *change* in voter preference over a six-month period.

The results:

- Political advertising converted only eight percent of voters from their original positions.
- The major effect of media appeared to be *reinforcing* beliefs originally held. In other words, advertising was more likely to get a committed voter *to believe more strongly* in his or her original choice than to *change his or her mind.* (This was before negative campaign ads.)
- In many cases, advertising did not have a direct effect. Instead, voters were influenced by opinion leaders—powerful people whom they respected—within their community. Media often worked *indirectly* by affecting opinion leaders who in turn affected other members of the community.

Lazarsfeld's study concluded that media had *minimal* effects, and that many of those effects were indirect and difficult to measure. Many scholars today continue to believe in the minimal effects theory.

However, later researchers reexamined strong media theories, and contended that media do have a strong influence, but it is difficult to measure. Most researchers today believe that the media have strong effects, sometimes indirect, and have woven themselves inextricably into our everyday lives.

The world of broadcasting, in fact, is a great succession of moments, like the ones Edward R. Murrow transmitted in the dark days of the Battle of Britain, and in the social drama reflected in television images of women reservists leaving husbands and children for military duty in the Middle East.

Those moments have been captured by a system of modern media that is stunning in its capabilities: we can be anywhere on the globe in an instant, and never be out of touch with entertainment, companionship, or news. With today's smartphones this is even more true since "everyone has a recorder" built into their phones.

Today, the study of media helps us understand the significance of broadcasting these events (see Connections: The Broadcaster and Social Sciences).

The nature of broadcasting, both large scale like ABC and small like a one-person micro station, continues to evolve. What was impossible technically just a few years ago is possible today. Radio and television stations use the Internet as an ancillary channel of information. Tech Talk provides some insight into what's happening.

Tech Talk

Web TV and Radio

In the last ten years we have experienced a revolution in the delivery of audio/video material via the Internet and on mobile devices. Today we frequently see people watching videos on smartphones while commuting to work on the subway or while they're relaxing in a park. Many car manufacturers offer high-speed connectivity in their vehicles so passengers can stay connected while travelling.

Tech Talk *(continued)*

A Look at Radio and TV via the Internet

During the last few years the fortunes of Internet radio have gone up and down. Several years ago, many radio stations started to rebroadcast their signals over the Web in anticipation of creating a new venue for listeners. Many people who worked in an office setting with a computer could now tune into their favorite radio stations while at work.

Royalties have provoked contentious arguments from musicians and Internet music services alike. In 2016, the Copyright Royalty Board voted to increase rates slightly and the new rates will remain until 2021. Services like iHeartRadio and Pandora have to pay higher royalties to play music.

Regardless of whether a station broadcasts its programs live on the Web, almost all radio and television stations maintain a strong media presence, usually on the Web and through a mobile app. Radio websites and Facebook pages have information relevant to their listeners, such as restaurant reviews, breaking news, and text features such as the current pop charts on their sites. Stations try to make these sites informational and fun to visit. Many colleges and public radio stations have successful Internet programming. Internet stations can run the gamut from local, live programming to national or international programming from the BBC or ESPN. Classical stations and alternative music stations are among the Internet services that offer a true alternative to commercial radio. Whether streaming services from Spotify and Apple will cut into Internet radio remains to be seen.

Television on the Web generally consists of sites that are affiliated with traditional TV/cable networks such as CBS's large site (www.cbs.com) or they may be "streamed" services such as YouTube or Netflix. Technological advances allow programs to be streamed in high definition and 4K resolution, with high-speed Internet connections. Hulu, Roku and others offer apps that viewers use to stream local and national broadcast services. These services, available on computers, on smart TVs and on mobile devices, are referred to as "Over-the-top" (OTT). Many viewers are switching away from expensive cable services and moving to streaming options from Hulu, Netflix and Amazon. Interestingly, many of these new services are providing original content, directly competing with traditional broadcast and cable networks.

Getting Started Online

First, you need to get online. Chances are you already have numerous apps and games on your phone, tablet, or computer. You probably have Instagram, Snapchat and Facebook accounts. You probably watch YouTube and may already listen to Pandora or iHeart Radio for music. The point is that you need to explore the different opportunities out there that are likely to use announcers and performers.

If you are a novice to the many web broadcasting opportunities, don't worry. Plenty of starting points are available to help you explore. Think about the apps that parallel the broadcast and cable world. Start looking for podcasts, Internet stations, YouTube channels and programming portals geared toward news, information and entertainment. Now look at the quality of the presenter. It is easy to find YouTube "how-to videos" with poor quality sound and lighting, but how did the performer do? Many professional sites are slick, but once again look at the performance aspect and judge the quality of the presenter. Learning what works and what does not will help you attain a critical eye as you start this journey. We'll deal with all of the aspects of presenting as we work through this text.

NOTE

1 Nielsen, Total Audience Report Q1 2016. http://www.nielsen.com/us/en/insights/reports/2016/the-total-audience-report-q1-2016.html. Accessed July 15, 2017.

Improving Your Speaking Voice

Most good broadcast voices are made, not born. True, many announcers have an extra share of native talent, but most of us learn effective vocal skills by practice.

This chapter lays a foundation on which you can build a clear, powerful, and professional-sounding speaking voice. After you have learned mechanics of posture, projection, and diction, you'll be able to practice those fundamentals not only during classroom sessions, but also lifelong, on the job.

These mechanics are important because a good-quality voice is an entry level qualification for almost any on-air position. In broadcasting, voice quality is one of the first points on which people judge you. In radio, it is just about the only one. Your voice is what you *are* to the listener. This text steers clear of the old "rounded tones and golden throat" approach to broadcasting, but having a pleasing voice is important.

Remember that the emphasis is on a *pleasing* voice, not necessarily a deep, booming, overpowering voice. Today, women are as likely to be announcers as men.

Talent coaches frequently point out that the most successful announcers are those who have learned, one way or another, to refine their speech patterns, often by removing offending regionalisms, and by learning to speak in a well-articulated style. It can take significant effort to overcome speech problems, and most successful anchors and reporters have worked hard to ensure that their speech is clearly understandable.

This chapter suggests ways to make the most of your voice, to use it as effectively as possible. We also discuss ways to eliminate problems that could disqualify you from on-air employment, such as diction problems, poor voice quality, a severe accent, and regionalism.

And we explain how to protect your voice from abuse by relaxing the mechanism. This technique also improves voice quality.

Voice instruction is worthwhile for anyone who speaks for a living, and it is of prime importance to an announcer. Often, voice and diction receive cursory treatment in broadcast performance courses. One reason, perhaps, is the feeling that the only way to deal with speech and voice problems is to get help from a professional therapist. And it's true. No broadcasting text could possibly cure stuttering or a severe speech impediment. For such disorders, consult a speech-language pathologist.

However, many problems broadcasters face are simply the result of bad habits, and this is where a full treatment of the subject can be beneficial. You *can* improve the quality of your voice by practicing some easy exercises. You *can* make your diction more crisp by acquiring an awareness of common problems and by practicing with an audio recorder or your smart phone. Many of the solutions are simple.

HOW YOUR VOICE WORKS

The vocal mechanism is a marvelous device and has certainly come a long way from the early days of human evolution, when the apparatus was primarily a sphincter that could be manipulated to form a grunt. We can still grunt, but we can also use the vocal apparatus to form an incredible range of sounds.

When you are working on exercises to develop your voice, it helps to know the structure you are using. For instance, tightness in the throat can be more easily overcome if you understand the musculature of the region. In **diaphragmatic breathing,** it's important to understand just where the diaphragm is and what it does.

You do not need to memorize all the structures of the breathing and vocal apparatus, so we show only the basics. For further information, investigate classes in basic speech production, almost certainly available in your institution.

This may come as a surprise but in addition to classes in normal speech production, you will benefit from exposure to singing instruction, even if you entertain no ambitions as a singer and have no talent for singing.

Vocal Anatomy

The mechanism that produces your voice is tied to your respiratory system (see Figure 2.1). This is important to know for a number of reasons, not least of which is the action of your diaphragm. Your lungs extract oxygen from the air, but they don't suck air in or propel it out. That function is performed primarily by your diaphragm, a muscle that extends across the base of your chest. It is connected by fibers and tendons to your sternum (breastbone) in front, to your ribs at the sides, and to your vertebrae in back. When you inhale, your diaphragm contracts, pushing your intestines down and out. That is why your abdomen should expand when you breathe in. When you exhale during speech, your diaphragm relaxes and is pushed upward by your abdominal muscles. Air in your chest cavity is compressed and forced out through your *trachea.*

The trachea is the airway leading from your chest to your *larynx.* The trachea is the point at which a number of airway tubes, including the bronchial tubes, are joined together. Bronchitis is an inflammation of the bronchial tubes; through experience with this common malady, most people are keenly aware of the location of the bronchial tubes. The larynx (see Figure 2.2a) is often called the "voice box." The larynx is

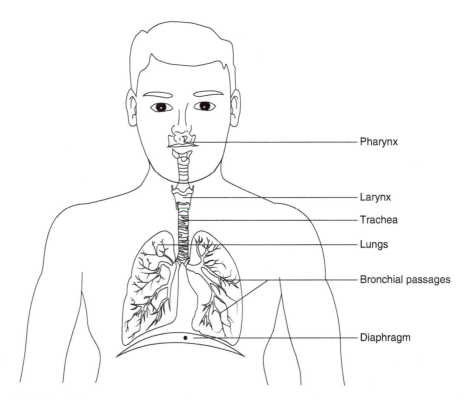

Pharynx

Larynx

Trachea

Lungs

Bronchial passages

Diaphragm

FIGURE 2.1 How you breathe.

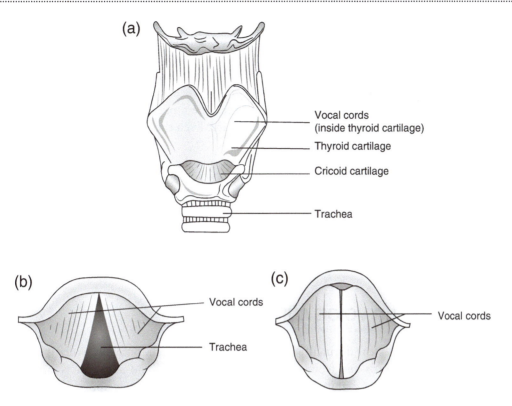

FIGURE 2.2 The larynx. (a) In this roughly tube-shaped structure, vocal cords are suspended across the tube. (b) Vocal cords open during quiet breathing. This is the view you would have looking directly down someone's throat. (c) Vocal cords closed during phonation.

cartilage, a tough, somewhat flexible and gristly material. Several different cartilages make up the larynx. The most important are the *thyroid* cartilage, which protrudes from the neck and forms what we call the "Adam's apple" (larger in men), and the *cricoid* cartilage, which connects to the thyroid cartilage. These cartilages form a roughly tubular structure in which the vocal cords are suspended.

The vocal cords—more properly called vocal folds, since they're not really cords—are membranes that come together across the cavity of the larynx. There are two folds, and during the process of producing voice, known as **phonation**, they stretch across the cavity. The easiest way to visualize the vocal cords is to see them as if you were looking down someone's throat, as shown in Figure 2.2b.

A number of muscles contribute to speech. The *intrinsic* muscles of the larynx are entirely contained within the larynx. The *extrinsic* muscles are outside the larynx and serve in speech, singing, and swallowing.

Above the larynx is the *pharynx,* the part of the vocal tract that exits into the mouth and the back of the nasal passages. Constricting muscles in the pharynx can close off the respiratory tract above the back of the throat. The pharynx connects with nasal passages above the back of the throat, the part of the throat you would see if you stuck out your tongue and looked in a mirror.

How Voice Is Produced

During normal breathing, the vocal cords are relaxed and are some distance apart, as pictured in Figure 2.2b. But during phonation, the folds meet and actually impede the flow of air through the larynx (see Figure 2.2c). Air escapes through the folds in short bursts only hundredths or thousandths of a second in duration. These bursts cause vibrations in the air. Combinations of tension and air pressure on the vocal cords produce various pitches and loudness.

Each small vibration is amplified to produce voice in the same way a brass instrument amplifies the sound from the mouthpiece. If you took the mouthpiece off a trombone and blew through it, it would produce only a weak, high-pitched squawk, the direct vibration of your lips. But when the mouthpiece is attached to the trombone, the acoustics of the instrument's piping cause an entire column of air to vibrate. Because of this effect, the musical note is heard, full of resonance and power. Likewise, a violin string just produces a scratchy noise when vibrated all by itself. The sounding board and the internal resonance cavities of the violin augment the sound of the string to produce a full, rich tone.

Roughly the same effect occurs in the human voice. The mouth and nasal cavities act as resonators, enhancing some of the harmonics (overtones) of the voice. Even the sinuses and the bones of the skull act as resonators.

Resonation in the nasal cavities is most apparent during the pronunciation of so-called nasal sounds, such as *m, n,* and *ng.* This becomes apparent when you close your mouth and hum; where does the air escape? The buzzing sensation of humming shows that you are producing resonance in the nasal passages.

You don't pass air into the nasal passages all the time. But nasal cavity resonance while saying *m, n,* and *ng* can enhance your voice. Resonance along the entire vocal tract enhances the quality of your voice.

Methods of developing resonance and other qualities of a pleasing voice are discussed later in the chapter.

EVALUATING YOUR VOICE AND SPEECH

It is worthwhile to make a clear distinction between voice and speech. Basically, *voice* is the vibration that emerges from the vocal cords and from resonance along the vocal and nasal tracts. *Speech* is how that sound is shaped and arranged within the mouth. The term *speaking voice* applies to the whole effect of voice and speech.

Making an honest evaluation of your voice and speech is one of the most productive things you can do in your career. Any voice or speech deviation is a handicap. Some performers have succeeded despite such deviations, but that is rare.

Evaluate your voice and speech by recording yourself on a smartphone (or with a digital recorder) and, ideally, with a knowledgeable instructor, speech-language pathologist, or vocal coach. You can start with Box 2.1, the "Self-Evaluation Checklist," later in this chapter. It is difficult to critique yourself. You hear your own voice through bone conduction or vibration, whereas others hear your voice after it has traveled through the air. Remember the first time you heard a recording of yourself? The difference between *your* perception of your voice and the actual playback was probably startling.

But a recording also has its limitations because we don't discriminate our own speech sounds with precision. Even people with severe lisps sometimes cannot tell they have a problem unless they are trained to listen critically to a taped playback.

Take advantage of critique from instructors and colleagues to identify problem areas, and listen critically to your recordings in an effort to develop self-critiquing skills.

A pleasing voice is helpful to a broadcaster, but an offensive voice is a real handicap. Voices that "turn off" listeners may result from problems in *quality, delivery,* and *breathing.*

Problems with Voice Quality

Have you ever developed a negative image of someone on the other end of a phone conversation, someone you've never met but have pictured because of his or her voice? Gravelly voices, for example, are not pleasant to listen to and certainly are a detriment for most broadcasters. Here are some of the most common negative voice qualities, possible causes, and suggestions for improvement.

Hoarseness. A raspy sound in the voice, often categorized as a voice that "sounds like it's hurting," is called hoarseness. This vocal sound may be a symptom of a pathological condition and should, if persistent, be checked by a physician. Most hoarseness results from overuse and improper use of the voice, such as cheering at a sports event, and can be compounded by too much tension in the vocal apparatus.

"Thin" voice. When a "thin," weak voice is the result of the way the vocal mechanism is formed, not a lot can be done about it other than to enhance the thin voice as best one can through good vocal habits. Often, though, a thin quality is the result of a lack of resonance. The two keys to increasing resonance are proper air support, including good posture and relaxation. Also, chronic inflammation and swelling of the nasal passages can cut off resonance.

(Try pinching your nose and talking; note how "weak" the voice appears.)

Gravelly voice. Whereas a hoarse voice typically has a strident "breaking" quality to it, the gravelly voice is usually low pitched, does not project, and is not melodic. Gravelly voices sometimes result from a simple lack of projection.

Note how gravel-voiced people often slouch and speak with the chin on the chest. Gravelly voices often result from speaking in a pitch that is too low. Better breath support, a higher pitch, and better projection can often ease this problem.

Problems in Vocal Delivery

Even when the vocal and breathing apparatus is working properly, a voice can fail to be pleasing because of poor delivery. We'll define five typical problems and give possible solutions.

Monotone. Failure to change pitch results in a monotone delivery. *Pitch* is the listener's perception of the frequency of a sound (its relative highness or lowness), as in the pitch of a note on a musical scale. A monotone can be extremely unpleasant to listen to and conveys the impression that the speaker is bored or boring. Speaking in a monotone can also irritate the vocal cords.

A speaker with a monotone should pay more attention to the nuances of the pitch rising and falling.

Poor pitch. Some people try to talk out of their ranges, too high or, as is sometimes the case with male news reporters, too low. One effect on the voice is an unnatural quality. Speaking at an unnatural pitch opens the door for vocal abuse, and a problem that would-be basses don't consider is that constantly talking at the bottom end of their range limits the expressiveness of the voice. When you are at the bottom of the range, you can only go up.

Finding a more comfortable and natural pitch often clears up the problem.

Singsong. A singsong delivery is characterized by a rhythm that rises and falls; it's a predictable voice pattern showing artificially wide and pronounced pitch swings—the "disc jockey voice." The problem isn't hard to eliminate once it has been recognized. Adopting a normal speech melody solves the problem.

Ending pattern. Many people end each phrase or sentence on the same pitch or series of pitches. A voice pattern that becomes predictable is boring and can be distracting.

Whininess. A whiny sound is often caused by speaking at a pitch that is too high and elongating vowels. "I tooooooold you this would happen . . . look at the mess you've gotten us into noooooo wwwwww." Awareness of whiny delivery is the first step in eliminating it, along with assuming a better pitch and shortening vowels. Whininess is also sometimes associated with an overly nasal delivery (too much air being diverted into the nose during speech).

Problems in Breathing

Poor breath control and the related problem of poor posture are often at the root of an unpleasant voice. Even though breathing is an automatic function, there is some technique involved in breathing properly for voice production. "Throwing your chest out" when you breathe is incorrect and counterproductive, because it is the abdomen, not the chest, that must expand significantly during inhalation for proper speech. Here are some typical problems and suggestions for alleviating them.

Breathy voice. The "Marilyn Monroe" or "breathy starlet" voice may be either a physical or a breathing problem. It can be caused by failure to bring the vocal folds together closely enough during phonation, so that air escapes while you are speaking. A common and more easily corrected cause of a breathy voice, however, is not having sufficient air reserves, so that the speaker "runs out of breath." More attention to proper phonation, proper vocal tension, and possibly professional therapy are indicated, along with better posture and breath support.

Voice with no "carrying power" Often the result of inadequate support from the abdominal muscles, lack of carrying power is compounded by lack of projection. Projection is simply the process of sending vocal sounds out of your mouth. Breathe diaphragmatically, and pay attention to posture.

Problems with Speech Quality

There are different ways to categorize speech problems, and our categorization is not the same as a trained speech-language pathologist would use. Instead, speech problems are discussed in terms of their occurrence and importance to the on-air talent.

The most common categories of sounds produced within the mouth and vocal apparatus are vowels and consonants. Among the consonants, different parts of the vocal apparatus are used to produce various sounds, including the following.

Fricatives. The source of these sounds is the gradual escape of air through a constriction in the mouth or vocal tract. Major English **fricatives** are *f, v, th, s, z, sh, zh,* and *h.*

Plosives and stops. An explosion of air (*t* and *d* at the beginning of a word) or suddenly stopping air flow (*t* and *d* at the end of a word) will produce these sounds. Major English **plosives** are *p, b, t, d, k,* and *g.*

Frictionless consonants. Included are semivowels, nasals, and laterals. Semivowels, *w, r,* and *y,* have a continuous, vowel-like quality in their pronunciation. An *l* sound is similar but is known as a *lateral,* because the breath exits from the side of the mouth. Another related type of sound is the nasal category: *m, n,* and *ng.*

When the sounds just described are omitted, distorted, added, or substituted for one another, speech problems occur. Here are examples of four typical deviations:

- **Omissions:** Dropping the *k* in "asked" so it sounds like "ast" instead of "askt."
- **Distortions:** Altering the *s* sound so that it comes out more like a *th* (lisp). Vowel distortions are also common, such as saying "pin" for "pen" or "min" for "men." Vowel distortions sometimes are traceable to a regional accent.
- **Additions:** Putting an *r* where it does not belong: saying "soar" instead of "saw."
- **Substitutions:** Saying *d* for *th,* as in "dese" and "dose" for "these" and "those"; or *n* for *ng,* as "bringin." This is sometimes called "dropping the *g,*" an error that also shares some characteristics of an omission.

Difficulties in sequencing sounds constitute yet another type of deviation, defined as follows.

- *Fluency problems (stuttering and cluttering):* **Stuttering** is a problem of rate and rhythm that is best addressed by a professional therapist. **Cluttering,** as an informal definition, involves telescoping sounds together, saying "vejble" for "vegetable."

Omissions, distortions, additions, substitutions, and fluency problems are terms used to identify specific speech deviations. How do they relate to broadcast announcing? Specific speech deviations are components of these overall problems: sloppy diction, regionalism, accents, and cluttering and rate problems.

Sloppy diction. Simple failure to pronounce sounds clearly is sloppy diction. Faults of this type include omissions, such as dropping the final *-ing,* which is a typical transgression. Although "lookin' " might be acceptable in conversational speech, it is not usually acceptable on the air. Sometimes substitutions are simply the result of social or cultural diction habits, such as saying "dis" and "dat" instead of "this" and "that." Substitutions, though, often require professional therapy. A lack of knowledge about the language can lead to additions, too, although this is not strictly a diction problem. For example, the adjective form of "disaster" is "disastrous," not "disasterous." The proper word is "nuclear," not "noo-cue-lahr."

Poor diction is a habit. "Lip laziness" accounts for many cases of sloppy diction, and failure to move the lips and tongue enough for crisp diction is a habit that must be overcome.

Here are some guidelines to help you tighten up sloppy diction.

1. *Self-evaluate.* Listen carefully: do you say "pitcher" for "picture"? Practice correct pronunciations.
2. *Do not "drop" final endings.* Be sure to pronounce *-ing* with an *ng,* not *n.*
3. *Practice giving full measure to all sounds within words.* The word "beasts" has three distinct sounds at the end. Say "beasts," not "beese."
4. *Watch contractions.* Unless you articulate clearly, the negative form of a contraction may sound like the positive form. If the announcer doesn't clearly pronounce the *t* at the end of "can't," the statement "The mayor said he can't remember being told the funds were missing" could be understood as meaning the opposite of the way it is written.

Regionalism. Although there is nothing wrong with speaking with a regional accent, regional speech is frequently a handicap to on-air talent. Yes, there are successful news reporters with New England accents, and radio personalities with southern drawls, but these are the *exceptions,* not the rule.

A regional accent in New York City, for example, may label you as being from Brooklyn or the Bronx. A pronounced regional accent may even disqualify you from getting a certain job. Often a person's regional accent can be reduced greatly by opening your mouth wide enough to enunciate the words correctly.

Foreign accent. A noticeable foreign accent can be a charming and engaging characteristic. In broadcast communication, however, the decoration an accent adds to your personality can be offset by the fact that it may under some circumstances interfere with clear communication.

In most broadcast situations, a heavy foreign accent is considered a detriment that can limit your opportunities and stall your career. If you speak heavily accented English, you should recognize this as a liability to your future as a broadcast communicator and take measures to deal with it. Professionals use a variety of techniques to reduce foreign accents (see the Focus on Technique box).

Cluttering and rate problems. Cluttering, or telescoping sounds, is different from sloppy diction because cluttering typically involves a problem with rate of speech and sometimes a lack of attention to communicating the message. The clutterer often jams words and sounds together because he or she is speaking too quickly. Many otherwise intelligible people become practically incoherent when they read aloud and rattle off the words at breakneck pace, with no phrasing. A clutterer who reads over the air frequently compounds the problem by just reading, not communicating. In other words, proper stress is not given to the words and phrases, so the reading comes out as a mashed-up jumble.

Focus on Technique

Accent Reduction

Although broadcast executives are more tolerant of foreign and regional accents today than in the past, anything that gets in the way of communication is an obstacle. On a realistic note, you will find that cable news channels with foreign correspondents and specifically targeted shows are the only places you might hear highly recognizable accents.

Accent reduction is difficult but not impossible. But it is very difficult if you try it by yourself, because you simply may not be able to hear your accent. Many Asian speakers, for instance, have trouble hearing the difference between *l* and *r*.

If you want to pursue a career in broadcasting, and if you have a foreign or regional accent, your best option is to consult a speech-language pathologist or a theatrical vocal coach. Speech-language pathologists are voice and diction scientists, and many are skilled in accent reduction.

(Ask, though; some might be more interested in reducing stuttering and have little experience in accent reduction.) Theatrical voice coaches are often highly skilled in teaching the building blocks of producing pronunciation; a good coach can not only teach a Swede how to pronounce English with a native US pronunciation but could also teach an American how to speak with a Swedish accent.

If these options are unavailable to you, you can still make progress with a partner, such as a teacher, colleague, or news director, and your *other* partner—an audio recorder. The key is to listen to yourself and listen to the suggestions of your native-speaking partner.

Here are some techniques you can use:

- Record and listen to network news anchors. They typically speak a more-or-less standard speech. Compare their phrasing with yours.

    For example, if ABC's David Muir (an excellent model of clear, unaccented speech) says, "floodwaters inundated the Midwest yesterday," play that part of the recording back and copy his pronunciation, rate, and stress.
- Practice the "musical" part of your delivery. Pitch changes and levels of stress are just as important to general American delivery as word pronunciation is. Rhythm and inflection, called *prosody,* not only are tip-offs for foreign accents but change meanings as well.

    For example: She is a light HOUSE keeper.

    She is a LIGHT-house keeper.

    Prosody is particularly difficult for Asians, who tend not to vary their patterns as much as do speakers of Germanic languages like English or speakers of Romance languages (Spanish, Italian, and so on).
- To practice proper English prosody, try reading rhythmic poetry aloud.

    Anything by Edgar Allan Poe is good. Simply by keeping the meter of the poem you will be forced into using native English stress patterns.

    In *The Raven,* for example: ONCE u-PON a MID-night DREAR-y, WHILE I PON-dered WEAK and WEAR-y . . .
- You will find it awkward *not* to stress the correct words and form the proper rhythm. If you don't mind a little good-natured silliness, try children's books by Dr. Seuss.
- Learn to say pitch changes *within vowel sounds.* If you listen to a native English speaker, he or she will make a considerable pitch change in the *oh* sound that ends "Hello." Generally, the sound will be elongated and drop quite a bit in pitch. Or, if the word is being

Focus on Technique *(continued)*

used as a question: "Helloooooooo . . . anybody hoooooome?" Both *oh* sounds will *rise* in pitch.

This is one of the biggest problems in accent reduction. Asians and many Romance-language speakers (such as Spanish speakers) tend to make their vowels short and flat. Once you realize this, you can begin to mimic the vowel patterns of native pronunciation.

- Move your lips. Ann Madsen Dailey, a speech pathologist with many years of experience in accent reduction training, notes that many accent problems, particularly with Russians, Indians, and Asians, stem from the fact that they do not move their lips enough to form English sounds. The *oh,* sound, for instance, can be difficult for anyone not used to puckering the lips severely enough.

- In general, pronounce the consonants and vowels *as far in the front of your mouth as possible.* This is something of an obscure concept, to be sure, but it basically boils down to this: As an example, when you say the *n* sound use the tip of your tongue up against the roof of your mouth *near the front teeth.* Chinese and Japanese speakers say the *n* by closing the back of the tongue, and the sound is made in the back of the mouth. For example, the *ooh* sound in "too" should be made far in front of the mouth, at the lips, which are pursed. Spanish-speaking people tend to make the sound in the back of the mouth. Try it if you are a native US English speaker—say "ooh" and don't purse your lips and make the sound short and without variation and you will produce a good imitation of a Spanish accent.

- Strive to move pronunciations farther forward in the mouth, and you will generally achieve more near-native speech.

- Slow down! It is very difficult to maintain your hard-fought native-US pronunciations when you talk too quickly. It takes considerable fine motor coordination for a non-native speaker to form an American *r,* and if you are speaking too quickly you will not be able to do it.

- There is nothing wrong with having two speech standards—one for the family and the neighborhood and one for the camera. People attempting accent reduction often face opposition and sometimes ridicule from those with whom they have day-to-day contact. That is a natural response—imagine how Americans living in Tokyo would react to other Americans who tried to adopt native-Japanese voice mannerisms. So live with this; you need not try to eradicate your cultural roots. Changing your speech patterns to adapt to the situation is common and reasonable. Doctors, for example, talk differently with other doctors than with their nonmedical friends. You have the same right.

- Improve your vocabulary! Probably the largest difference between native and non-native speech is the size of the vocabulary. If you are attempting to reduce your accent, you will sabotage your progress when you stumble over unfamiliar words. (Your rhythm and pronunciation will both be affected.) Look up unfamiliar words. Always keep a dictionary handy.

- Drill yourself on the difficult sounds. If *r* is your problem, say lists of words with that sound, and make sure you have an *r* in the beginning, middle, and end. Have a native speaker listen and critique.

A good collection of tapes is available to help you work with accent reduction. Dialect Accent Specialists, Inc. (https://learnaccent.com) offers an inexpensive and very good series of video- and audiotapes as well as residency programs.

Finally, in the last few years many very useful tutorials have been posted on *YouTube* that can help with accent reduction, and general American speech pronunciation patterns. Use these tutorials for practice. They're free!

These deviations reflect problems in **articulation**, meaning the joining and juxtaposition of sounds and words, rather than simple **diction**, which usually refers to the formation of individual sounds.

Cluttering and rate problems are common for people beginning air work.

The novice disk jockey sometimes tries to emulate a fast-talking pro who's practiced at speaking at an accelerated rate. These problems are most effectively handled by:

1. Slowing down the rate of reading.
2. Marking copy for effective understanding and delivery (shown in the next chapter).
3. Speaking clearly in an effort to communicate ideas, not just read words.

FLUENCY LIMITATIONS AND THE BROADCASTER

On-air performers who have **fluency** difficulties will have difficulty communicating effectively. If words are delivered at breakneck speed and articulation is poor, the effect is like hearing the music from a Broadway musical without the lyrics. The music may not sound too bad, but it is easy to miss the full meaning of the message that the composer intended to convey.

The broadcast announcer has a number of tools that can be used to help convey the full meaning of the words being read. If the rate is too fast or if articulation is poor, however, those tools don't get a chance to perform the functions they should. The effectiveness of *speech melody,* or **inflection**, is totally wasted if it flies by the listener too rapidly. Nuances of meaning are lost and the intended effect of the copy is diminished or eliminated.

An uneven rate of delivery can also cause inaccurate and inconsistent timing. When a television news anchor reads copy that leads into a recorded news package, people in the control room need to be able to depend on a consistent rate of delivery. To ensure that the recorded segment smoothly works, the playback segment must be started a couple of seconds before the anchor completes the lead-in. So an anchor who slows down at that point will "step on" the opening of the playback segment.

Timing

In media today, the increased use of satellite and computer automation means that timing must be more precise than ever before. On many stations in the past, a five-minute newscast could run over or under time by several seconds or more without anyone noticing. But if you know that the satellite programming will start exactly when the minute hand of the clock hits 12, you also know that five minutes is all you have. Anything less than that will create dead air. In radio that tight limit also applies to reading commercial copy and items like station IDs, promos, and weather forecasts. Similar requirements limit people who do narration and voice-over assignments. Timing must be an element of your delivery that you can control.

You must often adjust your rate so that you convey meaning even when conditions force you to vary from your usual rate.

The bottom line is that if you want to be effective as on-air talent in almost any type of assignment, you must know how to read copy precisely to time. Some top professionals can take a piece of copy, ask the producer how much time he or she wants filled, and read the copy in one take so that it hits the time limit exactly. But most of us need some rehearsal first. You must find ways to practice timing so that you can hone your skills.

One effective exercise to improve timing is to divide a piece of broadcast copy into sections, to be read in a stated amount of time. Read the copy over and over until you are able to read through to the end in the designated amount of time. Here's how to set up the exercise.

Copy has about ten words per line, on the average. Sixteen lines of copy would be about a minute's worth at a reading rate of 160 words per minute—a generally good rate for broadcast announcers.

Take a piece of copy with at least 16 lines, and mark the midpoint—eight lines down—with a mark that is easy to see. Place another mark at the end of the copy—16 lines down. Using a timing device that lets you easily see the number of seconds that have elapsed, read the copy through. See how close you can come to reaching the midpoint at 30 seconds. Did you complete the 16 lines in 60 seconds? Practice this over and over with various pieces of copy. With practice, you'll find that you will develop an awareness of how to read the copy at the proper rate to make it fit the proper time frame.

An Important Point About Timing

The point we're making is simple. Don't assume that you can simply ignore speech problems in rate and timing. Your problems may not be severe enough to require professional attention, but even relatively minor difficulties can severely hinder your ability to interpret copy effectively. The exercises at the end of this chapter can help you identify any problem areas you may have. For more help, consult a speech therapist or one of the many books on voice improvement.

One of the most comprehensive books is Utterback's *Broadcast Voice Handbook*.[1] Utterback has a wide background in voice and diction and has helped many professional broadcasters improve their vocal delivery. It goes without saying that the more good practice you do the better announcer you will become.

LANGUAGE AND THE BROADCASTER

Using language well is obviously of paramount importance to the broadcaster.

Unfortunately, there are no simple and all-inclusive guidelines for proper pronunciation and usage, and categorizing standards and definitions is very difficult. Scholars have debated the issues of dialects and standardized language for centuries without producing a completely definitive standard.

For example, what defines a **dialect**? In most basic terms, it is a variety of a language, but from what exactly does it differ? Is a certain dialect substandard?

What is standard?

It is useful to look at the language issue in the most basic terms, the terms most directly related to on-air broadcasters. This discussion includes pronunciation, which is obviously germane to a chapter on speech and voice. Also important, and included in this chapter to complete the discussion of language, is an examination of usage.

Two common terms encountered in on-air broadcasting are **standard English** and **general American speech**. Although these descriptions are sometimes used interchangeably, "standard English" is generally taken to mean the English language as it is written or spoken by literate people in both formal and informal usage, whereas "general American speech" can be defined as pronunciation of American English using few or no regional peculiarities. From the standpoint of pronunciation, deviations from general American speech are dialects resulting from regionalism or social circumstances.

Regional Dialects

Linguists identify dialects in terms of local and regional peculiarities in pronunciation. There are said to be four main regional dialects in the United States: Northern, North Midland, South Midland, and Southern. There are many distinct variations within these categories.

The exact scope of general American speech has always been elusive, but it has come to be used for all speech except that of New England and the coastal south.[2] Perhaps a better basis for judgment would be **network standard**, the unaccented speech of most newscasters and actors delivering commercials.

An unaccented form of American speech was thought to be spoken in Chicago, although clearly some speakers in Chicago do use regional speech.

In the early days of broadcasting, some organizations sent announcers to Chicago in an effort to eliminate regional accents.

Eliminating regionalisms in any manner is not easy. We're so used to hearing our own regionalisms (primarily vowel distortions) that we find it hard to distinguish regional speech from the unaccented speech used by most network newscasters.

An effort must be made to correct regionalisms, though. Vowel distortions caused by regional dialects can be distracting to a listener who, for example, expects to hear "boy," but hears instead "bo-ih" from a southern speaker. And many people find substitutions even more intrusive. The New England trait of adding *r*'s where they don't belong ("pizzer," "bananer") and dropping them where they do belong ("cah," "watah") can irritate listeners unaccustomed to the dialect.

As we noted earlier, you may not be able to distinguish your own regional dialect. If your instructors or colleagues tell you that you have a distracting regionalism, they're probably right. And if you can't identify and correct the regional distortion or substitution on your own, by all means ask a speech professional or coach for help in getting rid of it.

Social Dialects

Certain differences in pronunciation are apparent among groups that differ in educational levels or cultural practices. Standard speech is arbitrarily assumed to reflect the highly educated members of a society, so a similarly arbitrary definition pegs other **social dialects** as nonstandard.

Playwright George Bernard Shaw satirized the rigid British class system by reflecting its cultural differences in speech patterns. In *Pygmalion,* Shaw made the point that more attention was given to the packaging of the words than to their substance.

Still, it is important for a broadcaster to reflect the social dialect looked on as standard. You must use educated pronunciations and usages. Saying "dese" instead of "these" can reflect a nonstandard social dialect, as can loose pronunciation. "Whatcha gonna do?" is not acceptable speech for a newscaster. The appropriateness of loose pronunciations, however, clearly varies with the situation. You don't commonly intone every sound when asking a friend, "What are you going to do?" In informal situations, some loosening of pronunciation is acceptable.

Usage

The choice and use of words must be considered in evaluating standard language. Standard English, remember, is pegged to the educated speaker or writer. Use of double negatives, such as "haven't got none," is obviously nonstandard.

There is a more subtle point to be considered here, however. Although it is assumed that anyone contemplating a career in the broadcast media has the knowledge and ability to avoid such obvious blunders as "haven't got none," other lapses in grammar and usage can seriously detract from your image as an educated, standard English-speaking broadcaster. What is your impression of an announcer who speaks about a "heart-rendering" movie?

The usage is comically incorrect. (If you're in doubt, look up "rendering.") A lack of knowledge of the language also can mislead. One news reporter, for example, spoke of a city official's "fulsome" praise for a retiring teacher.

"Fulsome" is a word that is used as a synonym for "abundant" so often that its original meaning, namely, "offensive or disgusting," is rapidly becoming lost. Similar fates seem to be in store for "presently," "disinterested," and "infer." Use words correctly. Never guess in an on-air situation.

SELF-EVALUATION

It is important to be aware of any speech or voice problems you may have. Self-evaluation can help you assess your own speech so you can more easily identify and deal with problems that will hinder your progress toward achieving a more professional on-air delivery. Use the checklist in Box 2.1.

BOX 2.1 Self-Evaluation Checklist

A speech or voice deviation or a significant deviation from standard English or general American speech can slow the advancement of even the most intelligent broadcaster. It is important to keep an open mind to critiques and evaluations of voice, speech, and language. Although it is often difficult to perceive deviations in your own voice and speech, by constant monitoring with an audio recorder you can train yourself to be your own best critic.

Read through two or three pages of copy or a newspaper article. Then play back the recording and ask yourself:

1. Do I slur any words and sounds together?
2. Are my consonants crisp and clear?
3. Are my s sounds too harsh? Do my plosives (p's and b's) cause the mic to pop?
4. Are there any regionalisms or colloquialisms in my speech? Do I say "soar" for "saw," or "youse" for "you"?
5. Do I "drop" endings?
6. Do I read too quickly? Do my words telescope together?
7. Do I have a distracting voice pattern? Do I sound like a bad disc jockey?
8. Is my voice hoarse, harsh?
9. Am I speaking in a pitch range that is too high or too low?
10. Can I *hear* tension in my voice? Does it sound constricted, tight?

Note: Although self-evaluation is helpful, the difficulty of hearing your own mistakes cannot be overemphasized. If at all possible, have an individual analysis of your voice and articulation problems.

MAKING YOUR SPEAKING VOICE MORE PLEASING

The next step is to concentrate on some positive steps you can take for self-improvement.

Of primary importance to improving voice quality is posture.

Another critical aspect of a pleasant voice is relaxation of the vocal apparatus, which also plays the major role in preventing vocal abuse. Relaxation techniques are discussed in the section titled "Maintaining Your Voice."

The first step in improving your speaking voice is to learn correct posture and breathing.

Breathe Diaghragmatically

The suggestion to "speak from the diaphragm," which is a good one, doesn't make any sense unless the process is explained and understood. Using posture and breathing techniques will require forming good habits and breaking bad habits.

The first habit to cultivate is proper posture, contends David Blair McClosky, the late author, singer and voice therapist who coached presidents and broadcasters. In his book, McClosky recommends a posture in which your feet are spread comfortably apart and your weight is slightly toward the balls of your feet.[3] The key to the proper posture is to get rid of an exaggerated curve in your back. Keep your back straight and tuck your hips in, as shown in Figure 2.3.

This posture allows for proper breathing. Virtually all voice coaches point out that the abdomen must expand during breathing, rather than the chest. Although you may have been taught in elementary school to

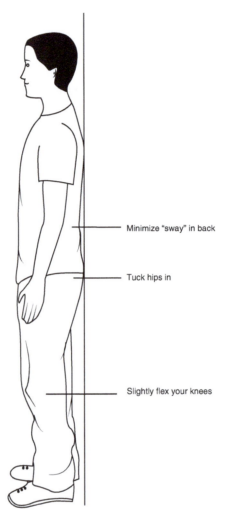

Minimize "sway" in back

Tuck hips in

Slightly flex your knees

FIGURE 2.3 A good posture for speaking. The goal is to minimize back sway and give your diaphragm and abdomen plenty of room for expansion.

"throw out your chest" when you breathe, that's not good technique. It doesn't let your abdominal muscles and therefore your diaphragm provide adequate support for the column of air in your vocal tract. If you are unclear about this, please take a moment to review the sections on vocal anatomy and physiology.

"Diaphragmatic breathing" is something of a misnomer because we have to use the diaphragm to breathe regardless of what scrunched-up posture we may assume. However, proper diaphragmatic breathing is accomplished when the contraction of the abdominal muscles pushes the diaphragm in and supports the column of air. This can be accomplished only if the abdomen is allowed to expand when the diaphragm pulls down into the abdominal cavity during inhalation.

Proper breathing compels us to abandon some of the typical vanities imposed by current culture, including the notions that we should be waspwaisted and that men should have swelling chests. For us to breathe properly, the abdomen must expand. Note the action in Figure 2.4 (b and c).

When the abdomen and the diaphragm have expanded, natural exhalation from that position, involving a contracting of the abdominal muscles, will produce the proper effect. Be certain you have used your diaphragm properly. One way to check on diaphragmatic breathing is to stand against a wall and press your fist against your abdomen. Proper inhalation will drive that fist away (Figure 2.4c).

(a)

(b)

(c)

FIGURE 2.4 Illustration of how to determine whether you are breathing diaphragmatically.

Here is one final test to see if you are breathing properly. Assume the correct posture and place your hands on your lower ribs (Figure 2.4a). Inhale. If your ribs move you are expanding your chest instead of your diaphragm.

This breathing posture works just as well in a seated position. All that will change is the position of your legs. Keep your back straight and your hips tucked in. Practice minimizing rib motion.

Avoid Exaggerated Diction

We've all heard the unnatural, affected delivery of the speaker whose diction is just *too* precise. We raise this issue because some people try to clear up imprecision in diction by swinging to the other extreme, which is probably a marginal improvement at best. Remember, English-speaking people do not pounce on every single sound in a sentence.

The best way to identify too-precise diction is, of course, to listen to a recording of yourself. It also helps to watch your mouth as you speak into a mirror. Exaggerated mouth and lip movements are often indicative of exaggerated diction.

Be Careful of Plosives

Even normal-sounding *p*'s and *b*'s can cause a microphone to pop—that is, to vibrate with an explosive noise because a blast of air has hit the mic element.

Sometimes, simple awareness of the problem and practice in controlling the force of plosives is enough. Speaking across the mic, rather than into it, can help. Or you might choose a mic that is less susceptible to popping.

All options are discussed in Chapter 4.

Women doing on-air work sometimes encounter resistance from listeners who claim their voices are harder to understand. For some people, especially older listeners with age-related hearing losses, this is true. For reasons dealing with acoustics and the functioning of the hearing mechanism, the impaired ear hears lower-pitched voices better than higher-pitched voices. A reasonable lowering of pitch can sometimes overcome this. Good projection and resonance can also resolve much of the problem.

Finally, be aware that many on-air diction problems can be solved by careful attention to copy interpretation. "Read for meaning," advises Ann Madsen Dailey, an author, consultant, and speech-language pathologist. "Use pauses where appropriate, stress key words, and use natural expression. Very often this can clear up the problems caused by poor habits developed by just 'reading out loud.'"

MAINTAINING YOUR VOICE

Broadcasters, like teachers and salespeople, often must contend with hoarseness, irritation, or just plain tiredness in the vocal apparatus. Even if the abuse is not serious enough to cause harm, no performer can communicate effectively when his or her voice is reaching the point of failure.

Good health and nutrition are important to on-air performers: They help you improve effectiveness the same way proper physical conditioning contributes to the performance of an athlete. Like athletes, announcers are called on to perform at specific times and places. That means you must perform well *then*—not just at those rare times when your voice sounds perfect. If you have to produce a quality vocal performance on a regular basis, you should try to be as fit as possible at all times. Eating sensibly, exercising moderately, and avoiding behaviors that harm your health will help you make sure your vocal tools are always ready to use to their best effect (see Box 2.2).

BOX 2.2 **Diet and Health Tips**

To get the most from your voice, follow a healthy lifestyle. The vocal mechanisms are physical, after all. Good health practices and proper diet help strengthen the vocal mechanisms and provide the energy that helps you develop an effective vocal delivery. Here are some basic tips that will help you keep fit and avoid the consequences of poor general health.

- *Get plenty of rest.* When your body is tired, the weariness will show up in your voice. A tired voice is usually higher pitched and lacking in strength. Announcers who try to perform with tired voices may wonder if they can even finish the shift. Attempts to "clear" the voice—frequent throat clearing and straining to lower the pitch—just aggravate the problem. The only effective remedy is to get some rest. Better yet, get enough sleep in the first place, and try to find some time for relaxation before starting assignments that require heavy use of your voice.

- *Exercise.* In addition to exercises that work the vocal mechanisms, engage in some form of regular, strenuous physical activity that works the major muscles of the body. This will strengthen your heart and lungs and give you endurance and overall energy. Your vocal delivery will reflect the general condition of the rest of your body. You'll be able to go longer with less strain, and the extra energy will give you a more forceful delivery when you need it. Of course, it is always wise to have a physical examination by a qualified physician before starting a strenuous exercise program—especially if you have been leading a sedentary life.

- *Watch what you eat.* A diet high in fat and low in nutrition contributes to fatigue and susceptibility to illness. The carbohydrates in whole grains and fruit, combined with adequate protein from various sources, will provide energy and help you maintain health.

  Don't eat too much fat, and pay attention to the nutritional values of the food you eat. If you are overweight, start a weight reduction program that helps you lose pounds over a reasonable length of time. Fad diets can endanger your health, and they usually don't work.

- *Don't smoke.* The constant irritation of heavy smoking can damage the vocal mechanism and greatly impair vocal delivery. Aside from the well-known risks to general health, smoking continually irritates the vocal cords. General irritation of the throat can result in excessive mucus production and the development of a "smoker's cough" that further strains the vocal mechanism. Over time, the general quality of the voice can change as the result of permanent damage to the vocal folds. Eventual lung damage can impair effective breath control and reduce the force of your vocal delivery.

Relaxation is the key to maintaining your voice. Proper relaxation also helps produce a pleasant, resonant voice. The exercises recommended in Box 2.3 really do work! Try them, practice them, and make them into a daily regimen.

Avoiding Vocal Abuse

"Vocal abuse" is any excess strain on the vocal apparatus, most notably on the vocal cords, that produces irritation. Symptoms of vocal abuse include hoarseness, a change in the character of the voice, fatigue or discomfort in the region of the larynx and throat, and a change in the basic pitch of the voice.

Vocal abuse can be chronic or acute. Chronic abuse develops gradually from improper vocal habits and excessive stress in the vocal mechanism. The results of acute abuse comes on suddenly, usually from screaming or a very hard period of speaking or singing.

Such abuse can result in a number of physical problems, including

- Formation of vocal cord nodules and polyps
- Excessive "bowing" (taking on a misshapen appearance) of the vocal cords
- Chronic irritation

One cause of vocal abuse is an abnormally low pitch. McClosky notes that when he was a university choirmaster and singing teacher in the heyday of the big-voiced announcer, a surprising number of students who reported voice problems to him were enrolled in the college's broadcasting school. They were trying to lower their pitch to the male ideal of those days.

BOX 2.3 Some Exercises To Relax Your Body And Throat

Professional singers and speakers perform many of these regularly.

1. Roll your head: forward, to the left, backward, to the right, and forward again. Repeat several times in each direction. This helps relax shoulders and neck.
2. Massage the muscles of your face. Work down from your hairline, and let your jaw go slack.
3. Thrust out your tongue several times, then let it hang limply over the bottom lip. Relaxing your tongue is important because the back of your tongue goes right down your throat. Tension here can interfere with vocalization.
4. Massage the area under your chin (Figure 2.5a) until there is no rigidity apparent. Learn to relax these muscles "on cue."
5. Grasp your lower jaw between thumb and forefinger and work it up and down until you overcome any muscular resistance. When you get good at this, you can bounce your jaw up and down with your forefinger (Figure 2.5b).
6. *Gently* massage the larynx from side to side (Figure 2.5c) until you eliminate rigidity and any "clicking" sensation.
7. Vocalize the word "hah" gently, using the *ah* sound as in "arm." Start vocalization high in pitch and then slide down the range of pitch. Initiate the vocalization as gradually and gently as you can.

BOX 2.3 *(continued)*

(a)

(b)

(c)

FIGURE 2.5 (a) Massaging under the chin. (b) Working the jaw. (c) Massaging the larynx eliminates rigidity.

Preventing Vocal Abuse

In addition to speaking in a natural tone of voice, you can protect your voice from abuse in several ways. Neri Holzer, MD, a Connecticut ear, nose, and throat specialist, offers these suggestions:

1. *Listen to what your larynx and throat are trying to tell you.* The body has several defense mechanisms, including pain and hoarseness. If these symptoms are chronic, reevaluate your speech patterns.
2. *Warm up.* Do some light vocalizing (humming, singing, and so on) before an extended on-air period or other time of vocal stress.
3. *Keep well hydrated.* When tissues lose moisture, they're more susceptible to damage. Have a glass of water on hand.
4. *Use amplification when possible instead of raising your voice.* A radio announcer, for example, can reduce strain on the voice by turning up the volume on the mic channel instead of shouting.
5. *Don't smoke.* Tobacco smoke directly irritates the vocal cords. Smoke indirectly irritates the cords by stimulating coughing. It is also a major cause of dry mouth, which can significantly impair your speaking ability.
6. *Avoid extensive use of the voice when you have a cold.* Using your voice then makes you more susceptible to vocal irritation. Also, avoid habitually clearing your throat.
7. *Look at your whole body for signs of tension.* Stress in other parts of the body can cause a reaction in the voice. Similarly, posture has an important role in keeping the vocal mechanism relaxed and working freely.

Vocal Relaxation Techniques for Protecting the Voice

Dr. Holzer's last point is important: having a relaxed body and vocal apparatus relieves much of the strain on the voice mechanism and allows the voice to function better. Voice therapist McClosky contended that relaxation is the precursor to any progress in voice development. Unless you can relax the muscles in your face, tongue, jaw, throat, and neck that interfere with the muscles controlling the vocal cords themselves, he says, "your singing and speaking will be muscle-bound" (refer back to Box 2.3).

Make these relaxation techniques a daily routine, and remember that relaxation exercises can be done at any time. Doing this routine during a break in a tiring recording session, for example, will help your voice immensely.

SUMMARY

Broadcasters need not force their voices into abnormally low pitch ranges. A pleasant voice, rather than a deep voice, is the hallmark of today's professional announcer. An artificially low-pitched voice is unattractive, and it can actually damage the vocal cords.

A basic knowledge of the vocal mechanism lets you identify the function of various parts of the apparatus when doing exercises to improve its function.

Vocal cords are suspended in a chamber of cartilage and allow air to escape in short bursts. Those short bursts create a vibration, which is amplified by the vocal tract and nasal passages.

Voice quality adds to your presence and persuasiveness, as does a good command of the language. See the Connections box at the end of the chapter for more about the role of persuasion in what we call *rhetoric*.

Evaluation of voice and speech is valuable for all on-air performers. Typical voice problems involve poor quality, delivery, and breathing. Typical speech problems are sloppy diction, regionalism, and cluttering.

Connections

• •

Rhetoric

The study of rhetoric, the art and science of using language persuasively and effectively, provides an excellent base for understanding the work of a broadcast announcer. When rhetoricians study communications, they focus on how communication influences beliefs or actions. And when we engage in any type of communication on radio, on TV, or simply in everyday life, we are often attempting to get our point across, to persuade people to our way of thinking.

Rhetoric in the broadest sense has been in existence since the first human could communicate, but it took its modern form and name during the 5th century BC when Greeks began studying oratorical technique, or *rhetorike techne.* In ancient Greece there were no lawyers, so if you were charged with a crime or if you brought an action against another citizen, you were compelled to speak for yourself. A group called the Sophists taught citizens how to make their cases persuasively.

Aristotle codified the field in about 330 BC when he compiled his work *Rhetoric.* Aristotle contended that the truth could be found and expressed through a combination of logic and elegance of speech. In this claim he differed from his teacher, Plato, who taught that persuasion could and should be carried out with pure logic.

Many of the concepts Aristotle wrote about are used today in analysis of persuasive communication. In fact, writers, speakers, and performers frequently use these concepts in their works: How do you "prove" an argument? Aristotle noted that there are three methods. A speaker must demonstrate:

* Ethos—A powerful, credible, believable character.
* Pathos—Style and substance that will stir the emotions of the listener.
* Logos—The use of logic to prove a point. Sometimes the argument is deductive, meaning that it works from general premises to a specific conclusion. Or the argument may be inductive, meaning that it provides many specific examples that lead us to a general conclusion.

Think about how effective broadcast communicators you have heard or seen use these principles. News anchors are often judged on their credibility—their ethos. The top-drawer music announcers relate the music to the emotions of their listeners, communicating pure pathos. And notice how many commercials feature copy that uses selective facts and a convincing announcer to communicate logos and draw the listeners or viewers to an inescapable conclusion.

Note that rhetoric has traditionally had some negative connotations: People sometimes regard it as the knack of persuading people regardless of the facts, the skill to mislead. Indeed, persuasive people can skirt the facts and lead listeners to an unreasonable conclusion. But that is another reason why the study of rhetoric is useful for an on-air person: Knowing how and why we are persuaded allows us to dismantle the arguments and see what makes them tick.

It is also important for on-air personnel to be familiar with standard American English and general American speech and to avoid significant deviations from these standards. An inappropriate rate of delivery and poor articulation can detract from the effectiveness of your vocal communication. Proper control of delivery rate also helps the announcer read to time limits—an important skill.

The broad task of making the speaking voice more pleasing begins with self-evaluation and isolation of specific problems. Continued work for crisp diction is important, but diction should not be overemphasized. It is also important to be aware of special considerations for broadcast work, such as using microphones properly.

Learning diaphragmatic breathing is the first major step in the long-term process of improving your speaking voice. Learning to relax is the second major step. In addition to preventing vocal abuse (a common problem of on-air broadcasters), relaxation increases resonance and improves the overall tone of the voice. Exercises can relax the vocal apparatus. A program of diet and fitness can help to ensure overall good health, which contributes to your ability to use your voice effectively at all times.

EXERCISES

In addition to practicing regularly the techniques described in this chapter, you can benefit by doing these exercises.

1. Pronounce the following pairs of words; record them if possible. Is there a distinguishable difference in your pronunciation? There should be.

picture/pitcher	saw/soar
wear/where	best/Bess
park/pock	peas/please
adapt/adept	aunt/ant
bowl/bold	pin/pen
can/kin	ensure/insure
kin/king	bad/bed

    An interesting variation of this exercise is to have a colleague or instructor check your pronunciation. An even more useful variation is to use each pair of words in a sentence. See if the distinction between the two similar words is still as clear during conversational speech as when the words are spoken in isolation.

2. Read through a line of poetry or other work and enunciate *every* sound in the sentence. Exaggerate to the point of silliness, but be sure to hit every consonant and vowel precisely. If you don't have poetry on hand, try this: "Speak distinctly, and rise above the babble of the crowd." The point of this exercise is to discover all the "hidden" sounds and variations of sounds we often gloss over.

3. Another type of diction practice is the tongue twister, which can be fun and interesting but probably not of extraordinary value. There was, however, a time when tongue twisters were popular material for radio announcer auditions, perhaps reflecting an overemphasis on mechanics, rather than on communication. Tongue twisters can bring about a healthy awareness of the accuracy of diction, though, so try these: Betty Botter bought some butter. But, she said, the butter's bitter, and if I put it in my batter it will make my batter bitter. So Betty Botter bought some better butter and put it in her batter, and the batter wasn't bitter so she opened a tin of sardines.

4. A variation on tongue twisters is a passage containing semi-nonsense words that must be read for *meaning*. Read the following paragraph so that the meaning is clear to a listener who has not heard it before. It is a very good exercise for showing how control of rate, pause, and inflection conveys meaning.

    Bill Bell builds bells. The bells Bill Bell builds bang and bong on Beele Boulevard. Bill builds bells with brass bell balls. Bell's bell balls build big bells. Bill Bell built brass ball-built bells for the Beal's bull, Buell. Buell's Bell-built brass bell banged when Buell bellowed on Beele and bore Bell's bells bong abroad. Bill Bell's bells, brass-ball-built for Beal's Beele-based bull Buell biased brass bell builders toward Bell brass ball-built bells. Boy![4]

NOTES

1 Ann S. Utterback, *Broadcast Voice Handbook*, 4th ed. (Taylor Trade Publishing, 2005).

2 David Blair McClosky and Barbara McClosky, *Voice in Song and Speech* (Boston: Boston Music Company, 1984). Used with permission.

3 David Blair McClosky, *Your Voice at Its Best: Enhancement of the Healthy Voice, Help for the Troubled Voice*, 5th ed. (Waveland Press, Inc. 2011).

4 Douglas Ehninger, Bruce E. Gronbeck, Ray E. McKerrow, and Alan H. Monroe, *Principles and Types of Speech Communication*, 10th ed. (New York: Scott, Foresman, 1986), p. 398.

Understanding the Message

The whole point of putting an announcer in a studio with a script to read is to convey a message to a listener or viewer. Whether that message is delivered solely by sound as in radio or with the added use of visual elements as in television, the objective is to translate what the copywriter had in mind, so that the listener ends up with the same idea.

The broadcast communicator is responsible for using all the skills and talents he or she can bring to bear to make sure the message is as effective as possible. This chapter addresses the basic responsibility of the broadcast communicator to understand the meaning of the message, and we outline techniques to improve the message's delivery. We will discuss (1) finding key words; (2) determining the mood, the pace, and the purpose of the copy; and (3) understanding that the goal is communicating, not merely reading. We'll also explore ways to mark copy for pronunciation, interpretation, and phrasing.

GETTING THE MEANING OF THE MESSAGE

The "message" is far more than just words. You must consider a variety of emotions and reactions when you look at words on paper, words that must be conveyed with meaning to each member of the audience. To compound the challenge, you must be sure that a faulty reading doesn't mar or blunt the meaning of the message.

An announcer conveys meaning by giving the copy an *interpretation* that communicates, through inflection and emphasis, something beyond the literal reproduction of the words on paper. Perhaps the words must be charged with emotion, or give a sense of excitement. You communicate these ideas *by first getting a clear and precise understanding of the message*. To do so, you must:

1. Carefully analyze the meaning and purpose of the **copy** (the topic of this chapter)
2. Communicate the words and phrases in such a way that the message has meaning and impact (the topic of Chapter 4)

Although years of experience can result in these two practices "coming naturally," the top professionals in the business never forget the need for understanding and communicating. "The most important ability an announcer can have is to interpret copy correctly," says Bill St. James,[1] host of United Stations' popular class rock show *Time Warp* and one of the industry's best-known freelance commercial voices. "You have to be able to read it as the guy who wrote it had it pictured in his head. And the other thing is that, when you get to this level, you have to do more than just read copy. You're expected to breathe life into it, to make it believable and human."

The point is often driven home rather vividly to beginners. Consider, for instance, this businessman's response to hearing a recording of a proposed commercial: "The announcer doesn't know what he's talking about . . . don't you people know anything about my business?"

One prospective news reporter lost a job he wanted very badly. The news director explained why when the audition tape was played back.[2] "Listen to how you read right through this line: 'the Republican coasted to an easy victory in a heavily Democrat district.' What the hell is this story about? It's about a Republican winning in a DEMOCRAT district."

Both performers were ineffective because they failed to understand the message.

To understand and communicate the message, you must identify *key words,* identify *pace and purpose,* and *communicate*—rather than just read—the copy.

Locating Key Words

The example we just gave of the news story shows what happens when the performer misses a key word. Finding those key words is the first step in analyzing the thrust of the copy.

Too often performers try to find key words by simply underlining every word that looks relevant. That approach is better than nothing, but if too many words are emphasized, they are no longer key words. Striking a balance is the goal.

One way to get to the heart of a piece of copy is to read it through and identify *three* words that summarize the thrust. This approach can give a surprisingly accurate reflection of which words are most important.

Theater set designers, who must come up with simple structures to convey complex messages, often play the mental game of distilling the entire play into a paragraph, then a sentence, and then a word. The set is designed around this word. This approach is oversimplified, but it does force you to think about the most basic meanings behind a play or any other form of communication. Key words are *those that accurately convey the meaning of the copy.* So changing key words can change the meaning of the copy.

For example, "Kim won the 10-kilometer run" is a simple statement. If you're looking for key words in that statement, you have to understand the context of the sentence. Is it an expression of amazement at athletic power? Turn it into a question-and-answer form to show it in a framework of a complete thought:

- "*KIM* won the 10-kilometer run? She hasn't trained in months!"

Changing the key word, then, can alter the perceived meaning. Let's complete three more question-and-answer pairs and show how context affects meaning.

- "Kim *WON* the 10-kilometer run? I thought she came in *third.*"
- "Kim won the 10-*KILOMETER* run? She said it was a 10-*mile* run."
- "Kim won the 10-kilometer *RUN?* I thought it was a *walk*athon."

Finding the key words may mean going through the original copy several times to clarify for yourself what the author had in mind. This is not a mechanical process, although mediocre announcers make it so. For example, in most commercial copy the performer can rightly assume that words such as "bargain," "inexpensive," "free," "new," "natural," and "modern" are key words. When reading the script look for words that are intrinsic to the message and that deserve stress, *always* the key words; a performer can mangle the message by not understanding it in context. How important is the word "new" in the following piece of copy?

The new line of Smith Hiking Shoes will give you a step up as you swing into spring activities. . . . Look great and feel great in . . .

The most important words here are probably "Smith Hiking Shoes," "look great," and "feel great"; "new" is really not important. Also of secondary importance are the words relating to spring. The word "new" is almost redundant because few shoe stores offer old shoes as their spring line. The purpose of this copy is not to communicate the idea that Smith Shoes are new. The purpose is to communicate the idea that Smith Shoes will make you look and feel great and will let you "swing into spring activities" in an upbeat way.

But let's take another example:

The new line of Smith smartphones, designed with the latest in digital technology . . .

Here, the word "new" assumes paramount importance. After all, a *new* smartphone, in these days of technological one-upmanship, is inherently more valuable than one of an older design.

The point is to avoid a mechanical approach to finding key words. Never assume that the most obvious choices are the words that convey the message.

Much the same caution applies to news copy. In news, there's really no stronger verb than "died." It conveys the most urgent event in our society, the loss of a life. But although there's no question that "four children *died* in a fire at . . ." is the correct interpretation of the copy, the word *died* isn't always the most important word in a message. For example,

The families of the four children who died in Tuesday's tenement fire are suing the owner of the building . . .

Is "died" the key word here? Not really. The most important words are "families," "suing," and "owner." Putting too much stress on the concept of death makes the listener think that the communicator is calling attention to a contrast between the families of those who died and those who didn't:

The families of the four children who *died* in Tuesday's tenement fire are suing the owner of the building . . .

According to this reading, the sentence ought to be completed with

. . . but the families of burn victims who did *not* die are not suing.

To sum up, finding key words is not a simple or mechanical process. It involves a thorough analysis of the copy. Marking key words in the copy helps the performer accurately communicate the thrust of the message.

Communicating Mood

Understanding the mood the copywriter wants to project helps you to give an accurate interpretation. By contrast, not understanding the mood can detract from the communication. Projecting an inappropriate mood or making an inappropriate change of mood can baffle the audience. For example, in one familiar situation comedy routine the newscaster mixes up his copy and blunders into a tragic plane crash story with the smile and upbeat tone reserved for the final "light side" piece.

Misreading the mood is seldom that obvious, but it can happen, and it can mar your delivery. So carefully determine the mood. It could be, for instance, any one of the following:

- *Carefree.* "Swing into spring with Smith Shoes . . ."
- *Sincere.* "Are you concerned about your health insurance?"
- *Romantic.* "Dinner by candlelight at the Copper Bottom Restaurant will be one of the most . . ."
- *Somber.* "Twenty-three miners were killed this afternoon in a cave-in north of the city of . . ."
- *Excited.* "Bob Smith Nissan has 30 cars ready to go at below wholesale!"

- *Humorous.* "A bank customer using an automatic teller machine in Los Angeles got more than he bargained for today when the machine spit out ten thousand . . ."

The relatively straightforward task of evaluating the copy for mood is done not so much to determine what mood the particular piece reflects as to find out where *changes* in mood must be expressed. A common problem for inexperienced or ineffective newscasters is not being able to *spot the points in copy where the mood must change.* When mood changes are not spotted in advance, the interpretation becomes inappropriate. At best, the announcer slides through the copy with an overall lack of mood. At worst, he or she catches the error and tries to change the mood at an inappropriate point, losing the real mood and sense of the copy.

Using Appropriate Pace

Pace is the rapidity of words, the overall rate of reading, and the rate of reading within phrases. You can make the most effective use of pace after you have acquired an understanding of when and why to vary it. In general, a speeded-up pace conveys a sense of excitement. Sometimes, that excitement can be panicky, harried: *You've got a problem . . . the system is crashing around you, everybody is looking at you, and you'd better make it right.*

But note that a change of pace is needed in the second part of the commercial:

. . . you'd better make it *right.*

At Telephone World Business Systems, we've been helping people like you make the right decisions for over twenty years. We've got the facts—not hype—and we can sit down with you and tailor-make a system that will do the job right.

We know it's a big decision, and . . .

Where would you vary the pace, and why? The first part of the commercial conveys a sense of time running out. That is as urgent a message as you can get. The pace, of course, is very rapid, almost breathless.

But the second part of the spot calls for a slower, more deliberate reading, "At Telephone World Business Systems, we've been helping people like you . . ." signals a change to a slower, deliberate, purposeful pace.

Get into the mind of the writer. What is he or she trying to get across? At this point, it's simply *you can stop panicking and come to Telephone World Business Systems, where we help people in the same situation every day, so calm down!*

An announcer who used the same pace throughout would mutilate this spot and lose much of its impact.

Determining the Purpose

What is the copy intended to do? Why was it composed in the first place? If you have answered these questions, you know the copy's purpose. Copy can persuade, inform, entertain, even anger. The communicator must understand the purpose before he or she can transmit the message accurately.

To understand the purpose, you have to understand more than what's on the paper. The more you know about the context for the copy, and the broader your range of knowledge, the better you can interpret the message.

For example, consider the intense advertising campaigns that competing cellular phone systems have engaged in since deregulation opened the door to competition.

To help interpret our imaginary Telephone World Business Systems spot, the announcer should be aware that the employee responsible for choosing a new phone system is under a great deal of pressure to make the right decision amid an intense advertising barrage. A valid interpretation must appeal to this theme.

Experienced professionals can lend an important sound to such copy through accumulated skills of emphasis and inflection. Understanding copy, though, will *always* help *anyone's* interpretation.

In addition, the announcer should understand the purpose of individual phrases in relation to the context. What would you perceive to be the purpose of the question "Why did this happen?" Standing on its own, it means little. It assumes varied significance when read in relation to the context. For example:

"Economists said interest rates fell sharply in the wake of the presidential election. Why did this happen?" Here, "Why did this happen?" is an expression of simple curiosity.

"Scientists found that the orbit of Pluto varied last year by hundreds of millions of miles. Why did this happen?" Now the question expresses wonderment.

"Speculation about whether the birds would fly north or south was ended today when they flew west. Why did this happen?" What caused the birds to fly west? Does it suggest that the speculation was unfounded?

"Ten people died in yesterday's apartment house fire. There were no smoke detectors in the building, which had passed a recent code inspection. Why did this happen?" The question now expresses outrage.

To sum up, understanding the purpose is essential. The next stage of the broadcast performance process—communicating the message—cannot be done effectively unless you know why the copy, sentence, phrase, or word is there in the first place.

COMMUNICATING VERSUS MERELY READING

Perhaps the ultimate example of reading instead of communicating was provided by an announcer with a fine voice but a lazy and mechanical approach to his work. The copy was designed to relate the sponsor's product to the weather, and the announcer was supposed to open the spot with *one* of the following *three* options:

- "What a beautiful, sunny day. . . ."
- "Look at all that rain. . . ."
- "We've had more than our share of snow. . . ."

But he read *all three*, and he failed to understand at first why the program director and the sponsor were so upset with his delivery.

That example is *not* too far-fetched. Similar mess-ups happen every day. Poor on-air performers can make hash out of commercial and news copy because they simply do not take the time to understand the message they want to communicate.

This is the sum of what we discussed in the previous section. A good broadcaster must incorporate key words, mood, pace, and purpose to communicate, rather than just read.

Most of us have heard "announcers" who have decided in their own minds "what announcers sound like." They deliver each message in a mechanical singsong. That is *reading*.

A *communicator* knows how the copy should be read and can get across the intent of the author. He or she does not follow a preset formula but instead approaches each reading with an open mind, looking for the thrust of the material. In most cases, the better performer is not necessarily the one with the better voice, but the one who makes the copy genuine, natural, believable, and true to the intent of the author.

After many years of practice, this ability can become second nature. Good performers develop that second nature by marking copy to indicate key words, pace, pauses, and in some cases mood and purpose. They also include methods of indicating pronunciations of difficult words. Learning to mark copy is one of the most important steps you can take toward improving your performance skills.

Marking Copy to Enhance Communication

To many, marking copy is more a learning process than a practical tool. Many performers don't mark copy. They rely on experience and ability to carry the situation.

Many announcers do not have the opportunity to mark copy. Commercials that are meant to be read live are kept in a copybook that is used by all staff announcers and would soon be obliterated if each staffer put individual marks on the copy. Newscasters must often read copy that is prepared by others and that is not assigned to a particular newscaster until moments before airtime. Most news copy is created on a computer and read off the monitor. Marking such copy is not practical.

What experienced announcers do, in effect, is to mark copy mentally. Beginners should mark as much copy as possible directly on the paper because the ability to do it mentally takes extensive practice.

However, all on-air people mark unfamiliar pronunciations, and such markings frequently are written right into the typed copy or wire service text. Marking copy for pronunciation is an integral part of understanding the message.

Phonetic Spelling. How do you show how to pronounce an unfamiliar word? Basically, you must come up with notations that will let you or another reader look at the agreed-on code and know how to pronounce the word. Such a system is known as *phonetic spelling*.

There are a variety of phonetic systems, and some are very accurate but very complex. The **International Phonetic Alphabet (IPA)**, for example, uses symbols not found in the English alphabet to indicate elements of pronunciation. The IPA is a valuable tool for linguists and other scholars, but its value for broadcast performers is limited for two reasons:

1. Not all broadcasters understand it. The IPA can help someone who knows it to reproduce pronunciations with great accuracy, but most broadcast copy is not written by people who will read it over the air. Even in newsrooms where broadcasters do write most of the news department's copy, much of that copy is read by other newspeople.
2. Many of the symbols in the IPA are not reproducible by standard word-processing and newsroom computer equipment.

The second problem also rules out the use of diacritical marks, such as those found in the dictionary. Most word processors can't reproduce markings such as ā and ī, easily.

Despite its limitations for broadcast applications, however, the IPA is a tool you should be acquainted with. The Appendix gives you a system for learning the rudiments of the IPA quickly. If you take a little time to familiarize yourself with the IPA, you will be able to use it—along with the other tools discussed in this chapter—to unravel nearly any unknown pronunciation you encounter.

As a readily available tool for everyday use, the best alternative seems to be the phonetic spellings used by the Associated Press (AP) Pronunciation Guide.[3] The AP uses a simple phonetic spelling system to convey how a name or other word sounds. It "goes along with the commonly accepted principles of English usage as to how vowels and consonants are sounded."

When an accent is indicated, the AP places a Teletype apostrophe over the letter or letter group that should be accented. As an example, in the style of the *AP Broadcast News Handbook*[4] the name Juan Martinez spelled phonetically would appear as *Wahn Mahr-tee'-ness*.

When you are constructing or interpreting a **pronouncer**, as it is called, use standard English usage and the guide shown in Box 3.1, from the *AP Broadcast News Handbook*.

Pronouncers are shown in all wire service copy destined for broadcast use. If you are doubtful about a word and don't have a pronouncer, try looking them up on one of the many helpful pronunciation guides available online, such as the Voice of America's Pro-nounce (https://pronounce.voanews.com/) or Forvo. com. Newspeople are responsible for determining the pronunciation of names of local newsmakers, a process that often involves making telephone calls to individuals, their families, or business associates.

BOX 3.1 The Associated Press Pronunciation Guide

Vowel Sounds

a bat, apple

ah father, arm

aw raw, board

ay fate, ace

e, eh bed

ee feet, tea

i, ih pin, middle

y, eye ice, time, guide

oh go, oval

oo food, two

ow scout, crowd

oy boy, join

u curl, foot

uh puff

yoo fume, few

Consonants

kh gutteral "k"

g got, beg

j job, gem

k keep, cap

ch chair, butcher

sh shut, fashion

zh vision, mirage

th thin, path

Source: Brad Kalbfeld, *AP Broadcast News Handbook* (New York: McGraw-Hill, 2001), p. 382.

Marking and Decoding Unfamiliar Words

To be able to approximate unfamiliar English words and words in foreign languages, it is worthwhile to get some exposure to foreign pronunciations.

For one thing, some pronunciations can't be approximated by phonetic spelling because the sounds are not commonly used in English. Also, sooner or later you will come across a foreign word and have no way to check it out.

The English-speaking announcer faces some additional problems, other than simply deciphering pronunciations.

Foreign Pronunciations

Many foreign words have been anglicized as a matter of convention.

In English, we speak of Munich, Germany; to speakers of German, the city is named *München*. Naples, to an Italian, is *Napoli*. Even when the spellings are the same, American pronunciations can differ from those of the original language. Paris, to a Frenchman, is *Pah-ree*. How does an announcer decide?

The best strategy is to combine knowledge of pronunciation rules with a good set of reference books, a broad education, and an observant personality. Suppose you need to say,

Our next selection is by Richard Wagner: the prelude to *Das Rheingold*.

Wagner is one of the names that is customarily pronounced with full inflection and adherence to native pronunciation. Most names in classical music follow this custom. Therefore, the *ch* in "Richard" is pronounced as a *k*. The *a*, as is typical of most foreign pronunciation, is close to the *a* in the American word "arm." The *w* takes the Germanic *v* sound. The title of the music needs little decoding except for the *ei* configuration, which is pronounced like the word "eye." Thus we have *Rih-kart' Vahg'-ner, dahs Ryn'-golt.*

Similar analysis can be applied to the following examples:

The Spanish region of Castile was originally divided into the provinces of New Castile and Old Castile, Known as Castilla la Nueva and Castilla la Vieja.

Note in this example that you would use different inflections when reading the English and Spanish designations of the same regions.

> Although not known as the most intellectual of Italian composers, Giacomo Puccini is one of the best known.

To begin your analysis, check the difference in pronunciation between the single *c* in Giacomo and the double *c* in Puccini.

Special Considerations for Foreign Pronunciations

Although this chapter centers on marking and understanding copy, some suggestions on delivering copy involving foreign words and phrases are appropriate to conclude the discussion.

- *Try never to be caught unaware.* Check copy thoroughly and phoneticize words. Be aware that foreign words can arise in almost any on-air work, not just classical music, international news, or sports. Check proper names with the people named, if possible, because even a common name such as *Gentile* can be and is pronounced "*Jen-teel'-ee*" by some people in certain locations. With some words, you may have little information about the word's origin or pronunciation, so it is wise to flag the word and check with an authoritative source, such as the radio station news director.
- Famed KQED-FM morning announcer Norm Howard in San Francisco put it in one of his broadcasts: "In the course of our work we often have to pronounce unfamiliar and foreign words—the names of opera singers, composers, places and names in the news, words from different ethnic and cultural groups, from alphabets other than Roman. This is all by way of saying that a few minutes ago I mispronounced the name of the polar bear Pike, and I want you to know that it is *'Peek-uh,'* not 'pike.' Such are the hazards . . ."
- *Do not hesitate before saying the word.* If you hesitate, listeners may think you are wrong *even if you are right.*
- **Bluffing sometimes is necessary, but don't get carried away.** One announcer, for example, recalls the time he was reading "cold" a list of boxing title holders, who in the lower weight classes were mostly Latin Americans. He did rather well except for his highly accented rendition of what he thought was the name of the featherweight champion, *"Teet'-lay Vah-caht'-ate,"* which turned out to mean "Title vacated."

Remember that although learning the basic pronunciation rules can help in many situations, there are exceptions to many of the rules. True competence in foreign pronunciation is best achieved by having some familiarity with the actual languages. Several semesters of foreign language courses will be very beneficial in cultivating pronunciation skills.

English words should also be marked and phoneticized. In fact, English is a very irregular language, and a simple set of rules to govern all English pronunciations cannot be devised.

What is "Acceptable" Pronunciation?

Most lexicographers (writers and compilers of dictionaries) define "acceptable pronunciation" simply as a pronunciation agreed on by convention among educated people. Pay attention to the way knowledgeable speakers pronounce words, and when in doubt about a word, *look it up in a reference book or reliable website.*

Some pronunciations are especially deceptive, and incorrect pronunciations have worked their way into common usage. See Box 3.2 for examples.

Marking copy with correct pronunciations is one of the first things you need to do when evaluating material. The next consideration is marking it for proper interpretation, for correct *phrasing.*

BOX 3.2 Examples of Frequently Mispronounced Words

Some really common words are also very commonly mispronounced.
Here are some examples:

- *Nuclear.* It's *noo'-clee-yahr,* not *noo'-cue-lahr.*
- *Status. stayt-us* is more widely accepted than *stat'-us.*
- *Data. dayt'-uh* is more widely accepted than *daht'-uh.*
- *Greenwich.* Say *"Gren'-ich"* to designate Greenwich, England, and Greenwich Village in New York City. Some small communities pronounce the same word *"Green'-wich,"* however, which points up the need for checking local usages.

If these words took you by surprise, consult a dictionary or other reference book and check out the following words and place names. Be sure you are pronouncing them correctly and not adding additional sounds.
For example, *"ath'-ah-leet"* is a common mispronunciation.

accessory	infamous	radiator	length
impotent	Moscow	Delhi	Yosemite
Spokane	La Jolla	Canaan	Cannes

Using Symbols to Aid Interpretation

The dictionary defines "phrasing" as a grouping together of words into a unit forming a single thought. Perhaps a more interesting definition from the broadcaster's point of view is the musical concept of phrasing, where many of the passages that combine to form a larger piece can also stand alone, each such passage, or phrase, expressing a more or less complete thought.

Musicians and composers use a variety of symbols to aid interpretation, such as a crescendo (<), indicating a gradual increase in volume, or a "retard" (anglicized contraction of *ritardando* and abbreviated in music as rit.), meaning a slowing of the tempo.

A broadcaster can do the same. Figure 3.1 shows some useful symbols for marking copy. The next section shows how these symbols can help you communicate the message by phrasing it properly.

Phrasing. Notice how the symbols in Figures 3.2 and 3.3 add to both the understanding and impact of the copy. Key words are identified and their relative strengths indicated. In the ethics story, there are many phrases that must be kept together for meaning and clarity, so they are bracketed for grouping.

The examples in Figures 3.4 to 3.5 take the marking process further and add some pauses and nuances. Observe how the jagged lines indicate a speeded-up tempo. You want to create a fast, harried mood for the first section. But when the copy must be slowed down, the change is indicated by the series of dots. The performer who marked up this copy realized that the second portion must be read in *deliberate* fashion.

Understanding the Message. The performer who marked up this copy also used a cue for a jingle at this point. He or she might also elect to use that cue mark for timing. The performer could indicate that the remaining copy must be read in a given time period.

<u>word</u>   underline for emphasis

word   underline twice for heavy emphasis

word/word   slash for pause

Word   to flag unfamiliar word or pronunciation

[One Complete Phrase]   brackets identify complete

Phrase or sentence   jagged line means speed up

phrase or Sentence   dots mean slow down

Word/word   cue note for production element or time cue

Excited!   marginal note for interpretation

FIGURE 3.1 Symbols for aiding interpretation.

```
     Two people are dead, four injured, in the wake of a violent
                                    Mahr-say'
explosion this morning at 443 Marseilles St. The names of the
victims are being withheld pending notification of next of kin.
     [The explosion and resulting fire] leveled the two-story house.
Investigators are currently on the scene. One fire official [who does
not want to be identified] told Eyewitness News that arson is a
possibility.
```

FIGURE 3.2 A marked news story.

[A study by researchers at Harvard and the University] of Utah says that <u>tiredness</u> can make people more likely to <u>cheat</u> or be <u>dishonest</u>.

[The Independent] reports that the study shows people were more likely to exhibit self-control and be <u>morally aware</u> in the <u>morning.</u>But in the <u>afternoon,</u>even those with the strongest moral compass were likely to <u>ethically fade.</u>

So-called Morning Morality is <u>more</u> likely to be apparent in people who have <u>high</u> ethical standards as a whole – meaning, presumably, that <u>unethical</u> people transgress more or less <u>evenly throughout the day.</u>

The erosion of ethics, the researchers concluded, can therefore result not from crises or stressful dilemmas, but merely from, in the words of the study, a ["gradual depletion of self-regulatory processes as a result of unremarkable daily activities"]

The study involved observations of subjects who played a game [in which a fudged answer earned a higher reward] and an [experiment in which they would associate <u>word puzzles with</u> the words "<u>moral</u>" and "<u>ethical.</u>"]

FIGURE 3.3 A marked news story.

You've been running from bank to bank, you've heard gibberish [*jibberish*]
and promises. You need a mortgage and time is running out. Well,
you can keep on running, or you can walk into Hypothetical Savings,
where qualified borrowers can get a fixed rate mortgage at 11 percent,
and no points. That's a fixed rate mortgage at 11 percent, and
no points. [single] The Hypothetical Savings Bank, member, FDIC.

FIGURE 3.4 In this commercial, markings help the announcer stress important points.

It's late July. August is right around the corner. It's time to shop
for fall clothes, but it's hard to get enthusiastic about wool and corduroy,
when the thermometer is pushing 90 degrees.

[So take a break from your shopping for fall] and enjoy something
tall and cool. [Come to the lunch counter at Woolworth's in the Park
Plaza Mall] and treat yourself to a "Sizzlebuster."

It's not exactly a drink. But it is cool, delicious, and
refreshing. The Sizzlebuster is made from six kinds of fruit mixed with
ice. There's no sugar added, and each one is mixed fresh at the time you
order it. [It's a smooth, tasty treat] that makes your whole body feel
cool and refreshed. [And this week] it's only $1.50.

So if you need a break from summer, and looking at heavy fall
clothing isn't cooling you off, stop at Woolworth's lunch counter and
get a Sizzlebuster. It's the cool thing to do.

A fine Italian restaurant is hard enough to find today [in this world
of Fast food] [and grabit and run.] And if you want to take time to enjoy
the quiet elegance of beautiful surroundings while you dine, you may
have given up hope.

But wait. There's Montinerio's [*Montinareeos*] Casa Italiano, where fine dining is
still considered a necessity of life. [The finest northern Italian
cuisine,] [expertly prepared by a master chef,] is presented to you in an
atmosphere of quiet Victorian elegance. [Your food is served with the
attention to detail that reflects the Old World grace and style] of the
finest European restaurants.

So forget the hurry-up world for a while. Put some style back into
your life. Come to Montinerio's Casa Italiano and see what life can be
like in the slow lane.

FIGURE 3.5 In this commercial, markings are helpful in identifying key concepts.

Phrasing and Interpretation. Consider how the examples presented show the ways in which phrasing can affect interpretation. The bank commercial was affected (see Figure 3.4) because the pace conveyed two very different moods.

Ineffective readers typically do not blend and match all the phrasing elements in a piece of copy. This frequently results in what might be called "mixed signals," for example, someone on television who is smiling but is clenching his or her fists.

You have to get your signals straight. There is some latitude in phrasing, but slow, deliberate phrasing would be inappropriate for most soft drink commercials, and quick, frenetic phrasing wouldn't work well for an insurance spot.

Rhythm and Inflection. The example of "Kim won the 10-kilometer run" in the section headed "Finding Key Words" illustrates the impact of inflection. Rhythm is also a powerful tool in conveying a message. The pause can create emphasis and, to an extent, suspense. Paul Harvey is an acknowledged master of the long, long pause, which virtually makes the audience beg for the punch line of his news story.

Rhythm incorporates change of pace, which is also a component of understanding and communicating a message.

In many cases it is not difficult at all to visualize the copy as a piece of music. Variations in rhythm, different inflections and emphases, and variations in loudness, intensity, and pitch all combine to provide a total effect.

Good writers know this, which is why they "write for the ear." Effective communicators recognize the melodic and dramatic features of what is written, and often compose their own words and **melody**. The Gettysburg Address, for example, uses a memorable rhythm. And one noted piece of advertising copy was delivered in an unforgettable way: "We make money the old-fashioned way . . . we *earn* it."

SUMMARY

Communicating a message is the first and most basic responsibility of an announcer. The announcer must think in terms of ideas, not words. Finding key words in the copy is a tool for understanding meaning and ideas. You may not always be able to mark up copy—after all, you'll read a lot of it from a computer screen—but do so when you have a chance, both for the improvement you'll notice in delivery and the practice in identifying key words. Getting the meaning of the message involves understanding and identifying mood, pace, and purpose. The goal is to communicate, not just to read.

Tech Talk

Research on the Web: A Guide for Announcers

On-air personnel must have a wide range of knowledge, and they are frequently called on to address current events, trends in music, and developments in the industry. The World Wide Web is an incredible resource for staying up to date in all these areas.

This is *not intended to be an all-inclusive list* but simply a series of starting points for performers who want to use the Web as a ready reference.

Check out the following sites.

Tech Talk *(continued)*

General News and Information

Journalist's Toolbox presented by the Society for Professional Journalists (https://www.journaliststoolbox.org/) provides a wealth of information for journalists. Included are links to major news aggregators (like NewsLookUp, Slate and Breibart) as well as links to many hometown newspapers around the United States. (A word of caution. The newspaper industry is changing rapidly. As a result you will find many links to small or local papers that no longer work.) Toolbox also provides links to electronic media news outlets as well. It is a useful all-in-one website.

For a quick scan of the world's and nation's top news, and searches of recent editions, try the *New York Times* . . .

www.nytimes.com

And the *Washington Post* . . .

www.Washingtonpost.com

Twitter has become an important tool for journalists to access brief reports and quotes from political figures regarding current news.

www.twitter.com

Search Engines

Major search engines like Google and Bing scan the content of websites and allow you to find websites that contain the key words you specify.

An excellent way to start your search is with

www.google.com or www.bing.com

For a guided search, try

www.yahoo.com

Library Links

Search the indexes of the Library of Congress for its extensive digital catalog including American documents, photographs and sound recordings.

https://catalog.loc.gov/vwebv/searchBrowse

For information about Congress go to

www.Congress.gov

Most states have a similar legislative website as well.

Journalism Links

The Poynter Institute features a wide assortment of links related to journalism along with examples of prize-winning stories and photographs and suggestions for improving writing and coverage. Search at www.poynter.org

Radio and TV on the Web

Check out the World Wide Web Virtual Library:

http://www.vlib.org

Broadcasters Radio Locator:

https://radio-locator.com/cgi-bin/finder?s=C

allows you to search for radio stations by call letters, location or format.

Tech Talk *(continued)*

Billboard Magazine has features about broadcasting and music:
  https://www.billboard.com
And you can find out a great deal about the TV news industry and see some job ads at
  www.tvspy.com
As noted earlier the AP Pronunciation guide is very useful:
  https://www.scribd.com/doc/39766501/AP-Pronunciation-Guide

Wire service phonetic spelling, although it has its limitations, works well within the constraints of word processing software, email, and typical newsroom operations.

Another important part of marking copy is identifying and decoding unfamiliar words and phrases. Key words are not always obvious. Often some analysis and digging are necessary to uncover the true meaning and impact of the piece. Noting key words is part of marking copy.

An announcer should make every effort to become familiar with the principles of foreign pronunciation. In addition to learning some language rules, it is important to know how and when to employ foreign pronunciation and inflection. In most cases it is best to follow the rules of pronunciation of the appropriate language but without trying to use the inflections of a native speaker of that language. Speak as you would imagine an educated American would, assuming some familiarity with the language in question. Never hesitate before you say a foreign word.

Names of contemporary newsmakers are pronounced as the person named wants. Names of foreign cities are pronounced according to conventional American usage. In the specialized field of classical music, however, foreign words receive full native accents and inflections.

The major component of marking copy is using symbols to aid interpretation. These symbols act like a musician's notation and guide the announcer to proper phrasing.

Phrasing—the grouping together of words into units forming single thoughts—affects meaning and communication. Marking copy identifies many of the signposts to meaning and communication. Also, it helps the announcer convey the proper rhythm and inflections of words and the melody of the words.

EXERCISES

1. Mark up copy you write or copy provided by your instructor. Split into groups of four and exchange copy.

   Compare similarities and differences. Discuss the differences and why you feel markups are right or wrong.

   Next, elect one person to read all four pieces of marked copy, following the markings closely. Others in the group may also do this, depending on time limitations.

2. Using news articles, pick three key words per sentence and write those words down. Do this for an entire article. Many long sentences will have more than three key words, so you will have to use your judgment in identifying the most important words. Be sure to use a straight news article, not a feature or human-interest piece.

   Read your key words aloud to a partner or to the class. Your partner or the class members must try to *reconstruct the story* from the three key words per sentence. When you read aloud, play out the words broadly and give them as much meaning as possible.

3. Write three approximately 30-second commercials for automobiles, and to the best of your ability write them "to ear." Make up whatever details you wish, but structure the commercials around these three concepts:

Commercial 1: To express elegance and love of luxury. Think in terms of rich leathers, classic interiors, and elegant lines.
Commercial 2: Youth, excitement, adventure.
Commercial 3: Practicality, dependability, durability, value to a growing family.

Have a partner or classmate give an interpretation of the commercials that you have written, aloud or on tape. Critique that performer. Work with him or her until you feel that each commercial is done correctly.

Compare your critique with the instructor's critique.

NOTES

1 Quotes used with permission.
2 The term tape is often used in the industry even though almost all files are now digital. Often the technology changes more quickly than the nomenclature.
3 Both the VOA Pro•nounce program and the AP Pronunciation Guide are freely available online.
4 Brad Kalbfeld, *Associated Press Broadcast News Handbook*, 5th ed. (McGraw-Hill Education, 2013).

4

Communicating the Message

Once he or she understands the basic message, the broadcast communicator must apply those skills to the actual delivery of information. Whether you're reading voice-over copy from a printed script or ad-libbing your way through the morning drive segment on the local radio station or reporting live from a breaking news event, the basic requirement is to generate a response from the audience.

In this chapter, we begin by discussing the basic principles of reading copy and then deal with some of the nuances. We discuss ad-libbing in detail. Finally, we'll examine two technical skills that are central to effective delivery of the message: mic technique and camera technique.

READING COPY

Why bother to sit down before a mic or TV camera and read a piece of copy? The answer is not as simple as it seems because, in addition to good mechanical delivery, a broadcast performer has several goals:

1. To communicate the message accurately
2. To convince the audience, on a *one-to-one* basis, that the performer understands and believes what he or she is reading
3. To breathe life into the message
4. To keep the listeners' and viewers' attention by giving energy to the reading

Accomplishing these goals involves proper use of your voice, a genuine and believable delivery, and the addition of style to the reading.

Using Your Voice

Proper use of your voice will help you considerably in communicating, in being convincing, in breathing life into a message, and in keeping the audience's interest.

A good voice is more than an "announcer voice." Today, you can be successful with what was once thought of as an average-quality voice. In news, the trend has been toward hiring on-air people who act more like journalists and less like performers. The commercial industry often needs voices that express humor or whimsy. Radio station managers and program directors search for true communicators who can reach specific audiences. Today that means hiring someone with a solid music background for that format rather than baritones with "rounded tones."

Two key elements of proper use of your voice were outlined in Chapter 2:

1. A healthy and relaxed vocal mechanism
2. The absence of distracting deviations, such as speech impediments or inappropriate regionalisms

Here we add a third key element:

3. A natural-sounding, genuine delivery

Creating a Genuine Delivery

A common beginning mistake is to put on an "announcer voice" and ignore the copy, focusing on the delivery as an end in itself. But even if you remember nothing else from reading this book, remember that the voice is only a tool and the message in the copy is what is important. Your voice *must not distract* from the message.

Some performers use the message as a vehicle for their voices, a practice that is neither productive nor professional. Actor John Carradine once said that one of the most valuable lessons ever taught to him was not to be "in love with my voice."

It is difficult to define the elements of genuine delivery because "genuine" implies a sound as natural and unaffected as possible. And yet, the broadcast studio is not a natural setting, and you certainly would not read copy the way you speak to a friend in a restaurant. Although some people advise announcers to talk as though they were speaking to friends in their living rooms, that's not, in a literal sense, what you want to do.

You must work in an unnatural setting and make your performance *appear* natural. You must make your message *resemble* the manner in which you speak to your best friend. If you listened to a tape of a conversation among friends, you would probably decide that it did not meet broadcast standards, especially in terms of diction and energy level.

A genuine delivery adds excitement and interest to a message without injecting artificiality. Mechanically trying to "punch up" copy can result in a strained, unnatural sound. That strained quality sometimes is a result of not paying attention to the phrasing of the copy. The delivery will sound much more believable if the words and phrases have been carefully analyzed and the copy marked appropriately.

Lack of artificiality is rapidly becoming one of the most desirable qualifications for an on-air performer. Today's performers in both broadcasting and new media are people who can communicate one-to-one. No longer do broadcasters *address* the audience. You could be on a *YouTube* channel viewed by only one person at any one time.

Top performers who conduct interviews on the air have become particularly adept at the kind of personal approach required of broadcasters today. One of the best in this format is Terry Gross (Figure 4.1), who hosts *Fresh Air*, an interview program heard nationwide on National Public Radio. She is particularly adept at establishing a close rapport with both her guests and her audiences. Although she has an excellent voice, she uses it *conversationally*, putting her listeners at ease as they join her to explore the personalities of her interesting guests.

STYLE

A style can also be defined as a particular and distinctive characteristic or mode of action. Style is a component of both writing and performing.

It is difficult to draw a line between a stylized delivery and an artificial delivery, and even more difficult to try to cultivate a style that works. Trying too hard can result in an affected, phony delivery.

Yet broadcasters, by the very nature of their work, are required to have something distinctive about their delivery and appearance. On-air people frequently become noted for their styles, and unless a performer has something unusual going for him or her, advancement may be difficult.

There is no comprehensive list of styles, nor should you adopt mannerisms based on the approaches given here. Bear in mind, too, that performers use bits and pieces of various style categories to form their own unique styles.

FIGURE 4.1 Terry Gross, who hosts *Fresh Air*, an interview program aired on National Public Radio, is noted for her ability to communicate one-to-one with both her guests and her listening audience.

Don't consciously wedge yourself into a style or copy everything a particular performer does. Do, however, remember that all performers pick up things from their colleagues. No one lives in a vacuum, and the way other professionals work must have an effect on each of us.

This eclecticism has plus and minus sides. Former *Tonight Show* host Johnny Carson admitted that some of his style was picked up from the late Jack Benny. The result was obviously successful because Carson hosted the show for more than 20 years.[1] On the other end of the spectrum is the speech pattern of NBC's former news anchor, Tom Brokaw. Brokaw has a very slight lazy 'L' pronunciation that people would *not* want to imitate, but he was a first-class communicator and an outstanding journalist.

Let's look at some style categories and representative performers.

Sophisticated. Lesley Stahl is an example of a performer who projects a sophisticated air. She projects intelligence, culture, and taste in her bearing, her phrasing, and in her appearance. She is one of only a very few performers who manage to present this image without seeming to be a caricature of sophistication. Despite this sophistication she is a strong journalist, comfortable asking tough questions to world leaders. Other *Sixty Minutes* journalists such as Steve Kroft and Scott Pelley also convey airs of cultured intelligence.

Authoritative. Someone who projects an air of importance and power comes across as "authoritative," a word that is overused in broadcasting to promote news programming. CNN's Jake Tapper (Figure 4.2) fits that role. Tapper, who graduated both Phi Beta Kappa and magna cum laude from college, hosts CNN's *The Lead* daily and *State of the Union* on Sunday. He is known for asking intelligent, difficult questions of both Republicans and Democrats alike.

FIGURE 4.2 Jake Tapper is known for the authoritative manner in which he poses questions.

Whimsical. Advertisers often seek performers who can project humor or vulnerability. The whimsical style works well in specific applications. Perhaps the best example of a host who successfully uses whimsy is former *Latenight Show* host David Letterman. You would not, though, customarily find this style in the evening news anchor. There are certain whimsical *elements* in newspeople and people related to the news business, including David Pogue and Mo Rocca on CBS.

Interestingly, since the election of President Trump, late night hosts Steven Colbert, Seth Meyers and Jimmy Kimmel have increasingly focused their opening monologues by poking fun at current events and political leaders. While this is not news, it impacts our consciousness about daily events in a whimsical fashion or often in a satirical way.

Folksy. Without peer in the "true-to-life" folksy approach to communication is *Today Show* host Al Roker. Roker is a very able performer who conveys great friendliness and personal charm. A performer who can master this style is sometimes able to parlay it into great trust and therefore great sales power. Walter Cronkite (Figure 4.3), one of the premier newspeople in the history of American broadcast journalism, projected the aura of an intelligent next-door neighbor. Cronkite's use of phrases like "By golly!" when covering a space flight and his overall friendly, informal style gave him tremendous credibility.

Dick Enberg was a well-known sportscaster who did play-by-play for many different sports on both radio and TV. His folksy style was appreciated by sports fans, particularly with his signature exclamation, "Oh, my" for exciting moments during athletic play.

Knowledgeable/didactic. Christiane Amanpour is noted for the knowledgeable/didactic approach. Her international background and strong use of facts lends credibility to her reporting and interviewing.

FIGURE 4.3 Walter Cronkite, one of the most famous news broadcasters in history, had a folksy charm.

Veteran PBS journalist Bill Moyers appears rather bookish and has a reputation as an intellectual, which he bolsters by his style. He often analyzes a story in a way no typical hard news reporter would.

Linda Cohn, long considered one of the pioneering women in sports reporting, is the superb ESPN anchor of SportsCenter. She is known for being a great storyteller, identifying key facts and elements in her delivery.

Perhaps the epitome of the didactic approach is Chris Cuomo, CNN's morning news anchor. Cuomo, who comes from a famous New York political family, always seems ready to debate issues with his guests, armed with facts and insights into the issues.

Aggressive or hard sell. Performers who seem to leap out of the radio or television set represent the aggressive approach. Mike Wallace made a living from this style. Some observers have noted the aggressive manner of Geraldo Rivera. Rivera's bearing and body language convey a sense of energy—even urgency, although he is noted more for an emotional rather than an intellectual approach. His combative style has caused controversy in his reporting at Fox News.

Physically appealing. When a performer's appearance becomes part of his or her persona, this physical appeal qualifies as a style element. However, an attractive on-air performer does not automatically fit only this one style. In the most blatant of cases, it is not difficult to see why an advertiser would feature models or other attractive performers. On a more subtle level, newscasters frequently benefit from an appealing appearance. Although attractiveness was certainly not the primary reason for their success, physical appearance has helped David Muir and Gretchen Carlson.

Sincere. Gayle King has turned sincerity into something of an industry, frequently giving her opinion during an interview on CBS Morning News and for her it succeeds. The sincere and trustworthy approach also works well for commercial spokespeople such as LeBron James and Julia Roberts. Former CBS News anchor Walter Cronkite is still recognized as the embodiment of the sincere and trustworthy news figure. Today David Muir projects a more vigorous form of sincerity, while

NBC's Lester Holt (Figure 4.4) comes across as a friendly next-door neighbor concerned about daily events.

Novelty. Usually people in the novelty category have distinguishing characteristics that make them virtually unique, yet they often have many imitators. John Stewart on *The Daily Show* was a perfect example.

Combinations of elements. The preceding descriptions of the categories are of course not definitive. Many performers cut across style lines, using several elements to hone their particular deliveries. For example:

- *Oprah Winfrey.* Oprah is perhaps the most unique talent in broadcasting today. She commands respect in covering important events but also can be seen as a spokesperson for a variety of products. She conveys authority through a combination of sincerity and a knowledgeable approach. Her viewpoints resonate with many Americans of all races. She has more than 11 million followers on Facebook and 41 million followers on Twitter.

- *Geraldo Rivera.* The style of this controversial television talk show host is remarkably effective in conveying to viewers the impression that he represents for them. He uses a "street-smart" image combined with a sincere approach. Rivera alternates the aggressive style of an investigative reporter trying to uncover wrongdoing with the image of a sensitive person who is only putting his guests on the spot because he has to get at some important issues.

- *George Stephanopoulos* combines a direct, "let's cut to the chase" approach with a thoughtful, reflective style that often comes through when he cohosts ABC's *This Week* show but seems

FIGURE 4.4 Lester Holt conveys great authenticity and sincerity in his on-air demeanor.

cheerfully upbeat every morning as host of *Good Morning America*. Much of the success of the ABC morning show is attributed to chemistry between Stephanopoulos and Robin Roberts, the cohost of *Good Morning America*. Roberts adds much to the show's style with her warmth and down-to-earth style.

DEVELOPING A STYLE

As we have said, developing a style requires a measured approach, not all-out imitation. It is a combination of assessing your own strengths and weaknesses, and experimenting with style elements that capitalize on your strengths. We list briefly several methods for developing a style.

1. Imitate performers who have style elements you would like to adopt. Do this during practice sessions and within the bounds of reason. Too much imitation can come across as a caricature of the person you are trying to imitate.
2. Before adopting stylistic devices, analyze *why* those styles are successful for the performers who use them. The foregoing section was intended to stimulate such analysis. Ask why the style element bolsters that person's performance.
3. Play up your strengths and make a realistic evaluation of your weaknesses *as you appear to the audience*. Aaron Frankel, Broadway director and acting instructor, points out to students that personal qualities do not always translate to the actor's stage identity. The same holds true for broadcasting. An extremely sophisticated and urbane performer may not *appear* as such on camera or on mic.
4. Experiment. That is what practice is for. If something works, add it to your store of knowledge and experience. If it doesn't work, discard it.
5. Learn from the techniques and successes of others, but do not ape their styles.

Nuances

Many intangibles are associated with communicating a message. Most are subtle, but such nuances often are key elements in getting the message across effectively.

Gestures, energy, and *body language* are some of the more important nuances involved in broadcast communication.

Gestures

As an exercise, try delivering a piece of radio copy while sitting on your hands. It's difficult, or should be. Gestures, even on radio, act to *color* the delivery by their association in our own minds with moods and feelings.

To turn the example around, adding gestures can help radio announcers add expression to their readings. No, the audience can't see the gestures. The audience can, though, sense the announcer's involvement in communicating an idea. Just record a lighthearted radio commercial while smiling and again while frowning. You'll hear the difference.

On television, gestures are obviously more apparent. A television lens magnifies many movements and makes them look exaggerated, so poor use of gestures can also have a negative effect on TV.

For example, restrain your head movement on television. A certain amount of head movement is natural in everyday conversation, especially among animated speakers, but it can be distracting on camera. Be especially conscious of restraining the movement of your head when the TV camera is on a tight shot.

Radio, audiobook, and podcast talent who plan to move into television should restrain their head movement, too. If you have practiced head-bobbing for years in the radio studio, it may be impossible to break the habit when you try to make a transition to television. Avoiding this mannerism from the start is easier than trying to break the habit later on.

Proper gestures, movement, and posture can reflect positively on performance.

We address this topic later, in a section on body language.

Energy

For many of us, putting energy into a piece of copy requires conscious effort. Low-key speakers appear fine in most normal conversation but can seem decidedly lackluster on the air.

Here is a gray area where the performer has to consciously "punch up" copy but must avoid artificiality. The only way to arrive at a proper compromise is through practice and critique. During practice, it's perfectly all right to overdo the level of energy (see Box 4.1). If it appears too "hyped," back off a bit. Fine-tune as you go along.

BOX 4.1 Guidelines for Projecting Energy

1. Show enthusiasm for the subject.
2. Project your voice and personality. As one director puts it, "try to jump right into that lens."
3. Vary your pitch and delivery, and be sure to avoid a monotone.
4. *Look* involved and interested, even in radio.
5. Maintain good posture when on mic or on camera.
6. Do not use excessive motion. Motion by itself will not inject energy. Appropriate and controlled gestures will.
7. Do not try to inject energy by using a high-speed delivery. Speeding up a monotone won't make it any more interesting.
8. Make every effort to appear and to actually be physically vigorous. Successful radio performers sound vigorous, and successful TV performers look and sound vigorous.

The most important aspect of energy and liveliness is that you cast yourself in the role of being extremely interested or excited by what the copy is saying, just as you would be interested and excited when telling a friend you've gotten a great job. That approach may be overdoing it a bit for some products, and much news delivery requires a more somber attitude. But energy is always an important attribute of a performer's talent, and it is worthwhile to cultivate these qualities. The guidelines in Box 4.1 will help you project energy and liveliness.

On the last point, note that most top television performers actually *are* physically fit. Tom Brokaw was physically active and an avid runner and cyclist, even while maintaining a busy schedule for NBC. People like Jake Tapper and Robin Roberts typify the vitality and energy that health and fitness provide. Cronkite was at one time a race-car driver, and his competitive vigor showed on air. Dan Rather was an energetic, though undersized, college football player. The point is that being in good physical condition never hurts and can help considerably in the effort to give energy to your on-air work.

Body Language

Body language has a powerful effect on a performer's appearance and delivery. It is really a combination of gestures, physical energy, and posture.

Body language reflects your attitude toward the audience. Pay attention to body language and your use of it. Some suggestions are shown in Box 4.2.

BOX 4.2 Use Body Language to your Advantage

1.   Make your body language show that you are open and at ease. Avoid crossing your arms in front of you, a posture that reflects a closed and defensive attitude.
2.   Reflect vigor in your posture. Resist the temptation to slump, which is a particular problem faced by TV performers when sitting at a desk.
3.   Use body language to project an interested attitude. Leaning slightly forward toward the camera lens gives the impression of energy and interest.
4.   Review videotapes of yourself in search of unconscious negatives in your body language. Do you clench your fists while smiling? Do you wet your lips, giving the impression of nervousness even if you are calm?
5.   Be aware of how your body language affects others. During an interview program, tenseness on the host's part often communicates itself to the guest.
6.   Maintain the posture and breathing habits demonstrated in Chapter 2. Good posture energizes a performance and improves breath support.

AD-LIBBING

Many people think of ad-libbing as a matter of opening the mouth and letting the words flow. Even the most experienced performer, however, is never sure exactly what will come out at a given moment. The result of a too spontaneous ad-lib is frequently embarrassment.

Most good ad-libbers have worked very hard to develop thought patterns that allow them to draw material together in advance, even only a moment in advance, and to use the material appropriately. Ad-libbing is a kind of role-playing, and even a second's rehearsal in that role gives the performer an advantage.

The ability to ad-lib (literally, to speak "at pleasure") is becoming one of the most important parts of a broadcaster's arsenal. News reporters today must ad-lib more often than ever before, thanks largely to modern live transmission technologies.

Components of an Ad-Lib

The first step in developing ad-lib talents is impossible to master in a quick lesson: it is the state of being well educated and conversational in a variety of fields. An announcer cannot fake knowledge. A news reporter must know the facts, a program host must know something about the guest's topic, and a radio personality must, if he or she ad-libs about local matters, be up on current events.

Step 2 in effective ad-libbing consists of learning how to do a quick encapsulation and rehearsal. Give some thought, even an instant's thought, to what you want to say. Break it into coherent, short, and simple thoughts and phrases. Mentally edit what you want to say. The biggest problem of most ad-libbers is their tendency to ramble on too long. One of the authors of this book, for example, was once assigned to ad-lib a 90-second piece from a crime scene live over the air. Just moments on the scene, and panicked by the thought of having to *fill* 90 seconds, he delivered a rambling, barely coherent report that went on for six unbearable minutes. The point? Ninety seconds is not really very long to ad-lib, and the report would have gone much better if the reporter had collected what few facts he did know, assembled them into three or four coherent thoughts, and ad-libbed without trying to fill. This would have turned out to be much closer to the 90-second requirement and would have made much more sense.

The same principles apply to the interview format. Some program hosts are more concerned with showing what they know rather than clarifying what the guest knows, and they ad-lib a halting and seemingly endless recitation of the facts during the show's introduction. *Less is always better when it means the difference between a coherent ad-lib and rambling.*

Here is a review of the principles of good ad-libbing, followed by an example:

1. Plan and encapsulate. Sum up what you want to say in a few mental notes.
2. Deliver the ad-lib in bite-size segments.
3. Keep it short.

Good ad-libbing involves giving a natural appearance to an unnatural action.

When we speak in normal conversations, we don't use the well-thought-out phrases of expert reporters. This is graphically brought home to people who read transcripts of what they have said in court testimony or legal depositions. What sounded quite lucid while being spoken seems almost unintelligible and semiliterate when reduced to the written word.

Thus, news reporters ad-libbing live over the air need to organize their material more carefully than if they were describing the scene to someone during a telephone call. Organization and as much pre-air planning as possible are needed. For example, take this scene approximated from a report of a major windstorm.

> This is _____ reporting live on the road. . . . It's really difficult driving because of all the debris in the road, and we don't know when the situation is going to be cleared up. The winds were very heavy, and because of all the debris in the road, police are banning travel. Like I said, it's difficult getting around because of the power lines and downed tree limbs . . . so police don't want people on the roads. No one is quite sure when the situation is going to be cleared up . . .

Had the reporter given a bit more thought to the coming ad-lib, the thoughts could have been broken down into three main points:

1. Police have banned travel.
2. Storm damage is heavy.
3. There is no indication of when the situation is going to be cleared up.

Breaking that down might take just five seconds, but the result would have been a significantly better report.

> This is _____ reporting from the mobile unit, one of the few vehicles on the road now because the police have banned travel in the wake of this evening's windstorm. Debris in the road has made driving virtually impossible . . . the city streets are littered with downed tree limbs and power lines. At present, police aren't able to give any indication of when the situation is going to be cleared up . . .

The same information is presented, and the report is shorter and more logical.

The principle of planning and encapsulating applies to all facets of ad-libbing. An afternoon drive radio announcer, for example, might want to ad-lib about the upcoming Fourth of July weekend. Instead of barging headlong into the ad-lib, she thinks, "I'll come out of the music, read the weather, mention how short the summer has seemed so far—it's almost the Fourth of July—then talk about some of the events coming up." In addition to being an accurate and coherent expression, an ad-lib should be able to pass the test of appropriateness and should be delivered with a professional-sounding flow.

Podcast announcers frequently ad-lib because they are not working from a full script for their programs. Many are not constrained by the same time elements as in radio, but it is important to consider the audience and apply the following principles to their performances.

Appropriateness. Just why do you want to ad-lib? To say something, or to hear yourself talk? Try to avoid the latter option. It never hurts to subject a planned ad-lib to this test. A radio personality whose primary purpose is to entertain still must deal in appropriate ad-libs, which touch on common experiences that have meaning to the listeners. In-jokes concerning station personnel, for example, don't meet this test.

Flow. Practice eliminating pauses and interjections. Saying "uhh" or making extensive pauses can become annoying to listeners. There is no reason, in most cases, for these delays to collect one's thoughts. Stalling and interjections are primarily nervous habits.

Although the principles just outlined are useful for just about any circumstance, certain tasks require individualized techniques. Let's look at some specific ad-libbing requirements of some typical broadcast performance situations.

Ad-Libbing in Radio

In radio today there is considerably less ad-libbing in general than there once was. Most modern radio music formats promote themselves as providing listeners with "more music, less talk." Often music is played back-to-back so announcements are confined to the breaks before or after commercials. So unless you are doing that kind of a show, a steady stream of patter from a "personality"-oriented announcer or disc jockey is counterproductive.

The key is that "less is more." Most radio shifts today call for the announcer to be the facilitator. It is her or his responsibility to make the program elements flow together and create an atmosphere where the audience feels comfortable. Announcers must blend with the overall sound that identifies the station and the format. Ad-libbing helps in that effort by providing information and by supplying transitions to smooth the process of getting from one program element to another.

In large-market radio, there are usually strict guidelines for announcers who work an airshift on a music program. In most cases, the music is the star. Announcers are expected to talk about things that will interest the particular types of listeners the station is targeted to reach. An oldies station that targets adults between the ages of 45 and 64, for example, wants its announcers to be knowledgeable about the music and the events that occurred when the music was first popular, who was in the band, what was their biggest hit and other information that will enhance a trip down memory lane.

Many stations will spend a great deal of money researching the music they play to determine how often a particular cut should come up in the playlist rotation and how the music should be blended to meet the desires of the audience. One major-market announcer who was fond of claiming full credit for attracting listeners to the station was invited by the program director to substitute polka music for his normal fare of contemporary hits to see if his sparkling presence was really the crucial element that held the interest of listeners. He declined the challenge. A talkative announcer who wants to be the center of attention can interfere drastically with a carefully designed music format.

Announcers who are permitted creative leeway are under fewer restrictions for the style and content of the program. In these programs (often aired in morning drive time), the personality is the focus. Personalities in major markets often work with a producer who helps put together ideas for the program and helps in the studio work necessary to make the material work on the air. Even though greater creative latitude is allowed on personality programs, there is no less attention paid to the content of the show. The host of a personality morning show, for example, often spends three or more hours after the airshift preparing for the next day's program.

What does it take to be successful in large market personality radio? Brad Murray, former station manager for Baltimore's WQSR, says you need to be creative, a good writer, and well informed. Many of the comedy elements used on personality shows are based on current topics in the news. Often morning shows feature a man and woman combination. The personalities must also be sensitive to how far they can go in flirting with the boundaries of good taste. Top radio personalities and their producers usually know when they're crossing the line, according to Murray. When they get into questionable areas, they ask for an opinion about whether or not to go with the idea.

Depending on which format you're working with, ad-libbing is either virtually nonexistent, as in some "lite" music stations, or is a major element, as in many contemporary hit radio formats. A brief look at several popular formats will show how widely ad-libbing requirements can vary in radio today.

> **Country.** Modern country formats are divided into several subtypes from the classic country hits of the past to "New Country"; contemporary hits by artists who frequently cross over to pop. As pointed out in the discussion of staff announcing responsibilities in Chapter 5, today's country music recording industry uses all the mixing techniques used in any other category of music. While some country stars hold to the traditional identifying characteristics of steel guitars and lyrics about truck driving and cheating in love and romance, most country music stations don't vary widely from many other formats in their overall sound.

The overriding principle of effective ad-libbing in a country format is "know the music and the artists who create it." Even though your ad-libbing will be restricted by the same "more music" constraints of all modern music radio, the ad-libs you do use will almost always touch some aspect of the current scene in country music, perhaps local venues or upcoming concerts.

If you are new to the category of country music (or any music genre where you're not familiar, for that matter), you'll need to get a quick education. There are several good histories of country music in book form. Check one or two out of the library and bone up.

For actual on-air ad-libbing, here are several principles to guide you.

- *Relate comments to what is going on at the moment on your station.* Don't start talking about the latest Hollywood gossip about Miranda Lambert if you've just come out of a cut from Chris Stapleton's latest album.
- *Don't depend on your memory of items in the news when making comments about the music or the artists.* Bring clips of information to the studio with you so you can briefly review the information before using it on the air. Chances are listeners are already aware of any news, and you'll lose all your credibility with your audience if you get the facts wrong.
- *Never make fun of the music or the artists.* Country music fans are fierce in their loyalties. Many country music fans regard their favorite artists as "family." Attempts by a radio personality to get a laugh by making comments about an artist are not well received. The same, of course, holds true for all music genres to some extent: listeners may also take offense at remarks about performers as diverse as Taylor Swift, Bob Dylan or Eminem.

> **Talk radio.** The growth of talk radio into sports, business news, and political conversation formats makes this an opportunity for budding announcers today. The announcer on talk radio must be able to ad-lib effectively about a wide number of topics. The major key is to be well informed. You should regularly read one or two major national newspapers and a good regional paper. Today these sources are available online and with mobile apps, making it easy to keep up with the latest headlines and stories. If your job has a specialty, such as sports, you will need to look at all the online sources related to that specialty. For news be sure to keep up with topics and people who appear on *cable talk shows* and other public affairs programs on television. Also, be sure to stay current with topical books that are being discussed in the news. Websites and apps like *The Hill, Reuters, The Verge, Huffington Post* and related news sites like *CNN, Fox, BBC, ABC* and the other major sources provide up-to-the-minute news and commentary.

In short, the talk show host, regardless of the specialty, has to be a well-rounded person who can articulate thoughts with clarity and style. Not an easy assignment, but there are many opportunities for work for those who do it well.

Ad-libbing in this format requires the ability to move quickly from one topic to another and to deal with a wide variety of people. And it's important to keep alert to what callers are saying so you can hit the "dump" button when callers' remarks are not appropriate for the air. Keep the following general principles in mind:

- *Bone up on the topic under discussion.* If you are speaking with a guest expert, familiarize yourself with the guest's background and with the books he or she has written. Read the background on topics in the news or on the Web that are scheduled for discussion.
- *Be careful about expressing opinions.* Unless your assignment calls for a personality who has strong opinions that are supposed to provoke listeners and guests into disagreement and conflict, soft-pedal your opinions.

   In general, keep your comments as neutral as possible, but don't be afraid to play "devil's advocate" to generate discussion.
- *Don't let yourself come through as a know-it-all.* The most effective host comments in talk radio are made with a certain degree of humility. If you are as well informed as you should be, you will be far more knowledgeable on most topics than the average call-in listener. Never forget, though, that the listener is the most important element of the equation. Treat all callers with respect, but don't get drawn into displays of emotion.

   Contemporary, Hot Hits, or Top 40. These stations often focus on songs on the current pop music charts. Listeners tend to be in younger demographics and relate to announcers who have a youthful sound. Ad-libbing should be used sparingly and often is not even allowed by program directors. Keeping the music flowing is the key here. Knowledge of the current music scene and the artists is important. Often the rotation of sounds is chosen by the program director, and there will be a rhythm and flow to the musical selections. It is the announcer who makes the connection with the listeners between musical sets and the station commercial breaks.

For those stations that feature a strong local morning drive show, the personality of the disc jockey can figure heavily into the sound of the station. Often the show has more than one host. Frequently a main announcer interacts with another, sometimes forming a male/female team, with one doing local news and traffic reports, and the second voice interjecting comments throughout the show.

This is the modern equivalent of the personality form invented by the famous DJs of the 1950s. Announcers maintain a steady patter laced with information about the music, the artists, traffic and weather. Various items of interest to young adults are interspersed, punctuated by humor that appeals to those groups. Local guests may be used. Energy is the hallmark.

   Adult Contemporary. The theory is that even if listeners may not particularly like what's playing at the moment, they will often stay around long enough to hear a selection they do like. But there must be music. This format tends to have greater diversity of music styles than many others in radio. It tries to draw from a bit wider spectrum of musical tastes. Many stations feature a broad playlist of the 1980s, 1990s to today.

Ad-libbing, when permitted, is very brief and usually is based on the weather, traffic reports, or comments on a current movie or a performance by an artist featured in the station's music format. Frequently the station will have an events calendar or community announcements that need to be read. These should be read conveying interest and excitement where appropriate. But, for ad-libbing purposes, it is not necessary to have the kind of in-depth knowledge of the music that country music announcers need. Because adult contemporary formats have oldies mixed in with more contemporary cuts, avoid ad-libs taking off from nostalgia that accompanies a selection.

The guidelines to keep in mind for ad-libbing in this format are:

- *Keep remarks very general.* The audience has a somewhat broader range of interests than those of other formats, so you may risk offending part of the group if you give opinions about anything.
- *Submerge your personality.* The announcer's role as facilitator is aided by a certain amount of anonymity. The music should form the central core of the station's sound. Ad-libs that draw attention to the personality of the announcer detract from this goal.
- *When in doubt, leave it out.* If you have any question in your mind about the appropriateness of an ad-libbed remark, don't say it. You'll seldom be worse off by passing up an opportunity to ad-lib. You may, however, regret having interjected an item that turned out to be inappropriate.

> **Classic Rock and Classic Hits.** These formats, as they exists on many stations, vary from mostly music to others that allow ad-libbing about the music, the artists and upcoming musical events in the local area. The classic rock format follows in the tradition of the early FM stations in the late 1960s, where album cuts from top artists were often interspersed with popular rock (not pop) hits of the day. Jocks like "Big Daddy" Tom Donahue in San Francisco and legendary progressive rocker Scott Muni in New York pioneered the format during the era when album releases became more important than 45 rpm singles.

The requirements for ad-libbing in these formats will of course vary, depending on the particular style of the station. The style of personality will often vary by time slot within the same station. There may, for example, be an outrageous style jock for a "Morning Zoo" program in morning drive time, a standard rock jock for midday and someone with deep musical knowledge in the evening. Some general principles can be stated for all three categories within this format.

- *Develop a humor style that reflects your listeners.* Take a lead from the *Saturday Night Live* and Stephen Colbert types of humor, but be sure to avoid the appearance of being a rip-off artist, who steals phrasing and material directly from these sources. Check out www.humor.com or other websites related to humor. Work on humor that meshes with these styles, but that bears the stamp of your own personality.
- *Keep up with the music and artists that constitute the format.* Read trade press articles about them and keep up to date on news about items such as new releases, concert tours, film appearances, and YouTube videos. Integrate this into your ad-libs. This is particularly necessary for the rock jock who relies less on humor. Most of the big rock artists from the 1970s and 1980s are still touring, often with other artists of the era. Keep up on concert schedules. Frequently stations promote the concerts locally with free tickets and a station presence at the concert. Be prepared to be at the concert and interact with fans and concert goers. Prepare a list of ad-lib topics and short items, and take it with you. The most important thing is to sound genuine and interested in the music that your listeners love.

Radio ad-libbing is an art that demands careful attention to context. A reticent talk show host will not succeed, nor will an all-too-loud adult contemporary announcer. Many announcers can effectively work in a number of different formats and quickly sense the requirements of ad-libbing. The key is that when it's done effectively, ad-libbing is virtually unnoticeable as such to the average listener. When it draws attention to itself, ad-libbing can detract from the impact of the format in general. The announcer who does so quickly becomes expendable. Adding vivid description can help the announcer bring a scene alive. In Focus on Technique we offer tips to would-be broadcasters.

Focus on Technique

See it on the Radio

One of radio's consummate ad-libbers is WCBS-AM's Rich Lamb. An award-winning 30-year veteran of New York all-news radio has covered the installation of a cardinal and the funeral of a first lady, the bombing of the World Trade Center, the visits of presidents and the city's final farewell to a firefighter killed in the line of duty.

His word pictures are vivid—and occasionally listeners pay a high compliment (accidentally or on purpose) and note that they've "seen it on the radio" after hearing his coverage.

Here are some tips he offered to student broadcasters:

- *Appeal to the senses.* "Flags snapping in the breeze . . . ," for example, paints a sight-sound picture and grounds the listener in an authentic environment.
- *Put yourself in the mood of the story.* "Mourners are lined ten deep along ten blocks of Fifth Avenue . . . ." Say it slowly and quietly, and the story of a firefighter's funeral will carry itself.
- Relating to the point above, *don't be afraid to use natural sound and let the story tell itself.* Lamb's advice: "Sometimes you just have to shut up."
- *Know the specifics.* When Lamb covered the firefighter's funeral, his background knowledge of city politics enabled him to inform listeners that one of the politicians closely involved was a former fire commissioner—a relevant point that affirmed the notion that this particular politician was not simply there to be seen.
- *Know the generalities*—in other words, have a healthy inventory of general knowledge. "A liberal arts education is extremely valuable," Lamb says. "You'll be surprised how much stays in your head and falls out of the right slot exactly when you need it."

Ad-Libbing on Television

Several television situations require announcers to ad-lib. On the local level, news, sports, and weather programming often call on announcers to ad-lib. Also at the local level are talent assignments involving hosting various community programs, and local morning talk or interview programs. Network-level announcing assignments that require ad-libbing include game show hosts, talk show hosts, sportscasting, and news reporting.

Some general guidelines for each category can help prepare you for the ad-libbing requirements of each of these assignments.

> **Local television.** Local news, sports, and weather talent need to be prepared to ad-lib in these general sets of circumstances.

1. *Between segments on the news set.* The concept known as "happy talk" brought ad-libbing to local news programs all over the country. The extremes of that idea, in which the conversation was specifically structured to convey the impression that the on-camera talent were great friends, has given way to brief segments of conversation that simply function as bridges between segments of the program.
2. *In live reporting situations.* The increasingly common use of live reports from the scene of a news event makes it necessary for reporters to ad-lib news reports that once would have been taped and

edited for broadcast. Live sports coverage also uses on-air talent to fill in spots between sports action with ad-libbed material.

3. *During weather shows.* The TV weather reporter is the only person on the news set who works without a written script. The basic information is given on the maps and charts, but it is up to the reporter to present the information smoothly. Today weather has increasingly become part of the important news stories as hurricanes, floods, fires and other large event seem to be more commonplace. The weather reporter may also find herself working from the scene of a natural disaster.

4. *During local talk shows.* Programs in which a host interviews area personalities and visiting celebrities require talent to ad-lib extensively to make the program run smoothly.

Network television. At the network level, ad-libbing is done by live news and sports reporters, talk show hosts, and game show hosts.

News and sports reporting requirements are similar to those at the local level, although the audience is larger. The same general abilities are required at network and local levels.

Game show hosts have special requirements. Generally, they must create an atmosphere of fun for the participants and the audience.

Talk show hosts at the network level are generally required to interact easily with guests and to move the conversation along so that it stays fresh and entertaining for the audience. Some shows, like ABC's *The View* invite famous personalities to comment on current news and social events. The host(s) needs to be skilled at maneuvering the guests through the show without seeming to be overbearing. More and more personalities may host a blog or Facebook page to interact with their audience.

Whether at the network or local level, each of these assignments requires announcers to draw on their experiences to make the unnatural seem natural. Those who succeed in that task draw little attention to their ad-libbing ability. That's the sign that they have succeeded.

It is difficult to draw general guidelines for ad-libbing in these different circumstances, but keep these several principles in mind:

- *Prepare yourself as well as possible before you go on camera.* If you are on the news set, for example, plan ahead with colleagues to establish the general sequence of the conversation. If no one knows what to expect, and everyone tries to jump in to fill up the dead air, viewers will sense the confusion, and the credibility of the whole news team will be in jeopardy. If you are reporting live, list what you will say in sequence.

  Do the same thing for live sports reports.

- *Don't be a slave to your pre-set plans.* The best ad-libs are indeed "off the top of your head." The trick is not to have blind faith that something will occur to you once you're on the air. If you have prepared properly, you'll have an idea of what you will say when you are expected to ad-lib. If something better occurs to you later, go with it.

- *Try to think ahead about what exactly will take place during the program or program segment you're involved with.* Not all situations requiring ad-libbing are live, but many are. The more you can anticipate what will happen, the more confidence you'll have. Relaxing and feeling confident improve the effectiveness of your ad-libbing. The same goes for taping sessions. There is a certain amount of leeway for error in some ad-lib situations, but the more professional you are in the session the better you'll feel about your performance.

Ad-libbing in performance situations is the ultimate test of a professional. Those who do it well have considerably broader opportunities for advancement in broadcasting than do those who can simply read a prepared script.

We'll discuss ad-libbing more as it fits in with other aspects of various performance situations, in later chapters.

PLAYING TO MICROPHONES AND CAMERAS

The rest of this chapter deals with techniques of playing to microphones and cameras. Mic technique and camera technique are major components of basic announcing skills, and they significantly affect a performer's ability to communicate a message.

In broadcasting, the equipment necessary to put the broadcast over the air is a prominent part of the performer's work. The ability of a performer who does not know how to deal with mics or cameras can be seriously compromised by technical errors. By extension, a performer knowledgeable about equipment can enhance his or her performance. Some mics, for example, tend to flatter voices of certain types.

A basic communication model (see Figure 4.5) shows that anything that hinders transmission of a message from sender to receiver is known as *interference.*

Today microphone technology has progressed and most performers use lavalier mics that can be worn on clothing and are fairly inconspicuous. Many are wireless. This provides the performer with freedom of movement and the sound quality of good lavalier mics is quite good. However, in the field this may not be the case. A performer who is uncomfortable and unfamiliar with the tools of the trade may generate a great deal of interference. Every performer does not have to be a technician. Only a basic knowledge of mics and camera technique is required for skillful on-air work, but that knowledge is essential.

The Microphone

A microphone reproduces sound by means of a diaphragm within the instrument. The diaphragm vibrates in response to sound. Sound is a vibration of molecules in the air or other medium. The diaphragm of the mic responds to that sound in much the same way as our eardrums respond to sound. The mic then converts the vibration of the diaphragm into an electrical signal, which can be transmitted or recorded. The process of converting one form of energy to another is known as **transduction.**

What does this mean to the broadcast performer? Various microphones respond differently to sound. To use the instruments properly, performers should be aware of at least some of these differences.

Microphone types classified by internal electronics. Mics are classified in a number of ways, including by their internal electronics, the pattern in which they pick up sound, and how they are used (such as in studio or hand-held).

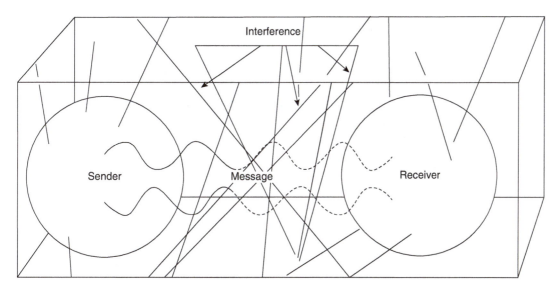

FIGURE 4.5 A basic communication model.

This sounds confusing and it can be, but you'll understand what we mean when you finish reading this section.

The mics most common in broadcasting are the **moving coil**, and **condenser** types. Other types such as **ribbon** and **piezo** (also known as a contact mic) are found in recording studios but are generally not used in television or radio on-air work.

Moving coil: The diaphragm vibrates in sympathy with the sound that activates it. An attached conductor moves through a magnetic field and creates an electrical signal. Moving coil mics, such as the Sennheiser MD 46 cardioid mic (Figure 4.6) are regarded as rugged and versatile and are used extensively in fieldwork because they feature low handling noise and good protection from wind noise. An ElectroVoice RE20 is a standard studio mic.

Ribbon: A thin foil ribbon is suspended between two poles of a magnet. Vibrations move the ribbon; the moving ribbon creates an electrical signal. This mic is not very rugged, but many broadcast performers like a ribbon because it is said to impart a warm, rich quality to the voice. While some specialty microphone companies do manufacture ribbon mics, they do not make up a large proportion of the industry. Interestingly, some announcers covet ribbon mics and pay thousands of dollars to buy and maintain them. The RCA 77DX (Figure 4.7) is a good example; it is still used by some announcers who find that the ribbon element flatters their voices. But ribbon mics do have their disadvantages, one being an extreme sensitivity to wind. Popping of plosives (*p*'s and *b*'s) is very evident on a ribbon mic.

Condenser: An electrical element called a *capacitor* stores an electrical charge. Actually, "condenser" is an old term for "capacitor" that happened to stick as the name for this type of mic. An electrical charge is applied to the diaphragm and a capacitor plate. The vibration of the diaphragm produces a change in capacitance, which is transduced into an electrical signal. Condenser mics provide the highest quality of sound reproduction with excellent sensitivity. A good example is the Neumann U87, shown in Figure 4.8. For a performer, this can be an advantage and a disadvantage. Extreme sensitivity provides the intimate "presence" so in tune with many FM radio formats. Conversely, a supersensitive condenser mic picks up a great deal of unwanted sound, such as breathing, mouth noises, and console operation.

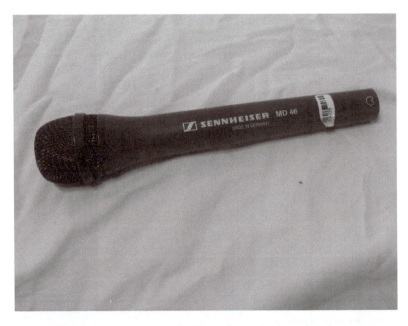

FIGURE 4.6 The Sennheiser MD 46, a rugged, dependable moving-coil mic.

FIGURE 4.7 This classic mic, the RCA 77 DX, has not been manufactured in decades but still is an icon. Many are still in use. The mic was renowned for its rich tone.

FIGURE 4.8 The Neumann U87 is one of the finest microphones made, with extraordinary sensitivity. It is used in high-end studios and is popular for music recording.

Microphone types defined by pickup patterns. Another major consideration in mic technique is knowledge of pickup patterns. The major pickup patterns are omnidirectional, bidirectional, and cardioid.

The **omnidirectional** mic picks up sound from all directions equally well (except from the very rear of the mic, where the actual mass of the unit blocks sound reception). A very simplified representation of the omnidirectional "pickup pattern" is shown in Figure 4.9a.

The pickup pattern chart packed with the mic would contain concentric rings representing the relative volume in units of sound intensity called *decibels*. Technical details are beyond the scope of this book, but if you are interested in exploring the role of sound and audio in broadcasting further, we suggest you consult *Modern Radio and Audio Production* by Hausman, Messere, Benoit, and O'Donnell.[2]

For the performer, an omnidirectional mic is especially useful in hand-held operations where background noises are desired, as in many news applications. The **bidirectional** pattern (Figure 4.9b), which is characteristic of the ribbon mic, is sometimes useful in a two-person interview if it is not possible to mic each talent individually.

"Cardioid" means heart-shaped, which describes this pickup pattern (Figure 4.9c). Remember, these patterns extend in three dimensions, so you can approximate a cardioid mic's pickup by imagining it to be the stem of a gigantic apple.

A cardioid pickup pattern is useful to the performer in that it cancels out sound from the rear. That feature is often essential in "combo" operations where a radio staff announcer operates the console and other equipment. If noise from the background were not canceled, the listener would be treated to a wide variety of clicks and thumps.

A related area worth mentioning is frequency response. Frequency response is a complex subject, but basically it means the range of frequencies that can be picked up by an audio system, and because of differences in this response, certain mics emphasize certain pitches and deemphasize others. One notable characteristic of cardioid mics is known as the "proximity effect," an emphasis of bass frequencies as the

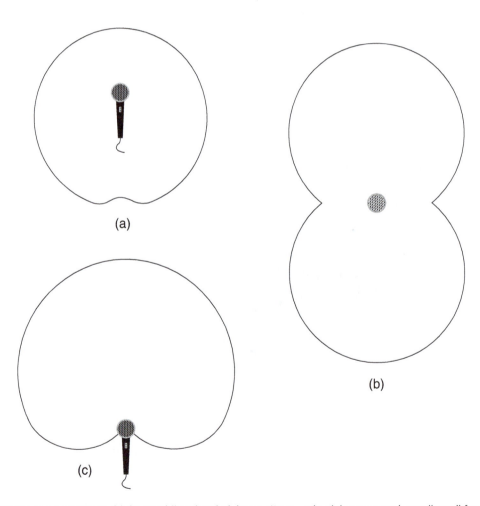

FIGURE 4.9 Three mic patterns. (a) An omnidirectional pickup pattern—mic picks up sound equally well from all directions. (b) A bidirectional pickup pattern—mic rejects sounds from the sides, hears only front and back. (c) A cardioid (heart-shaped) pickup pattern—mic rejects sound from the rear.

performer moves closer to the mic. This can be good or bad, depending on the announcer. Some mics emphasize the frequencies that lend clarity to speech, such as the higher frequency sounds of consonants. These types of mic are quite useful when maximum intelligibility is required.

Still other mics have switchable patterns. The user, for example, may select a "flat" response for music (all ranges of frequencies receiving equal emphasis), or a "bass roll-off," where the bass frequencies are deemphasized, to defeat the proximity effect and lend greater clarity to speech.

Microphone types by use. We differentiate microphones meant for hand-held use and studio mics. Hand-held mics, as you might expect, are meant to be gripped in the hand and have some electronic sound treatment that reduces handling noise.

Compare this with a "studio mic," such as the Shure SM7B (Figure 4.10).

The SM7B is a large, heavy mic that clearly would be of little use in a hand-held situation. It is a *dynamic cardioid* mic (do you see how the standard descriptors now make sense) and is prized for its warm tone and excellent noise rejection. Many announcers like it because it is not so sensitive as a condenser and does not reproduce so much in the way of breathing or mouth noises.

Some mics are meant to be clipped to the performer's clothing. They are generally referred to as lavalier or lapel mics (Figure 4.11). Both terms are a little misleading in that a lavalier is named after a piece of jewelry that hangs around the neck, as these mics originally did. And the lavalier, or *lav,* can be clipped to any type of clothing as long is it's in the mid-to-upper chest area.

Sometimes you want to mic someone so the mic is not visible. In this case, you might opt for a shotgun mic, so named because of its shape (Figure 4.12). Shotguns have a very narrow pickup pattern, meaning that they focus in on what's directly in front of them.

FIGURE 4.10 The Shure SM7B is a popular studio microphone known for its warm tone and excellent noise rejection.

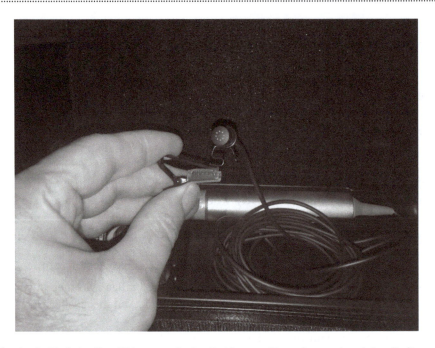

FIGURE 4.11 The Audio-Technica Pro-70 is a popular lav that is versatile and rugged and despite its small size produces a robust sound.

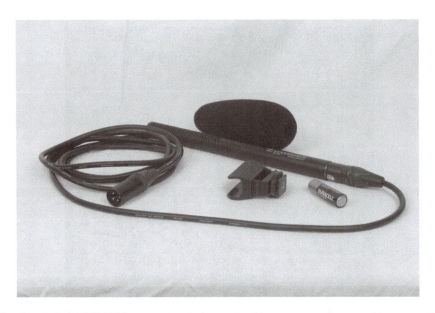

FIGURE 4.12 The Sennheiser MKE 600 is a popular shotgun mic. It has a narrow focus and is an excellent way to mic a performer's voice while not picking up—or at least de-emphasizing—background noise.

MICROPHONE SELECTION AND USE

Selection and use of microphones can affect the performer's image and appearance. Someone other than the performer usually selects the mics, although experienced announcers do develop a preference for particular mics and use them when available. More important for the entry-level performer is knowing how to translate the information just presented into effective performance. Some practical suggestions are given in Box 4.3.

BOX 4.3 Tips for Using Microphones

1. Positioning yourself closer to a mic will provide a more intimate feel to your reading. This is particularly true of the supersensitive condenser mics. Be aware that the intimacy can be accompanied by a strong increase in the audibility of mouth noises, such as lip smacking and teeth clicking.
2. Working closer to a mic with a cardioid pattern will lend a deeper quality to the voice. It also may muffle the sound reproduction, which is why some station engineers cover the mic with a thick foam wind filter. The filter mechanically keeps the announcer back from the mic.
3. Wind filters, which come in many shapes and sizes, can sometimes help the announcer who is operating outside in windy conditions or has a problem with popping plosives. These filters, also known as *pop filters,* simply block some air movement.
4. When speaking into a mic, maintain the same relative distance from the instrument. This depends on the piece you may be reading, of course. For an intimate feel you might want to move in closer to the mic, but be sure to maintain that same distance throughout the reading so that the intimate feel is consistent.
5. How close should your mouth be to the mic? The answer depends on your individual speech pattern, the mic itself, and the effect desired. As a *general rule,* six inches, about the length of a dollar bill, is a good working distance.
6. You will want to work closer to the mic in noisy situations. Move farther away from the mic if you have a deep, powerful voice and tend to sound muffled during playback.
7. If you have problems with popping plosives, avoid ribbon mics. With ribbon mics, position yourself and the mic so that you can speak across the diaphragm, not directly into it.
8. *Hard-sell* pieces generally sound more convincing when the announcer moves back from the mic. The perspective offered more adequately reinforces the hard-sell message than does a close-up, intimate perspective.

Learning proper mic technique requires an investment of time and a willingness to experiment. You must also ask questions of engineering and production personnel, who are usually willing to help you with any aspect of mics and their use.

PERFORMING ON VIDEO

The equipment of television places a variety of demands on broadcasters. Mic technique is not very important because mics in TV are usually clipped to the performer or hung from booms. The unblinking eye of the camera, however, can flatter a performer, or poor camera technique can hinder the performer.

Playing to the Lens

One of the major problems faced by newcomers to TV performance is difficulty in becoming comfortable with the properties of the TV camera lens.

To play to the lens, work as follows.

1. When you look at the lens, *look directly at it.* Even a small diffraction of the angle of your gaze will be very apparent to the viewer.
2. Take an occasional glance at the studio monitor so that you know what kind of shot you are in. When the lens is on a close-up, you must be careful to restrain movement and gestures.

3. Use proper eye movement. Some of us glance to the side when carrying on a conversation. Although not particularly bothersome in normal conversation, this habit is extremely distracting on TV. A camera lens will mercilessly pick up this movement, and the performer may look "shifty-eyed." When you break contact with the lens, it is much better to glance downward than to glance sideways.

The subject of camera changes is addressed more completely in Chapter 7 on television news, but it is worthwhile to note that changing the gaze from one camera to another is a good talent to cultivate. Do not make a glassy-eyed rotation of the head. Instead, pretend you are changing conversation partners at a party.

Posture and Bearing

Movement and posture are important elements of camera technique. To use movement and posture to improve your on-camera appearance, try the following:

1. *Learn a standard stance and practice it.* This is particularly important to announcers who read while seated at a desk. Considerable practice often goes into developing a good-looking and consistent body position. Desk-sitting announcers should practice using the full-front or three-quarters postures (see Figure 4.13). The goal is not to slump and to avoid unnecessary movement, while appearing reasonably relaxed.
2. *Don't fidget.* Excessive blinking, table tapping, and constant wetting of lips will imply that you are ill at ease, even if you are not.
3. *Don't use mechanical expressions.* The "raised eyebrow" that some viewers think implies skepticism may simply be a gesture that the newscaster has affected. Not only does it not mean skepticism, it doesn't mean *anything* unless you are Stephen Colbert who frequently uses it for comedic effect in his opening monologue.

The newscaster's pasted-on "concerned face" can often appear ludicrous and can be offensive to some viewers who know that you really are not ready to break into tears. Some viewers may feel that a maudlin expression is an insincere attempt to appear emotionally moved by a tragedy that is being reported. However, avoid smiling during the reporting of serious or somber news.

Eye Contact

Now that prompting devices (more in this in a later chapter) are common in TV stations and even in home studios, maintaining eye contact isn't as difficult as it once was. Devices such as the TelePrompTer consist of a mirror that is angled over the camera lens. A special camera takes an image of the news copy, and that image is projected onto the mirror. The newscaster or other performer can see the script, but it does not interfere with the camera's view.

You will, though, be required to read directly from copy in many circumstances. TV news, late-breaking events, election coverage, and so forth all require you to read from printed copy and still maintain good eye contact.

Maintaining eye contact involves the ability to read ahead a sentence or two in the copy. This skill is valuable for radio announcers, too, because it allows them to monitor clocks and look at equipment they are operating. Reading ahead also allows you to spot errors in copy and allows a moment or two to adjust. To cultivate eye contact, use the following guides.

1. Practice reading one sentence ahead of the point in the copy you are reading aloud. This is not as difficult as it sounds, and experienced communicators can often digest entire paragraphs in advance of the words they are reading aloud.

FIGURE 4.13 Camera positions for announcers. (a) The three-quarters position is frequently used when on-air talent is seated at a desk. (b) The full front position creates a more direct feel.

Push yourself during practice sessions to scan as far in advance as possible. Reading ahead helps in more ways than maintaining eye contact because you will be digesting and repeating back ideas rather than words.

2. When reading from a hand-held script, avoid looking up at monotonously regular points. Don't, for example, get into the habit of glancing down at the end of each sentence.

3. Although prompting devices have simplified the problem of making eye contact, they do require some measure of skill. For one thing, a performer using a prompter must avoid staring too directly into the lens. It's natural to keep an eye on the lens, though, so remember to glance down occasionally.

4. Announcers with poor eyesight need the prompters placed close to them. Otherwise, they will stumble over the copy and squint. But performers with very dark eyes must be wary of having the prompter and the camera lens too close because the movement of their eyes from word to word will be apparent and can be distracting.

Energy

One of the most important elements of camera technique and on-air performance in general is the *ability to infuse energy into a performance,* and the most common defect is a lack of that energy. Consider these three remarks overheard or read recently:

- "Be as vibrant as possible," a TV talk show producer recently told a guest for an upcoming segment. "There's something about the medium that robs energy."
- "If you sat next to the announcer on the set," a weather reporter told a trainee as they watched the host of *Good Morning, America,* "he'd blow you away. But on the air he has just the right level of energy. You need that kind of energy in your performance."
- "I am returning your tape," wrote the news director. "Your appearance is good, your voice is outstanding, but your energy level is very low. If you don't care about what you are reading, why should the viewers?"

It is better to inject too much energy than too little. First, what you think is too much might be just enough after the lens and camera have "robbed" the energy. Second, it will be easier to back off than to try to add. Finally, the potential to influence an audience is important to realize. We close this section with a discussion related to the ethics of broadcasting (see Connections).

Connections

Ethics

Because questions of ethics pervade almost any discussion of mass media, this book deals with case histories of on-air people faced with ethical dilemmas.

Understanding ethics is vital to an on-air performer for a number of reasons. First, though the on-air performer often receives undue credit for the work of a large team of production personnel, the announcer also receives some of the blame if there is a lapse in factuality or ethics.

Second, you can recover from almost any career stumbling block other than an ethical lapse. Factual mistakes are generally forgiven in time, so if you make a horrible but honest blunder it is not a career-killer. A reputation for connivance or dishonesty may follow you from market to market and dim your employment outlook.

In some instances reporters exaggerate the facts, as was the case with MSNBC's Brian Williams. Williams lost the coveted anchor position at NBC *Nightly News* as a result. Make sure your stories are accurate.

So what is ethics? There are at least two definitions of ethics, the first being "the branch of philosophy which studies questions of right or wrong." The second definition comprises the more common understanding of the term, and identifies "ethical" behavior with "good" behavior.

The word *moral* is sometimes used synonymously with *ethical,* although morality usually refers not so much to philosophy as much as to prevailing customs. We have a tendency to use the word "moral" in matters dealing primarily with those customs and not with fundamental questions of right or wrong. For example, we would be far more likely to describe marital infidelity as "immoral" rather than "unethical." Another point of usage: "Ethics," when used to refer to the branch of philosophy, is usually treated as a singular noun, such as "Ethics is a controversial subject." If you refer to individual collections of ethical principles—"My personal ethics are quite flexible"—the word takes a plural form.

Connections *(continued)*

If you elect to study classical ethics, you'll find that an immediate benefit is the revelation that ethical problems have had essentially the same structure for centuries. In a way, it's comforting to know that you are not the first person to confront a problem.

So here's a simple (and admittedly simplistic) crash course in ethics.

An initial point of analysis, and a widely accepted one, begins with the two camps into which philosophers tend to fall when discussing ethics: they usually are termed *consequentialists* or *nonconsequentialists.* Some gravitate toward the middle, advocating an approach that adds up the pluses and the minuses and produces an average, or *mean,* that balances the two extremes.[3]

Consequentialists generally believe that instead of attempting to judge whether an act itself is right or wrong, the judgment should be predicated on the *outcome.* John Stuart Mill and Jeremy Bentham were noted consequentialists. They advocated a type of consequentialism called "utilitarianism," the course of action that produces the greatest good for the greatest number, or as Mill put it, "the greatest happiness." (Note that this is an oversimplification; Mill and Bentham shared basic ideas but there are differences in their philosophies, which are beyond the scope of this discussion.)

In short, consequentialists will argue that the ends justify the means, and that *motives* are not a particularly relevant factor in that analysis. If someone saves me from drowning, a consequentialist might argue, it makes no difference if he saved me out of the goodness of his heart or because he wanted to get his picture on the six o'clock news. I was saved, and that's all that counts.

Nonconsequentialists, on the other hand, contend that *results* are not the standards by which we should judge an action; *motives* are. Immanuel Kant was the most widely recognized nonconsequentialist, and his philosophies still guide those who advocate adherence to the "categorical imperative." The categorical imperative means that each person should act as if his or her "maxim should become a universal law." Kant might argue, for example, that you have no right to steal food even if you are lost and starving. Stealing is wrong, he would contend, under *any* circumstances. It cannot *become right* when it proves convenient, because if everyone adopted that handy and painless approach to ethics, we would see theft become rampant as people bent their ethics to fit the situation.

One way to conceptualize ethics.

                    Golden Mean
Consequentialist   Nonconseqentialist

Ethicists who have taken the middle ground essentially put their trust in the individual's judgment. In other words, a person attempting to come up with an ethical solution to a problem would aim for a point halfway between excess and deficiency. Aristotle called this the *golden mean.* He claimed it was the quickest path to excellence, and that virtue is the mean between extremes, a mean that can be determined not by blind adherence simply to consequences, or simply to motives, but to "rational principle . . . that principle by which the man of practical reason would [make a decision]."

Consequentialist, nonconsequentialist, and golden mean thinking are used every day in analyses of ethical problems. Here is an example.

Suppose you are scheduled to anchor the six o'clock news and your department becomes embroiled in a controversy about whether or not to use the name of a suicide victim. How could you apply this framework to the decision?

Connections *(continued)*

In general, most broadcast news departments do not air the names of suicide victims if those people are essentially private persons and the suicide an essentially private act. That is a *nonconsequentialist* rule, grounded in the quite decent categorical imperative that families have already suffered enough at this point, and there is little to be gained by dragging the name of the victim out into the public spotlight. So we just won't use the name of the victim, ever.

But things don't always work out so neatly. Let's assume that the suicide victim was a popular young man, the captain of the football team, a person who seemingly had everything going for him. A *consequentialist* might argue that this is a case that merits breaking the rules. Why? Because it shatters the myth that only lonely, reclusive people take their own lives. Teenage suicide is indeed a growing problem, and potential suicide victims often drop hints or display symptoms disclosing that they are at risk. Friends and family members who find it impossible to believe that popular kids kill themselves, though, frequently ignore those symptoms. "Sure," a consequentialist might argue, "using the victim's name will cause the family pain, but in the long run we'll save lives."

An advocate of the *golden mean* might search for a reasonable middle ground. Perhaps the story could be handled in such a way as to avoid identification of the victim. Family members, if they were willing, could be unidentified and be interviewed in silhouette, and thereby pass along their valuable, albeit tragic, experience to family and friends of other teens.

Those are the most basic approaches to one common ethical dilemma. You will find those rationales (consequentialist, nonconsequentialist, and golden mean) served up at some point during almost every ethical debate. But remember that they are not foolproof formulae. They could hardly be foolproof, since consequentialism and nonconsequentialism are diametrically opposed to each other. But they help to illuminate our thinking patterns by shedding light on whether we are thinking and arguing from a consequentialist, nonconsequentialist or golden mean point of view.

But what's the point of "illuminating our thinking patterns" or determining the rationale from which we are arguing? Simply this: once we understand why we reason a particular way, we can take a step back and gain a clearer perspective of our thought process. We can also, by examining our thinking and the well-established criticisms of *nonconsequentialist, consequentialist,* and *golden mean thinking,* search for flaws in our ethical reasoning.

Here are some examples of ways in which we might sift through our reasoning process.

Nonconsequentialism: Pro and Con

Arguments in favor of nonconsequentialism. Nonconsequentialism is a philosophy with a noble heritage, and within the context of our example (the suicide victim) it offers many strong points. Why should we suddenly decide to break a rule because we *think* it will produce some benefit? What proof can we offer that airing the name of the suicide victim will prevent further suicides?

And another point follows: If we're not going to stick to a rule, what is the point of having it? Rules are meant for the tough choices; you cannot simply choose to invoke them only in the easy cases.

Those are the arguments nonconsequentialists use to bolster their case. But their opponents can peck away at that logic.

Arguments opposed to nonconsequentialism. Critics of nonconsequentialist reasoning argue that clinging to a categorical imperative is, in itself, logically inconsistent. Why? Because a nonconsequentialist says that consequences don't count—but at the same time, he or she is

Connections *(continued)*

anticipating consequences. By imposing a rule prohibiting the use of suicide victims' names, for example, aren't we *predicting* consequences—*assuming* that we will besmirch the name of the victim, disgrace the family, "glamorize" suicide, and so forth?

Also, it is arguable that we are indeed blocking an act of good will—bringing the issue of teenage suicide more directly into the public spotlight—by blind adherence to a rule. Perhaps these are special circumstances that should cause us to change our thinking. We cannot adapt to unfolding situations if we are obsessed with following rules.

Consequentialism: Pro and Con

Arguments in favor of consequentialism. Basically, the previously stated rebuttals to nonconsequentialism serve as the consequentialist's platform when he or she defends the concept that the ends justify the means.

- We should not be hidebound to a set of inflexible rules. We can adapt.
- We can look past the immediate situation and can do what will provide the greatest good for the greatest number.
- We do not anticipate consequences while pretending to ignore them.

Arguments opposed to consequentialism. Consequentialists also take their lumps in ethical analysis, though. As mentioned above, the consequentialist argument about "preventing teenage suicide" sounds appealing, but how do we really know what the outcome will be? Will breaking our rule and running the story deter teenage suicide? Maybe.

Maybe not.

Doesn't it make sense to base our decision on the premises of which we are sure: Our policy which, for good reason, protects the privacy of the families of terribly disturbed people who, confronting their own private demons, take their own lives?

The Golden Mean: Pro and Con

Arguments in favor of golden mean thinking. The best we can hope for is to make a rational decision based upon what we know. Instead of trying to predict the outcomes, and instead of clinging to an inflexible rule, we must add up pluses and minuses and come to a reasonable decision halfway between the extremes.

Arguments opposed to golden mean thinking. While the idea of adhering to a *golden mean* is appealing, self-reference problems are involved. After all, if you are the one making up the two extremes you can still wind up with a distorted mean. ("How many people will I murder today, one or ten? Oh, let's compromise and make it five.")

On a more realistic level, let us also note that a compromise is not always the best solution. Because this is first and foremost a journalism text, we need to point out that there simply *may not be a reasonable middle ground* when reporting an event of this nature. You could not hedge indefinitely; it would be ludicrous to write a story about "the captain of the Central High School football team, whose name is being withheld." Also, if the event occurred in a public place, and many citizens witnessed rescue units dashing to the high school, you start a panic by going on air at noon with a story saying "a student died by suicide this morning at Central High" and not naming the student.

SUMMARY

In the most basic terms, reading copy involves using the voice to facilitate expression, and communicating the *ideas* with an unaffected delivery. The way the announcer does this involves the element of style. Polished performers often borrow style elements from professionals they admire, and you can do the same. However, developing a style must never be outright imitation.

Many of the announcing skills needed to communicate a message involve nuances. Gestures are a nuance that can improve expression even in radio because they add an intangible element of communication. Gestures must be carefully controlled because the television lens magnifies gestures and they can detract from appearance. Energy is another nuance, and a performer should always infuse energy into on-air work. A third nuance is body language, which can subtly convey many impressions to the audience. A talk show host tensely holding the arms across the chest, for example, will convey the image of a withdrawn and up-tight person, a feeling that may be communicated to the audience and to guests on the program.

An increasingly important basic announcing skill is ad-libbing. To be effective, an ad-lib must be kept brief and must be thought out in advance, even if the announcer can devote only a moment to planning. Break down what you want to say into distinct ideas, and make mental or written notes of those ideas.

Both radio and television performers need to develop the ability to ad-lib. Ad-libbing in radio requires knowledge of the audience and the format. Ad-libs must blend well with other elements of the overall station sound. The "more music, less talk" concept used by many stations requires music show hosts to make ad-libs short and effective. Talk radio hosts need to keep up with current events and to move quickly from one topic to another. Television situations that require ad-libbing include news, sports, weather, talk and interview programs, and hosting movie shows.

Camera and mic techniques are crucial in communicating a message. An announcer who knows how to work effectively within the technical constraints of the media and who can take advantage of the properties of mics and cameras will look and sound better. Microphones have varying electronic elements and pickup patterns. The elements are moving coil, ribbon, and condenser. Patterns are omnidirectional, bidirectional, and cardioid. An example of mic technique involves moving closer to a mic for a more intimate perspective.

Camera lenses pick up and magnify any deviation of the eyes from a direct angle to the lens, so a direct gaze, without eye shifting, is important. The properties of a TV camera also require polished movement and posture. Eye contact bolsters contact with the viewer, and cultivating the ability to read ahead in the copy allows greater eye contact as well as improves communication skills.

The most common mistake in television, and to a great extent in radio, is failure to project enough energy.

EXERCISES

1. Cast celebrities in the following hypothetical commercials. Write down which celebrities you would choose for each spot, and what elements in their styles will reinforce the particular message to be communicated.

   a. A radio bank commercial specifically geared toward attracting young customers.
   b. A radio bank commercial geared to attracting mature investors with a great deal of money.
   c. Narration (off camera) for a television documentary on the great science fiction movies of the 1990s.
   d. Host (on camera) for a TV special on the earth's volcanoes.
   e. Host (on camera) for a humorous look at small-town America. The host must *not* imply anything demeaning about small towns; the humor must be good-natured.

2. Experiment with different body positions as you read several pieces of copy. Record the readings on audiotape. Use these modes:

    a. Slouching in a chair
    b. Standing
    c. With gestures
    d. Sitting on hands
    e. Smiling
    f. No expression

3. Practice ad-libbing. Take the following exercises seriously; they can be very effective and useful. Using a portable audio recorder, try the following:

    a. Describe a scene (a busy street corner, looking out a window, a sporting event—anything) for 60 seconds or so. Make it compelling, and more than just a physical description of objects.
    b. Clip an action news photo from a newspaper and ad-lib a description of the scene (about 60 seconds' worth).
    c. Ad-lib a brief commercial from the following facts:

        *   There is a Washington's Birthday Sale at the Acme House of Furniture.
        *   Everything is marked down 20 percent.
        *   There's a complete selection of Nordberg Scandinavian furniture, including teak desks and coffee tables.
        *   Acme will be open all day tomorrow from 9 till 9.

    Before you start, let us complicate things a bit. Do this commercial twice: once as you think it should be done for a Hot Hits radio station, and once for a Classic Rock station.

NOTES

1 Johnny Carson was a master performer and television host as was his successor Jay Leno. You can see highlights of their work at *YouTube*. Looking at some of their clips is instructive to note that each has a unique style in their performances. Their performances look effortless but resulted from years of working in the field.
2 Carl Hausman, Fritz Messere, Philip Benoit, and Lewis O'Donnell, *Modern Radio and Audio Production*, 9th ed. (Wadsworth, 2013).
3 This structure and analysis is adapted from Carl Hausman's *Crafting the News for Electronic Media* (Wadsworth, 1992), and Carl Hausman's *Crisis of Conscience: Perspectives on Journalism Ethics* (HarperCollins, 1992).

Radio Staff Announcing Today

Over the past decade the radio industry passed through a period of unprecedented change in the way it used announcers. On some radio stations and for certain airshifts, technology has supplanted the staff announcer altogether. For example, many stations use a live announcing team for their morning drive-time show but then switch to voice-tracking for their midday show. For stations that use voice-tracking software, the staff announcer has been replaced with a board operator, a person who may or may not have any announcing experience. The actual air talent may or may not work at that station. Many announcers now appear on several different stations in different radio markets, prerecording their shows in advance. Some stations use a satellite service for times when they don't have a live announcer.

Where staff announcers exist in today's radio station, they do far more than just read copy and introduce music. In addition to informing, persuading, and entertaining, the staff announcer must reinforce the station's overall sound quality and format. Staff announcers provide linkage between the station and the listener and the wider community it serves.

In some instances, a computer program has replaced the disk jockey's ability to select music within the station format. The program manager may preselect production elements and the rhythm and pacing of the format to reinforce the basic programming strategy of the station. Despite continuing technological innovations, the staff announcer still has to make the station sound cohesive and interesting. If the format happens to be fast-paced contemporary hit radio, for instance, the staff announcer is expected to convey energy and to inject the right amount of humor to provide an entertaining accompaniment to the music.

Modern radio is very specialized. Formats are targeted for well-defined segments of the population. In radio today, on-the-air performance is measured by the announcer's success in attracting listeners among the station's target "demographics" (population). The primary goal of a staff announcer, whether doing a live shift or voice-tracking, is to attract and hold the interest of the audience segment that the station needs for attracting advertisers.

Although reaching those particular audiences is their primary goal, announcers also must know how to operate equipment and how to organize time and perform the tasks integral to on-air work. Small- and medium-market stations usually require the announcer to work in "combo," operating the mixing console (Figure 5.1) and manipulating discs and program material, while announcing.

In this chapter, we outline the operational and organizational skills required for effective on-air performance in modern radio.

THE STAFF ANNOUNCER'S JOB

In a broad sense, the duties of a staff announcer can be classified as *performance, operations,* and *organization*. Although these categories of duties overlap, they categorize the typical staff announcer's job as well as any other classification. Understanding these categories provides valuable insight into some of the

FIGURE 5.1 WGLS General Manager Derek Jones working a combo shift.

operational and organizational tasks that are not heard by the listening audience but that still play an important role in the staff announcer's job.

Much of this chapter centers on programming and technology, rather than on what would strictly be considered announcing, and you may wonder why. Well, programming has been evaluated in such detail because *programming and the role of the performer have become inseparable.* Although 20 years ago an announcer could rely on a good voice and a glib tongue, today a program director can replace a good voice with a computer and a music service. Therefore, the choice to keep a live announcer on the air is a conscious choice the station management makes. A competent and skilled performer is one who can work effectively within a format and can reach that target audience better than can a technological solution.

Performance

Performance includes introducing music, entertaining with humor, and reading commercials, weather, traffic reports, sometimes news, and routine announcements such as time and temperature, school closings, and so on. It also includes the air personality's general patter, which can range from occasional ad-libs to extended comedy monologues.

Operations

The duties associated with getting program elements over the air by means of station equipment (computers, CDs, microphones, the mixing console, and so forth) are called *operations.* This category involves such duties as the off-air recording for later replay of in-studio programs or material fed via the Internet or a network line. Taking readings of the station's transmitting gear also falls in this category.[1] Another operational duty assigned to some staff announcers is answering telephones and taking requests. Many radio stations pay close attention to telephone calls, using them as an informal research tool.

Never forget that a heavy responsibility can rest on the shoulders of the on-air person during periods of emergency or natural disaster. On-air staff—and sometimes this means the staff announcers as well as newspeople—must pass along crucial information about storm warnings, floods, and other imminent dangers. While most stations have important phone numbers posted, every on-air person *must* be familiar with the appropriate contacts at local police, fire, and emergency management agencies. In addition, the radio console operator is generally responsible for monitoring the Emergency Alert System.

Organization

Organizational duties vary from station to station. For stations that use computers to automate the program selection, frequently the music and the commercials have been programmed into the station's computer. The announcer does live announcements at intervals designated in the program.

While most stations have music and commercials stored on computer hard drives, there may be other stations where music is on CDs, Here, the duties may include pulling music from the station's library in preparation for an airshift and refiling them when the shift is completed.

Generally all announcers who also run the board have other duties that include filling out the station's program logs and lining up commercials and, if the format is not preprogrammed, choosing music in advance of airplay.

Typical Duties

The nature of radio is constantly evolving. Small stations that service local and rural areas with live local news, swap shops and live coverage of local events are few. Many AM stations have been automated or are affiliated with a satellite network programming service. Many small FM stations have joined together, rebroadcasting a single program to provide a common service to a wider geographical area. Thus, there are many types of stations and many different potential scenarios for the staff announcer. With our three categories in mind, we've chosen what we think is often seen as typical duties in small, medium and large markets. Let's watch some staff announcers at work, focus on requirements of the job, examine the equipment used, and discuss the role of formats in the working world of the staff announcer. The responsibilities of an air personality vary tremendously from station to station. In smaller operations, the announcer may even be responsible for vacuuming the studios. In the top markets, an air personality is just that: an entertainer expected to project a personality, with very few or no operational or organizational chores.

The following job descriptions and working conditions may be found for stations in the market sizes given. All names are fictitious.

Small-market country FM with AM automation

Juan is the morning person at this station, which is housed in a prefabricated office building in an open field next to the transmitter and antenna. The station serves a city of 19,000. The FM station is partially automated and the AM is fully automated.

Juan arrives at the station at 5:00 a.m. to get ready for the day. He signs on at 6:00 a.m. His performance duties include acting as host of the morning music show until 10. He will also read news headlines (on the hour), talk about the weather and local events during his shift. Commercial reading is an important duty. Juan is known for his ability to ad-lib a commercial, and local sponsors furnish him with fact sheets. The fact sheets rotate as local merchants announce sales and other promotions occur. At 10 the station switches to an automated music service (Figure 5.2) until the afternoon drivetime. During this time, Juan may cut a commercial or two. After he goes to lunch, he may return to the station for some more production work or he may go visit clients for the station.

Operational duties include culling local and national headlines from the Web or a news service, developing material about the country music scene, taking transmitter readings at intervals during his shift, running the board for his own program, running the production board when cutting commercials, and operating all the studio equipment. Another responsibility on Juan's shift is to keep the AM automation running. There is very little to do for the automation as the program is streamed from a satellite and a computer plays the commercials and IDs.

Organizational duties include filling out logs and, because this is a hometown station, putting together his own music playlist for his show, monitoring the Web for news headlines and weather forecasts and other items of interest.

FIGURE 5.2 Modern software allows the flow of music to be partially or fully automated.

Summary: Although not a particularly accomplished performer, Juan is well known in the community. He is expected to be reasonably knowledgeable about the music he plays and to be able to communicate effectively on the air. He is in actuality a "personality," but much of his job involves operations and organizational duties.

Small-market FM adult contemporary

Lisa, a college student, is a part-time staff announcer at this station, which barely survives in a town of 32,000. The station plays mainly contemporary pop songs, although there is some music from the 1990s and later. Physically, the station consists of an on-air studio, a small production studio, and two offices. The news service was removed when the owners fell behind in their payments to the service provider. News and weather headlines are now gathered off websites like CNN and WeatherUnderground.

Performance duties include acting as a host of a music program and reading an occasional commercial or public service announcement.

Operational duties include running all station equipment. From 7 a.m. until 10 a.m. on Saturday, Lisa will run the board for her own music show, and from 10 until noon she will act as engineer for an ethnic music program hosted by a local businessman, who supplies the music for this program.

Organizational duties include making standard log entries, filing music not available on the computer and copy, vacuuming the station, and emptying ashtrays and trash cans. Occasionally Lisa helps out with a live remote from a store opening or similar events. Lisa works for a little more than minimum wage, as do most of the employees at the station. She receives no benefits of any kind but can supplement her salary by selling time to local merchants.

Summary: Lisa's primary responsibilities are operational: putting CDs and records on air, running the board, and so on. She is not a smooth air personality, nor is she expected to be.

Small- to medium-market AM/FM station

George is an announcer on the FM. He plays classic rock and works the afternoon shift. The station is located in a city of 80,000 and is very successful. Headquartered in a reasonably modern building in the center of town, George's station has modest but modern equipment, all of which is well maintained.

Performance duties include introducing music which is preprogrammed on a computer. George can insert a very limited number of songs into the playlist if he receives requests. He has the opportunity to add some light patter, and he reads commercial copy and weather.

Station policy prescribes back-announcing; that is, George gives the name of the song after it has finished, usually in a set of two or three songs.

Operational duties include running the board for his show and for the local news anchor. He also must hit the network newscast at the top of the hour exactly and open the network channel on the board.

Organizational duties include planning music *backsells* (the back announcing of songs), taking occasional phone calls, and keeping the program log.

Summary: George is expected to maintain a light, pleasant tone throughout, to give brief intros to the music, and to back-announce the songs. Voice quality is important, but there is not much emphasis on personality. Some knowledge of the type of rock music featured is needed.

Medium-market adult contemporary FM

This station has a rigidly programmed contemporary hits music format, and heavy emphasis on news, traffic reports, and other useful information. It serves a city of 250,000. The station has several translators so it serves a wider geographic area. Jay, the afternoon staff announcer, also deals with numerous promotions and contests. His shift runs from 3 p.m. to 7 p.m., although he reports to work at 11 a.m. to handle the heavy production load assigned to him.

Performance duties include heavy ad-libbing, fast humor, and banter with callers who are participating in promotions and contests. Jay has a desktop computer for recording callers and he can do some limited editing on the fly before airing call-ins. Jay reads an occasional commercial, but most commercials are recorded.

Operational duties include the complex job of running the board, which involves handling incoming air traffic reports and frequent prerecorded station identification announcements, inserting commercials and caller comments, and running the console for the news anchor.

Organizational duties are minimal; music is preselected and programmed into the station computer. Commercials are also programmed on the computer and are sequenced between music sets by the program director.

Summary: Jay is expected to run a tight board, making sure his talk between music sets is smooth and comes over the music outros, and he needs to be an excellent ad-libber. He is a good communicator and provides listeners with an entertaining four hours of music, information, and humor.

Medium- to major-market FM modern rock

Angela works in a very high-tech environment. The equipment is state-of-the-art, and there is a great deal of glass in the spacious studio setup. On Angela's shift, from midnight until 6 a.m., she plays an adult contemporary format with some album cuts for a loyal audience in a city of 650,000.

Performance duties include projecting a hip, laid-back style and ad-libbing about the recording artists. She also reads, in her style, short news summaries she prepares before her shift and then edits through the airshift.

Operational duties include running board, a relatively simple job because most of the music is programmed on the station computer. Angela has some flexibility and can program and play certain requests into the computer's rotation.

Organizational duties include programming the computer and taking requests. Requests must be logged because station management wants to know what listeners want to hear.

Summary: Angela is expected to project a certain personality over the air, the aura of the laid-back aficionado of a particular kind of rock music. In addition, she is required to ad-lib about the music and, therefore, must be extremely knowledgeable.

Major-market all-talk AM

Barbara hosts the 10 a.m. to 2 p.m. shift in a station located in a city of almost two million. She sits in a fairly small studio separated by glass from her engineer, who runs the console. There is a producer for the show who uses a special telephone hybrid to screen incoming telephone calls. To Barbara's right is a device that identifies each caller by first name and hometown. To her left is a tablet computer allowing her to do quick research on Google.

Performance duties include conversing with the callers and, indirectly, with the rest of the listening audience, and providing information on the topic being discussed. She conducts interviews and reads commercials.

Although Barbara has very few operational duties, her organizational duties include heavy research into the topics being discussed, including a ritual morning's reading the local newspaper, one or two of the major national newspapers and the major news portals on the Internet. Barbara also must be knowledgeable about the topics of discussion with interview guests and frequently checks their twitter feeds to keep abreast of current opinions.

Summary: Barbara is expected to be a lively conversationalist and an interesting person in general. She must be a superb ad-libber and interviewer. Also, she is a true one-to-one communicator, an absolute must in the business of talk radio. A comprehensive knowledge of current events is taken for granted.

Major-market adult contemporary FM

Bob has the afternoon shift in a network-owned and operated (commonly called an O&O) station in a city of several million. Located in a downtown skyscraper, the studio is lavishly furnished and even equipped with a fireplace, a holdover from the golden days.

Performance duties include introducing music, giving informal patter between cuts, reading commercials, and introducing the news. Bob will cut some other commercials, but not as part of his regular job. He will be paid extra, and very well, for any voice work he does in addition to his airshift. After his shift, Bob will spend another hour voice-tracking programs for two other smaller stations the network owns. He is paid extra for his voice-tracking work.

Operational duties include nothing more than turning on his mic. An engineer in another room runs the console.

Organizational duties are limited to keeping track of the commercial scripts and other announcements handed him by an assistant. After his shift, Bob will record a summary of community activities for the station to air throughout the day and he will voice-track and then record a series of song intros and other patter for the two smaller stations.

Summary: Bob is expected to perform flawlessly. Sponsors pay thousands of dollars for commercials and expect him to bring that copy to life. He has an exceptional and distinctive voice, which has made him wealthy.

The examples given do not cover every situation in radio staff announcing. They do, however, illustrate three rules that generally prove true—see Box 5.1.

BOX 5.1 **The Division of Labor in Large and Small Stations**

1. Facilities and equipment tend to be better in larger stations. Of course, there are poorly equipped, rundown facilities in major markets, and state-of-the-art equipment can be found in smaller markets. But in general owners of stations in larger markets have more money at their disposal, hence, they also have newer equipment and better physical plants. Today most production and programming is done on computers so there is less overall maintenance required for station operations.
2. The staff announcer is responsible for fewer operational and organizational duties in larger markets than is the case in smaller markets.
3. An air personality is expected to be more professional and talented in larger markets. That person usually will have proved his or her abilities in progressively more demanding arenas before reaching a major market.

JOB REQUIREMENTS

The tools and experience necessary for an air personality vary with the particular needs of the station and the size of the market. The format, a concept that is examined in more detail shortly, also shapes the requirements.

Smaller markets often seek the so-called jack of all trades. The reason: small-market staff announcers simply do not have the support staffs available in larger markets, and must therefore absorb some of the duties that are relegated to other specialists in larger markets. It is not unusual, for example, for a small-market announcer to double as an engineer. A small-market announcer with no technical training will often be trained to perform routine maintenance on equipment, or do production work for the station. Air personalities may also participate in station sales, act as play-by-play announcers, host live remotes at store openings or write copy.

In larger markets, positions are more specialized and require more narrowed and refined talents. The ability to do an interview is useful in small markets, but it is vital to the radio talk show host. What passes for engaging humor in a small market may not captivate audiences in New York, where whole formats evolve around the gag-telling ability of the staff announcer.

Basic requirements for a staff announcer in any market or format include a working knowledge of music and the ability to garner an in-depth knowledge of a particular music style if the situation requires. Familiarity with good grammar and pronunciation is a must. Also important is the ability to work with equipment because almost every staff announcer must start in a small or medium market and run his or her own board. Lack of this ability definitely hinders a career.

A clear, expressive voice, free of speech and vocal defects, is almost mandatory.

Some announcers can turn an odd speech pattern into a trademark, but the odds are against anyone with a distracting defect in his or her delivery.

A resourceful personality and the ability to perform well under pressure are definite pluses. A college education is helpful, but rarely specified in the job description. However, being well educated in a general sense is extremely worthwhile for any performer.

EQUIPMENT

As mentioned earlier, operation of equipment is a major portion of a staff announcer's job in most small and medium markets, and a "tight board" is important. Mastery of equipment is not the be-all and end-all of staff announcing, however. Being an air personality involves genuine communication, not just manipulating the console. Unfortunately, some air people become fixated on equipment and gimmickry at the expense of developing an engaging personality and real communication skills.

Even production specialists are wise to avoid thinking of hardware and technical operations instead of focusing on concepts and communication of a message. With that point understood, do recognize that confident operation of equipment is important. Here is a short introduction to some of the equipment found in a typical radio station.

Console

To the uninitiated, the console (Figure 5.3) can seem like an intimidating and complex collection of switches and slide faders. But although the hardware can be complex, the concept is simple. The console is the Grand Central Station of the control room, and has three main functions: routing signals, mixing signals, and amplifying signals.

> *Routing:* The console is able to take the output of a sound source such as a microphone or computer and send, or route, it to the transmitter or to some recording device. A variable resistor called a fader ("fader pot") governs the loudness of the audio signal. Audio is comprised of varying

FIGURE 5.3 A slide-fader console, otherwise known as "the board." It's simply a mechanism to put different audio sources on air.

electrical signals, which transmit sound. There is also, in a typical console, an on-off switch that governs the pot. Further details are provided at the end of this discussion.

Mixing: An important duty of the board operator is to mix signals, such as music from a CD or a computer and voice from a microphone. The console allows multiple audio sources to be put over the air at the same time. For example, if the computer is brought up on Fader 1, and the microphone on Fader 2 the operator, by judgment and experience, will set the correct balance between music and voice.

Amplification: The electrical signal strength of most components in the radio control room is very weak, and the console must amplify these signals to a level high enough to feed the transmitter or a recording device.

Line amplifiers in the console boost the incoming signals to usable levels. The various signals can be combined together. The console performs these functions by means of the faders, which are manufactured in the form of vertical sliders. The on-off switch is commonly known as a "key" (even though it may be a button).

An important element to understand regarding console function is the key, which is generally a button that selects or turns the fader on. Consoles usually have two or more output channels. The audition channel and the program channel may be separate buttons. Audition is an off-air channel, used for private listening and frequently for off-air production work on the on-air console. The program channel is the on-air channel. When a channel's fader is keyed (switched on) to program, the audio source it governs is fed to the transmitter. Today many radio programming systems allow the operator to send the program signal out for distribution while also recording from audition to a recording device such as a computer.

An alternative to the audition channel is the cue channel, which feeds a signal to a small speaker usually located in the console or headphones, without putting that signal over the air. One useful application for the cue channel is in listening for the point in a song at which the announcer wants to begin a cut. Then the music can be paused so that at a specified time, the music will begin at the desired point. Another is to cue up request call-ins from one of the station's computers.

Computers

Computers are the primary playback device in broadcasting for music reproduction today. They are also programmed to play back commercials, spot announcements and station IDs. To some extent, computers

FIGURE 5.4 Sophisticated but intuitive broadcast automation packages allow easy control of many program elements.

can also replace the staff announcer when the installed software allows the station to voice-track segments of their programming.

Modern broadcast software such as Skylla and Caliope allows a staff announcer to automate many of the functions that used to be done manually by the board operator. On stations that have tightly formatted music playlists, the program director or music director can preselect the music and the name of each song will appear in the order to be played. Commercial breaks are also programmed into the software program or if the shift is live, a virtual cart machine allows access to commercials and jingles.

Popular types of automation software (Figure 5.4) are exceptionally versatile and allow integrated control of many sources.

The modern automation systems integrate with digital consoles so that only a standard Ethernet cable is required to connect between the console and the computer. Sounds on computers will usually be recorded in either an MP3 (MPEG audio layer 3) or WAV file format.

LEGACY AUDIO EQUIPMENT

There are a number of legacy audio formats and devices and you may find them still useful in a variety of radio stations. Here is a brief summary.

Compact Discs

Compact discs or CDs (see Figure 5.5) use a digital, microcomputer-aided system to play back sounds, so they give what some feel is a truer rendition of recorded sound than MP3s. The compact discs play with

FIGURE 5.5 A CD player built into a rack.

FIGURE 5.6 Here's a turntable that is hidden away until needed. LPs are not dead. According to Billboard.com nearly 14% of all music sold was on a vinyl LP.

display track numbers and track times, so there is less need to cue discs than there was when analog turntables were dominant, and there is less chance of damaging CD recordings. Modern broadcast CD players can be programmed into a station's console to start or stop but automation is difficult. Some machines record as well as play back audio tracks.

Turntables

Turntables (Figure 5.6) are essentially record players, but they differ from the home variety in several respects. A broadcast turntable is a heavy-duty unit that has a plate (the part that spins) that can be manipulated by hand to cue a record to a point just before the music starts. Few radio stations use turntables today, but we include them in this discussion because you will still find them in some production setups. For the broadcast performer, working with turntables is basically a matter of learning to cue discs properly and to start them smoothly.

Minidiscs

Minidiscs are recordable magneto-optical devices that allow the user to perform basic editing functions in addition to recording and playing back audio. Minidiscs can be cued to play back tracks instantaneously, and each minidisc can record as many as 255 tracks or about 74 minutes of audio. Most minidiscs have been replaced by solid-state recorders that use some memory card such as a CF or SD memory card.

Reel-to-Reel Tape Machines

Tape reels come in several sizes, including 10½-, 7-, and 5-inch widths and the tape itself is generally 1.4-inch wide for most broadcast applications. Audiotape has a Mylar or acetate base coated with iron oxide—a fancy name for rust. The iron oxide coating can pick up magnetic impulses and store them by means of the arrangement of the particles. The pattern is encoded onto the tape by the heads of the tape machine. Typically, a tape machine has an erase head, a record head, and a playback head, and the tape crosses the heads in that order.

A variant of the reel-to-reel tape machine is the cassette recorder. High-quality cassette machines were often found in production and air studios to make dubs or backups. Today flash drives and the Internet have replaced the need to make cassette dubs.

Cartridge Machines

The cart machine comes in two varieties. The digital cart machine is essentially a hard-disc recorder with features that provide for the easy recording, naming, and selection of audio tracks. Play back of the track is instantaneous and cueing is done simply by selecting the name of the track or the track number. Digital cart machines are often found in studios where the staff announcer is live and takes requests from listeners or uses many sound effects (SFX) or jingles for the show. Sometimes, a computer is set up as a digital cart machine.

The analog cart machine used a single loop of tape that did not need to be rewound because it contained a continuous reel of lubricated tape that feeds from the middle of the spool. An inaudible tone automatically stopped the tape when it reached the point where the recording was started. These machines are not used today.

Other Gear

Other types of equipment are available to an on-air performer, but their use is best addressed in a production course. Production skills are indispensable to a radio staff announcer because the duties of radio performer and producer usually overlap. In fact, the ability to use equipment often plays a major role in the overall effectiveness of the communicator. (Just read through the trade journals and note how many help-wanted advertisements for on-air positions specify expertise in production.) Consider too that if you lack the ability to run the board competently, your performance will be compromised.

No matter how good an announcer's voice and delivery may be, constantly flubbed program elements will detract from the message.

FORMATS AND THE STAFF ANNOUNCER

In radio today, the format identifies stations and differentiates one station from another. One primary duty of a radio staff announcer is to reinforce the station's format.

Formats center on more than the choice of music. The format is built by the style of announcing, by the overall pace of program elements, by the choice of announcers, by the sound of commercials, even by the choice of microphones. Any sound element must reinforce the format.

For example, certain adult radio formats center on the "laid-back" air personality who communicates in an intimate way with the listeners. Stations using this format often equip the air studios with highly sensitive mics that pick up breathiness and mouth noises, important components in projecting the "personal" feel. Also enhancing that feel, of course, is the style of the air personality and how well he or she works within the format. Many NPR announcers seem to exhibit this quality.

In decades past, a typical announcer had a powerful, versatile voice and was called on to do widely differing tasks. A typical shift might have involved reading news, introducing a wide variety of music, hosting a live band show, and reading loftily worded commercials.

Glibness and a good voice often were sufficient qualifications for an announcer's position. Auditions usually consisted of tongue twisters and sometimes classical music pronunciations to test the announcer's mechanical ability to render words and phrases.

Today, much more emphasis is placed on communicating a particular message. The news reporter, for instance, is expected to have more than just a voice. He or she must project understanding of the news, a perspective gained only by a professional journalist. Although there are few classical music stations today, announcers must show in-depth understanding of the music, not simply the ability to correctly pronounce titles and composers' names.

The specific formats of modern radio call for special abilities and characteristics by the on-air personality. Following are some examples of how an effective on-air communicator must work within a format to reach a particular audience segment.

Adult Contemporary

In what is known as the adult contemporary (AC) format, radio station programmers typically try to reach the young adult audience, usually defined as women listeners aged 25 to 54 or 25 to 49, depending on the particular *demographic* sought. Demographics are statistical representations of populations.

The demographic data obtained from a study of an audience's density, distribution, and vital statistics are intensely important in the station's overall sales and programming effort. In short, a commercial station's goal is to "capture" a demographic range and sell that distinct audience to advertisers who want to reach a specific group.

An interesting outgrowth of demographics is psychographics, statistical breakdowns of the audience by lifestyle. Researchers have developed such colorful psychographic designations of audience segments as "minks and station wagons," or "shotguns and pickups." In any event, radio stations use demographics and psychographics to shape their sound toward reaching a clearly defined audience.

Although adult contemporary programming varies widely within the format, it usually consists of a mixture of light rock, with a greater proportion of former hits from the 1980s and 1990s. Current popular hits are used, but AC programmers steer away from heavy rock or hip-hop.

To work effectively within an AC format, consider these suggestions:

1. Avoid artificiality. Extremely patterned, singsong "disc jockey" voices are not popular, nor are voices with odd characteristics. Often soothing and friendly female voices are used.
2. Maintain an even pace, not frenetic but certainly not laid-back.
3. Be well organized. AC radio relies heavily on the transfer of information (school closings, notes of community interest, traffic, weather, etc.). Usually there is more talk during morning and afternoon drivetimes.

In hiring AC announcers, it is not unusual for program directors and station managers to specify "a performer who can provide companionship." This job description might translate into projecting the personality of a friendly and amusing next-door neighbor. As one program director put it, "the kind of person you'd like to have at your cocktail party."

Adult contemporary listeners are thought by many to be easily irritated—meaning, prompted to tune out. Whatever you do, don't be an "irritant," which is actually so common that it's a standard term in radio. See Focus on Technique for more.

Focus on Technique

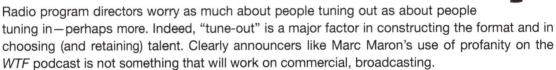

How Not To Be an "Irritant"

Radio program directors worry as much about people tuning out as about people tuning in—perhaps more. Indeed, "tune-out" is a major factor in constructing the format and in choosing (and retaining) talent. Clearly announcers like Marc Maron's use of profanity on the *WTF* podcast is not something that will work on commercial, broadcasting.

What this means is that one of the top priorities of a radio staff announcer is to keep from irritating listeners. This usually does not mean simply being personally agreeable; a lot of "personality or shock jocks" would actually be an "irritant" and "tune-out" factor to listeners if they suddenly became mild mannered. However, the era of the "shock" jocks appears to be on the decline.

The point: Tune-out happens when listeners don't get what they expect.

If they want to hear the music and the jock talks over it, they tune out. If they want to hear the jock talk and he or she doesn't—ditto. With Internet services like Pandora, Spotify and others, music is available 24/7. So listeners tune into stations because they want to be entertained or hear information with their musical preferences.

Here are some tips for avoiding what program directors (PDs) call "on-air irritants."

- *Too much hype.* Most staff announcers are toning down their deliveries. The "growling voice" and "in your face" delivery is out of favor in all but the hardest-format stations.
- *Too many reminders about how much music you are playing.* Interviews with disaffected listeners confirm that when you continually stop the music to tell people how much music you are playing—TEN HITS IN A ROW!!—you irritate the audience. Remember "less talk" means you must talk less."
- *Endless "pre-sell" on the music sweeps.* "TEN IN A ROW, COMING NOW, YES, TEN IN A ROW" may induce a listener to push a button before the sweep starts.
- *Laughing at your own in-jokes.* Air people sometimes like to convince themselves they are funny but this doesn't always seem entertaining to the listener.
- *Stepping on the end of songs.* Listeners may actually want to hear the ending and will resent you talking over it or dumping out of it completely. Research shows listeners are irritated by missing the ends of current hits.
- *Stepping on a "cold" ending.* On a related note, don't talk over the end of songs that end cold.
- *Getting tricky with the call letters.* Radio stations often use "handles," such as "Mix 101," that have no real relation to their call letters. As a result, when stations give the required legal ID (a direct statement of the call letters and station location) at the top of the hour, just say the call letters and don't make an enormous production of it.
- *Always talking over the beginning instrumental and butting up to the start of the vocal.* Focus groups say this is an irritant, and it is often heard as the announcer's self-indulgent exercise.

Pop Contemporary Hit Radio

The category that used to be referred to as Top 40 but now is commonly called contemporary hit radio (CHR) is oriented toward the younger listener. Often, stations are zeroing in on the 18–34 age bracket, although it also includes younger listeners. The format is fast paced, with many different program elements interjected in short periods of time. A jingle may be followed by a commercial, which butts up to a very short station promo, which overlaps the beginning of the music cut, while the announcer "talks up" to the vocal.

To be effective in hit radio, an announcer should

1. Project a high energy level but not offensive or overtly loud.
2. Have a good working knowledge of the music. The hit radio announcer won't be required to engage in lengthy discourses on the performers, but knowledge of new releases and up-and-coming acts is necessary. Ignorance of the music and musicians will quickly become evident. Remember, many listeners get frequent updates about their favorite performers via Facebook, Instagram, and other social media sites, and they attend concerts by the performing artists. Websites such as Billboard, Rolling Stone and Spin can provide useful information.
3. Handle control room equipment smoothly. Practice is necessary to run a "tight board," which is essential in this fast-moving radio type.

If you opt for a career in hit radio, remember that you must be able to sustain enthusiasm for the format and for the music. Trends in music come and go, and even announcers in their early twenties often find their tastes moving away from current hits. But on-air enthusiasm must always be evident.

Country

Country has evolved over the past two decades. Today it appeals to a wide demographic of adults 25+. Country & Western was an older style typified by twanging guitars and whining vocals. Some of those elements can still be found in country today, but for the most part country is considered a mainstream part of popular music, featuring more sophisticated arrangements and orchestral backgrounds to supplement the guitars.

Suggestions for country music air personality work include the following:

1. Study the music and artists. Many listeners are devoted fans, so the announcer must have good working knowledge. *Nashville Country Daily* and *The Boot* are good places to read about current stars and upcoming musical releases.
2. Have genuine interest in and appreciation for the music. Enthusiasm for country music is hard to fake.
3. Develop an understanding of factors that relate to the country music scene. Many performers tour extensively and interact with their fanbase. Gone is the day when country music listeners were thought to be rural folk or farmers. Some of the most successful country music stations in the nation, in fact, are located in large cities. However, if you do serve a rural area, remember that farming today is a big, sophisticated business, and a modern farmer is just as likely to read the *Wall Street Journal* as the dairy association newsletter.

Country music can be a satisfying format in which to work because country personalities often attain celebrity status in their markets. This means that an announcer in this format should have a strong desire to communicate and an interest in individuals and the community.

Classic Rock and Classic Hits

These formats of rock music have evolved in many directions, from some stations that focus on the best-selling rock artists of all times to some stations that primarily play music from the late 1970s through the 1980s.

Typically, classic rock stations feature songs from the Beatles, the Eagles, Fleetwood Mac, Rolling Stones, Elton John, Journey, etc. although some stations focus on heavy metal and harder rock. Classic hits on the other hand will include a broader mix of Top 40 hits from those decades.

Here are some hints to help you function successfully.

1. Having a mature-sounding voice is an asset because many listeners to this format are 35 years old and older. They grew up with this music and often assume you did too.
2. Ad-libbing is less important than in other formats because the format relies heavily on longer sets of music. But those spots must be delivered with precision because copy is slotted less frequently and sponsors may be paying a premium for commercials that will stand out.
3. Always maintain a friendly, personal approach but be knowledgeable about the music being played.

Album-Oriented Rock

Although long record cuts and heavy rock are staples, within the album-oriented rock (AOR) format are a myriad of music types and demographic targets.

Probably no other format is involved in such precise "narrowcasting," or targeting of a very specific audience segment. One station in the market might, for example, focus on so-called "modern" rock, whereas another might tend toward more "classic" selections.

In any event, an AOR announcer must have a good working knowledge of the field because he or she will be expected to ad-lib at some length about the music and the artists.

Other suggestions are as follows:

1. Use an intimate and conversational style. This is virtually the hallmark of the AOR announcer.
2. Study the particular jargon and lifestyle of the listeners, their slang expressions, the concerts they attend, the clothes they wear. If it's modern rock, bands tend to be more current, usually within the last five years, so it is important to know the music well.
3. Strengthen your ability to ad-lib effectively and at some length. Ad-libbing is important to most radio announcers, but with some AOR formats, particularly with music from the 1970s and 1980s, it requires a conversational approach and requires superior skills.

   As with country music and classic rock, interest in and knowledge of album-oriented rock is difficult to fake.

Talk Radio

Talk radio has been around for many years but only recently has emerged into a variety of different formats such as all sports, all politics, etc. The entire rationale is to elicit responses from listeners who phone in and comment on various topics.

To function effectively in the talk radio format, follow these three rules.

1. Read as many newspapers and informational websites as you can. Knowledge in a wide variety of areas is essential. A talk-show host caught unaware of an important trend or news development can appear foolish. If it's a sports show, call-in guests and listeners know a seemingly endless amount of detail. You must be knowledgeable about players past and present.
2. Develop and practice the interview skills presented in Chapter 8. Many talk radio shows feature an interview segment. If there is no guest, the host must use the same skills to elicit responses from callers.
3. Pay particular attention to time and timing. The talk-radio host must know when and how to wrap up a discussion to hit the network news or other program element. Also, he or she cannot afford to be caught short, without material to finish a segment.

Talk radio requires the ultimate in one-to-one communication skills and a genuine interest in people and events. Glibness and superficiality are apparent immediately.

Other Specialized Formats

These include classical, all-jazz, urban contemporary, religious and foreign language formats. New formats evolve regularly, and existing formats split into narrower categories. During the early days of FM, "rock" was a reasonably accurate description of a station's format. Today there are many variations of this format, ranging from new age to classic rock to modern rock and soft rock.

The narrower the format, the greater the knowledge required of the announcer.

While there are only a small number of classical music stations, an announcer for this format must be an expert in classical music. Besides knowing enough to program music, he or she must be able to discuss the pieces themselves and the life and times of each composer.

DAYPART

A station's programming varies within the day, and programming elements in a particular daypart will differ from other time periods in the same station. A daypart is a segment of several hours, generally identified by the audience tuning in. In a typical adult contemporary station the morning period, usually from 6 a.m. to 10 a.m., is known as drive time, or *morning drive.* (In some commuter markets, drive time starts slightly earlier.) As you might guess, that term relates to the heavy listenership as people commute to work. Drive time also includes people in their homes, preparing for the day's activities. These listeners typically are assumed to be eager for news and information, and for a bright companion to get their day started.

As the daypart changes, so do the station's programming elements. The midday format, designed for listeners from 10 a.m. to 2 or 3 p.m., may include special program elements like the "at work request hour" if the audience has a great many office or factory workers. Typically it was thought of at many stations as "housewife" time but as more women entered the workplace this changed. The approach of a midday announcer would be geared toward women. Delivery might be slower; there is not as much flow of news and information, and no traffic reports. Because the listeners have longer periods in which to listen, some stations may feature longer features and interviews while other stations may provide live call-in requests.

Later comes "afternoon drive." Here, the input of news and information is stepped up as listeners once again take to their autos. Afternoon drive is generally a bit lower keyed than morning drive.

In the evening, the station's listenership typically skews toward younger listeners. The announcer may gear his or her approach to high school or college students studying while listening to the radio.

Overnight segments have become more competitive for the advertiser's dollar. Once thought of as virtually a throwaway, the modern overnight shift often has substantial numbers of listeners, sometimes a very devoted audience. Listener composition typically changes throughout the overnight period. From midnight until 2 a.m. much of the audience may consist of people who have not yet gone to bed, whereas 2 a.m. to 4 a.m. often is the domain of night workers. Starting at 4 a.m., the emphasis may shift slightly to incorporate very early risers and those who need to get ready for work. Overnight on-air radio staff announcers often gear their approach and program content with these periods in mind. Overnight operations are frequently automated to some degree. Tech Talk provides a look at how computers can be used to assist a staff announcer.

TECHNIQUES OF RADIO STAFF ANNOUNCING

To communicate effectively with the target audience, an air personality must combine natural talent and experience, along with the ability to master equipment (see Tech Talk, below).

Tech Talk

Live Assist and Automation and More

Integration of station automation and social media applications are changing the way announcers do their business. And it's a safe bet you will encounter such high-tech equipment at one of your future job sites—perhaps the first one. You'll be expected to demonstrate at least some familiarity with the way modern applications work.

With audio production software (see Figure 5.7) you can manage music libraries, cut and paste audio clips, record news actualities, customize voice tracks, dub in commercial spots and let different announcers repurpose content for different programs, such as for Internet feeds. The software can be used as a fully automated system or live-assist, with a satellite service or with any combination of these.

New social media applications provide stations with the ability to interact with listeners via the Web. Coupons or special offers are sent to listeners at the exact moment the listener hears the spot on the radio can increase the value of the station to the advertiser. Other software allows for increased listener experiences as listeners download and customize their mobile apps. Features within the app allow stations to repurpose special shows or program segments, and allow the audience to enter contests.

As a staff announcer, your responsibilities may also include specific segment work in the social media app realm. Audience feedback via Facebook, listener request lines and via mobile apps plays an important role in providing information for program managers, as do ratings.

The computer takes the place of more legacy playback devices, such as cart machines or minidiscs. Instead, the audio elements—such as commercials, jingles, sound effects, and

FIGURE 5.7 Touchscreen automation that allows the announcer to "fire" program elements.

Tech Talk *(continued)*

music—are stored on computer hard drives. The announcer/operator uses a mouse, or in some cases a touchscreen, to activate audio elements.

In many cases, the events stored in the computer are "ganged" together so that several events fire in sequence. This practice is known as "live assist." Of course, the computer provides the option of ganging all program elements together and completely automating the station, which is an option some station owners elect to pursue. In this circumstance, the announcer may be called on to record all his or her commercials, narrations, record intros, and other program material in one sitting, and to program the computer to run music, commercials, and narration in the proper sequence.

Not all stations have converted to computer-driven programming, and some small stations probably may not for the forseeable future. The fact is that old-style equipment still works well and in some cases it is more cost effective to do things the old-fashioned way.

Some elements can be taught, but skill as a staff announcer comes only with experience. Experimenting to determine what works and what doesn't is an invaluable part of the learning process.

Finding Personality and Perspective

You can also learn a great deal by listening to other air people, selecting elements of their styles with which you can be comfortable. Of course direct imitation is not the goal, but most accomplished radio air personalities could name five or six other broadcasters who influenced their styles.

One guideline that almost never fails is this: be conservative when you first start out. An inexperienced announcer who tries to emulate another personality probably will produce a poor imitation at best and possibly a ludicrous flop. What seems like side-splitting humor to a novice announcer may simply sound inane to the listener.

Start slowly. Get comfortable with the station's equipment, program schedule, and format.

Be careful of ethics. You will probably encounter people who want favors and/or want to do you favors. In addition to ethical considerations, there are laws governing what you can and cannot do when you are a radio announcer. While not a comprehensive guide, this chapter's *Think About It* provides some background.

Think About It

Free Stuff

Music announcers are often called on to make appearances at events, sometimes acting as master of ceremonies or simply lending publicity to the gathering. In addition to putting in an appearance, the announcer frequently is expected to "plug" the event on-air ahead of time.

Stations have varying rules and procedures about such appearances, and the federal government has drawn up rules governing what sort of "reward" an announcer can receive for saying things on the air or playing certain kinds of music.

The biggest taboo is "payola," meaning cash, drugs, or other gratuity given to an announcer to play certain music. (Giving or accepting payola is not only against station rules, but it can

Think About It *(continued)*

also be a crime, punishable by fines or imprisonment.) The Federal Communications Commission (FCC) regulations against payola were instituted when it became obvious that some staff announcers were making more than their salaries by playing and plugging music, but that concern persists today. In the last few years the FCC has launched a variety of investigations into payola practices at some US radio stations.

Another taboo, rigging contests, was codified in federal regulations after the quiz show scandals of the 1950s. What happened was this: Contestants on quiz shows, placed in "isolation booths," would grimace, bite their knuckles, and publicly wrack their brains to come up with an answer—usually as the clock was ticking off the final second. It all seemed too dramatic to be true. And of course it was.

The advertising agencies that produced the programs were selecting the most telegenic performers and feeding them the answers. Congress and the FCC put a halt to that with Section 509 of the Communication Act of 1934, making it a violation of federal administrative law to fix a contest. Current FCC rules state broadcast stations must fully and accurately disclose the rules of a contest to the listeners. Even so, a 2016 study found that over half of 18–44-year-old listeners felt contests were rigged.[2]

A practice known as "plugola" straddles the line between legality and illegality. There are regulations about plugging (making mention of) products on-air, but as media ethicist Jay Black notes, the process has now become more "refined," particularly in the film industry. Producers seeking authenticity in their movies make extensive use of easily recognized brand name products—cars, soft drinks, beer, cigarettes, junk food, and so on—for which they are paid fees by the product manufacturers and advertisers. The practice has become so widespread that agents openly advertise their product placement services in trade journals, such as *Advertising Age*.[3]

An announcer who makes an occasional appearance at a night club, with his station's approval, and plugs that night club on air is committing no crime. But here is a question for consideration: Suppose you find that because of the popularity of your radio program, you can get away with frequent plugs of your favorite club? The club obviously likes having you there, and gives you free drinks. Soon the free drinks become free meals. And soon the free meals become a nightly occurrence.

Do you think you have crossed an ethical line? Do you think that the fact that most staff announcers don't make much money justifies your arrangement? Where would you draw the line?

Ad-lib with discretion. Experience and airtime will point up your strengths and weaknesses. You may find that you have a definite flair for humor. If so, expand on that base *slowly*. Here are two techniques for developing an on-air personality and a perspective from which to approach air work.

1. *Use imitation and trial and error.* Listen to other personalities and identify the elements in their deliveries that you can adapt to yourself and your station. The key here is to listen critically, both to others and to yourself, to determine whether that joke, approach, or style really works.
2. *Polish your delivery with the audience in mind.* Put yourself in the place of a listener, a listener you believe to be typical of your station. Would you, the listener, find that remark funny, or tasteless? Is that five-minute feature compelling or boring? Use this acid test before and after a program segment.

The artistic and technical aspects of delivering a commercial are evaluated in Chapter 10. See Box 5.2 for three techniques of commercial delivery that relate specifically to the radio staff announcer.

Entertaining with Humor and Taste

As stated, the development of a personality, as the term applies to on-air radio work, is largely a matter of trial and error and experimentation. Humor and entertainment value, which are important facets of that on-air personality, must be balanced by good taste.

When experimenting, consider that *humor* must be funny. That sounds tautological, but a scan of the radio spectrum suggests otherwise. Three points on humor during an airshift:

1. Avoid in-jokes.
2. Think before you say it. Is it really funny?
3. Don't keep repeating the same line. Listeners will notice.

Many radio air personalities subscribe to humor services that provide one-line jokes or humorous talking points for a fee. These lines can be incorporated into the patter, and with practice they will sound original and topical. The danger with subscription humor is that you may not adequately make written material "your own." If a joke sounds as though it is being read off a sheet, it will fail.

Entertainment is really what the whole business is about. The overriding goal in the element of entertainment is to get and keep the attention of the audience. The audience must be interested in a commercial, a record, or a public service announcement. Therefore, you must be interested, and you must sound interested.

It's easy to let down your efforts on commercials. However, as commercials pay the bills they are important, and sponsors and management will notice if you are not giving your all.

BOX 5.2 Hints For Commercial Delivery

1. *Avoid "going flat" on commercials.* One of the biggest problems encountered by an announcer pulling an airshift is a general flatness imparted to commercial copy. If a spot is not prerecorded, a radio staff announcer must read the same copy day after day for weeks. (One author of this book once worked at a radio station where a client's copy remained unchanged over a 15-year period. It became a badge of having earned your credentials as an announcer at the station to have the chance to read this classic, enduring copy on your airshift.) Today more commercials are prerecorded, only a few spots may be read live by the airshift announcer. The result: a mechanical, lackadaisical approach, often because the announcer doesn't really know anything about the product or the sponsor. Avoid this by getting to know your copy.

   Keep your energy level and enthusiasm high by reminding yourself that this is where you directly earn your paycheck. Remind yourself that the client has only you and your ability to interpret the copy as a means of persuading listeners of the value of his or her commercial message.

2. *Do not use the same rhythm, pattern, and inflections for every commercial.* Each commercial is an individual work and must be analyzed in terms of its own intent. What is the goal of the spot? To whom does it appeal? Why? To avoid mechanical reading, you must have an understanding of these points.

   Find the key words and use the techniques of marking copy described in Chapter 3. But vary your vocal delivery so that each commercial comes across to the listener as distinct and unique.

BOX 5.2 *(continued)*

3. *Read what is written.* The quickest way to get into trouble as an on-air announcer is to take liberties with a client's commercial copy.

    The key guideline in 99 percent of the situations in which you are asked to read copy live is to *play it straight.* Don't change words, or rearrange the order of presentation. And avoid the temptation to make gratuitous remarks about the copy before, during, or after reading it. If you think you can do a better job of writing the copy, talk to the sales representative and make suggestions. Don't take it on yourself to punch up someone else's copy on the air. In most cases the copy has been cleared with the client, and most clients are quite specific about what they want said and what they don't want said in their radio commercials. The exceptions are commercials in which an announcer is asked to ad-lib a commercial from a fact sheet. When that situation occurs, it will be very clearly stated on the copy sheet.

Good taste varies, to some extent, with the composition of the audience. A staff announcer is expected to avoid material and presentations that would offend the audience, unless the announcer's style is one of being offensive. There are, of course, some announcers whose style is built around bad taste, a provocative method of enticing listeners to tune in. But for most purposes good taste is still the name of the game.

In the demanding work of an air personality, there is considerable pressure to be funny and to come up with things to say. Often, this pressure may lead you to say things you shouldn't. When in doubt, especially at the beginning of your career, err on the conservative side.

Some radio announcers' careers are impeded by amateurish attempts to be outrageous or exceptionally funny. Understand that unless and until you attain the stature of a Stephen Colbert or some local equivalent, a station manager will be far more concerned with complaints of sponsors and listeners than with your freedom of expression.

Analyzing Yourself and Others

How do you keep improving your skills? One major advantage of being in the broadcast business is the ease of making comparisons. Analyzing the strengths and weaknesses of others can significantly help your development.

Listening to yourself is important. Recording a show is an excellent tool. In some stations, monitoring airchecks (a recorded segment of an actual airshift) is a requirement of the job.

Also, solicit the opinions of others. Friends and co-workers may sometimes tell you what they think you want to hear, but often they will be strikingly honest. Feedback may sometimes be tough on the ego, but it is worthwhile.

Sometimes announcers stop learning at a particular phase, perhaps in a small or medium market. Those announcers may never get any better because of a lack of talent or, more probably, because the situation does not force them to improve. If there are no expert programmers critiquing airshifts, and if competition does not force continual improvement, the announcer will not grow professionally.

Always remember that the very best announcers got that way by comparison and critique. At one major-market station, for example, the entire air staff receives a daily critique from the program director.

Careful analysis and self-critique are vitally important to honing on-air skills. Listen to yourself; then listen to others. A good-quality radio with a long antenna can bring in an astounding number of stations. You can immediately compare your performance with others all over the region. At night, when AM radio waves travel farther, your comparison can extend halfway across the nation.

When analyzing the deliveries of other announcers, refer to *Nielsen Market Survey* information (https://www.nielsen.com/content/dam/corporate/us/en/docs/nielsen-audio/market-populations-and-rankings.pdf) and the Radio-locator (https://radio-locator.com/) to identify information about the station and the locale (market) as this will help your analysis by showing exactly what format and market size you're listening to.

Airchecks

You will hear an amazing variety of material. On a major-market adult contemporary station, for example, a twist of the dial turns up a noted personality interviewing via telephone a public relations man trying to promote a product.

Announcer:	Can I tell you something?
P.R. Man:	Yes, of course.
Announcer:	No offense, but you're kind of a jerk. Has anybody ever told you that?

This announcer makes a career out of being offensive.

Changing stations to a medium-market hit radio station, the listener encounters a robotic screamer who makes a living out of endless repetition.

(Jingle)
Hey, that's Justin Timberlake
(Station ID)
Everybody wins at _____! Nineteen after ten! Comin' at ya with . . .

At a small-market country station, the announcer takes a more original approach:

Well, howdy. C'mon in. Get set for some mighty fine country music.
We've got Carrie Underwood coming right up . . .

This air personality has developed a unique personality and plays the role well. Even his speech pattern, a virtual "country dialect," reinforces his image.

But on the neighboring adult contemporary station, the announcer is not doing so well.

And that was *Just the Way You Are* by Bruno Mars. And there's Bob coming in the studio . . . he's been over at Hank's office and we know what they've been talking about . . . heh, heh . . .

In-jokes just don't bolster communication between the air personality and the audience.

But in another state, an FM AOR personality plays personal communication to the hilt.

How's it going? Wow, what a day, huh? Sunny skies and all day. The weather was just great . . . just great. Jessica, who's working in the stockroom of Marshall's, just called in and says she's depressed about having to work on such a beautiful day, and she thinks a double shot of Taylor Swift might improve things . . .

She ad-libs a few remarks concerning Swift's last concert tour.

In Toronto, an announcer at a large AM station that plays some oldies and middle-of-the-road music, tending toward nostalgia, ad-libs beautifully.

. . . When Doris Day started singing with *Les Brown and His Band of Renown*, nobody thought her style would make it, but after recording *Sentimental Journey* things really took off . . .

The announcer, one of the best in the business, gives an insightful and interesting background into the music. How did he get to that plateau? Presumably by doing his homework, listening to himself and to others, and always trying to improve. In the fast-changing world of the radio staff announcer, staying still is, in reality, moving backward.

SUMMARY

Radio staff announcing is a complex job, involving entertaining, informing, and providing companionship. The duties and responsibilities of an air personality vary among particular stations and particular markets. Typical jobs involve performance duties, operational duties, and organizational duties. Performance is on-air work. Operations include operation of station equipment. Today knowledge of software becomes increasingly important. Organizational duties include keeping logs and filing music.

In general, the larger the market, the greater the emphasis on performance duties. This means that the large-market performer must be a superior on-air performer and will generally have fewer operational or organizational duties.

Most announcers have operational duties, though, and even those who do not have operational duties certainly have to run the board at one point in their careers. The board is a mixing console allowing the operator to mix, route, and amplify signals from sound sources. Sound sources include computers, microphones, digital recording equipment, possibly compact discs, and other devices.

Techniques of radio staff announcing include developing a personality and perspective, a task that involves trial and error, listening to and incorporating suggestions and feedback, and assessing one's performance from the point of view of the audience.

Delivery of commercials is an important part of the staff announcer's job. Two techniques that relate specifically to this task are maintaining energy and enthusiasm and varying delivery. These two techniques are particularly important because radio staff announcers often "go flat" when confronted with many commercials to be read in a shift.

Important to the staff announcer are humor, entertainment, and good taste. What is funny to the announcer may not be funny to the audience, so it is important to subject prospective humorous remarks to the acid test: is it really funny, and will it amuse a listener? The listener expects to be entertained by listening to a radio personality, and there is no surer way for an air personality to be entertaining than to enjoy what he or she is doing. But any humor and entertainment must be subject to the rules of good taste, and evaluating program elements and potential ad-libs with that in mind is worthwhile.

Radio staff announcers have a distinct professional advantage in that they can easily listen to others and compare their performance with that of announcers in local and distant areas. Use a copy of *Broadcasting/Cablecasting Yearbook* to find additional information on the markets to which you are listening.

EXERCISES

1. If you have access to a production facility, combo a five-minute music show. Pot down the cut after the music has been established, and move into another piece of music. The timing is approximate, but the content must include:
    a. an introduction to three discs
    b. a weather forecast
    c. a public service announcement (PSA)
    d. station identification
    e. one commercial
    f. two time announcements

Do this with any style of music and style of delivery with which you feel comfortable.

If at all possible, write your own commercial, PSA, and other material. If production facilities are not available, just read the copy into a tape recorder and pretend the records have played.

2. Repeat Exercise 1, but use music and delivery reflecting these formats:

   a. fast-paced hit radio, with a target audience of very young teens;
   b. easy listening, with a very affluent, middle-aged target audience;
   c. album-oriented rock, with a target audience of rock aficionados in their early twenties.

3. Select the largest and best radio station you can receive in your area and listen for 15 minutes at a time during three separate dayparts. Write down your impressions of the air personality, and describe that individual's

   a. timing
   b. pace
   c. general approach
   d. use of humor

   Do not undertake an extended discussion; just make brief notes. Also, note production values, such as how tightly recorded material is played together and integrated.

   If possible, listen during morning drive, midday, and afternoon drive.

   Compare and contrast the air personalities on the dayparts.

NOTES

1 Many of these operations are automated today, but they may still occur at some locations.
2 Radio Ink. "Are you rigging your contests?" https://radioink.com/2016/09/19/are-you-rigging-your-contests/. Accessed January 30, 2018.
3 Jay Black and Jennings Bryant, *Introduction to Media Communication*, 4th ed. (New York, Brown and Benchmark, 1998), p. 550.

News Announcing Basics

Perhaps the most personally satisfying area of broadcast performance is news. News stands out among broadcast performance specialties because it is a distinct profession with its own professional standards, operating principles, and ethics. This chapter and the next one are devoted to broadcast news, and both chapters address the special qualities that comprise the news operations of radio and television.

Very few newspeople are employed simply to read news on the air. A major part of the day-to-day duties of broadcast newspeople is involved with preparing the news broadcast. The on-air newsperson must be able to gather, write, and produce some of the audio and visual elements that give form and context to broadcast news stories. Even those few individuals at the very top level of broadcast news have some involvement in assembling the elements of the on-air news product. And those people got to the top of that lofty pyramid because they were skilled journalists who advanced through the ranks. It is beyond the scope of this book to offer a full course in journalism, but Chapters 6 and 7 provide a broad view of the journalistic principles that relate most directly to on-air performance.

Broadcast journalism offers rewarding opportunities for talented and skilled broadcast performers. In television, news offers the greatest number of opportunities for entry into the medium. To succeed in this specialized area, we advise you to include some training in journalism, both broadcast and print, in your preparation. You should also become well grounded in other academic areas, such as economics, political science, English, foreign language, geography and sociology.

BROADCAST NEWS

In an overall sense, a journalist in a broadcast setting is under the same obligations and constraints as a print journalist is. The responsibility for accuracy and completeness is no less demanding in radio and television than in a newspaper. Broadcast news takes on some additional importance, however, because of its immediacy. Broadcast and cable, like radio, are the media most capable of responding instantly to breaking news. Obvious breaking news events can be captured on smartphones and posted to the Web almost immediately, but it is up to media organizations to provide context for what happens. Today the impact of broadcast news is often considered to be greater than that of the print media as newspaper readership declines.

This impact was brought home vividly during the extensive coverage of US war efforts in the Middle East and coverage of devastation of hurricanes Harvey and Maria. The immediacy of live reports of events that were taking place as we saw them, and the ability of video to convey the effectiveness of our war efforts and the rescue efforts during natural disasters, were just two elements of coverage that print could not duplicate. Television, with the help of smartphones and satellite hookups, allowed people at home to experience breaking news in ways that have never before been possible

Often, broadcast news is looked on as something like show business, and many such criticisms have some justification. For example, the trend toward "happy talk" news programs of the 1970s produced, at the extremes, some inane results. And, in recent years some cable news networks have exhibited more concern for ratings than for accuracy.

The power of the rating point in broadcast news is undisputed. No commercial operation, whether broadcast or cable, can afford to ignore audience considerations in news programming.

But the charge that broadcast news is "pure show business" is false, and the source of much of this notion—namely, print critics—is recognized. As web-based and mobile news sites have impacted local newspapers greatly over the past ten years, local broadcast news has taken on more importance in reporting community events. Print news sources are not exempt from the need to attract an audience, either. Newspapers, which have paid great attention to graphics, artwork, and readability, also show awareness of the "entertainment" function. Today some of the major newspapers such as *The New York Times* are also providing video segments within their web and mobile apps sites.

A commonsense look at the state of American broadcast news journalism shows that although show business plays an undeniable role, there is a great deal of quality, integrity, and inventiveness at every level of the profession.[1]

STRUCTURES AND CONTENT

The structures of broadcast news fall into several broad categories that overlap. They are presented here to give an idea of the news functions, not to present a definitive listing.

Newscast

In its simplest form, a newscast involves nothing more than reading aloud a string of news stories. In longer form, such as television news, the newscast is a mixture of breaking news and feature material. In essence, the newscast is a planned and structured assemblage of news, which encompasses some of the following forms.

Report

One element of a newscast, the report, deals with a single news item. It can take many forms, such as the *voice report* on radio, where the reporter delivers a minute or so on a news topic. The voice report, or voicer, is signed off with the reporter's name and affiliation, such as "This is Frank Lombardo reporting for WAAA News." The radio voicer can be expanded to include an actuality, or snippet of an interview or other relevant audio from a newsmaker or news event. Incorporating an actuality into the voice report produces what is known as a **voice-actuality.** This might consist of 10 seconds of the reporter delivering the first section of the voicer, an interview segment cut in for 20 seconds, then the reporter finishing up with a 10-second close and signing off. Longer form voice-actualities sometimes include "wild sound," sounds of the event without words, to add impact to the report. Actualities without a voice report wrapped around them are often used within the newscast. Sometimes actualities are simply introduced by the newscaster.

Television's version of the voicer is often referred to as a **stand-up.** The structure of the radio voice-actuality piece, when done with video, is usually called a **package.**

Interview

The exchange of information and ideas is often the crux of an entire news show, such as *Meet the Press.* The subject of interviewing is covered in detail in Chapter 8. When portions of an interview are used in a news report or newscast, they become actualities.

Documentary

A documentary is a relatively long piece done in dramatic style. Generally, a documentary focuses on one issue and has a plot line. A documentary usually reaches a conclusion and makes a point. "Documentary" is clearly distinct from "docudrama," which is a dramatic reconstruction of an actual event in which actors representing real people work from scripts based on eyewitness accounts and the public record.

Hard versus Soft News

Hard news generally deals with breaking stories and ongoing events that are newsworthy because of their immediate impact on listeners and viewers. **Soft news,** sometimes called *feature news,* is not necessarily linked to a time element or to a story of immediate impact. For example, the story of a fire in progress is hard news, whereas a follow-up report on the lives of the people thus made homeless crosses into the soft news category.

In many stories, soft and hard news overlap. An investigative report on the influence of organized crime in city government may uncover hard news, or material that becomes hard news.

REQUIREMENTS AND DUTIES OF THE JOURNALIST

Broadcast journalism requires a number of specialized skills and talents. Aside from the standard requirements for other broadcast assignments, the following attributes are helpful and in many cases essential.

A Broad Education

Knowing something about a wide variety of subjects is a great plus for a broadcast journalist. Proper pronunciation of words and names is largely a function of formal and informal education. It is also important to have an awareness of world events. For local reporters, a thorough knowledge of the local politicians and current local issues is essential. After all, you can't report the news without understanding the context in which events occur.

Writing Skills

Almost all broadcast news on-air people are required to write copy. Today a reporter is likely to create segments for broadcast and the station's corresponding website and mobile app. Remember, too, that occupants of read-only positions generally got there through previous news positions in which they employed writing skills. You *must* develop the ability to write for the ear in broadcast style, a topic addressed later in this chapter.

Ad-Lib Skills

The ability to ad-lib is especially important for the voice report, which in modern radio and television is frequently delivered live over the air. New remote gear means that more news pieces are done live from the field, and with improving broadcast technologies the ability to ad-lib will become increasingly important in broadcast journalism.

Interpersonal Skills

Newsgathering personnel must sometimes prod, flatter, or browbeat news sources, depending on the situation. The ability to extract news requires finely honed interpersonal skills. Also, you are likely to encounter difficult situations in dealing with news sources, and often you must be particularly sensitive to the feelings of someone who is emotionally distraught.

News Sense

Few of us are born with news sense, but someone lacking it cannot determine what is news and what is not and cannot assess the relative importance of stories. A journalist develops this ability largely through experience and guidance from other professionals.

NEWS STYLE AND IMPACT

Style in broadcast news, in a general sense, concerns the way the news is presented. From a performer's standpoint, the desired result of a particular style is to draw attention to the news, not to the newscaster. Exceptional news personalities are usually highly regarded because they make the news coherent, exciting, and immediate for the listener or viewer, not because they are handsome or beautiful.

Yet popular folklore would have us believe that the typical news anchor is chosen exclusively because of his or her looks and voice. There is a kernel of truth in that, but journalistic know-how and the ability to communicate and convince are the deciding factors in hiring for most anchor jobs.

The factors that make any broadcast journalist able to communicate and convince include believability, energy, and authority.

- *Believability.* A newsperson with a believable style is able to communicate without artificiality, inspiring confidence in the truth of what he or she has to say. Believability is enhanced by forthright speech devoid of any artificial patterns and by knowledge of news and current events.
- *Energy.* Broadcast news performers are expected to inject energy into their delivery, to keep listeners and viewers interested. To succeed in this, the performer must be interested in the copy.
- *Authority.* The element of authority—a variant of believability—convinces the audience that the newsperson knows what he or she is talking about. Viewers and listeners almost always can tell the difference between a mere reader and a real reporter.

Broadcasters are required by the very nature of their jobs to have something distinctive about their on-air appearance and delivery, and style is important to newspeople as well as to other on-air personnel in broadcasting. Style—which includes the elements of believability, energy, authority, and miscellaneous personality traits and other elements discussed in Chapter 4—is a major factor in the success of many journalists. Box 6.1 gives some examples of newspeople who project various styles.

As these examples suggest, an effective communicator of news must develop beyond being a reader of copy. An important part of broadcast journalism is the interpretive role played by the newscaster, the energy, believability, and authority the newscaster imparts to the copy.

Box 6.1 provides some examples of how style fits into the news delivery.

BOX 6.1 Examples of News Delivery Styles

- *George Stephanopoulis.* Host of ABC's Sunday morning news/politics program *This Week* projects an aura of calm believability and political savvy. Stephanopoulis should sound like he knows about politics: Before coming to ABC News, Stephanopoulis served the Clinton White House as a senior advisor. During the weekday his personality is much friendlier as one of the hosts of *Good Morning America*.
- *Scott Pelley.* The no-nonsense approach of this veteran *Sixty Minutes* reporter and network news anchor conveys the image of someone who understands the essential elements of the story he is working on. His style is low-key and nonconfrontational, but he conveys to

the audience that he is not going to be satisfied with the answers he receives until he gets the truth. Viewers get the impression that Pelley is carefully building his story bit by bit, filling in pieces that will eventually result in a complete picture.

- *Cynthia McFadden.* This *Nightline* reporter has a straightforward approach which enhances her authority and believability. McFadden is a pleasant, serious journalist who does not hesitate to show her concern with the news. Her investigative pieces often add depth to ABC's *World News Tonight.*

FIGURE 6.1 George Stephanopoulos exudes an air of believability emanating from his background in politics.

NEWSWRITING BASICS

Newswriting is a complex field, and shelves full of books have been devoted to it. This introduction describes some basics of newswriting that are particularly useful for the on-air performer.

Why is newswriting important for on-air people? First, to succeed as a journalist, you must be able to write. Second, understanding how a news story evolves greatly enhances your ability to communicate facts and ideas.

Let's follow a radio news story from beginning to end. A radio news reporter hears from the police and fire scanner that there's a fire at a major furniture warehouse. She immediately calls the fire department, confirms that there is indeed a fire at that location, gets the name of her informant, receives permission to record the call, and gathers pertinent information.

Q: What's happening right now?
A: Two alarms have been called in. The call came in at 10:47 and we sent the first units. When the deputy chief arrived, he figured we needed another unit, so a second alarm was called in.
Q: Has anyone been hurt?
A: Not that we know of, but rescue firefighters are searching the building right now.
Q: Do you have reason to believe that people are still inside?
A: No, the manager of the building says all employees are accounted for, but we have to check as a matter of routine.
Q: Could you describe the extent of the fire?

A: At last report, the building was about 50 percent engulfed. I just talked to the deputy chief on the scene and he thinks the roof might collapse, so the firefighters on the inside are going to have to get out pretty soon.

Q: Any danger to other buildings?

A: We don't think so. There's not much wind, and no buildings connect to the warehouse.

Q: Do you know what caused the fire?

A: Nope, no idea at this time. Listen, I gotta run because there's another call coming in. Call me back in 15 minutes or so and I'll know more.

From this information, the reporter can construct a story. Granted, it is far from complete, but that's what the reporter has, and she must go on the air with it in the next couple of minutes.

The first step is to write the lead, the first sentence of the story. The two primary categories of leads in broadcast writing are hard leads and soft leads, but there are many variations. A hard lead is a straight presentation of information, the major factors of the story. The soft lead is a more leisurely approach, designed to stir interest.

In the case of a fire story, an immediate piece of breaking news, a hard lead is called for: A two-alarm fire is racing through the Hoffman Furniture Warehouse at 511 Clinton Avenue West.

The lead sentence in broadcast newswriting is usually shorter than a lead in a newspaper or website entry because broadcast news is written for a listener instead of a reader. If who, what, where, when, and why are all in the first sentence, a listener will have trouble comprehending it.

A newspaper lead might look like this:

A two-alarm fire raced through the Hoffman Furniture Warehouse at 511 Clinton Avenue West today, causing no injuries but heavily damaging the building, District Fire Chief Stanley J. Kusinski said.

That is a good newspaper lead, but even though considerations of "why" have been omitted, it would be difficult for a listener to digest.

The radio lead just given is more appropriate, and when followed by other important details, it forms the basis for a short, punchy story:

A two-alarm fire is racing through the Hoffman Furniture Warehouse at 511 Clinton Avenue West. No injuries are reported. All employees are reportedly accounted for, but officials on the scene are conducting a room-by-room search. The building is 50 percent engulfed in flames, and firefighters worry that the roof may collapse.

The initial report was called in at 10:47 this morning. When officials arrived on the scene, they called for additional apparatus.

Fire officials say there's little danger of the fire spreading to nearby buildings. The cause has not yet been determined.

This story could also be written to include an actuality recorded from the telephone interview.

A two-alarm fire is racing through the Hoffman Furniture Warehouse at 511 Clinton Avenue West. No injuries are reported. All employees are reportedly accounted for, but officials on the scene are conducting a room-by-room search.

Here's how District Fire Chief Stanley Kusinski describes the scene:

"The building is about 50 percent engulfed. I just talked to the deputy chief on the scene and he thinks the roof may collapse."

The initial report was called in at 10:47 this morning. When fire officials arrived on the scene, they called for additional apparatus.

Fire officials say there's little danger of the fire spreading to nearby buildings. The cause has not yet been determined.

The story will be updated throughout the day, and the lead will progress through several stages:

Fire officials have finally left the scene of a stubborn, smoky fire at the Hoffman Furniture Warehouse . . .
Investigation continues into the cause of this morning's fire at the Hoffman Furniture Warehouse . . .

When a story is no longer breaking news, the lead may change from a hard lead to a soft lead:

It was an exhausting day for local firefighters, as 24 volunteers battled a stubborn blaze that burned for more than 7 hours . . .

In writing a television news script, the same general principles apply. The difference is that in television you will have the added element of pictures to deal with and your facts will be put together in a different way.

Using the same fire example, but in television scenario, we can illustrate the differences in approach. There may be less rush to get something together to put on the air. In radio, a regular newscast is usually scheduled a short time after the station's newsperson gets word of the story. As we have shown, the story can be developed over time as more and more details become available. In television, there are far fewer times when news can be broadcast. Usually there is an early evening and a late evening news block, and some stations have a news report at noon.

Because local television has newscasts at specific times in the broadcast day and because it relies on pictures to tell much of the story, a very different approach is needed when a news story breaks. More work needs to be done to get the pictures that will tell much of the story, and more people are needed to do the work. Here is how the job will be set up.

1. Using the facts she has gathered, the reporter does an on-camera "bridge" as a transition between segments taped at the scene.
2. The reporter does an on-camera "stand-up," which will conclude the package when it is edited for air.
3. The reporter and cameraperson (if there is one) return to the studio.
4. The reporter writes copy to be read by the anchor in the studio as live "voice-over" audio while taped pictures of the fire appear on the screen.
5. The package is edited and prepared for use on the air.

The actual amount of writing involved in putting this package together is minimal. Much of the reporter's responsibility centers around quickly gathering essential information, selecting the items that best tell the story, and integrating the information with visual elements of the story.

A major consideration in writing the copy for a package like the one described here is how closely to follow the video. There is a fine line between ignoring what is on the screen and writing too directly about it. It would sound silly, on the one hand, to say, "This is a fire that erupted this morning." People can *see* there is a fire. To have the anchor say, "This is a fire," uses valuable time to provide information that the viewer already has. On the other hand, if you are showing firefighting action, this is the wrong time to talk about the progress of the investigation into the cause of the blaze.

When a television news director receives word of a breaking news story such as a major fire, a reporter and a news crew will likely be assigned to go to the scene and do the story. Several factors may influence how the story is handled at this point.

Let's assume that the story breaks a couple of hours before a scheduled newscast. If the news director feels the story is fairly important, a live remote may be set up to bring viewers the reports directly from the scene as the story develops. If the story is regarded as less important, the news director may tell the reporter to prepare a "package." A package usually runs somewhere between 45 seconds and 2 minutes. It includes taped pictures of the news event, and interviews with key people connected to the event. The reporter also records on-camera reports at the scene.

Whether coverage is live or packaged, getting the story ready for the air requires the on-camera reporter to coordinate several different activities.

We'll use the fire example to illustrate what a typical television reporter would have to do to get the story on the air.

1. Arriving at the scene of the fire, the reporter tells the cameraperson to get some shots of the fire and the firefighters battling the blaze.
2. The reporter locates the fire official in charge at the scene and does an on-camera interview.
3. The reporter locates workers who have evacuated the building and gets on-camera reactions from two or three of them.

The proper approach at this time might be to give an overview of the facts about the fire. The appropriate lead-in to the script might read:

> Fire officials are still not sure what touched off flames that engulfed this Clinton Avenue furniture warehouse this morning. The facility is owned by the Hoffman Furniture Company. No one was injured in the blaze, which caused an estimated 200 thousand dollars' worth of damage to the facility.

Another consideration in writing the on-camera material from the scene is to avoid using material that may change later. For example, if you were to report in your stand-up that "officials are unsure if anyone was injured in the fire," your video becomes useless if the question of injuries is answered before your report is aired. If you are in doubt about elements of the story, leave it out of your report from the scene and let the anchor fill in the information when the report airs.

Today many stations are using live remotes and in these situations, the anchor asks the reporter a question, such as: "<Name of Reporter> were there any injuries reported?" In this instance you would report with the information that was current at that time. Often the question is arranged before the reporter goes live on the scene. This technique is meant to give the reporter a way to demonstrate her knowledge about the situation.

As a final note, read your copy aloud as you write it. This is something most broadcast journalists do automatically. It helps you write in a style that is easy to read. For example, the phrase "sixty-six separate series of incidents" might look fine on paper, but when read aloud, problems quickly become evident. Reading your copy aloud is also necessary to determine how long it runs.

Television script writing makes unique demands of reporters. The major consideration is to be as brief as possible and yet to convey a lot of information.

It takes a bit of practice to master the techniques of "tight" writing, but once mastered it becomes almost automatic.

PRESENTING MATERIAL

The goal of broadcast newswriting is to communicate facts quickly and accurately. There is little room for excess words. The same principles apply to ad-libbing live reports. In fact, because of the immediacy of broadcast news and the need to get a story on the air as quickly as possible, many reports from a news performer are half written, half ad-libbed. Often reporters in the field make a couple of notes of the story's main points before going live. The roles of performer and journalist are inseparable.

To effectively present written or ad-libbed material, keep in mind the points highlighted in Box 6.2 and discussed in the text.

First, *use attribution correctly and when necessary*. Attribution is the association of material reported with the source of information. Failure to use correctly attributed information is a common mistake among beginning news reporters.

Controversial statements must always carry attribution. "Chemicals in the village water supply were responsible for the death of 5-year-old Heather Smith" is a statement that must be attributed to a qualified source. An appropriate attribution might be "according to County Director of Public Health Frank Johnson."

Statements of opinion must be attributed in news reporting. For example, "The mayor badly bungled the handling of the school bus strike" must be attributed to the source, such as "according to the Democratic members of the city council."

Legal charges must be attributed. If police arrest a suspect in a bank robbery, the phrases "police have charged" or "according to police" must be incorporated into the statement. It is wise to attribute all information on arrests or charges to the official source. One important reason is that streetwise criminals frequently give names and addresses of other real people when being booked. If you report, "John Jones of 211 Front St. held up the First National Bank" without attribution (such as, "according to Detective Frank Andrews of the city police physical crimes unit"), you are opening the door to legal problems if indeed the bank robber appropriated John Jones's name. This point is not purely academic; it's a troubling area for journalists. The use of false and or stolen identities—someone else's name, address, and even place of employment and Social Security number—is occurring with great frequency today. By the time police sort out the arrestee's real identity, the damage may be done; so always attribute the charges to the legally constituted source.

Caution in handling crime stories is crucial because legal boundaries concerning lawsuits against news organizations are not always clear. Use "alleged" or "accused" when referring to someone charged with a crime. Even this caution is not always a blanket defense should the charges be proven false. Lawsuits concerning crime reporting are not very frequent in daily journalism, but the possibility always exists.

A commonsense guide to the problem is to use attribution when there is any doubt about the *factuality* and *verifiability* of the statement. For example:

- "The governor visited City Hall today" does not need attribution because it is a fact verifiable by photographs, TV footage, and eyewitness accounts. Viewers and listeners will not expect explicit attribution, nor will the governor's office demand it.
- "The governor will not run for reelection" demands attribution. The statement could, for example, be attributed to the governor: "Governor Masters made the surprise announcement during a press conference here at City Hall." Or, attribution could be made to "a statement from the governor's press secretary." A veteran reporter sure of his or her story and facts may link the statement to a "highly reliable source close to Governor Masters." In any case, the factuality and verifiability must be proven, to the largest extent possible, directly within the story.

Note that in broadcasting, the attribution is often given at the beginning of the sentence: "Police said that a human body has been found in Southtown Gorge," instead of the newspaper type of end-of-sentence attribution, "A human body has been found in Southtown Gorge, police report."

Second, *paraphrase quoted material*. For the most part, direct quotes are not used in broadcast writing. The quote is usually paraphrased. Continual reference to a direct quotation, such as "quoting now," is distracting, and is used only when necessary for absolute clarity in the case of controversial or sensitive material.

BOX 6.2 Summary of Pointers for Effective Presentation

1. Use attribution correctly and when necessary.
2. Paraphrase quoted material.
3. Keep sentences short.
4. Use clear sentence construction and word choice.
5. Write for the ear.

Third, *keep sentences short.* Usually 20 to 25 words is the top limit. Although a number of word formulas have been developed, common sense is the best guideline. Simply break up longer sentences in a natural place, and be aware that keeping sentences short is particularly important in ad-libbing. An occasional long sentence is all right, however; continual short, choppy sentences become repetitive in rhythm and unappealing to the ear.

Fourth, *use clear sentence construction and word choice.* Listeners cannot go back and reread what you just said. Avoid using words easily confused by listeners, such as *can* and *can't.*

Fifth, *write for the ear.* The material is meant to be read aloud, so read it before putting it over the air. If it doesn't *sound* right, redo it.

ETHICAL ISSUES

A successful journalist must earn the trust and respect of the public. Certain canons of ethics apply to the job, and they are important to any performer who functions in news. Practices and policies vary from station to station, but two terms germane to any discussion of journalistic ethics are *right to privacy* and *libel.*

The Right to Privacy

Possibly the reporter's first encounter with the right to privacy will involve the recording of a newsmaker's voice or image. In a few cases, you can record someone without his or her permission. Obviously, you do not need permission to record a press conference. In other cases, though, the line becomes blurred.

If you approach someone in a public place with microphone in hand and explain who you are and what you are doing, you're on solid ground to report or broadcast. Entering a private office or residence is another matter and should be considered case-by-case with your news executive.

Telephone interviews can cause problems because the interviewee may later claim to have been unaware of the recording. To protect yourself and your station, a mechanical beep tone is useful if you are at your station's control room. If you're in the field most smartphones can be used to record, so it is always wise to notify the person before you begin an interview and get his or her consent *on tape.* Be sure to learn your station's individual policy governing recording phone calls before you air any portion of a recorded conversation. Also, laws governing recordings vary from state to state so be sure you know the laws pertaining to your location.

In many cases the right to privacy is clear-cut, but in many cases it is not. Hidden-camera interviews and other investigative techniques should be used only under the supervision of an experienced news executive or attorney.

Sometimes the right to privacy is not so much a legal issue as a moral one. Does the grieving widow of a slain police officer have a right to privacy? Is she unnecessarily traumatized by having a microphone thrust in her face and being asked for comment? Common sense and good taste deny the right to invade her privacy just to get a story. By contrast, newspeople have swarmed over artificial heart recipients, and concern has been expressed that the patients' rights to privacy were being trampled. However, because these surgery patients consciously chose to participate in medical experiments of profound significance, the public's need to know seemed to legitimately take precedence over the individuals' rights of privacy.

The right to privacy also depends on whether the individual involved seeks notoriety. A person who is defined as a public figure, such as a politician or a performer, has sacrificed a considerable amount of right to privacy by entering the public spotlight. This has a bearing on the legal interpretations of damage to reputations, known as *libel.*

Libel

Some recent court cases have demonstrated there are very few clear-cut answers to the question of what constitutes libel. Basically, *libel is the act of issuing or publishing a statement that damages a person's reputation, defaming his or her character and exposing him or her to ridicule.*

Simplistic definitions of libelous versus nonlibelous statements are worse than none at all because there are many gray areas within the law. The interpretation of libel laws is subject to change according to new court decisions.

To consider briefly the most basic points of libel as they apply to a news announcer, examine the contention that truth is a defense against libel. On close examination, you can see that this is a somewhat simplistic concept because truth is not always easily definable. If a reporter alleges that the subject of a story is an incompetent physician, can that charge be proven? If the word *incompetent* is used, can it be defined and verified? Has the physician been convicted of malpractice?

Yes, truth is a defense against libel, but often the question revolves around the recognized definitions of the words and terms used in the news item. As journalists Ted White, Adrian J. Meppen, and Steve Young put it,

> *Proving the truth is not always easy, and the proving must be done by the writer or reporter. If you referred on the air to a labor leader as a racketeer, you had better be prepared to show that he was convicted of such a crime or that you have conclusive evidence of such activity that will stand up in a court of law. Otherwise, you and your station management could lose a lot of money if your report does not fairly and accurately reflect the public record.*[2]

Another defense against libel is *privileged communication*. For example, you cannot be sued for repeating remarks made by members of Congress from the floor of the legislative chamber or judges in open court; those remarks are privileged communications. Certain other public statements and records are also privileged. In cases less clear-cut than judicial or legislative remarks, always check with a senior news executive if there is a possibility that the statements could be interpreted as libelous.

A fair comment against a public official or public figure is not libel. Someone who runs for public office, by the very nature of that act, exposes himself or herself to public comment. The courts have ruled that people who seek publicity have, for all intents and purposes, less protection under libel laws. However, "fair" and "accurate" are subjective terms; a reporter does not have *carte blanche* when dealing with public figures. An irresponsible and unfounded statement against a celebrity can still be actionable (serve as the basis for a lawsuit).

Malice and reckless disregard of the truth are the primary factors a public figure must prove to wage a successful libel suit. As was the case in 2016 with Blake Shelton's suit against *In Touch* magazine. The court ruled that the magazine telling its readers that Shelton went to rehab for an alcohol abuse problem was false and libelous. The judge said the magazine knew that they published the story knowing that Shelton had not been in rehab and that was clearly proof of malice.

Be aware that libel law interpretation changes as courts make decisions and set new precedents and that libel laws differ from state to state. It is very, very difficult to predict what the interpretation of libel laws will be if any gray area is entered. When in doubt, always check. The information presented in Box 6.3 is only a collection of general guidelines.

BOX 6.3 A Primer on Privacy and Libel

First and foremost, remember that what follows is a brief summary of libel and privacy law—not specific legal advice. Laws differ from jurisdiction to jurisdiction. So when in doubt, consult with a senior news executive or your station's attorney.

The *Legal Information Institute* at Cornell University defines **libel** as defamation expressed in print, writing, signs and any communication that injures a person's reputation, exposes someone to hatred, contempt, or ridicule. Beyond that, libel can be established if the person suffers loss of respect or if he or she is harmed in some way.

BOX 6.3 *(continued)*

Certain things must happen for libel to be committed. Usually in case law these are called *elements of libel.* They are *publication, damage, identification,* and *fault. Publication* is self-explanatory, except that the word also applies to something disseminated over the airwaves or over the Internet. *Damage* can be emotional or monetary, but libel suits are often brought because a story causes loss of income to a business. Probably this is because balance sheets are easier to document than emotional suffering.

Identification, again, is relatively self-explanatory, but for the purpose of this discussion it's important to remember that identification usually means specific identification of an individual. Groups rarely sue for libel. Of particular importance to the broadcast journalist is avoiding accidental associations of people and events, such as using so-called wallpaper video showing a car repair establishment to illustrate a story about car repair scams. Someone whose shop is identified by the video may indeed have a viable libel action against you even if you chose that person's shop only as cover video. (*Cover video* simply refers to pictures used to illustrate a television news script.)

The fourth element is *fault.* It must be shown by the plaintiff that the information was incorrect and fulfilled the other elements. (Note that simply being incorrect does not expose you to a libel case. If you say someone is 6 feet tall when he is really 6 feet, 2 inches, there are very few instances where that would be construed as a mistake that caused damage.) Public people—that is, people who have thrust themselves into the public eye—must prove fault to a higher degree. They must show that the reporter disseminated the information knowing that it was false, and with the intent of causing damage. This is called the *actual malice rule.*

There are a number of defenses against libel. For the purposes of our discussion, we will group these defenses into the categories of *provable truth, privilege, fair comment,* and *public figure exposure.*

- *Provable truth,* as mentioned in the text, goes beyond simply knowing in your heart that the allegation is true. It must be documented and specifically proven in court. That is why newswriters frequently avoid words such as *incompetent.* This term is rather nebulous, difficult to prove, and you would be in a better position to simply list your documentation, rather than use the catchall term *incompetent.*
- *Privilege* applies to statements made on the floor of a legislative body when that body is in session, or in court when court is in session. These statements are granted what is often called *absolute privilege,* and a reporter enjoys *qualified privilege,* meaning that he or she is protected from libel action as long as the remarks are repeated fairly and accurately.
- *Fair comment* simply means the right to express an opinion. A journalist has every right, for example, to criticize a play, a restaurant, or a public performance. However, that criticism cannot include embellishments of the truth or unrelated and irrelevant personal attack. For example, a Supreme Court opinion handed down in 1990 held that an opinion column could be subject to libel action because it dealt with a serious issue—for example, an implication that a local high school coach committed perjury.
- Finally, *public figure.* Our concept of public figure exposure stems back to the 1964 Supreme Court case of *Times v. Sullivan.* In that ruling, the Supreme Court held that the American spirit of valuing free and robust debate causes a public official to expose himself or herself to public criticism. As a result, a public official—in this case a southern police commissioner—enjoys less protection.

Decisions following *Times v. Sullivan* broadened the definition of a public figure to include famous persons as well as elected or appointed officials. More recent cases, however, have

BOX 6.3 *(continued)*

moved the pendulum in the other direction, affording more protection for well-known people who are not public officials.

Privacy

Privacy actions are far less frequent than libel litigations. A good share of privacy case law, in fact, does not relate to news operations. For example, many privacy cases involve appropriation of someone's image for advertising without that person's consent.

The areas that should concern a news reporter are invasions of privacy, which in some way embarrass a person or portray that person in false light. The issues are far from clear-cut. For example, successful privacy actions have been brought against news organizations that have carried "Where are they now?" stories that brought up true but embarrassing tales of what someone did decades ago.

The defenses against privacy actions are as complex as the laws. However, as a general guideline you should remember that an item that embarrasses someone must be newsworthy—a difficult concept to determine.

But judgments can and have been made against news organizations that pictured people in embarrassing situations simply for the sensational impact. Second, being a reporter does not give you the right to trespass. Third, you should be especially careful when dealing with minors or anyone who might be deemed to have diminished capacity to knowledgeably agree to be interviewed or appear on air. Finally, subjects of certain news stories do lose their right to privacy just because of their bad luck. However, be aware that laws do protect the privacy of victims of certain crimes—especially sex crimes. Remember that, even though there will always be exceptions, when someone seeks publicity, or is the subject of a current legitimate news story, you are probably on safe ground.

RADIO AND MOBILE APPS NEWS

Radio news can be the most immediate of all media, particularly in large urban areas where there are full-time news operations. When people need to find out about a breaking news story, such as a weather emergency, they turn on the radio. Today mobile apps and the Internet news sources have come to rival radio's ability for immediacy in reporting breaking headlines, so let's review some news operational techniques that are common to both radio and mobile news.

Most all-news stations have mobile applications so this discussion would apply to both situations. Modern news operations work under the basic journalistic principles described earlier. This section deals with some of the specialized methods and equipment by which news is gathered and structured, and with the equipment used by radio reporters. For simplicity we are going to refer to this section as gathering radio news, though clearly it applies to any reporters gathering news for websites, podcasts, mobile apps, or any other audio-based service. Techniques and operations relating to delivery, formats, and news services are examined later.

Gathering Radio News

In radio, newsgathering consists of obtaining facts and sound sources. This can be done at a very basic level by one person working with a telephone and a telephone recording device, as demonstrated by the example of the reporter covering the furniture warehouse fire by phone. On a more sophisticated level, radio newsgathering can involve a staff of street reporters equipped with high-quality smartphones, tablets or portable recording gear, covering specialized beats. Large radio news operations have people in charge of editing and production, though today's sophisticated phones and tablets have a variety of editing capability available for reporters to use in the field.

All radio news operations are under the command of a news director. In small stations, the news director may be the only newsperson on the payroll. In large radio stations, he or she is an executive in charge of large budgets and staffs. The radio news director usually reports to the station general manager or the program director. Today many stations have a person under the news director who is in charge of social media and the station's online presence. Often the reporter's material will be uploaded to a Facebook page, the station's app, or some social media app. As a result the lines between radio and television reporters are being blurred by today's technology.

The concept of actuality is very significant in radio news. Gathering actualities by phone or with a digital device such as a tablet, digital recorder or some other recording device has become one of the radio newsperson's primary responsibilities. News stations are not content simply to read stories over the air; somewhere in most newscasts there is actuality material.

Actualities can consist of an interview segment or a **wild sound bite**, that is, sound other than interview speech, recorded at the scene of a news event. The scream of sirens, for example, could be incorporated into a piece as a wild sound bite. Wild sounds might consist of the chanting of crowds on a picket line, or the roar of flames in a four-alarm fire. When an actuality consists of an interview segment, it is usually less than a minute long, more often less than 30 seconds. Longer actualities are used in documentary pieces.

The reporter must choose a compelling piece of actuality rather than running an entire interview. When gathering and editing down an actuality, the reporter looks for responses that express opinion or give greater focus to the central issue of the story. A politician's description of what he or she thinks a budget cut will do to the district is far more interesting than a recitation of budget figures. An eyewitness account of an accident is much more compelling than that person's reaction to the accident.

In general, when choosing actuality, remember:

1. Statements of fact made during the interview are best used in writing the script.
2. Statements that express emotion or opinion are best used as actualities within the news report.

Radio Reporting Equipment

The basic radio reporting tool is the digital recorder and a good-quality microphone (Figure 6.2). Today it is possible to use flash drives or SD cards with digital recorders. This simplifies the process of transferring the audio file to an editing device like a laptop.

In radio news operations a journalist uses a small production studio (see Figure 6.3c) containing necessary equipment and an electronic link between the telephone and the recording gear such as a portable tablet. Almost all editing is done on a portable device. Actualities can then be loaded into the station's playback system for retrieval throughout the broadcast day. Today many cars are equipped with Bluetooth and Wi-Fi, allowing tablets and smartphones to connect to the station's network as soon as the report steps into the car.

Practices vary among individual stations, but usually there is a standard method of labeling the segment with the name of the person being interviewed or the reporter filing the actuality, the length of the interview, and the **outcue**. The outcue is the final word or words spoken on the tape. Labeling an actuality with an outcue is a must because it indicates when the newscaster is to begin speaking again. Multiple actualities should be labeled sequentially or with a unique identifier (for example, Fire 1, Fire 2, and so

FIGURE 6.2 A good mic wired into a portable recording device, even a cell phone, produces excellent quality audio and is the workhorse of modern radio news.

Source: viktor95/Shutterstock.com.

forth). An interview used as the basis of a story that incorporates two actualities would look like this in script form:

CITING FAILING HEALTH, STATE SENATOR MARGARET BLANK TODAY ANNOUNCED HER WITH-DRAWAL FROM THE UPCOMING RACE FOR REELECTION.

//BLANK #1//

. . . As I'm sure you're aware, I've had several operations within the past four years, and while my health is relatively good, I don't think I'm up to the strain of another term in office.

THE SURPRISE ANNOUNCEMENT HAS THROWN LOCAL REPUBLICANS INTO TURMOIL AS THEY JOCKEY FOR A SPOT ON THE PRIMARY TICKET. AS TO HER POSSIBLE SUCCESSOR, BLANK WON'T PLAY FAVORITES OTHER THAN TO SAY,

//BLANK #2//

At this point, I'm not endorsing anyone. I will pledge to oppose, though, anyone who plans to cut aid to education in our district.

THAT STATEMENT IS INTERPRETED BY SOME OBSERVERS AS A BACKHANDED ENDORSE-MENT OF CITY SCHOOL SUPERINTENDENT PAUL WHITE, WHO HAS EXPRESSED AN INTEREST IN BLANK'S JOB.

The computer files for this cut would be labeled

- Blank #1:09 (term in office)
- Blank #2.08 (in our district)

The format of capital letters for announcer copy and lowercase letters for actuality is used in many news operations, although practices vary. It is a good practice to have the actuality written down, though, in case the computer fails and you are obliged to paraphrase the statement.

Radio news reporters often feed cuts back to the station using a Wi-Fi network or a cell phone. Depending on the length of the cut, it is possible to get the report on the air in a matter of minutes. It is also common for reporters to use the cell phone to give live reports from the scene of the event.

Today's sophisticated technology is helping the newsgathering in many ways. Focus on Technique discusses how audio edition software can be used to speed news preparation. Although a reporter can certainly do a decent job reporting live from an event without sophisticated hardware, the new technologies give stations an edge. But as radio news becomes more highly competitive, the use of high-tech equipment has provided stations with the means to connect with listeners on a variety of platforms and in a variety of ways. These new capabilities give radio stations the ability to compete with other media.

Focus on Technique

Digital Editing

The computer is an integral part of today's radio station. Computers provide both audio and editing capabilities along with providing management of billing and record keeping. For the broadcast journalist, the most visible aspect of the computer's advance is the digital audio workstation (DAW). It may be a software-configured computer (both Macs and PCs are popular) or it may be a stand-alone device. Radio production personnel commonly use DAWs in recording and mixing commercials and promotions; in those cases, the performer may not have any idea what's happening at the computer terminal.

But newspeople frequently must combine performance with some hands-on knowledge of DAW operation.

Digital editing is surprisingly simple. In the most basic terms, it follows a standard cut and paste formula with which most people are already familiar on their word processors. Editing is a three-step process:

- First information is digitized, meaning that audio sent to the computer is converted into a digital format. "Digital" simply means "made of numbers," and that's what happens to the sound signal. The computer sound card samples the sound thousands of times per second and constructs a numerical pattern that represents the recorded sound. A "waveform" (see Figure 6.3a) represents the sound. The peaks and valleys in the waveform represent the relative loudness.
- Using the computer mouse or track pad, you can highlight a portion of the audio that you want to edit. The block can easily be cut from the rest of the waveform (see Figure 6.3b), leaving you with an edited waveform that has joined the two parts of the actuality, now ready for air.
- Mobile devices are capable of editing as well making it possible for the reporter to edit the actuality in the field and send it back to the station for immediate playback (Figure 6.3c).

FIGURE 6.3a The waveform represents the sound recorded into the computer.

Focus on Technique *(continued)*

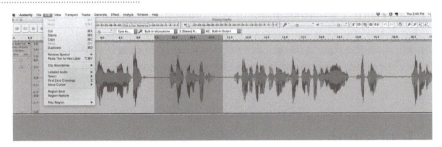

FIGURE 6.3b The highlighted area represents the sound portion that will be cut. After cutting the unwanted portion, the segment will be ready for use.

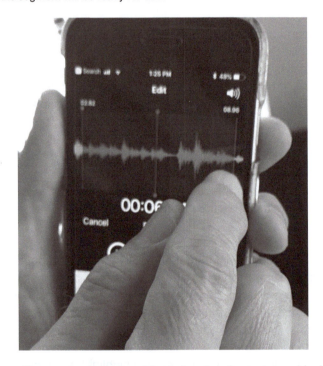

FIGURE 6.3c Waveform editing can be done on mobile devices too. A reporter could edit the segment in the field and upload it back to the station for immediate playback.

There are a number of different software packages to use. In most cases software will allow you to undo a bad edit; if you make a mistake you can undo it and start over. Other systems create separate regions that are edited, preserving the original sound. Each system has its own unique features.

- Finally the information may be stored on the computer's hard drive or on a central server. It may then be called up for playback later or dubbed onto a digital cart for playback during the next news segment.

Systems vary in operation and complexity, of course, but you'll find that the basic pattern in Figures 6.3a–c is common to most systems you'll encounter.

Digital editing has other advantages beside simple precision, by the way. For one thing, you do not have to edit in a "linear" fashion—meaning in a line, from beginning to end. You can edit in any order that you want. Second, digital editing is nondestructive, meaning that you do not have to physically cut or erase any of your original material. Should you make an editing blunder, you can tell the computer to "undo" the edit.

Radio News Operations

Typically, a radio news anchor is responsible for gathering, editing, and reading news. The operations involved include making calls to police and fire agencies and scanning newspapers and wire services for important stories. Working with news service material is covered later in this chapter. Here we mention the practice, common in radio, of rewriting stories posted on media websites or from the local newspaper. This practice should be pursued with caution, because when a newspaper story is wrong and a radio reporter rewrites and uses it, the radio reporter is wrong, too. Local news outlets such as newspapers vigorously object to radio reporters' use of stories gathered by their staff. Nevertheless, the newspaper and local media outlets will always be an important source for the broadcast journalist, and once you have verified the story and done some additional checking and gathering, you are ethically entitled to use the story. It is a good idea to provide attribution for the story when appropriate.

There will generally be pieces left over from the previous shift or the previous night, such as a report on a city council meeting. The morning news anchor would certainly want to include such material in the early reports, but the council story may be rather stale by noon.

Stories must be written and rewritten throughout the morning. The reporter will follow up on tips from the public, items broadcast over police scanners, and story assignments set up in advance. Street reporters will cover stories in person, and often the morning anchor will take to the streets later in his or her shift.

These are the most basic operations. Now the journalist-performer must take the raw material and make it compelling.

Painting a Picture with Words

A radio journalist must make people visualize a story in the theater of the mind. The writer, who must choose the words and phrases, shoulders much of this responsibility. The performer, who may also have been the writer, has to read accurately with expression and meaning. This is really important to the journalist who has to ad-lib a report from hastily scrawled notes, but it is also vital to the podcaster and the long-form reporter who want to hold their audiences.

In these cases, those words and phrases must paint a picture that is coherent as well as vivid.

The techniques for understanding the message (Chapter 3) and for communicating the message (Chapter 4) apply here. Some additional suggestions follow (highlighted in Box 6.4).

1. *Describe events with imagination.* Your words are virtually all the listener has to go on. Your ability to describe can be dramatically improved with practice, so practice as much as possible. One program director of a major-market all-news station advises reporters to practice describing anything: ride along in the car and describe the countryside; look out the window and describe the neighbor's fence. In your descriptions, pay attention to details, such as the exact color of leaves or the shape of a yard.
2. *Include sound in the story.* Can you get the sound of a fire engine into your street report? By all means give it a try. Also, don't be afraid to incorporate the acoustics of the environment into your story, such as the sound of wind on a report concerning fast-moving brushfires. Do *not* manipulate sound elements in a way that will affect the content of the story. For example, do not use sounds of strikers chanting *recorded during the morning* as an element of a story covering the situation *in the afternoon*, when there were no strikers outside. Also, never use a sound effects record or other device to fake sound elements for a news story.
3. *Make accurate mood changes.* In radio, you have only your voice to communicate changes in moods, and this has to be done with precision because stories are typically short. One of the most common complaints about poor radio news announcers is the lack of mood change between and among stories. Mark copy to reflect changes in moods. Do not use the same pitch, pace, and rhythm for a report on a double homicide and for a story on a senior citizens' outing.

BOX 6.4 Summary of Tips for Vivid Communication

1. Describe events with imagination.
2. Include sound in the story.
3. Make accurate mood changes.
4. Use and stress vivid words.
5. Pay attention to clarity in using actualities.
6. Develop a system for gauging time.

4. *Use and stress vivid words.* A television shot of a smoky fire speaks for itself. In radio, you have to paint a word picture. Do not touch important words too lightly. If you are writing or ad-libbing, never be content with pedestrian phrasing. For example, which description is more vivid and compelling?

    - "There is a great deal of black smoke coming from the upper window."
    - "Greasy black smoke is *boiling* from the upper window."

    Simple words can paint vivid word pictures; there is no need to become flowery and lurid. Edward R. Murrow's historic word pictures of London during World War II were effective primarily because of the simplicity of the images and the straightforwardness of his delivery. Murrow used vivid small details to bring the picture to life in the theater of the listener's mind. He was not content, for example, simply to tell the listener that bombs were exploding. Instead, Murrow described the burn marks in pavement scorched by hot shrapnel. He was never content simply to describe the sight of people scurrying underground; he invoked other senses, too: "You cannot believe the stench of the air raid shelters."

5. *Pay attention to clarity in using actualities.* If you play an actuality during the delivery of a newscast, identify the speaker *before* and, if possible, *after* the actuality plays. It is best to do this by gracefully including the name of the speaker, such as "Professor Campbell of Georgetown went on to say . . ." If that is not possible, a simple declarative sentence will do: "That was Professor William Campbell of Georgetown University."

6. *Develop a system for gauging time.* Time yourself reading copy whenever possible so that you become able to look at a piece of copy and immediately gauge its length in airtime. Radio news often operates under extremely rigid time requirements, and it is important to be able to estimate how much copy can be read in an allotted time period.

Your reading rate will probably be about 150 words per minute (wpm), although rapid news readers sometimes reach about 200 wpm. Rate of speech is much faster on a long-form announcement, such as a newscast, than on a 30-second commercial. You can determine your standard long-form reading rate simply by timing a minute's worth of reading and counting the words.

Knowing the average number of words per line of copy will simplify word counting. Most standard word processors average about 12 words per line of copy, but that will vary with different script formats.

If you read 150 wpm, and your script averages 12 words a line, *you now know that 13 lines of copy will fill one minute.* Knowing how many lines of copy you read per minute is the most valuable method of time approximation.

Skilled announcers who must "stretch" copy often develop a method of prolonging vowels and gently slowing the reading rate so that the stretching is not noticeable. You would not want to use this method for stretching a 3-minute newscast to fill 5 minutes, but it is helpful when it appears that 5 lines of copy will fall 5 seconds short.

When news copy is running too long, it may be a simple matter to drop a line or two in the story. However, be sure you are thoroughly familiar with the story so that you don't drop vital elements, such as attribution or a punch line. With experience and a complete understanding of the story, you will be able to ad-lib a brief conclusion rather than just dropping some copy.

Fitting News to Station Format

There was a time when broadcast news was looked on as something of a burden, to fill FCC requirements. A pleasant development, especially for the journalist, was the discovery that news could make money. As mobile devices and Wi-Fi networks have improved many music stations stopped providing a local newscast, but over the past 10 years some music stations have started to reintroduce short local news features, but the vast majority of local news is found on the all-news station. For those audiences they want well-done news reporting, and advertisers are willing to pay for exposure on a newscast. This is usually because the top of the hour breaks the music format with the station ID and advertisers can 'sponsor' a news update during that break time.

All-news and talk radio of all genres make money, particularly because the listening audience for these formats tend to be more affluent. For these listeners the news must reinforce and complement the sound of the station. This is accomplished in a variety of ways, using every kind of component, from the produced opening of the newscast to the style and pace of the newscaster to the selection of the news itself.

A modern radio journalist must be able to vary his or her delivery to fit the sound of the station. Some all-news stations feature a revolving series of headlines every 20 minutes. Their reporters need to be sharp and to the point. Other stations, particularly NPR stations, have a much more laid-back reporting format. Unless you have the luxury of having an assured career with one particular format, it is highly advisable to practice flexibility in your delivery. Listen to what works at other stations, and practice communicating effectively within other formats.

News and Talk Formats in Radio

In 1965, New York's WINS became the first radio station to make a success of an all-news format. Many greeted the idea with skepticism. The nay-sayers felt that audiences wanted news only in small chunks. It seemed unlikely that anyone would stay tuned to one station for continuous news.

In 1965 WINS proved that the format could succeed, and in the nearly six decades since its inception, the all-news format has become viable for stations in many markets. WCBS in New York, KYW in Philadelphia, and WPOP in Hartford, Connecticut, all have used the format to become some of the most successful stations in the country. In addition to those listeners who keep their radio dials tuned to all-news stations for the entire time they are listening to radio, many listeners tune in for brief updates on what is happening. This high turnover of news enables all-news stations to perform well in the category of ratings known as "cume" ratings—ratings that count the number of different people who tune in to a station during a certain segment of time. The all-news format is demanding for on-air news readers. The hybrid format of news/talk combines news programming with listener call-in programming.

Many of these stations feature nationally syndicated shows during morning or evening dayparts. The station's entire sound depends on the style in which the news is presented. That style is a function of (1) the length of news stories and news segments, (2) the selection and arrangements of news stories, and (3) the reading style of news readers.

The on-air performer must be able to maintain a presence over time that is sustained only by the sound of her or his voice. To do so requires considerable skill in several areas.

- *Rate.* The successful news reader at an all-news station must move along at a comfortable pace. If the rate is too fast, readers will miss important elements of the story. If readers are too slow, energy is lost, so the listener's attention is likely to wander. The most effective rate is one that strikes the reader as a comfortable conversational rate.

- *Inflection.* Inflection is probably the most crucial element of a news reader's delivery in the all-news format. A singsong rate or monotone delivery can be deadly. One is distracting but the second could literally lull listeners to sleep. (Incidentally, we have interviewed radio listeners who say that they use the all-news radio station in their vicinity to help them fall asleep at night. A news reader must guard against inflections that unduly emphasize this characteristic of the format.) Vary your inflection enough so that patterns do not repeat. If you tend to drop pitch every time you come to the end of a sentence, for example, the pattern quickly becomes noticeable. Be aware of your inflection and adjust it to avoid repetitive patterns, while guarding against inflections that do not fit the style of the copy.

- *Timing.* All-news radio is delivered in timed segments. A common promotional phrase used by one all-news station is "Give us 10 minutes, and we'll give you the world." Announcers must be precise enough in delivery to be able to read news scripts exactly to time, so that segments end on the dot at the right time. Very often news readers read copy that ends just before the station joins its network for its newscast. Networks begin their segments at the precise time scheduled. If a local news reader runs over or under the time allotted for the copy adjacent to the news, the cue will be missed.

- *Pitch.* Announcers who use a pitch that is too low or too high will stand out because of the length of time listeners have to discern the fault. A common fault among some inexperienced male announcers is to try to hit an unnaturally low pitch. This can be deadly to all-news performers because an inappropriate pitch stresses the voice. Eventually the constant voice strain on the all-news format will likely impair the announcer's ability to use his voice. Find the correct pitch for your voice, and the delivery will sound better and conserve your voice.

- *Error-free reading.* The most important hallmark of a good news reader in any circumstance is the ability to read copy without stumbling and with accurate pronunciation. Of course, everyone stumbles at some point, and in a format that demands that you continue reading without interruption for 15 minutes or so at a time, there is much more opportunity for stumbles to occur. Announcers who consistently have trouble reading copy smoothly, however, won't last long in an all-news format. There are no second takes in live on-air work. The performance must be as close to flawless as possible or it becomes distracting to listeners.

- *Proper pronunciation.* Words and names must not be mispronounced in all-news radio. Listeners associate the credibility of the station with the news reader on the air. If you mispronounce the name of a newsmaker or a place name, you can bet that someone listening knows you did it. Your credibility and that of the station is compromised. In the all-news format, credibility is everything. If listeners don't think you are knowledgeable about the news you're reading, they won't continue to listen.

In general, the key to giving a good performance in an all-news format is to be very solid in the principles that apply to all-news reading. Credibility is crucial. In the all-news format, the elements of effective performance are emphasized by the long periods when your talents will be on display. Flaws are magnified many times over, whereas the absence of flaws won't be noticed much. That is as it should be. Remember that the important element of the format is the news. Your job as news reader is to showcase the news. The most effective performers are noted by average listeners, not because of their outstanding voice and delivery, but because they communicate. The trick is to make the listener think it is easy to do that.

News Services Today and Tomorrow

News services are an important cog in all-news operations; they provide a link to news sources not available at the local level. From the standpoint of news operations and technique, a local reporter does well to gain a thorough understanding of these services because they are effective tools for making the station's entire news effort more effective and professional.

New applications for computers and mobile devices, like *iHeart Radio* have made it possible for listeners to choose a wide variety of news sources. Satellite radio also has expanded choices for news audiences. SiriusXM provides news feeds from CNN, Fox, NPR, BBC, Bloomberg, MSNBC along with other information channels.

One familiar news service available to radio stations is the hourly newscast provided by radio networks through an online or satellite link. Because of the increasing importance of formatting, network newscasts are sometimes provided in different forms for various stations, with one feed tailored for music stations and another for stations serving an all-talk or sports audience. Networks also provide features that can be broadcast live or recorded for later airplay; in some cases, they furnish voicers and actualities for use in local newscasts.

News services, previously known as wire services such as the Associated Press, typically provide information via satellite feeds in the form of ready-to-broadcast copy but they also provide an online service that can be streamed to mobile devices. This includes newscasts, feature material, state news and archived material.

Wire services offer localized feeds known as "state splits," which can be quite useful to newspeople on slow days. You can further localize a state report on aid to education, for instance, by calling city or town officials and asking for comment.

Wire services do such a capable job that some local operations become overly dependent on the wire, which results in what is commonly termed a "rip-and-read" operation. The best use of a wire service is as a supplement to an active news operation.

For stations that assemble national newscasts at the local level, audio services provide actualities, voicers, and voice-actualities for integration with wire copy. The wire service feeds a copy describing the cuts, known as a **billboard,** which lists the cuts by number, time, content, and structure. These cuts are fed according to a regular time schedule. A tone precedes each cut so that newspeople can cart the cuts, starting the cart machine at the end of the tone.

Many private organizations provide news feeds in return for the exposure.

Colleges and some professional associations offer material free to stations in return for exposure.

SUMMARY

Radio news is a sophisticated business, requiring much more than an ability to read aloud. In addition, reporting for radio is changing as more stations post their news on their website or by providing mobile customers with streaming services. The radio medium offers a unique blend of immediacy, intimacy, and drama. The broadcast news field is dominated by journalists; therefore, a newsperson is bound by the responsibilities and ethics applied to all journalists. Although it undeniably has elements of show business, broadcast news is a serious and formidable type of journalism.

The general structures of broadcast news include the newscast, the report, and the interview. The documentary is a long form of broadcast news containing dramatic elements. Broadcast news content generally can be categorized as hard news or soft news. Hard news deals with breaking stories. Soft news presents feature material.

The basic requirements of a broadcast journalist include a broad-based education, the ability to write, the ability to ad-lib, the ability to interact with people, and the possession of a news sense. Style is an important element for an on-air broadcast journalist. The journalist must project believability, energy, and authority.

Anyone who aspires to a news anchor position must know how to write. Most newspeople do their own writing, and even those who no longer write the material they broadcast achieved their positions by being skilled writers and journalists. Broadcast news consists of a short but informative lead, followed by a succinct and compelling recitation of the facts. Among the skills to be mastered in writing or ad-libbing a news story are correct use of attribution and the ability to paraphrase quoted material accurately. Using short sentences, using clear sentence construction and appropriate word choice, and writing for the ear are also important.

Ethical issues affect the broadcast journalist, who must have a basic understanding of when and how someone's image or remarks can be recorded. Because the issues of right to privacy and libel are complex, and the related rulings are subject to change, you must ask for guidance by your news executives when dealing with sensitive issues. *Think About It* tells about a famous reporter, Edward R. Murrow, and his clash with Senator Joe McCarthy. This box poses questions aspiring journalists should ask.

Think About It

Do you drop your "objectivity" when you're sure you are right and there is a crisis?

The man who set the standard for a modern broadcast announcer and journalist—in fact, the man who pretty much invented the persona of the on-air reporter—was Edward R. Murrow.

Murrow was trained in public speaking, not journalism, and he went to work for CBS as an administrator. But when World War II began in Europe, Murrow put himself behind the microphone. Later, beginning in the 1950s, he appeared on television and became the nation's most recognizable broadcast journalist.

It was probably inevitable that Murrow would clash with another key figure of the 1950s, Joseph McCarthy.

Joseph McCarthy (Figure 6.4) rose to political fame on his credentials as a war hero. He called himself "Tail Gunner Joe," referring to the position of the soldier who defended a bomber from a position near the tail of the airplane.

FIGURE 6.4 Senator Joseph McCarthy's reckless tactics—during hearings to expose what he termed "The Red Menace"—were the focus of a series of CBS television broadcasts produced by Fred Friendly and Edward R. Murrow that helped to discredit the man who called himself "Tail Gunner Joe."

Think About It (continued)

But McCarthy was never a war hero or a tail gunner. His habit of making up details for personal benefit would stick with him through his political career.

McCarthy rose to national prominence by exposing "The Red Menace," the threat to US security posed by alleged communist sympathizers and infiltrators. McCarthy again did not let facts get in the way of his career. He recklessly accused hundreds of people of having communist leanings, ruining lives and careers. Almost all of these accusations were made without proof or even anything that remotely resembled evidence: McCarthy would claim to have a "list" that never materialized, a list from high government "sources" who were never named.

Edward R. Murrow and his partner Fred Friendly wanted to produce a program that exposed McCarthy. Murrow had sterling credentials from his years as an on-air correspondent. Friendly, who worked behind the scenes, was a respected producer. For a series of programs called "See It Now," they gathered film showing McCarthy at his worst: bullying, waving sheets of paper that contained the "lists" that never materialized, spewing "facts" that were simply untrue.

McCarthy's political career was doomed after that, and though he tried to counter-attack, Americans had experienced a big dose of the real Tail Gunner Joe and did not like the taste it left in their mouths.

That, anyway, is the skeleton of the story. "McCarthyism" had become a common phrase that lives on today, meaning guilt by association and blind bigotry against assumed "enemies."

But here is the rest of the story, followed by some rather difficult questions.

McCarthy was a clever schemer, but the news media were responsible for making him so brutally powerful. Reporters, both from print and the newly emerging broadcast organizations, often repeated his patently bogus claims without checking them out.

McCarthy staged events that had no real meaning; he would often call a press conference to announce that he was calling another press conference tomorrow. (Historian Daniel Boorstin calls this a "pseudo-event.") And it is not inconceivable that many of the news media were themselves terrified of McCarthy, who leveled charges of communism against his political enemies—meaning anyone who dared challenge him.

Also, viewers watching the final program in the series are struck by the fact that it is not so much an objective news report as an editorial.

Murrow took a stand and went after McCarthy. According to CBS News Anchor and Managing Editor Dan Rather, "he knew it and felt uncomfortable about it . . . The question is still relevant. When do we go from telling the story into interpretive reporting?"

The famous closing Murrow delivered also seems somewhat over the top by today's standards:

We will not walk in fear . . . we will not be driven by fear into an age of unreason, if we dig deep into our history and our doctrine, and remember that we are not descended from fearful men. Cassius was right. "The fault, dear Brutus, is not in our stars, but in ourselves," Good night, and good luck.

(Consider viewing the movie "Good Night and Good Luck" which deals with these events.)
Put yourself in the place of a reporter covering modern stories that have similar parallels.

• Suppose, for example, a senator tweets a scandalous charge of sexual impropriety against another politician. Would you, as a reporter, repeat the tweet, attributing it to the senator, or would you hold off until you personally had checked it out? Would your station post the tweet on its website? What would happen if other reporters simply repeated the charge (as they probably would); would you risk being hopelessly behind on the story? And suppose

Think About It *(continued)*

the senator making the charge was way off base. Would you stop quoting him in the future? At what point?

Today respect for journalism and reporting has been called into question as political leaders respond to reported headlines as examples of "Fake News." Would being wrong hurt your standing among your listeners or viewers?

- What would you do if you concluded that the senator was just a bald-faced liar? How far would you feel compelled to go to prove this? Would you allow him equal time on a show you produced to show him for what he is? Would you try to *balance* the program?

What, exactly, constitutes "balance?" Are you obligated to give balance to the story?

Also, would you call your viewers to action at the end, telling them, "We will not walk in fear?"

The foregoing principles apply to both radio and television news. For radio news specifically, you need to have an understanding of how radio news is gathered and structured. A basic component of radio news is the actuality, the recorded sound of a newsmaker or event. Radio actualities can be inserted into a story in a number of ways.

Radio news anchors and reporters are generally responsible for gathering, editing, and reading news. Sources include news services such as the radio networks and streaming services, offered by private organizations.

Radio journalists must be able to paint a picture with words. This process involves describing with imagination, including sound in the story, making accurate mood changes, and using and stressing vivid words. To preserve clarity and flow in the word picture, the announcer must pay attention to clarity of stories and actualities, and be able to gauge time effectively.

News is a component of the station's overall format, and the news effort and news announcers' deliveries must be compatible with the station's overall sound.

EXERCISES

1. Take five local stories from the newspaper and rewrite them into broadcast style for a 3-minute newscast. Record the newscast, making sure it runs *exactly* 3 minutes.
2. Write brief, descriptive phrases for the following circumstances. Feel free to take some liberties because you are not operating from a strict factual base, but keep within the bounds of reason. The goal is to use descriptive, colorful adjectives and punchy verbs. Use the active, rather than the passive, voice. For example,

- *Circumstance:* A tractor trailer carrying chemicals tipped over on the expressway and broke open. The payload of chemicals went onto the highway.
- *Description:* A tractor trailer ruptured, spewing chemicals onto the expressway.

Get the idea? Take out those flat-sounding words, and make the sentence paint a picture. Try these circumstances:

- *Circumstance:* An escaped convict was shot and killed while running away from the police.
- *Circumstance:* A tree was blown over by the wind. The roots were pulled out of the ground and stuck up in the air. The falling tree broke through the roof of a house.
- *Circumstance:* An angry Senator Jacobs called his opponent a liar. Jacobs said his opponent should withdraw from the race. Said his opponent was lacking in morals. *Hint:* Come up with variations for "said" and "called."

- *Circumstance:* Tractors were driven by farmers into the grounds of the state capitol. Onlookers were frightened by the onslaught of tractors. *Hint:* Use the active voice.
- *Circumstance:* People at a funeral walked past a casket, walking slowly. The wife of the slain policeman began to cry loudly as she passed the casket. She leaned on top of the casket.

3. Select one of the newscasts created in Exercise 1 and critique it. Rate from excellent, fair, to poor on the following categories:

   a. Were ideas presented clearly?
   b. Was energy level sufficient?
   c. Was there an adequate change of mood between stories?
   d. Were all pronunciations correct?
   e. Was delivery natural sounding?
   f. Did the reader sound interested in the material?

   Compare your evaluations. If there is disagreement among critics, play back the recording and examine the specific instances. Be prepared to defend your criticisms.

NOTES

1 Readers please note in the past few years some politicians have raised questions about media creating "fake news" as a way to win ratings or cause political chaos. This text does not deal in political matters and suggests you examine these claims carefully and draw your conclusions based on facts.
2 *Broadcast News Writing, Reporting, and Production* (New York: Macmillan, 1984), p. 55.

7 Television News Announcing

Much more is involved in on-air work in television news than sitting before a studio camera and mouthing words convincingly. Television newspeople function as a part of a team that must work closely together to get the news on the air. Television news reporters and anchors are expected to know how to put together a story from start to finish in a short period of time. So they must be able to write clearly and quickly and be familiar with the basics of video production. The performer must have a firm grasp on how television news is gathered, structured, and produced. You simply cannot do the job without understanding the basics.

TELEVISION NEWS BASICS

A tremendous amount of advance planning and thinking about content is necessary for TV news coverage. Getting each report on the air involves a technical crew and a reporter. So personnel must be scheduled with care so that all important stories during the day can be covered, with flexibility for breaking stories.

After the story has been recorded, the pieces are assembled and a script is written. The finished report must pass the scrutiny of the station's news executive(s), who decides whether it will be used. Sometimes news reports do not pan out, and they are pulled. Because today's technology allows almost instantaneous gathering of information, news items are bumped to make room for more timely stories. The entire process is often harrowing, always exciting. This section examines the basics of the business, including gathering the material, structuring it in a form useful for telecast, and putting it over the air within a newscast.

How TV News Is Gathered and Structured

Television news operations vary quite a bit in scope, depending on market size and other factors. A small-market newsroom might house only four or five full-time employees, but a major-market operation may have close to a hundred participants.

Although the particulars of staffing differ from station to station, the basic functions of the TV newsroom are roughly similar in all markets and operations. In larger markets, with bigger staffs, the operations are more specialized. Basic functions include administration, production, gathering, and reporting.

News administration. This function, headed by a news director, involves decision making on news coverage and maintaining the journalistic integrity for the station. The news director also has responsibility for staffing and budgeting. News directors in major-market stations often find themselves rather removed from actual newsgathering, having to focus instead on fighting for budgetary allotments, new equipment, and additional personnel. The news director of a small station may supervise only two or three other reporters and will cover stories and perhaps anchor the evening newscasts, as well. News directors look for upcoming events in the community and try to schedule the crews' week accordingly.

The number of administrative layers in a news department varies according to the size of the department. Most medium-market stations employ an assignment editor, whose responsibilities include scheduling crews and reporters and assigning and developing stories.

In summary, the functions of news administration are:

- Personnel and budgetary management
- Decision making and editorial policy
- Planning coverage of news

News production. News production was radically transformed by development of lighter, more easily portable video equipment and transmission facilities. Today newsgathering is digital and technology allows multiple ways to gather news video and information. The result is that news is produced faster and more easily than in the past.

Production duties range from the basic technical jobs of such staffers as audio specialists (Figure 7.1), to the producer, who is in overall charge of assembling the production elements of a newscast and often some editorial elements. The producer reports to the news director. In larger news operations there may be a managing editor or assistant news director who in in charge of the day-to-day operations.

Within the production function are such specialists as camera operators in studio and in-field producers who put breaking news on live from mobile or satellite links (Figure 7.2), studio assistants, control room operators, and field producers. A field producer, as the name implies, supervises the production function outside the studio. The job description varies in different markets, however. In very large markets and networks, associate producers and assistant producers work under the field producer's supervision in gathering news from the field.

In larger markets all duties become more specialized. A major-market operation may have one or more people responsible for electronic graphics, and the graphics designer may be an executive who

FIGURE 7.1 Audio specialists are an integral part of news production work. Running an audio console requires concentration in order to properly maintain the proper "levels."

FIGURE 7.2 News is frequently broadcast "live" from the field using state-of-the-art remote satellite trucks like this one.

supervises the entire "look" of the newscast. Some people specialize in editing, the process of arranging and rearranging the raw materials of news into a final product.

Although not strictly a part of the production function, broadcast engineers keep equipment maintained and operating, as well as supervising ongoing technical functions. A particular requirement for production engineering concerns live remotes, where a microwave unit or other technology can be used to transmit directly from the news scene.

In summary, duties of news production people include:

- Operating equipment needed to record or air the news
- Presenting visual elements, such as graphics and making sure talent and sets look good.
- Editing and assembling raw materials

> **Newsgathering and reporting.** Once news administration has assigned stories, journalists must gather the facts, outline the story elements, write copy, and deliver the copy to the camera either in a field report or as an anchor segment during a newscast. In larger markets, full-time writers compose copy, do research, and to some extent edit and revise copy. In some large markets, writers are assigned to work with a reporter in the field, a function bordering on field production. Today, as news coverage has expanded in many markets, more and more field segments air live within the newscast. This requires the field reporter to provide a lucid news segment using a combination of field notes and ad-libbing.

The primary duties of the newsgathering and reporting arm of the television news effort include:

- Assembling facts and writing stories or presenting stories live
- Working with the production crew to get visual and aural elements such as interviews and cover shots
- Delivering the news copy

The various functions interact a great deal. An on-air member of the newsgathering and reporting arm cannot operate without understanding the other functions and working closely with staffers in the other areas of television news.

HOW THE TV NEWSCAST DEVELOPED

In the early development of television, a newscast was radio with pictures, and very few pictures at that. Typically, newscasts were no longer than 15 minutes and featured a camera focused unblinkingly on a news **anchor**, a personality who virtually carried the show.

The evolution of the modern newscast came about through experimentation. At the local level, stations expanded coverage of sports and weather into separate segments. But even through the late 1960s, the local news was often done halfheartedly; it might feature only one or two short film pieces juxtaposed with the anchor reading.

At the same time, broadcast executives began to realize that the newscast could produce revenue for the station. That revelation brought about gradual but tremendous change. For one thing, the increased competition for audience shares sparked innovation and creativity as news and station executives sought new ways to attract viewers. The many developments that have changed the news picture since the 1960s include the supplanting of film cameras with portable video gear, vivid graphics, fast-moving and evocative formats, and *the increasing focus on the newscaster as an informer, performer, and personality.*

Personality did, indeed, become important in the content of most TV news shows. Packaging became and remains a prime issue. Specialists advise on the impact and acceptability of elements within the newscasts, from newscasters to news writing, from selection of stories to the color schemes of sets and criticism has been aimed at the use of consultants and the trend to make newscasts more entertaining.

Some of that criticism has been balanced by the vigorous pursuit of ratings by station management. Many seasoned journalists and critics feel that accepting consultants' recommendations was selling out to show business and that news judgments were being subjugated to non-news considerations designed solely to increase revenues.

Station executives are motivated by a desire to survive. Rating points translate into salaries and jobs, including the salaries and jobs of the news staff. So ratings are important for the health of the station and the very existence of the news operation. It is common to see anchors providing some light-hearted banter at the station break and at end of the newscast but today the newscast has evolved into a reasonable balance between journalism and show business. It is important to realize that the on-air reporter must meet a variety of requirements, for both journalism and entertainment.

The Typical Process

On-air news work is generally done under extreme time pressure. Here is how a television news operation might handle a typical day's developments.

> 9 a.m. The news director arrives at work, scans the files of upcoming events, and discusses stories with the assignment editor. The assignment editor looks over scripts done by the two early-morning newspeople and arranges for news crews to be sent out.
>
> Among the major preplanned stories today are a news conference on police sting operations, a meeting of the mayor's task force concerning whether a new municipal building will be constructed downtown, and the arrival in town of a famous country singer. The celebrity's imminent arrival is causing great excitement, and the news department's "Live Eye," will be stationed at the airport. Breaking stories include a brush fire threatening to spread in the far western region of the county and a state police manhunt for an escaped convict.

Some of the feature stories, known around the news department as "back of the book" material, were photographed yesterday but are being edited together today. The feature piece is a three-part series on adoption, running tonight and the following two nights.

The producer begins putting together a rundown of the stories that are being considered for the newscast. This rundown will change many, many times before the 6 o'clock news. The producer and the assignment editor discuss some of the visual elements of the stories, too.

Throughout the morning, the assignment editor is in telephone contact with reporters covering assignments in the field.

Handling the Changing News

1 p.m. There are now several other breaking stories. A tractor trailer has overturned on the expressway, and a photographer is dispatched to the scene to take footage of the accident. A writer will gather facts over the telephone and write a script for a voice-over. Tonight, the anchor will read the story off camera while the video of the accident rolls.

3 p.m. The newscast is beginning to take shape. Writers are composing some of the script material that will hold up throughout the day, "timeless" stories that won't change by 6 p.m. Some reporters have returned from field assignments, have written up their scripts, and are working with production people in editing together the package.

The manhunt for the escaped prisoner continues, so a script will not be written until shortly before airtime. If the situation does not change, some cover video that was shot early in the day will suffice for the voice-over.

Production people are looking at and editing videotape, making decisions on the amount of time to allocate to each story.

4 p.m. The producer and the news director find themselves with several files of video that have been edited on nonlinear systems.

These segments include the following:

- Four packages (stories filed by reporters), including the reporter's introduction and closing, along with an interview segment and other material.
- Seven pieces of cover video, to be used while an anchor reads over the footage. In the case of the truck accident, for example, there will be a shot panning the scene of the accident, and the anchor will read the story over the video. Total time for the voice-over is 15 seconds.
- A segment of the three-part piece on adoption. Editing was finished late in the afternoon.

Each time a story is added or subtracted from the storyline the station's news computer system automatically updates the running order. Video segments and graphics are placed in the rundown.

4:40 p.m. Here is what the producer and news director do not have:

- Any idea when the country music star will arrive. Her plane was supposed to land shortly before news time, but it is going to be late. The producer has been checking the star's Facebook page, Twitter feed and other social media to see if there is anything that might become a useful backstory for the 11 p.m. news.

  (The assignment editor is given the responsibility of coordinating with the air charter service to figure out when the plane will arrive.)
- Any footage of a serious house fire that broke out minutes ago. One person is believed dead. A crew is on its way.
- Anything new on the manhunt.

5:05 p.m. The list of stories is firming up. The production staff is choosing the artwork, which will be projected behind the anchors; the sports and weather people are preparing their segments (details on this in Chapter 9); and the assignment editor is beginning to think about the 11 o'clock newscast. He has to cover several meetings and schedule the crews for their dinner breaks.

5:35 p.m. A voice on the police scanner indicates that shots have been fired at the site of the police manhunt. No further information is available by phone from the state police. There's no time to get a crew out and back, and no one knows for sure what the shots mean.

Meanwhile, the control tower at the airport says the plane will be only five minutes late, allowing plenty of time for coverage by the Live Eye. The arrival of one of the country's most famous country stars certainly is a major story, but the shots fired at the manhunt site indicate the potential for an even larger story. Was the convict shot? Was a policeman shot? No one knows, and there is no time to find out, for if the Live Eye is to reach the remote site by airtime, it must leave the airport now.

"Go to the search site," the news director orders. His reasoning: any deaths or injuries occurring in the manhunt would amount to a major story. Also, the manhunt is in the third day with no end in sight, and the other two local stations have backed off coverage; thus there is potential for a scoop. No one here knows where the competitors' remote vans are, of course, but it's worth a gamble to be the only station in town to have coverage of the capture—if, indeed, there is a capture.

One other point influences the news director's decision. Tape of interviews with the music star's fans waiting at the airport has already been fed back to the station. Instagram and Facebook entries are reviewed. Is there an ancillary story to cover about a local fan?

6 p.m. Airtime: the anchors introduce themselves and tease (read a short piece of copy that tells viewers about top stories coming up) the top stories of the evening. One anchor must ad-lib, from hastily assembled notes, the introduction to the live manhunt coverage, the signal for which is just coming over the air.

The reporter covering the manhunt has just arrived and has absolutely nothing to go on other than the sound of shots, heard a half-hour ago. She tries to reach out to the police but they are too busy so she ad-libs a brief stand-up from the scene, giving some background on the search and the convict, who is believed to be hiding in the woods. Then she indicates that the story will be followed up shortly.

Back at the studio, anchors read through their scripts, several copies of which have been distributed to the producer, the director, and the audio director. The news computer has automatically updated all changes and the finished script is displayed on the station's teleprompter. Anchors will read some stories straight to camera, do voice-overs for taped footage, and introduce reporters' packages.

During a commercial, the director cues the anchors: "We're going to the Live Eye right after the commercial." The anchor again must ad-lib an intro. This time, there's dramatic live footage of a wounded prisoner being led to an ambulance. Also played back is video made moments ago showing the actual capture. The reporter on the scene must, of course, make sense of all this and communicate the excitement of the situation to the viewer.

This action is produced by a corps of on-air performers who, as we have seen, must not only speak to the camera but must also work within the technical constraints imposed by television. Part of their job is to create material under intense time pressure and to be able to communicate with accuracy and completeness.

Moreover, almost everyone involved must be able to use technology to tell a story. The way you "tell" in video is through assembling the fragments you gather during the reporting process.

Although extensive examination of production is beyond the scope of this book, Focus on Technique does offer a basic introduction to what almost any announcer in television news will need to know to communicate via video.

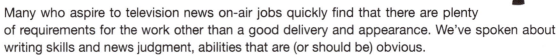

Focus on Technique

Overcoming the Editing Obstacle

Many who aspire to television news on-air jobs quickly find that there are plenty of requirements for the work other than a good delivery and appearance. We've spoken about writing skills and news judgment, abilities that are (or should be) obvious.

But on-air reporters need to be able to understand the editing process.

Often, they must "cut" their own material; at the very least, they must be able to give coherent instructions to the person operating the editing equipment. While it is surprising how often on-air candidates fail to learn how to edit. Perhaps it is fear of the equipment or the reluctance to admit ignorance of the process. *But every television journalist must know the rudiments, at a minimum.*

If at all possible, take as many courses as you can in broadcast journalism and TV production. Many newly graduated journalism students have learned some of the basics and these skills come in handy looking for that first job.

If you are entering the journalism profession without this knowledge, get hands-on experience in editing as soon as possible.

Here is a basic introductory "crash course" that will familiarize you with the process and how it's done. Remember that despite variations in editing equipment and software packages, the technique is the same.

Editing Basics

The process of editing can be confusing, especially to those without a background in television production. If you are going to be manipulating a computer workstation that is used to edit video you do not need extensive familiarity of the controls. While software packages can be very complex, it is not our intention to go through all of the capabilities of editing software. This overview will explain the process you would use to develop a news package. You will need to get some instruction in the specific system that you are going to use as they vary from station to station.

Let's start by stating exactly what editing is and what we're going to do. Editing is the process of manipulating video and audio so that the shots are arranged into a specific order. It may mean that not all the material shot on camera will be used and that some of the material may be used out of the order that it was shot. For example, a news crew may arrive on the scene of a fire that's already well in progress. The cameraperson may immediately start shooting footage of the firemen's progress in battling the blaze while the reporter begins gathering details and facts that will be used in his story stand-up. After the cameraperson has shot footage of the blaze, the reporter records an interview with the chief. The cameraperson may then shoot the reporter detailing the events on the scene of the fire (with the fire in the background over the reporter's shoulder). The order of the shooting looks like this in block form.

We have three separate segments and they were shot in the order shown in Figure 7.3a, b, and c.

Through the editing process, the order of our final package will be quite different. We'll start first with the reporter's stand-up detailing the event, then edit in the interview with the chief, next we insert some of the fire footage over the audio of the chief's comments, go back to a shot of the chief ending the interview and then finish with a shot of the reporter for a closing wrap up. The final order of shots will look like that shown in Figure 7.3d.

This edited arrangement is fairly typical for a news package at the scene of a fire. Note that because of the editing process it will not matter which shots were recorded first or second or last. We will edit the segment in such a way to tell the viewers the story in a logical way.

Focus on Technique *(continued)*

a. House fire in progress
   shot 1

b. Reporter interviews fire chief
   shot 2

c. Reporter does stand up—
   both open and close are
   shot at the same time
   shot 3

d. Edited Package

Opening shot
Shot 1

Interview with
fire chief
Shot 2

Insert fire video
over voice of chief
Shot 3

Back to fire chief
Shot 4

Reporter's closing
Shot 5

FIGURE 7.3 Raw footage.

In news, you'll generally be doing "cuts-only" editing, meaning that your story will be done with one video segment edited right next to another in a logical order. There will be no dissolves or special effects because these effects are generally not used in hard news package segments.

To make the package described in Figure 7.3, we will have to choose the appropriate video footage, note the appropriate beginning and ending points, and then place these segments together to form the seamless package.

The process of shooting, selecting, and ordering shots is not difficult, and with some practice, you and your cameraperson will get into a routine that will help it become second nature. However, that doesn't mean that gathering the news and shooting the news footage is easy or routine. For example, this story would be quite different if the fire crew rescued someone from the burning house. Perhaps you would have interviewed the firemen who did the rescue and then asked for comments from the chief.

There are many different news editing software packages available from very simple systems that work on laptops, such as Apple's iMovie to more professional systems by Avid, Adobe and others. **YouTube** provides many different video tutorials that demonstrate how to create a news package using these systems.

The power of modern programs is astonishing, and brings the ability to edit video not only to television stations but to independent producers. Generally, only standard computer hardware— although it needs to be fairly high-end—is required (Figure 7.4).

Once you determine which system your organization uses, we recommend that you avail yourself of the tutorials available both on YouTube and from the software company's websites. They will provide you with a basic understanding of how the systems work.

Learning the basics of editing is good for any television journalist as it will strengthen your ability to look for shots and story angles that will go together smoothly. So, even though you may not be called upon to edit your news piece, it is likely that understanding the process will make you a more effective reporter.

Focus on Technique *(continued)*

FIGURE 7.4 A standard computer, some editing software, and preferably two screens is all you need for basic video editing.

This extended examination of a "typical" day shows the primary difficulty, and appeal, of the challenging field of TV news. It takes a great deal of stamina just to cope with the pressures and physical activities of the job. Also, you must learn to be calm in a high-pressure environment. While experienced performers may look comfortable and relaxed, the actual physical environment is anything but calming (see Figure 7.5.) And, of course, considerable skill and experience are necessary to be able to deliver a story coherently to a camera. The work of a television reporter may look easy, but this is only because of many reporters' competence and ability to work under pressure and because these on-air journalists have acquired a grasp of techniques and operations.

TELEVISION NEWS TECHNIQUES AND OPERATIONS

Until now, our exploration of TV news has centered on the structure and elements of the operations. This section examines the considerations of newspeople who actually go before the camera, the techniques of effective delivery and working on the air with the tools of the TV news trade.

TV News Delivery

TV news delivery incorporates the general principles described in Chapters 3 and 4. The following areas are specific to the on-air newsperson.

   Phrasing. Giving the impression that you understand what you say is extremely important. As phrasing relates to TV news, the important element is to group words together in natural-sounding patterns and to communicate thoughts, rather than words. It is crucial to be "on top of" the copy, reading a sentence or phrase ahead. Getting lost in the copy, or hesitating in your delivery, can seriously impair credibility.

   Pace. You can improve your chances of success in television news by developing a proper pace, a pace that is not rushed yet conveys energy. Equally important to an anchor is development of a *steady* pace. Production people have to roll video segments (which may be on a hard drive or an inhouse network) according to the news anchor's reading of a script, and constant speeding up and slowing down plays havoc with this process. In your drill and on-air work, strive for a consistent pace.

Emotion. A newscaster must be able to communicate feelings as well as facts. The expression of feelings, however, should not be maudlin or phony. A mechanical "sad face" on a newscaster who is narrating a story that truly *is* tragic, borders on being offensive. Although it is natural for people's facial expressions to reflect emotion, television is not a natural medium. Some practice is necessary to acquire a serviceable technique.

Review tapes of yourself to judge your expression. The most common mistake is the adoption of robotic expressions obviously called up to match the story. Scan tapes for the "sad face" or "happy face," and modify these expressions in further air efforts.

The next most common problem in expressing emotion is giving mixed signals: for example, maintaining a stern and rigid posture when reading a light story. The practical reason for mixed signals or improper expression may simply be that the on-air person is thinking about the next camera change or trying to remember when the next package will be introduced. Focusing on the thoughts and ideas of the story can eliminate mixed signals caused by lapses in concentration.

Interest. A news reporter in any situation must *show* interest in the subject at hand. Practice is essential because it is possible to be extremely interested in the copy and still appear indifferent because of poor delivery technique.

Ideally, you should practice on camera. If that is not possible, recording yourself with a smartphone will do. Get any airtime possible to develop your skill of projecting interest in the story.

Projecting interest involves enthusiasm for the task at hand and involvement in the material. Remember that you cannot evince genuine interest in a subject of which you have no understanding, so a wide-ranging knowledge of current events will help.

Finally, determine as much as possible *why* each story is of interest to you and your viewers. Does the city council's action translate into higher taxes? If so, stress that connection. If you grasp the essential points, your manner and communicative abilities will get the message across.

FIGURE 7.5 You don't typically have a lot of time to get comfortable in the studio, but it's wise to get in as soon as you can and make sure everything's ready and your nerves are calm.

Credibility. Related to the need to understand the material and for the viewers to understand you is the viewer's faith in what you say. Polls regularly show that news people are among the most trusted people in America. Trusted newscasters are perceived as honest and impartial and as experienced and intelligent enough to understand the news and give a fair rendering.

This concept affects the American tradition of using journalists as on-camera performers. A news director could hire much better-looking readers from the ranks of actors than from the world of journalism. This has in fact been tried—but without much success. The actors, people without news backgrounds, do not project credibility. Some successful news anchors do not have backgrounds in journalism, but they are the exceptions, not the rule. While political commentators on various cable networks come from many different backgrounds, there is an increasing focus on journalistic background for broadcast anchors; aspirants are well advised to develop a strong background in journalism.

There is no magic formula for developing credibility. It may largely be a function of avoiding negatives: do not mispronounce local names, do not use poor grammar, do not be uninformed or appear to be uninformed of local news and newsmakers, and do not look sloppy.

Contact. On a tangible level, contact means eye contact. On an intangible level, the concept of contact is defined by how well an on-air performer seems to move off the screen into the living room. Many of the subtleties can be developed after a good grounding in the proper techniques of eye contact, particularly in news reading and interviewing.

One trademark of on-air professionals is knowing what to do with their eyes. For example, note how interviews often portray the questioner as being calm, forthright, and direct, while the guest (or victim) appears nervous and shifty. This often has to do with eye movements, natural movements that the TV performer has learned to override. Many of us, during conversation, shift our eyes downward or to the side. While quite normal during conversation, shifting of eyes, especially from side to side, is both apparent and distracting on television. It inevitably creates a poor impression.

The only way to correct eye contact problems is by viewing and critiquing tapes. Remember, you must maintain steady and unwavering, but not glassy-eyed, contact with the lens. Even being slightly off in gazing at the lens is perceptible.

Ease. While TV news can be nerve-wracking, your viewer doesn't understand that. The viewer sees you as company in the living room. That's why it's important to feel comfortable in your environment. Advance preparation (Figure 7.5) is important. It's important to arrive in studio as early as possible, make sure things are working and that you are prepared.

Field Reporting in Television News

The job of the field reporter is crucial to the success of any station's news programming. Prerecorded or live news packages are the building blocks of television news programs. Without them, even the most talented, credible news anchor would be useless. The days are long gone when a news program could be carried by a "talking head" reading copy. Television news today depends on pictures. And those pictures are gathered and explained by field reporters and news crews.

The job of a television field reporter requires resourceful men and women who can quickly grasp the news value in a variety of situations and make solid news judgments in a short period of time. They must be able to shape the story, plan the sequence of events, gather the visual elements of the story, write a script, and do on-camera work—all very quickly and often several times a day. Several specialized skills and techniques are used by effective field reporters that must be mastered by anyone who aspires to this kind of work. Bear in mind that the immediacy of on-camera fieldwork requires that reporters be guided by a strong sense of ethics (see Box 7.1).

BOX 7.1 **The Ethics of Field Reporting**

Television field reporters need to be keenly aware of the standards of excellence and fairness that govern their role as journalists. Many news departments and several national associations have codes of ethics. Many of those codes, including the code of the Radio Television News Directors Association (RTNDA), insist that video be used in such a way as not to alter its context. You should not use a cutaway shot, for example, that makes someone appear furtive or nervous when that might not really be the case, or if a subject's nervousness is simply normal stage fright and not an indicator of guilt.

Suffice it to say that television news reporters have powerful tools in their hands. Misrepresentation for the sake of sensationalizing a story or to introduce drama simply cannot be tolerated. The cardinal principle of television news reporting is to tell the story accurately. Don't embellish or distort. Never manipulate information to prove a preconceived idea of how the story should go together. Hard work and persistence pay handsome dividends for those fortunate enough to work in this exciting profession.

Those who engage in shady practices and clever manipulation seldom last long.

Getting the information. The first thing you must do at the scene of a news event is find out what's going on. Generally you will get some information about the event when the story is assigned. Usually, though, the information is very sketchy, and sometimes it is wrong. Moreover, in fast-breaking stories things may change rapidly. So you must catch up on the facts as soon as possible after arriving on the scene.

The best way to start is to try to find someone in a position of authority. If the event involves breaking news, getting information may mean just walking up to someone who looks as if he or she should know something. At a fire, you need only ask any firefighter who is in charge. When it is not immediately obvious who is in charge, just start asking questions of people in the vicinity. It usually won't take you long to get to the right person. There is usually only a limited amount of time that a news crew can spend at the scene. Other stories may need to be covered, and the report still must be edited for broadcast, so there is always a need to work quickly.

While the reporter is looking for information, the camera operator can be getting shots of the general activities at the scene. When it is time to edit the story, there will be a need for video that shows generally what is going on at the scene. Shots of firefighters at work, or striking workers picketing a work site, or crowds gathered at the scene of a homicide are some examples of video that can be shot while the reporter gets information.

On-camera interviews. Lining up the interviews is the next priority for the reporter. First you need to decide who should be interviewed on camera. Some events require bystander reactions. At other times you'll want a spokesperson who can respond to questions about an organization's activities or a police investigation, for example.

The neighbors of a gun-wielding homeowner who has taken a hostage might provide insight into the person's recent behavior that can shed light on the reasons for his or her actions. A homicide victim's relatives and friends might provide comments that set the story in context. An official spokesperson for a college can talk about the institution's response to community complaints about a noisy fraternity.

Interviews fill out the news story factually and help convey its human dimensions. Field reporters must develop a good sense of which subjects will best add the necessary impact to the story. Once you have decided whom you want to interview, sometimes you must persuade them to appear on camera. People at the scene are often shy about going on camera, or may simply not want to get involved. Officials of organizations are often fearful about their comments being "taken out of context." Or they may fear looking foolish when a difficult question is posed.

In such circumstances, be persistent without being annoying. Coax, rather than browbeat. If you can reassure subjects that they are talking to you as a reporter and not to the camera, they are more likely to relax. You can reassure them that serious mistakes can be edited out, and that they can stop and try again if they make a mistake or say something that they suddenly realize they shouldn't have said. Use this technique only when necessary, to reassure particularly nervous subjects. If you make such an offer routinely, you may encounter subjects who ask for endless retakes to improve their performances. Others may feel that they have the prerogative to ask you to edit out any comments that, on reflection, they decide may be misinterpreted.

When conducting the interview, follow the techniques of effective interviewing described in Chapter 8. Avoid long interviews. This will help in editing, and minimize the uneasiness of the subject. Don't be afraid to keep questioning the subject, though, if you don't immediately get the answers you need. Keep in mind that you are looking for those few seconds that provide a key element of information or add insight to the story.

Usually the reporter stands near the camera and slightly off to one side. Have the interview subject look at you, not at the camera lens. It is generally not good to have a lot of background activity when you're interviewing someone. The viewer's attention should be focused on the subject of the interview and on what is being said. If your video shows a lot of activity in the background, the viewer's attention is likely to wander away from the subject. Often reporters use tight close-ups for interviews. This technique eliminates background distractions and lets the person's facial expressions be seen more easily.

> **Cutaways and Reverses.** When you have completed the interview, you will usually have your camera operator shoot cutaways and reverses. A **cutaway** is any shot that can be edited into your interview segments to make smooth transitions when you want to edit out some of the interviewee's comments without breaking continuity.

If you butt together two segments of tape showing the interview subject at two different times of the interview, you most likely will get a sudden change in facial expression or bodily position. This jump looks unnatural and is distracting to the viewer. To avoid this, a different video element, the cutaway, is inserted at the point where the edit occurs. This eliminates the jump cut and establishes smooth continuity.

Some news organizations, though, now prefer using jump cuts rather than covering the cut with video. The reason is that a jump cut emphatically demonstrates to the viewer that something has been taken out of the tape, and the time frame of the statements compressed.

One reason for the increased use of jump cuts is that technology is now available that creates a dissolve effect. This technique is often used in CBS news reports, for example.

Some shots that are commonly used as cutaways are a group of reporters at a news conference, firefighters at work, an emergency vehicle with flashing lights, a cover shot of a building, crowds at the scene, or even a street sign (a street sign achieves the added function of locating the news event visually).

> **Reverse shots.** These are shots of the reporter doing the interview. They are shot from behind the interview subject—a reverse of the shot featuring the interview subject. Reverses are commonly used as cutaways. Reverses can also be used, however, to re-ask a question. This is usually done only when it is deemed useful to show viewers how the reporter asked a particular question. If a

question draws a dramatic response, featuring hitherto unknown information, it may be desirable to show viewers how the question was asked.

Be careful when you do such a reverse shot. It is important to try to duplicate the original question word for word. Inflections should be the same, as should the facial expressions of the reporter. Of course, this can be done without the interview subject in the shot, but usually you'll want to have the subject visible when the "re-ask" is shot. Never use this technique just to convey the impression that you can ask tough questions. It is considered a serious breach of professional ethics to create a false impression through editing techniques.

When your camera operator is shooting reverses, to be used as cutaways, the mic is usually off. The reporter needs to appear to be listening to the subject of the interview, so that the reverse appears to have been taken during the interview. Good reporters try to keep the subject talking. They use this informal conversation with the interview subject to get further information that may help put the story together. The subject is usually more relaxed at this time than when the mic is live. This may be the time that a subject gives you something that he or she didn't feel comfortable saying while the mic was on. Such information will often make your story just a bit better than the one done by the competition. It can also provide information useful for your stand-up or in writing copy to be read in the studio by the anchor.

Stand-ups. The **stand-up** gets its name from the fact that it is shot with the reporter standing up in front of the camera at the scene of the news story. When the story is edited into a package back at the studio, the stand-up can open and close the report. Stand-ups are almost always done as the last segment recorded at the scene. (As we pointed out earlier, it is increasingly common for reporters to do their opens and closes live from the scene during the newscast.)

You'll write short pieces of copy for delivery during your stand-up. This copy usually must be memorized before you go on camera. There are no prompting devices in the field, and you don't want to read word for word from your notes.

Memorizing your open and close should not be too difficult. You wrote it, so you probably have played with several versions of the copy before you got it the way you want it. By the time you've written it to your satisfaction, it will be well established in your mind.

When the camera is running, though, many things can keep you from concentrating on memorized copy. There are usually bystanders watching. You have to think about your cue from the camera operator, your facial expression, and the inflection and rate of your delivery. Most of the time you don't need to be concerned to get each word exactly the way you have written it. As long as your delivery is smooth and natural, altered phrases won't matter much.

Occasionally, though, the situation is such that you must stick to exact wording. If each word is vital, be sure to take the precaution of over-memorizing your copy. One technique that helps you memorize copy verbatim is to build the piece in your mind sentence by sentence. Repeat the first sentence over several times until you have it fixed in your mind. Then repeat the first two sentences over and over. Next repeat the first three sentences, and so on. In this way you'll be reinforcing your memorization of the earlier parts each time you add a sentence.

Another technique is to focus attention on the words at the beginning and end of each sentence. Most people who get lost trying to deliver memorized copy segments, do so at the end of a sentence. They get through one or two sentences fine, but they can't recall the next sentence. To avoid this, memorize the words that form the transitions between sentences. For example, memorize the last word in the first sentence in conjunction with the first word in the second sentence, and so on.

If the stand-up is complex, remember that there is no shame in glancing at your notes. Key words, on a notebook that is held just out of the camera shot, can help you move from point to point. Even the top pros sometimes use their notes in stand-ups. If you do use a notebook that you want to keep out of the shot, by the way, be sure to tell your camera operator to keep the shot tight enough so the notebook does not show. When you use a notebook with key words, write in large letters with a black felt-tip marker so it will be easy to see.

Some reporters have opted not to worry at all about memorization. They rely instead on electronics. It is a relatively simple matter for a script to be read into a digital recorder or a smartphone. The reporter can then play back the recorded piece through an earpiece while speaking into the camera.

Bluetooth ear monitor systems can help a reporter connect a recording device with wireless earpiece. Professional audio companies offer high isolation earpieces that can connect via a wire looped through the back of a jacket or shirt and then connected to the recorder. The reporter simply presses play/pause to control the system. These systems may be particularly useful in high noise situations. This method can take some practice to master, but it can provide for impressive eye contact during delivery of a long or involved story in the field.

Reporters in field doing a live remote will wear an interruptible foldback (IFB) earpiece that allows the reporter to hear cues from control booth or respond to questions from the studio anchor. These devices are necessary in order to ensure that the reporter will start the live segment on cue. These IFB devices have an in-studio setup for the news anchor that allows on-air talent to stay in communication with the control room. The device may be wireless or there may be a loop mounted under the anchor desk. Separate loops can be provided for each member of the news team and at various locations in the news studio, for example in the weather map area.

Dealing with Crowds. When you show up at a news scene with a camera crew, you automatically become a "moron magnet," to use a phrase coined by one frustrated field reporter. People often want to get behind you and perform, while you're on camera trying to do a stand-up or when you're conducting an interview. Several things can be done to cope with this kind of situation.

If you have trouble with crowds in the background, try doing your on-camera work against the wall of a building or, if you happen to be near a body of water, next to the waterline with the water in the background. Sometimes you can get permission to use private property where public access is restricted. If police are on the scene (at a demonstration, for example), crowd interference can sometimes be minimized by setting up near a concentration of uniformed officers.

Sometimes you can get rowdy crowds out of the shot, but their noise interferes. In that case, try holding the mic close to your chin. That usually minimizes background noise. Sometimes you must deal directly with the crowd and try to reduce the incentive for interference. Veteran television reporters have developed several techniques that sometimes help in this kind of situation. One technique used occasionally by one author of this book as a field reporter was to co-opt one member of the group. In a group of rowdy kids, for example, he would seek out the biggest, toughest-looking member of the crowd and persuade or pay him to act as an enforcer (encouraging the use of intimidation rather than physical violence).

If you have a television monitor in the field, have the camera operator take a tight head-and-shoulders shot of you. Place the monitor where the would-be troublemakers can see it. They'll note the fact that their background activity is not in the shot, and sometimes that will discourage further antics.

One reporter says he tries to wear down the crowd by doing an endless number of takes of the same script. Eventually the crowd gets bored and leaves. Then the reporter doesn't roll until the crowd departs. Then the reporter does his real take. He says the phony takes help him smooth his delivery and memorize his copy.

Sometimes there is no alternative but to appeal to a sense of decency. It sometimes helps to point out to disruptive kids that immature, idiotic behavior may prove embarrassing when they actually see it on the air. Worse yet, their friends, parents, and teachers will also see it.

A final point about dealing with crowds: it is important that the reporter realize his or her responsibility to protect the camera operator, who is extremely vulnerable. When the camera is running, the operator is looking straight ahead. He or she can't see trouble coming.

WORKING TO THE CAMERA

One factor that complicates good contact is the multicamera setup unique to the TV news studio. You will typically face two or three cameras (Figure 7.6). An anchor must shift his or her attention from one camera to another without interrupting content and flow. An audience does not notice when a performer does camera changes well. But those who make camera changes poorly do call attention to the process.

If you find camera changes difficult (and some performers do), pay attention to the sort of movement by which you naturally change glances, during a party, perhaps. Use the same natural motion you use to address another person.

Often the transition can be made easier by a brief glance at the script; that is, down. In fact, brief downward glances are a good idea even if you are reading from a prompting device. An unblinking stare is rather unnerving to the viewers. When changing from one camera to another, you may choose to take a short downward glance at the script and then raise your gaze to the other camera.

Here are three additional points on working to the camera. First, TV cameras are equipped with tally lights to indicate which camera is on air. If you look to what you think is the proper camera but there's no tally light, you must make a decision. Do you hunt for the right camera or wait for the director to follow you and punch up the camera to which you are looking? Generally, a floor director's cues and gestures can help sort the situation out. Discuss this matter with the director in advance, and always follow the floor director's instructions.

Because the floor director cannot speak to you, he or she must rely on gestures, and you must understand these gestures. Figure 7.7 shows some of the more common cues used by floor directors. Television news and interviewing are the most common areas in which you will encounter floor directors.

Second, in many news systems the teleprompter script is automatically generated from the news story filed. The output image from the news computer is displayed on the prompter screen. That image, projected on a mirror directly in front of the performer's camera lens (the script is visible to the performer but not to the viewer), produces a "roll" in which there are only several words per line. Precisely timing the roll—the job of the crew member who operates the prompting device—is demanding. See Box 7.2 for some tips on using the prompting device.

Third, remember that changing cameras will also result in a closer or wider shot. Because of the visual requirement of the medium, transitions between identically framed shots are almost never used. Close-ups

FIGURE 7.6 Announcers often face an array of cameras, and it's critical to know which one to talk to and when you will change.

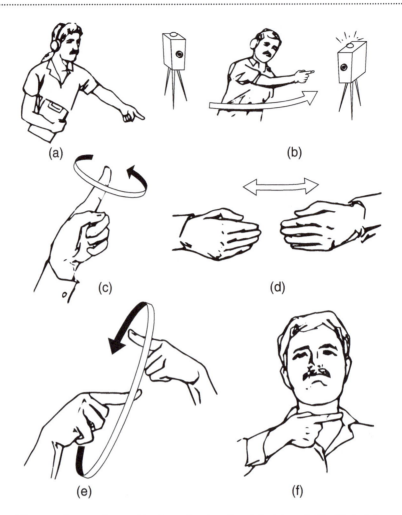

FIGURE 7.7 Some of the cues frequently used by floor directors in a television studio. Signals in common usage vary among stations, so always go over the signals with your floor director before air or taping time. A pointed finger (a) means "You're on!" A sweeping and pointing motion (b) indicates a camera change. One finger twirled (c) is often used to mean "speed up." A motion imitating stretching a rubber band (d) means "stretch" or "slow down." Two-handed twirling motion (e) means "wrap up." Finger drawn across throat (f) means "cut."

call for caution in movement. Move too much, and you will be out of the frame. Wide shots allow for more expressive gestures to make up for the increased perceived distance between the performer and the viewer.

In news, a medium shot includes part of the desk and the newscaster. A close-up includes the head and shoulders, while an extreme close-up generally shows the face from the chin to the hairline.

Robotics

Many television news studios today are equipped with automated cameras—sometimes referred to as robot-operated cameras, or simply robotics. The distinguishing characteristic of studios using these camera systems is that there are no camera operators in the studio. The cameras are programmed to respond to commands conveyed electronically from the control room.

Robotics are generally used in situations in which camera shots are fairly simple and there is not much need for cameras to move around. The most commonly found robotics studios are news sets. NBC television has used automated cameras on its evening news broadcasts and in other news-type programs since 1988. Today many local news studios have converted operations to robotics as well.

BOX 7.2 **Some Tips on Using the Prompting Device**

It is often difficult for announcers to pick up the tricks of the trade when reading from a prompting device (see Figure 7.8). Some hints:

- Read the prompter at a steady pace. That way, the operator of the device will have a better handle on your reading rate.
- Although it is tempting to try to compensate for variations in the crawl speed, remember that it is the newscaster's job to set the pace and the prompter operator's job to follow. Don't get involved in a game of catch-up. Dictate your own speed—but be sure you read at that speed steadily.
- Some performers find it a great help to read a specific line of the prompter crawl. Try reading the third line down. This usually gives you some cushion above and below. Once the operator perceives that you are consistently reading the third line, he or she will be able to develop a steadier hand in operating the device.
- Remember to look down from time to time. The audience can be unnerved by an unwavering stare. Also, remember that you must keep your place in the written script that you hold in your hand. If the prompter breaks down—and it often does—you'll need to go immediately to the written script.

FIGURE 7.8 Using a prompting device is not entirely an intuitive action. It takes practice.

Nevertheless, it can be somewhat disconcerting to on-air talent to work in a studio with no human operators at the camera positions. In many robotics studios, there is still a floor director to cue talent to the proper camera and to alert the announcer to impending shot changes. In these studios, air people need to learn to concentrate on the floor directors and trust the cues they give. You need to disregard other camera movement in the studio and work to the camera that is currently operating. Although this is also true of cameras operated by people, the potential for distraction increases when unmanned cameras start to move around, seemingly on their own.

Some news operations use completely automated studio operations and if there is no floor manager, the talent will get the cues directly from the technical director (TD) via an earpiece. Usually the talent and TD have worked out an understanding for providing cues.

In cases where there is no floor director, you need to pay attention to control room directions received through your earpiece. This can be distracting while you are reading, but with practice you will be able to take in the comments of the director in the control room while seeming to be fully engaged with your viewers. If you become confused, ask questions during commercial breaks or prerecorded segments.

Today's automated cameras are commonplace and extremely reliable, but should one start to move improperly during a shot, the on-air talent should try to adapt as much as possible. There isn't much you can do if a camera starts to pan or tilt away from you as you are reading. You can't move with it, so you'll just have to play it straight and hope that control room people quickly fix the problem. In such a situation, you might lose sight of the prompting device on the camera you're working to. If that happens, use your script. If possible shift to another camera's prompter, even though that may temporarily distract the viewer. Probably it is best simply to read from your script, looking up when possible to see if the situation has corrected itself. It is wise to practice doing that from time to time anyway, in case a prompting device develops problems at some point.

Ad-Libbing for News

Even the finest readers stand little chance of success in news if they cannot **ad-lib**. From the standpoint of the field reporter, ad-libbing is the name of the game. Anchors must be able to speak extemporaneously in introductions to breaking stories or for coverage of special events such as elections.

Some special considerations apply to ad-libbing in news situations. First, you are doing news and will be held accountable for what you say. Liberties with the truth cannot be taken. A storm of controversy can erupt over an ill-chosen phrase used in relation to a sensitive story. Always ad-lib in phrases

1. *That you know to be factual.* If you are repeating a statement of opinion or conjecture, be sure to qualify it as such.
2. *That are not subject to misinterpretation.* Using shorter sentences and phrases can help keep meanings clear.

Time is limited for newspeople ad-libbing stories. You may not have the luxury of doing five or ten takes. During live coverage, of course, there is no second chance.

The process of compartmentalizing and encapsulating thoughts outlined in Chapter 4 is applicable to news ad-libs and helps both in ensuring accuracy of facts and in producing mistake-free takes. To apply the principles of Chapter 4 to a news ad-lib, consider the following framework:

1. *Be well informed about the issue.* You must be able to call up names, facts, and figures.
2. *Do a quick encapsulation of thoughts and rehearse, mentally or out loud, what you are going to say.* Break up the ad-lib into complete thoughts. List those thoughts, either mentally or in a notebook, before speaking.
3. *Deliver the ad-lib briefly.* Do not be concerned with stretching for time, and never try to expand without adequate information. Strive for a definite ending of the ad-lib, a brief conclusion or summary.

PRODUCTION EQUIPMENT

A performer does not always have to be an expert on production, but knowledge never hurts. Such expertise enhances ability to work creatively and within technical constraints and also will help you earn the respect of production people on the news team. In many cases, especially in small markets, the on-air person will have to do editing and other production work. Here, of course, a good grounding in production is essential. Reporters in the field often call their own shots and must be aware of the visual rules of assembling TV news. Our discussion of working with equipment is only the briefest of introductions to the tools of the trade of modern television.

Studio Cameras

The studio camera, as shown in Figure 7.9, is a large camera equipped for smooth movement across the floor. It has a zoom lens. Attached to most newsroom cameras is a prompting device.

Camera and on-air people work in the studio. The studio must be adequately lighted so that the audience can see the talent and the set without unnecessary shadows. The studio is connected electronically to the control room (see Figure 7.10). In the control room, production specialists such as the director, the technical director, graphics, audio and others put the program elements over the air.

Portable electronic newsgathering (ENG) cameras produce a signal that is recorded on some type of recording medium, such as a memory card. Many ENG cameras also provide a wireless signal to the remote truck where the signal can be recorded, broadcast live or streamed online. Recorded material can be dumped into a computer for editing. Video recording formats have evolved over the years but most systems record using an MPEG 2 or MPEG 4 standard. This means the recorded image can be edited on a wide variety of systems.

Some recent ENG cameras can stream video over a 4G/LTE cellular network and this allows the field producer to transfer files back to the station wirelessly where an editor can begin working with the files while the reporter stays to continue coverage.

As we noted earlier in the chapter, the process of editing involves cutting together various video segments to tell the story in a compelling way. The software used in editing allows the operator to assemble the raw stock in virtually any sequence wanted.

FIGURE 7.9 Skilled camera operators can significantly enhance the visual impact of the news program.

FIGURE 7.10 All elements come together in an orchestrated way in the control room, where the director and other staff mix audio and video from many sources into the final product.

Audio can be dubbed separately from video, so a voice can be recorded separately and added over cover shots.

Integrating Technical Tasks

A performer needs to understand how the technical aspects of TV affect him or her. As shown throughout this chapter, an on-air journalist must have a base of technical knowledge, if only for decoding the typical TV script.

As performers become more comfortable with technology, they frequently invent shortcuts and adopt laborsaving devices. Here are two examples.

1. *"Slating" takes in a field report.* Many journalists find that identifying the cuts on the tape makes the editing process much smoother. A slated cut is easier to find and easier to edit: "This is the introduction to the bank robbery story, take two, rolling in five, four, three, two. . . ." This cut would not be hard to extricate from a reel of material. The countdown would also aid in cueing up the tape for the editing process. It is best, incidentally, to avoid saying the number "one," since there's a chance of that part of the countdown winding up on the air. Skip over the number, but give a silent segment in the same rhythm. Start the report where you would ordinarily say "zero."
2. *Carrying and using a small audio recorder.* If your crew does not have editing capability in the field this allows you to capture the interviews and stand-up material that also have been recorded on the video. On the way back to the station, the field journalist can play back the audio, using it as a guide for choosing sound bites.

When time is tight, virtually the entire script can be written in the notebook during the trip back to the studio.

These are just two examples of how an understanding of the technical function can make work simpler for the performer. There are others, and after some trial and error you will certainly invent your own.

RECENT TRENDS IN TV NEWS

Television news has undergone a gradual but significant change. The widespread, sophisticated use of technologies such as light weight, digital field equipment, drones, smaller remote trucks and improved microwave transmission technology let TV news producers air remote broadcasts live from almost anywhere and almost anytime. Smartphone video has improved to such an extent that stations sometimes use this material to supplement their own footage. Add to this a host of new syndication services that focus on the "news you can use" variety of feature material, and even stations in the smallest markets in the country can offer their viewers a level of professionalism undreamed of even five years ago. A wider variety of news stories and features can be presented on a regular basis, and production quality is maintained at the highest levels. Streaming online has become an important add-on service for many news operations. As a result, viewers have come to expect more from both the station and its news staff.

When it comes to actually putting the newscast together, stations today have installed computerized news automation systems that streamline the process of developing and delivering newscasts. Modern computer editing systems by Avid, Sony and others provide a high level of sophistication even in moderately priced workstations. Stations that have invested in such systems have increased flexibility in organizing and arranging stories for broadcast, and producers can update material right up to the time that a story is actually aired. Online feeds make it possible for viewers to follow breaking developments closely.

With this increased capability, stations can more readily attract and hold the attention of their audiences. And the trend in many markets toward devoting more airtime to local newscasts means that the increase in numbers of news features and expanded coverage through live remotes need not necessarily displace harder news stories.

Stations that once received feeds only from the network with which they were affiliated can now look at several sources and choose the feeds that best fit their style and time requirements. Stations can do a better job of reporting on important national stories and can present feature material that would otherwise cost so much to produce that it would not be profitable. Weather-related reporting has expanded thanks to sophisticated computer software and the growing use of weather radar. Sports reporting is also greatly improved by the availability of a better selection of taped highlights from major games and sporting events from all over the country.

It is important for those who want to enter the field of television news to be familiar with these technologies and services and to develop the skills needed to work effectively with them. Let's look at some of these developments a bit more closely.

Live Remote Coverage

Twenty years ago, live broadcasting from a remote location was a novelty for most TV journalists. As stations began to explore the capabilities offered by live remotes, they often seemed to be straining to find uses for the technology. Live reports from the scene of news events usually implies that the event is important enough that it merits live coverage that includes the very latest information. Unfortunately, some events that received such coverage very often just happened to be going on while the news block was on the air. Viewers are often left wondering why a reporter had to be on the scene to report immediately on the latest developments, when the news event was relatively unimportant in comparison with other happenings in the area.

Live reports may often serve only as an expanded stand-up in a news package that features segments taped earlier. Brief on-camera interviews are sometimes included as a part of live remote coverage, but fewer attempts are made to convey the impression that the live presence is necessary to bring viewers the latest developments. Live reporting is used in such situations to add interest and variety.

The concept of using live remotes to provide viewers with the latest developments in an ongoing story can still be important, however, when breaking news is unfolding moment by moment, as when news organizations report on natural disasters like hurricanes. Viewing audiences have become used to live reports and frequently can interpret the significance of the story covered.

Sportscasts also benefit from live coverage. The sports anchor can increase audience interest in the sports segment by reporting from the spring training camp of the local baseball team or from the scene of a major golf tournament in the area. Nothing much changes about the arrangement and variety of stories covered. The lineup is usually pretty much the same as it would have been anyway. The station shows its interest in the event and its capability of keeping up with developments through the live presence at the event. As in news, live interviews from the scene often add a dimension of interest as well.

If reporters are allowed to move off the news set and out into the community, the feeling is conveyed that the station is interested and involved in the community. (One medium-market television station used its live remote capability to move the entire news set out to various community locations for several days while their studio set was rebuilt.) Stations can use this capability to increase audience interest and attract viewers in a particular community.

Although some view this as a questionable compromise, when the practice is used judiciously, little harm is done to the integrity of the news.

In general, on-air talent must be more flexible when dealing with live coverage. The stand-up you deliver live on camera from city hall will be done in one take. If you usually flub the first two takes of your stand-up, you will want to practice getting through your material with no mistakes. Your announcing style on a live report can be more relaxed than is usually the case in a package. The whole idea of the live report is to convey immediacy. If your live report looks well-rehearsed and tightly scripted, you won't come across appropriately.

This doesn't mean you don't need to prepare. If anything, you generally need more preparation for live reports than you otherwise would. You may need to fill additional time or to respond to questions from the anchor in the studio. There is always some uncertainty about how the live segment will unfold. The better you have prepared by becoming completely informed about the situation, the better able you'll be to respond to any unexpected circumstances that may arise while you're on the air.

Syndicated Feature Services

Not too many years ago, most TV news directors depended solely on the network they were affiliated with to provide feeds of news events that took place outside their coverage area. The same was true for sports highlights needed for the local sports segment. Today, though, stations have available to them several news feeds that can be picked up and used by anyone who has a couple of satellite dishes to receive them. First, many television stations are now owned by a large conglomerate allowing news operations to share video and reporters. Also, services like CNN's Newsource provide global coverage of news events and more stories each day than some stations can even look at. These services provide affiliates and independents a wide variety of news feeds supplied by stations from virtually everywhere in the country.

CNN offers its two hundred affiliates 24-hour service. Its sole product is news, so it need not interrupt other programming to provide live coverage of breaking news. Affiliates may broadcast news-breaking special reports as they occur. Thus CNN affiliates were able to tap into live reports during the mass exodus of refugees from the war-torn regions of the Middle East. During the continuing civil war in Iran, stations carried live reports from CNN reporters. Affiliate stations are allowed to excerpt package features from *Headline News* to carry in local news programs.

Most networks, the Associated Press (AP), and CNN Newsource are contract news services that provide a daily series of news feeds including national and international breaking stories, features on topics such as medical and science news, nutrition and women's issues, and sports highlights. This allows local news directors to integrate this material into local newscasts, using local announcers for voice-overs and intros.

TV news directors also have available to them a large selection of syndicated feature material that can be integrated into newscasts in ways that give viewers the impression that the segments were produced locally. Products such as *Consumer Reports TV News*, produced using the resources of the Consumers' Union (which puts out *Consumer Reports* magazine) provide stations with short features several times a week.

Typical syndicated packages run about 90 seconds, and stations receive three features a week. Depending on market size, features might cost a station anywhere from $3,000 a year to $40,000. The packages usually feature a split-track audio, which allows the station to use its own talent to narrate the piece rather than using talent of the original producers. This conveys the impression that the reports are produced locally.

Many stations find that using syndicated feature material lets them cover specialized news beats, such as business reports and medical news, without the considerable expense of producing the material themselves. According to Walter Gilbride, a syndicator of news features, many news directors find that using such material frees up their own reporters and resources to do a better job of reporting local features.

Some stations use the syndicated material as the foundation for five-day-a-week segments on a particular topic, such as health or money matters. The voice of the reporter is used in the syndicated material and the station's own reports (usually featuring a local angle on the general topic) are produced by the same reporter. Often, by the way, that local reporter is a member of the profession most closely related to the topic area covered in the reports. A local doctor is often used as the reporter on feature segments about medical topics, for example. If the syndicated material is integrated smoothly, and local production quality is matched to that of the syndicated material, the audience will have the impression that the station produces all five reports each week.

The increased use of syndicated feature material and satellite and online news feeds requires reporters to be able to mesh effectively with the styles of those who produce the syndicated packages. In hiring, this may mean that news directors will be looking for more generic styles for some slots than they might look for in others. The announcer whose style seems generally reminiscent of news reporters may be more useful in some circumstances than a reporter with a distinctly individual style. In contrast, some openings in television news may require reporters with specialized knowledge and with expertise in specific areas. Rather than emphasizing on-air talent, for example, a station may want to fill a slot that covers a distinctive beat such as crime reporting, politics or consumer affairs.

Another consideration for on-air talent when working with syndicated feature material is that the appeal of the feature material is its usefulness to viewers. The material itself is of paramount importance. The role of talent in such circumstances is to localize and smooth out the presentation of the material but not necessarily to draw attention to the reporter.

Preparing for the Modern Marketplace

To prepare for the changing requirements for on-air talent in television news, try to become adept at a variety of styles. Take the time to watch the news reporters on as many different stations as you can. Take note of both the differences and similarities. See if you can categorize various newspeople by the styles they use. Do styles change for various types of reporting—a feature on how high school students choose a college, for example, compared with a news report about citizens who oppose the construction of a landfill near their housing development? Can you tell what elements of rate, inflection, energy, and facial expression are responsible for defining the style? Through close observation of many different newspeople and styles of presentation, you'll begin to know how to adapt your own delivery to create different styles.

The next step is to practice the different styles. Write scripts of your own that are representative of different assignments you have noticed in your analyses of various TV news operations. Practice the scripts using various styles of delivery. Notice how inappropriate some scripts sound when they don't fit the news story. Work on nuances of inflection and rate that make the delivery particularly effective.

Beware of overdoing it, though. Remember you are trying to draw the viewer's attention to the story, not to you. Get feedback on your performances from others. Don't just go to professors or other broadcasting students—try to find people who are *not* familiar with the devices you're using. They will be in a better position to tell you how you might be coming across to the average viewer.

In Chapter 12, when we talk about ways to prepare for your first broadcasting job, we stress the importance of broadening your academic background beyond the field of communications or journalism. Syndicator Walter Gilbride, who has studied television news operations all over the country, recommends that students get a solid educational background in areas that might be helpful in reporting on specialized areas. Gilbride says that news reporters trying to report on complex topics such as AIDS or personal finance, often make fundamental mistakes that could have been avoided if the reporter had some formal education in the area. For those interested in crime reporting, for example, one approach might be to major in communications or journalism as an undergraduate and go on for a master's degree in criminology. Other experts recommend a double major as an undergraduate.

Newsroom Automation

One of the most dramatic advances in television news in recent years is the development of computerized newsroom systems. With sophisticated computer hardware, running specially designed software programs, modern television newsrooms can streamline all their news functions in ways that add speed and quality to news coverage.

State-of-the-art digital newsroom software provides word processing, sorting and filing of service material, a scriptwriting format program, a rundown program that will automatically sequence and update the order of stories, and an archiving capability for keeping stories that have already aired. These end-to-end systems provide both newsroom automation capability along with the ability to distribute to multiple platforms. Such software has many advantages. For the TV station, breaking news can be updated instantly without the need to laboriously refigure how the update affects the timing on the local show. Producers can instantly check on the status of any story and find out if it is ready to go on the air. With some software programs, tapes can be controlled automatically.

The impact of computerized newsrooms on on-air talent is great. The modern television newsroom requires a familiarity with computers. Basic operations are not difficult to master. If you can operate word processing systems and understand how computers control systems, you will be in the best position to make the latest technology function to enhance the station's competitive standing.

On-air talent must be adaptable and ready to make changes in stories right up to the last possible moment before air. Reporters have to follow developments on breaking stories more closely and be prepared to update them when new information becomes available. It may be necessary to update copy many times before the story actually hits the air. Anchors must be ready for last-minute changes to the story rundown. They must be able to cope with last-minute script changes while maintaining their professional manner on camera. Reporters need to ensure they are current for both station and online dissemination.

For producers and news directors, computer automation means that it is easier to assemble the news. It is simple to determine the status of the newscast at any point in time, and to monitor the progress of individual stories as they are being written. With this technology, people responsible for putting the newscast together will be expected to provide more timely stories than in the past. To do so, they will need to closely monitor reporters and news crews and follow the progress of breaking stories that are subject to change. In simplifying the physical assembly of the newscast, computer automation also demands more minute-to-the-minute decision making on the part of news executives.

The skills you will need to cope with automation include good journalistic judgment and computer literacy. A pleasant appearance and the ability to read copy smoothly will not take anyone far in television news. People who want an on-the-air news position increasingly need to provide a certain degree of technical capability in addition to a solid on-air presence.

APPEARANCE

It goes without saying that good appearance helps a television news performer. In fact, news requires exact attention to certain aspects of your appearance because your credibility as a news person is involved. The following brief guidelines are particularly helpful for newspeople.

Clothing and Hair

For men, the choice of clothing is really not an issue. New anchors wear a virtual uniform of suit or sports jacket and tie. Women have a wider choice, but most newswomen stick to simple clothes with basic lines. For field reporters, simple and durable clothes are an advantage because the afternoon's story may involve slogging through a potato field. More and more, we see reporters wearing a jacket or windbreaker with the station's logo. Box 7.3 gives some basic tips for achieving a good appearance.

Beware of a tendency to dress inappropriately for the role of a newsperson. Steven Osborne, former news director of WOR-TV in New York (now WWOR-TV in New Jersey), says that he's noticed a trend among some television newspeople to present themselves as fashion plates. "They should remember that they are newspeople, not aristocracy," he says. High salaries and their position as celebrities in the community often provide an affluent lifestyle for newspeople, but on the air they should not draw attention to their socioeconomic status through their appearance, says Osborne. "Clothes shouldn't say 'Look at me—I can afford nice clothes.' "

He notes that too many of today's television newspeople drip heavy jewelry or wear expensive clothes when covering stories on location. He recommends simplicity when it comes to clothing. Men should avoid heavy plaids in coats. Ties should have relatively simple patterns. Women should watch out for loud patterns and outlandish colors. Hairstyles on women should be conservative, not flashy. Nora O'Donnell on *CBS This Morning* is an example of a stylish news anchor.

Another crucial tip is to *get a good haircut!* Find a barber or stylist who will work with you to get the style you want, and request the same person for every visit. Frequently, television stations will trade out advertising for haircuts at a particular salon.

Men often do not pay much attention to their hair, and it shows. To improve the neatness of your hair dramatically, get it cut every 2 to 4 weeks. One warning: tell your regular barber that you will be getting frequent cuts and that you want a relatively *small* amount of hair taken off each time.

Men also usually do not experiment with styles as much as women and do not receive as much guidance from stylists. Experiment with different lengths and partings to show off your best features and to camouflage poor features. Box 7.4 provides some hair tips for both men and women.

Makeup

Professional makeup kits are available at many television facilities. These provide talcum-based makeup in stick or cake form. Makeup experts also use a variety of special effects to add wrinkles, paste on facial hair, or make a character appear threatening. For most television applications, you won't need the type of theatrical makeup used to create characters in acted presentations.

You'll probably be content with:

1. *A compact containing an oil-absorbing makeup.* The makeup should be a shade darker than your normal skin tone. For most work, you don't need special theatrical makeup; the stuff available from the drugstore will do just fine. Make sure to apply it in short, downward strokes. Don't smear it when applying. The advantage of a compact, by the way, is that it can easily be used in the field and carried in your pocket or bag.
2. *Eyebrow pencil.* Eyebrows are expressive features, but some people have wispy or very light eyebrows. An eyebrow pencil or mascara brush is a useful tool for both men and women.

Don't be afraid to experiment. Try different types of makeup and see what works best for you. Remember, though, the final criterion in judging how well it works is not how you look in the mirror, but on the monitor.

> ### BOX 7.3 **Guidelines For Dressing Well on the Air**
>
> 1. *Avoid complex patterns.* Herringbones can cause a wavy effect, especially when photographed by older cameras.
> 2. *Check with your station engineer regarding the chroma key color.* A chroma key is one device used to remove a background from a TV scene and insert a new image, usually a slide behind the newscaster. In modern facilities, the clothes versus chroma-key problem is not serious, but older gear may be insufficiently selective as to which shade of blue, for instance, it chooses to eliminate. If your clothes are too close to the chroma key color, they may be replaced with the keyed image.
> 3. *Avoid stiff clothing.* Men seated at news desks have a particular problem with stiff-woven jackets bunching up behind the neck. A tailor can take out the "roll" in the upper back and keep the collar down.
> 4. *Make sure clothing is not restrictive.* Tight European-fit double-breasted jackets are not a good choice for a weather reporter who has to move and gesture.
> 5. *Avoid too masculine a look in women's clothes.* There was a time when women entering the field felt it necessary to wear man-tailored clothes. Those times are pretty well past, but simple women's clothes are still advisable. Frills and bows have a habit of coming out of place and can also be distracting to the viewer.
> 6. *Be conscious of what your clothing looks like from the rear or side.* The camera may occasionally catch a view of you from an off-angle. Men, be sure your jacket covers your middle when you sit.
> 7. *Avoid extreme cuts of any clothes.* Although bizarre or unusual clothes may build an image for an actor, newscasters have never gained recognition for their style of dress, except for the very low-key style represented by the late Peter Jennings. Jennings dressed conservatively and with a European flair, a very subtle differentiation from other newscasters.
> 8. *Avoid gaudy jewelry.* The camera has a tendency to emphasize and, in both a literal and a figurative way, to magnify. A large pair of earrings may look grotesque on the air.
> 9. *Remember that cameras also magnify girth.* If you need to lose weight, lose it now, before cutting audition tapes. If you have a blocky appearance, concentrate on clothes that lessen that impression. Women can do especially well with V-necks. Stocky men must avoid checks, blocks, or any lateral design element. Stick to plain colors or vertical pinstripes.

Skin, Teeth, and Eyes

Developing a skin care regimen is a healthy idea for both men and women. In lieu of experimenting with various preparations to clear up skin problems, visit a professional. Dermatologists can frequently clear up long-standing problems that have not responded to inexpert trial and error.

Teeth deserve the same special attention. As you will notice from a quick scan of local channels, TV newspeople hardly ever have bad teeth. A cosmetic tooth problem could cripple your on-air career, so attend to those conditions now. Invisible braces, teeth whitening and bonding can correct a variety of problems.

Eyeglasses may become part of a newsperson's style, but in general they are distractions, another barrier to contact between the news reader and the viewer. That is why many on-air people opt for contact lenses. Modern lenses are easy to adapt to and even people with moderate astigmatism can be fitted with contacts. In addition, soft and gas-permeable lenses are more comfortable than the old-style hard contact lenses.

The major drawback to contact lenses is the difficulty many people encounter in adjusting to them. Yes, it is difficult to adjust to foreign objects in your eye, and it may take months or a year to become comfortable with the idea of wearing contacts and *not wearing glasses*. If you cannot see well without glasses, it would be worthwhile to investigate this option.

Image

All these appearance factors add up to that semi-tangible concept of an image. Although there is no prescription for a proper image, do weigh various appearance factors and make sure they don't work against you. A good appearance is important. You need not be strikingly beautiful, nor particularly good looking, but you must be well groomed and have a generally attractive appearance as a news performer.

BOX 7.4 Style Your Hair to Enhance Your Appearance

- Short hair makes weak facial features seem stronger.
- Long hair camouflages too-strong features.
- Long hair in back emphasizes the jawline and can make up for a weak jaw area.
- Attention can be drawn away from a large nose by hair that projects higher on the head and farther out from the forehead.
- Parting the hair higher (closer to the center of the head) visually narrows the face. Parting hair closer to the temples widens the face.
- A lock of hair down on the forehead breaks up a too-wide or too high forehead appearance.
- People with very round faces should avoid very short hair.

Remember, too, that image and credibility are much more than simple matters of cosmetics. Physical impressiveness will never compensate for a lack of professional or intellectual depth.

SUMMARY

Television reporters are journalists as well as performers. TV news is a team effort, and many people are involved in coverage of news events. The basic components of a TV news organization are news administration, news production, and the gathering and reporting of news.

The typical television newscast has evolved over the years. In the early days of television, the newscast was little more than an audio newscast with a picture of the reader. Today, many different program elements are integrated into the newscast. Gathering and assembling news events for a TV newscast involves teamwork, quick decisions, and hustling by reporters and crews. In addition, news and production people must be flexible because the typical television newscast is often being put together seconds before airtime.

Television field reporting requires good judgment and the ability to work quickly. The field reporter must be able to interview with skill and write, memorize, and record copy on camera. Other duties of the field reporter may include directing the activities of the camera operator and dealing with crowds.

Television news delivery involves proper use of phrasing and pace, as well as the expression of emotion and interest. News reporters must project an aura of credibility. Contact with the viewer is enhanced by smooth use of prompting devices and good physical eye contact with the camera. Working to the camera is an important part of TV news delivery, and in the studio it involves making frequent transitions from camera to camera and following the orders of a floor director. The news reporter must be aware of tally lights and must realize that the relative closeness of the shot will change when the director changes cameras. Field reporters work in a variety of conditions and must be prepared to ad-lib live when reporting.

Ad-libbing is an extremely important skill for the newsperson. A reporter must be certain to ad-lib in words and phrases that are factual and are not subject to misinterpretation. The same techniques used in basic announcing are applied to news ad-libbing.

Television news involves working within technical constraints and working with equipment. Equipment includes cameras, prompting devices, and the studio and control room in general. Modern digital technology has enhanced newsgathering.

Many TV stations use live reports from the scene of news events. There is also increased use of syndicated feature material and footage obtained via drones, smartphones and online, some of which is localized by using a local announcer as the reporter. Most newsrooms are automated with computers that make it possible to update stories right up to the moment they are aired.

The TV news announcer should understand the technical aspects of the field well enough to take advantage of them in preparing for his or her performance. Slating cuts to keep track of edit points and using a portable audio recorder are two examples of integrating technology into one's work habits.

Television news requires particular standards of appearance. Part of being a successful news reporter is paying attention to clothing, hair, skin, and teeth. Contact lenses are often useful. All the factors of appearance and performance add up to the newsperson's image. However, success in TV news is not a matter of cosmetics. You must be a first-rate journalist and a competent performer.

EXERCISES

1. Design and execute a mock-up newscast. This is an ambitious three-day project, but worthwhile if you have the time and facilities.

    Day 1: Elect or ask your instructor to appoint a news director, who will appoint

        a. The head of production for the class news department
        b. The head writer
        c. The assignment editor

    Those three people will then choose classmates to work under their direction. You will need approximately 25 percent of the class working in production, 50 percent in writing, and 25 percent as on-air people. The assignment editor will choose on-air people. The duties are as follows:

    - *Production people* will design the newscast with whatever equipment they have available. If there is no video equipment, the newscast will be presented to an audience. Production people will determine the construction of the set, placement of cameras, and so on.
    - *Writers* will each decide on one story, preferably an easily done local story. The stories will be assembled in the next class session. Each story must be no longer than one minute when read.
    - *On-air people* will file some of these stories as taped reports, if equipment is available, and the two anchors will coordinate the newscast.

    Day 2: The news director and all three department heads will meet to decide story assignments and other production details. If remote gear is not available, reports will be delivered directly to the camera or audience during the newscast.

    Day 3: Now prepare the final lineup and assemble the script; this must be done in less than 15 minutes. The newscast itself is to be 20 minutes long, and must start *exactly* 15 minutes after the start of class.

This set of guidelines is intentionally open-ended. The duties and time frames must be adapted to circumstances in class. Also, particular sequences and responsibilities are not specified because in an actual TV news situation, getting organized and figuring out who will do what, and when and how it will be done, is half the battle.

In this exercise, *teams* will have to decide what can be done and what resources can be allocated, all within a time limit. If you are selected to work on the air, you will certainly find that the backup and cooperation you receive go a long way in determining how good you look on air.

2. Do the following exercise, strictly to time. It is a good one to do during class and in front of other class members.

Your instructor will clip a daily newspaper and assign stories to class members. You will have 10 minutes, no more and no less, to study the story and take as many notes as you can fit on one side of a 3-by-5 index card. Your goal is to ad-lib a 1-minute report before the class, with each class member giving a report according to random selection. If facilities allow, tape the reports.

Maintain as much eye contact as possible. *Hint:* Copious notes crammed on the 3-by-5 card will not necessarily be as helpful as a concise outline.

3. Choose a network or well-known local news reporter for each of the following hypothetical assignments. Pick the person you believe could do the best possible job and explain why in one or two paragraphs. Specify what qualities of this reporter would make him or her the best choice for the job.

a. A host for an hour-long documentary on the stock market. Technical information must be made interesting to a wide audience.

b. A host for a morning news/entertainment program in an industrial city where audience research shows that many of the workers arise at 5 a.m. and want a show and host to brighten their day.

c. A reporter for a 10-minute segment on the plight of the homeless in New York City.

d. A reporter to do a 5-minute feature on inflatable furniture.

e. A host for a 15-minute feature on fine wines.

f. A reporter to confront a tough big-city mayor on charges of corruption in municipal government.

g. An anchor to handle the first reports of possible outbreak of a war involving the United States. You would likely want someone adept at presenting breaking information, someone who inspires confidence and remains calm under pressure.

h. An interviewer to talk to the mother of a servicewoman killed in one of the initial skirmishes of the war.

The Craft of Interviewing

Ask a simple question and get an answer. It seems simple enough to do.

But when you're a journalist, getting the right answer is more complicated than it might seem.

Whether you're talking about print journalism or radio or television, the interviewer's skill can spell the difference between a news report that actually contains news and one that merely fills space or time. Interviews can be tough. Some interview subjects are extremely nervous on camera. Some are unresponsive or evasive. Others talk only about their own specific interests no matter what question is asked. To add to the pressure, the broadcast newsperson often works under rigid time and technical constraints. Regardless of the obstacles, though, you as a reporter are charged with the task of coming up with an interview that is logical, informative, and interesting.

The focus of this chapter is to explore and demonstrate the principles and techniques that will help you conduct an effective interview. Whether the interview forms the basis for television news, a radio talk format, or an entire program in which a single guest is the subject of an extended interview on a variety of subjects, a succession of pat, bland questions will not provide much useful and lively information. Successful interviewing involves three steps:

1. Determining the type of interview and adjusting the approach accordingly.
2. Preparing for the interview, which involves selecting questions and topics, narrowing the topic for a logical discussion, prescreening guests, and doing a good deal of homework.
3. Executing the interview, which entails proper attention to the logistics of an interview, making it flow logically, and avoiding major pitfalls.

TYPES OF INTERVIEWS

A broadcast interview is not always conducted in a comfortable chair in an air-conditioned studio. With the advent of modern television gear, television on-air personnel find themselves in a wide variety of situations, which boil down to two basic types: the **actuality interview** and the **studio interview.**

The actuality interview is generally a straightforward attempt at obtaining information. The studio interview can be of several varieties, ranging from brief personality interviews to in-depth discussions of serious and complex topics.

Actuality Interview

An **actuality** is a response or statement from a newsmaker, which is typically edited and used in another format, such as the "package" described previously, or used in a newscast after an anchor's introduction.

The key to successful actuality interviewing is obtaining a response in a form that *can* be edited out and used, perhaps, in a 90-second report. You're looking for short, succinct answers, so the way you phrase each question is important. Often, the actuality interview is conducted on the scene of a news event with a hand-held microphone (Figure 8.1).

Ways to devise questions are suggested throughout this chapter.

Studio Interview

Although parts of an interview conducted in the studio may be used as actuality, most studio interviews are meant to be broadcast in full, with a definite beginning, middle, and end.

Generally a specific amount of time is allotted for a studio interview, but usually there is more latitude in time and content than is the case for the actuality interview.

Dealing gracefully with time restrictions is one of the most difficult aspects of interviewing. An interview to be edited can run to virtually any length, but a talk show type of interview must make its point and wrap up when the clock (and the director) says so. This means that pacing within the interview must conform to the time frame. A half-hour interview should not reach an emotional peak in the first 5 minutes and coast downhill from there. Likewise, important questions should not be left unanswered at 28 minutes into the program.

The broadest categories of studio interviews are the personality type and the issue type.

- The *personality interview* explores the life or career of an important or well-known individual. Entertainment value comes into consideration here. In most cases, the interviewer is expected to keep the session reasonably light and engaging.
- In the *issue interview,* the personalities of the guest and host are less in focus than is the topic at hand. The interviewer, generally a program host, is expected to highlight various points of view and present them fairly. In-depth analysis and discussion are frequently used in the issue interview.

FIGURE 8.1 The actuality interview is generally a short opportunity to get a meaningful response, so you want to make the most of it.

How the Type of Interview Affects Style

Keep the foregoing distinctions in mind because style and execution of the interview differ for each type. The elements are not mutually exclusive, of course, for there certainly can be entertainment in a talk-show presentation of an in-depth analysis of a serious topic. But if discussion of a serious topic is too flip, the results can be offensive.

Likewise, the interviewer will not want to adopt for an issue interview the same style that would be used in an actuality interview. Have you ever watched a half-hour talk show that seemed to consist of nothing more than an endless, hypnotic interrogation? What you were seeing was a host who asked for a specific fact or reaction but neglected to ask the guest to *discuss* the issue and *analyze its meaning*. The chance to discuss and analyze is the main strength of the studio interview, and failing to take advantage of it can lead to an awkward and boring product. Listening carefully to responses can help you develop relevant follow-up questions.

Regardless of the type of interview, the goal is the same: to obtain interesting, relevant, and provocative responses. Some factors will be out of your control, but the most important aspect is your responsibility: you must adequately prepare for the interview.

Preparing for the Interview

Much of the interviewing you will do is off-camera/off-mic interviewing. Although at times the interviewer barges in with lights burning and cameras rolling, most interviews are set up well in advance, and information has been gathered before the videotapes or audiotapes roll. The information-gathering process might involve calling the interviewee and putting together some basic facts before inviting him or her to the station for a studio interview. If it is someone who holds a political office you will probably want to research the issues that faced that person when she ran for that office.

> **Preparing Questions.** How much information to gather before turning on the cameras or mics is a judgment call. On one hand, too little preparation before the tape rolls can result in a clumsy session, and it will be obvious to the audience that it was thrown together at the last minute. At the other extreme, too much advance preparation can result in a "flat" interview over the air. The interviewee who is responding to the same set of questions for the second or third time may sound as if he or she is being very patient with a slightly stupid interviewer.

Also, too-extensive preparation can put guests on guard, giving them a chance to prepare evasive responses to questions they'd rather not answer.

There is one other important point. Many people will be reluctant to give you the most mundane information when you start the conversation with microphone in hand. Some subtle, low-pressure questioning in a conversational tone, done off-mic or off-camera, often elicits a much better response for the air. One additional advantage of preparatory information gathering is that guests are very hard put to omit or refuse to comment on information they have already given to you or confirmed before the tapes rolled.

> **Importance of Research.** Research is an important factor in interview preparation. An interviewer's lack of knowledge is usually very apparent once the conversation starts.

Never let cockiness and overconfidence seduce you into walking into an interview unprepared. Preparation should always be a priority for two major reasons, one obvious and one not so obvious:

1. You can conduct a much more intelligent interview by being well informed.
2. You can fulfill your responsibilities to management, your audience, and yourself by not letting outrageous statements slip by unchallenged.

For example, let's say you are a talk-show host and your guest, the leader of a neighborhood group, assails the city for not providing enough low-income housing. After the program airs, you receive an angry call from a city official who informs you that there have been low-income units sitting vacant for months. This situation was highlighted at the city council meeting last week. It made all the papers. Where were you?

Some basic research would have allowed you to question your guest more closely, challenging the assertion by citing the recent council discussion.

Lack of preparation in the following areas can also lead to on-air gaffes or unnecessarily dull interviews:

1. *Not knowing the political opinions of your guest.* Politics color responses, and if you do not know a guest's politics you will have trouble filtering out the party line. Or you might fail to follow up on an important statement by not realizing when a politician has opposed the party line.
2. *Not knowing or not completely understanding the vested interests of your guest.* For example, if your guest is employed by an organization or lobbying group to promote a particular product or belief, it is your obligation to know this and point it out to the audience. It is also important to find out if a politician has any personal interest in a particular piece of legislation, or what boards of directors a banker serves on. Knowing the background of, and reasons for, a guest's position on a subject is vital to an open, complete interview. Only careful questioning and research in advance will determine whether the guest is an impartial observer or a paid spokesperson. Having incomplete information in this respect is, in effect, a distortion in itself.

Research Material and Resources. One good way to prepare for an interview is to check through newspaper or magazine clippings on the topic, and the best place to start is with a newspaper database. While there are professional databases available, it's likely that you'll be able to find enough basic information on Google News or searchable websites of news organizations, including local newspapers and other news organizations.

Another avenue for a local search is simply to ask questions of co-workers, friends, and neighbors. You cannot accept everything they tell you as a fact, but the leads you gather can be useful in opening other areas of research.

Writers of nonfiction, who use this technique extensively, gather a great deal of material just by continually broaching a subject among various groups, even at cocktail parties. It is often surprising how a casual conversation can steer you to an appropriate resource or helpful individual.

Selecting a Guest and Topic. One final note concerning research and preparation: the success of an interview, especially a studio interview, depends on selecting a guest and a reasonable narrowing of the topic.

By prescreening guests, you can sometimes avoid having to deal on the air with someone who is too nervous or obstinate to give a productive interview.

Unfortunately, there are no foolproof predictors of a guest's performance. Oddly, the guests who initially, off-camera or off-mic, appear to be the most blasé about the prospects of being interviewed are often the ones who "freeze up." Your initial dealings with a prospective guest may lead you to believe that he or she either is not interested enough to give an enthusiastic interview, or is covering fright by adopting an uncaring attitude. If this happens, you will have to work harder at making the guest feel comfortable.

You might boost the guest's ego by explaining how pleased you are that someone of his or her stature or knowledge of the subject has agreed to be interviewed. Try to make the reticent guest more self-confident.

One way to avoid trouble is to put the guest at ease and explain what is going to happen during the interview. This is especially appropriate for TV talk shows, where there is a great deal of motion on the set, and some noise also.

The setting probably is unfamiliar to your guest and is likely to be perceived as threatening. Remember, the guest who has not been briefed may not understand what's going on. It's not unusual for a guest to turn and stare at the wild gesticulations of a floor manager who's trying to get your attention. Guests have been known to freeze in panic as a camera ominously slides toward them.

Think about it from your guests' standpoint. Explain, while you are preparing to go on the air that there is a great deal of activity in a television studio, but none of it need concern them. Let guests know that they should not look at the monitor, and warn them specifically that cameras may move. Remember that radio can be intimidating to guests, too, and a pre-air orientation can be calming to an interviewee. A good time to reinforce the importance of the interview is when you meet with the guest just before the actual recording or airing of the program.

Creating a personal relationship is useful in allowing the guest to understand that you value her or his time. Make it known that you will respect her or his point of view, even though you may disagree with that viewpoint. These discussions should also serve as a vehicle for you to narrow the topic. Often, a guest will press you for a specific list of the questions you plan to ask. As suggested earlier, giving out a list of questions before airtime is not a good idea. First, the guest may respond with rehearsed, flat answers. Second, if the guest assumes that these are the *only* questions to be covered, he or she may balk at any question that was not on the list.

To lay the groundwork for the interview, however, a definition of the areas to be discussed is necessary. For example, your initial off-camera/off-mic discussion with a state economic development official may prompt you to narrow the topic to explore the revitalization of your city's downtown area, rather than a shotgun-type discussion of the official's office and what it does.

CONDUCTING THE INTERVIEW

A successfully executed interview is usually the result of a three-pronged effort to:

1. Get an interview that is appropriate for the format or intended use, also making sure that the topic is of interest to the target audience.
2. Work effectively within technical limitations (such as time limits) and performance considerations (such as opening and closing the show, keeping the interview flowing, and making the program run smoothly).
3. Elicit responsive answers from the interviewee.

Let's examine these principles of interview execution in detail.

Appropriateness of the Interview

News interviewers are frequently sent out to obtain a specific fact ("What will next year's tax rate be?") or reaction ("What is your opinion about the sentence given to the defendant?"). Often the fact or reaction is edited down into a short piece that can be inserted into a newscast.

Technical and Performance Considerations

An interview is not a natural situation, although a skilled broadcaster can make it appear so. If an excellent interview has the character of a conversation in the host's living room, it is because the host is skilled in working within the technical limitations of the TV or radio facility and equipment.

The graceful wrap-up that appears so simple and easy is probably a product of preparation, experience, and instinct.

Following are some suggestions on ways to work within the confines of broadcast structure and format and to deliver a professional-appearing performance.

Specific techniques of the question-and-answer aspects of the interview itself are discussed later in this chapter.

Preparing Introductions and Closings

Do not put too much faith in your ad-libbing abilities; you can ruin an otherwise good talk show by flubbing the beginning or the end. On a talk show, the host is responsible for setting the scene properly. Four elements should be part of an opening: 1. What the topic is; 2. Who the guest is; 3. Why the guest is worth listening to; 4. *Why the audience should care about the topic.*

The final factor is vital. A show on economics might be of little interest to viewers or listeners unless you explain that the prime rate will determine whether they can buy new houses. A show on food additives won't have much appeal unless you specify that certain additives, which may be harmful, may be in the food your audience and your audience's family will eat for dinner. It is generally good practice to write notes on the openings and closings and use them for reference.

Preparing Questions and Follow-Up

Prepare questions, but don't be a slave to your list. Preparing questions helps to focus your own thinking about the thrust of the interview. A prepared list can be a lifesaver when an unresponsive guest fails to give answers that lead into other questions. A list of prepared questions is useful, but it should not be the end-all of the interview.

Here is an excerpt from an actual interview.

Interviewer:	Mr. _____, what do you think of the majority leader's actions?
State Representative:	To be honest, it makes me feel ashamed of the whole system. This sort of thing just takes the heart out of you, and I don't feel right associating with the system. I don't think I'm going to run for reelection.
Interviewer:	Now, what do you think of the chances for a tax hike next year?

This interviewer stuck to a prepared list to the point of ignoring an unexpected answer and managed to miss a major story. Always listen to the answers to your questions and follow up when appropriate.

Keeping Audience Attention

A major responsibility of an interviewer, of course, is to keep the audience from tuning out. Lack of interesting material is a major culprit, but distractions also steal the audience's interest from the subject at hand. See Box 8.1 for some suggestions for avoiding distractions and keeping the viewers' and listeners' interest levels high.

BOX 8.1 Suggestions For Holding Your Audience

1. *Don't make meaningless noises.* You might say "uh-huh" 30 times in a normal conversation, but it appears downright silly on the air.
   "I see," "yes," "right," and "you know" are other verbal tics to be avoided.
2. *Fill in your listeners and viewers from time to time.* The first piece of advice usually offered to play-by-play sports announcers is "Give the score, because if the listener doesn't know the score, you're not doing your job." The same advice, to a lesser degree, goes for talk

BOX 8.1 (continued)

show hosts. The audience won't always know exactly what the interview is about if they tuned in late or weren't paying attention, and it is up to you to fill them in, perhaps after a commercial: "We're back with Dr. Frank Adams, who is telling us how to get in shape for spring sports. . . ." That's all it takes.

3. *Stick to the subject.* If you are talking to a fire chief about ways to prevent house fires, you do not want to get into an extended dialogue about the social problems that cause arson. Some examination of that issue is important, and probably necessary, but it should not take over the show. Be particularly wary of guests who wander into controversial areas that are not within the boundaries of their expertise.

4. *Establish the guest's qualifications, and reaffirm them from time to time.* The audience wants to know why they should bother listening to your guest: "We're talking about poison prevention with Dr. Janice Jones, who is a toxicologist, a specialist in the study of poisons, and is head of University Hospital's Poison Control Center. . . ."

5. *Don't assume too much knowledge by the audience.* If you are conducting an interview about vacation travel, remember that a good share of your audience may never have been on an airplane. Likewise, don't assume that every viewer or listener has an up-to-date knowledge of current events.

If the discussion starts at a level beyond the knowledge of a good share of your audience, you will lose the attention of many listeners and viewers. Set the groundwork simply and completely, giving information that will be obvious to some members of your audience but not to others.

If the conversation gets complicated ask for clarification. Don't try to steal the show from your guest. Remember, the audience is listening and watching because of the guest, not because of you.

FIGURE 8.2 Larry King, often regarded as one of the best interviewers in the history of broadcast media, was non-confrontational but not afraid to ask direct questions of the powerful—in this case, Russian leader Vladimir Putin. 8 September 2000.

Source: Presidential Press and Information Office, http://www.kremlin.ru/eng/text/images/127086.shtml.

BOX 8.1 *(continued)*

If you were the star, the station wouldn't bother cluttering up the set with interviewees.

And never forget that an interview is a conversation. While he is now largely retired, you can find video of Larry King in abundance on YouTube and other video channels. King is regarded by many as one of the finest broadcast interviewers in history. Watch King and note how he makes every interview a dialogue, a back-and-forth, even when the dialogue is with a powerful subject (Figure 8.2)

King never attempts to be the "star" of the show. Instead, he draws out the unique talents and perspectives of his guests.

Dealing with Time Restrictions

One of the most awkward aspects of a talk show format is dealing with the clock. A good segment can be spoiled by having to cut off a guest in midsentence with a frantic closing.

One of the most frequent questions guests ask before going on the air is how they will know when to stop talking. Try telling your guest, "Just watch me. You'll know when it's time to wrap up." You usually don't have to do anything special; having the guest tuned into your body language cues is often enough. After all, can't you tell when someone is in a hurry, regardless of whether that person states it verbally? If you find that the subliminal approach doesn't work, and you are having trouble getting out of the show in time for commercials or the program end, you may elect to set up some sort of cue with guests.

Using Your Guests' Talents

Although the principle of taking advantage of a guest's talent sounds obvious, many interviewers have become infatuated with the technique of asking comedians about the tragic aspects of their lives. A little of this is all right, but a little also goes a long way. Be sure to give your funny guest an opportunity to be funny. The audience expects this and will, by and large, be disappointed if it doesn't happen.

Eliciting Responsive Answers

Despite the considerable overlap between the performance considerations just discussed and the specific techniques of questioning discussed next, it is productive to concentrate on some of the methods used by interviewers to obtain logical, reasonable, and useful responses. Here are some principles and their applications.

> **Avoiding Dead-End Questions.** Sometimes an interview can grind to a halt because the questions just don't lend themselves to lively conversation. There are two main methods of preventing this from happening.

1. *Avoid asking questions that can result in yes or no answers.* Instead of saying, "I gather you don't think this is fair?" try asking, "What do you think is unfair about the situation?" A yes-or-no question may be very useful, however, if you are trying to pin down a guest who is being evasive.
2. *Avoid obvious questions, and avoid obscure questions.* Do not ask a politician who has lost an election if he or she is disappointed. On the other end of the scale, do not start off an interview by quizzing a scientist on the molecular structure of a high-performance ceramic, unless you are doing an in-house presentation geared for people who have a technical understanding of the subject.

Getting a Complete Answer. Often, through accident or intent, an interviewee fails to provide an entire answer, or leaves an issue hanging. The hallmark of a skilled interviewer, however, is the ability to elicit complete answers to his or her questions. This often involves waiting for an answer to be completed or, at the end of a response, stating that the question hasn't been answered completely. To get a complete answer, use the following techniques.

1. *Wait out a noncommunicative interviewee.* Some people might not be willing to give complete answers, but some are simply terse and shortspoken.

   When you need a more complete answer, just keep looking at the interviewee. He or she will get the message that more is expected.

   If the interviewee is trying to evade giving a full answer, he or she may just stare back at you—but that is an answer in itself. Usually, though, interviewees will give in before you will.

2. *Point out that you are not getting an answer, and repeat the question.*

   Never be afraid to say, "Excuse me, Senator, but that's not what I was asking. My question is . . . " Many public figures are experts at avoiding unpleasant questions and at giving the answer they want to give regardless of what is asked. It's up to you to get the interview back on track and not let the evasive answer go unchallenged.

   For example,

Interviewer:	Do you expect another round of layoffs?
Corporate Vice President:	We anticipate a very healthy turnaround of the economic situation, especially when our new division opens in 18 months, when we actually expect to add jobs to the payroll.
Interviewer:	I'm glad to know the long-range job situation looks good but what about the immediate future? Do you expect another round of layoffs before the new division opens?

3. *Take your responsibilities seriously when looking for an answer.* Do not become pontifical on the subject, but remember that a broadcast interviewer is, in effect, a representative of the public. You have a right to ask questions and a right to a reasonable answer.

Always be polite, but never let yourself be cowed by a high-ranking official who is 30 years your senior. Never mind how well the interviewee says he or she knows the station manager. Do your job, and remember that you are not doing your job if you let yourself be intimidated.

Understand Why Questions Backfire. In an interview situation, the host can inadvertently create negative impressions of himself or herself and of the guests by falling into the traps of mincing around unpleasant questions and being a cheerleader.

1. *Don't be hesitant about asking unpleasant questions.* Suppose you are interviewing a former convict who now works with a children's group. Questions about why the guest was in prison and what he or she learned from that experience are unavoidable, so ask them straight out and don't hedge. Your inclination to preserve the dignity of your guest is perfectly natural. Remember, though, that a direct question will be far less damaging to your guest's dignity than will a mincing, indirect approach, which leads the audience to believe that the subject is distasteful to you.

2. *Avoid being a cheerleader for a guest.* You may be interviewing a celebrity whom you greatly admire, but your audience won't be well served by having you gush all over him or her for 30 minutes. Maintain your perspective.

Forcing the Issue

Perhaps the clearest distinction between a poor interviewer and a good one is that the good interviewer keeps the discussion focused on a central theme, whittling away verbiage to keep answers understandable and to the point. Two valuable techniques for focusing the issue are *using transitions* and *paraphrasing*.

First, focus the issue with transitions. People being interviewed for talk shows or for newscasts may wander from the point, either by accident or because they want to avoid the topic under discussion.

The interviewer can politely steer the conversation back on track by using a smooth transition. For example, assume that you are interviewing a home economist on the subject of budget-saving meals. The economist has mentioned the inexpensiveness of Chinese cooking, but has gotten off on a tangent about the benefits of Mandarin versus Cantonese spices. You can gently return the conversation to the subject by saying, "Yes, Chinese food is very good and very inexpensive. Are there other ethnic foods that represent good bargains?" This gets you back to the topic of budget-saving meals tactfully, without making an abrupt jump, and the conversation can continue naturally. You may, of course, want to be abrupt when an interviewee is obviously trying to duck a question.

In some cases, the guest might stray from the point because he or she has an ax to grind. For example, the head of a police union, asked if a strike by uniformed officers would endanger residents of high-crime neighborhoods, might overlook the question and begin a discourse on how the city failed to bargain in good faith. If you want to preserve the ambience of the interview without taking a blunt approach at that particular time, you can use a gentle transition: "Well, the collective bargaining has been going on for months, with no solution in sight. But it seems that the situation in high-crime areas during a police strike could be an immediate problem, and I wonder if you could tell me . . . " If the transition fails, you may elect to resort to the more direct principle of stating flatly that the question hasn't been answered. This heavy-handed technique, though, is generally more useful in an interview that will be edited than in a talk show. The reason? If you start pressing a guest 5 minutes into a half-hour talk show, you may have 25 tough, uncommunicative minutes ahead.

Second, focus the issue through a paraphrase. In many cases the answer you receive from a guest simply won't make much sense, either because the guest cannot express it better or because he or she does not want to say it more clearly. For example, a politician being quizzed on government finance might say, "Well, as the people of this great state know, budgets are tight in this day and age, and some form of revenue enhancement may be in order to preserve the programs that have made this great state a leader in . . ." One way to make sense of such a response is to paraphrase what you think the interviewee just said and see if he or she agrees with it: "Governor, do I understand that you are saying there may be a tax increase next year?" Now you are forcing an answer and focusing the issue. The governor can agree with what you said, back off from what he said, refuse to make a specific statement at this time, or blandly offer another waffling answer. A more detailed response is necessary, and you may have finessed him into predicting a tax increase in plain English.

Keeping Statements Fair. Interviewers are not required to judge the validity of every statement made by every guest, but they are responsible for challenging what appear to be unfair attacks and illogical or unsupported statements. As a representative of the public, you have a duty to call attention to unfair or misleading statements.

Specifically, you must balance both sides of the issue and keep the discussion logical.

1. *Balance the issue.* A trend in talk shows is to invite several guests with opposing views and let them battle it out before mics and cameras.

Guests on the same show may differ widely in their eloquence and communication abilities, so it is up to you to see that an aggressive guest does not trample a less-skilled interviewee. You may have to play devil's advocate, just to ensure that all sides of a matter are fairly represented.

Your most important responsibility as a pseudo-referee is to make sure that if charges are made, they are supported or are clearly identified as unsupported allegations or personal opinions. Potentially damaging allegations should not be left hanging. Try to resolve such matters before moving on to the next point. The next technique may be quite useful in this regard.

2. *Keep the discussion logical.* A discussion of formal logic is beyond the scope of this book, but if you have the opportunity for further instruction in logic, take advantage of it. Essentially, it is your responsibility to ensure that the statements presented by your guests are factual, and that the conclusions and inferences drawn make sense. Here are some examples of lapses in logic that should make your antennae tingle:

- An interviewee says that all homosexuals are dangerous deviates and that "Dr. Smith" has proven it. Don't let something like this go unchallenged.

Who, exactly, is Smith? What is he or she a doctor of?
Exactly what does the proof that is claimed consist of?

- A guest says, "ten people died in yesterday's fire because there were no smoke detectors." This is a dangerous type of statement because it may be true, though unprovable, and even if it's not true at all (seven victims were in a narcotic stupor, two were unattended infants, and the guy who set the fire left a suicide note in a metal safe), there's an element of validity that tempts the broadcaster to violate the rules of logic.
- A politician running for reelection contends that the fears of the elderly in a certain rundown neighborhood are groundless. He cites statistics indicating that an elderly person has less chance of falling victim to street crime in that neighborhood than a young person does.

Statistics are very difficult to sort out, but a broadcast communicator should always be prepared to challenge them. In the case of the politician and home for the elderly, the interviewer remembered that the neighborhood in question contained a very large nursing home.

Interviewer:	But Mayor _____, don't these figures include residents of the _____ Nursing Home?
Mayor:	Well, yes.
Interviewer:	There are hundreds of elderly people in that nursing home, and many of them are bedridden. They couldn't be victims of street crime if they wanted to. *Doesn't this cast some doubt on your statistics?*

You will not always be able to score this type of coup, of course. But a healthy understanding that statistics can be extremely misleading if used with self-serving intent may shed light on many illogical contentions put forth by interviewees.

For a little more in-depth discussion on logic, please see the Connections box below.

Connections

• •

Logic

In this chapter we have referred to the obligation of an interviewer, especially a talk show host, to keep the discussion logical—that is, to keep it within the bounds of reason.

Connections *(continued)*

A skilled interviewer can gain insight from the study of logic, the academic field dealing with the validity of arguments.

The most simple application of logic is that an argument is valid if the premises on which the argument is based are true and if they relate to the conclusion in such a way that the conclusion must follow from the premises.

For example, consider the classic syllogism, which is a three-part way of coming to a reasoned conclusion:

1. All Greeks are mortal.
2. Socrates is a Greek.

   _____

3. Therefore, Socrates is mortal.

Note that logical deduction does not "prove" that the assumptions are true, only that there is a valid relationship among them.

The "valid relationship" is what matters. For example, you can see that this syllogism does not carry a valid relationship:

1. All Greeks are mortal.
2. Socrates is mortal.

   _____

3. Therefore, Socrates is a Greek.

Suppose Socrates were Swiss. Could he still be mortal? Statement #1 does not rule that out. The Swiss can be mortal, too. Premise #1 doesn't say that *only* Greeks are mortal. And therefore the validity of the argument is ruined.

Several classic logical fallacies relate directly to the broadcast interviewer.

We will list and describe them briefly here, but you can explore these and other fallacies more fully in a course on logic; such courses are offered at most colleges and universities.

Cause and Effect

Because something happened before another incident does not *necessarily* mean that it caused the incident. For example: There were no smoke detectors in the building, the building burned down, and five people died.

Are you being logical if you broadcast, "five people died because there were no smoke detectors in the building?" No; you cannot prove the argument from that premise. Suppose one of the dead was an unattended infant?

Suppose one of the dead set the fire to commit suicide? Without further evidence, you cannot jump to such a conclusion. Remember: Just because there is a consistent relationship among actions, there is not necessarily a cause and effect relationship. After the rooster crows in the morning, the sun comes up. Does the rooster cause the sun to rise?

Ignoring the Exposure Base

If you don't know the field from which the evidence was drawn, you cannot ascertain the validity of the conclusion. If, for example, a poll indicates that nine out of ten respondents favor a particular measure, you must ask how the respondents were drawn. Did they phone in their responses voluntarily? Are they members of a specific group?

Connections *(continued)*

Fallacies of Vacuity

Empty arguments can be persuasive if you don't recognize the empty (vacuous) premises. Often, fallacies of vacuity involve simply restating the argument in different words and pretending that a valid deduction has been made. For example, a talk-show guest says: "The draft is morally wrong, because it is wrong to force someone to join the armed services." Regardless of whether the premises are correct (and remember, in logic we do not judge the premises, only the relationship between and among them) the "conclusion" is flawed because it is simply a restatement of the premise. Forcing someone to join the armed services *is* the draft. Simply restating the premise does not make it valid.

Here is another example:

1. It is always wrong to murder human beings.
2. Capital punishment involves murdering human beings.
3. Therefore, capital punishment is wrong.

Restating the premise in different words and using it as another premise is illogical, and in this case, we have simply called capital punishment "murder" and in a circular fashion used that as an improper premise to "prove" the argument.

Example from R. J. Fogelin, *Understanding Arguments,* 3rd. ed., Orlando, FL: Harcourt-Brace, 1987.

Drawing Out Reluctant Guests. Fear is a strong element in the performance of a guest. Being on the air *can* be frightening, even to experienced performers. Remember, too, that some people simply are not verbally oriented.

A "man of few words" can be admirable in many respects, but he may not make an ideal interviewee. Two ways of getting a guest to open up include *personalizing the questions* and, if the situation really deteriorates, using your list of *disaster questions*.

Personalizing questions is a useful technique because guests who are afraid of repercussions often are reluctant to give complete and responsive answers. A lower-level manager of a social program, for example, may be very edgy about providing specifics because he or she "can't set policy." If you are confronted with such a situation, avoid questions that make the guest seem to be a policymaker. Instead of asking, "What is your agency's position on . . . ?" try the following approach: "What sorts of things is your agency doing to overcome . . . ?" This approach is *very useful* when dealing with workers in a highly structured bureaucracy.

Some people do not fear repercussions; they just don't like to talk, aren't very interesting, or don't care very much about getting their messages across.

For some reason these people can and do appear on talk shows, so you need to know some techniques for opening them up.

A good way to elicit a response from an untalkative guest is to ask, more or less, "What does your program (service, etc.) mean to our audience? How could it affect them?" Even the most uncommunicative guests will be reluctant to admit that what they do with their lives has no impact on other people.

This is what makes personalized questions good "disaster questions," as discussed later. Such questions also lend themselves to follow-ups.

Sometimes, however, interviews just go badly, and you must be prepared for that rare guest who "clams up." The reasons may be varied, but often they are seated in people's ignorance of the impression they make on television or radio. Thus a guest may sit as tight-lipped as a murder defendant for 30 minutes to keep from appearing "too gabby," or "undignified." But at the conclusion of the program, he or she will turn to the host with a worried look and ask, "I didn't run off at the mouth too much, did I?" In such situations, when a guest only mumbles monosyllabic answers, you may need some of the following *disaster questions.*

1. "What are some of the personal success stories you've had in your experience with the program (agency, organization, etc.)?" It is a rare guest indeed who doesn't have something he or she is proud of and willing to talk about at greater length.
2. "Why did you get into this line of work (support this cause, etc.)?" This is an intensely personal question, and even the most uncommunicative guest will not let it slide.
3. "What advice would you give to someone starting off in this line of work (interested in supporting a similar cause, facing this problem)?" Likewise, personal questions, which give an opportunity for the guest to draw on his or her experience, are very difficult to slough off.

This is not the definitive list of disaster questions, and you might want to develop some of your own. The key, of course, is the personal angle, an angle that just might help in all your interviewing tasks. Why? Because the prime factor in any type of interview, with any purpose, is *what the subject means to people.* People and their lives, not facts and theories, are what interests an audience.

SUMMARY

Interviewing can be made difficult by a number of factors, including rigid time restrictions, nervous guests, and interviewees who want to use your program as a soapbox. Overcoming these obstacles and conducting a successful interview involves determining the type of interview (that is, studio or actuality), preparing for the interview, and doing the interview.

Preparing for the interview involves drawing up a list of questions and doing research. Selecting the guest and topic is often the interviewer's responsibility, also. Doing the interview entails effectively working within technical restrictions and performance considerations, and eliciting valid responses that are appropriate for the format or intended use of the interview.

The technical restrictions and performance considerations just mentioned involve openings and closings of interview segments, proper use of prepared questions and following up on questions, and keeping listeners' and viewers' attention. Time restrictions must be dealt with effectively, and the interviewer must grasp the techniques of closing an interview segment gracefully.

An interviewer must be concerned with getting a *response,* not simply an answer. Techniques to spur continued conversation and get complete, relevant answers are essential.

Some questions backfire for reasons not immediately apparent. Reasons may include interviewer hesitancy toward asking unpleasant questions or, conversely, an obvious "cheerleading" attitude toward the guest.

Skilled interviewers know how to focus an issue. They do this through use of devices such as transitions and paraphrases.

The interviewer is responsible for keeping statements and allegations fair. Inherent in this responsibility are the tasks of balancing issues during an interview and keeping the discussion and contentions within the bounds of logic.

Some guests are very frightened or simply uncommunicative. Talk shows with such guests can be disastrous, but the technique of personalizing the question can often elicit good responses. Every interviewer should be prepared with a list of "disaster questions"—material that can be used at any time and almost always will resurrect the interview. Such questions involve explorations of the individual's personal success stories or lifelong goals, and usually are not sloughed off by even the most uncommunicative guest.

EXERCISES

1. Ask a classmate or co-worker to read a newspaper article on a particular subject and to take notes. Your job is to interview him or her for five minutes on that topic.

   This is a realistic type of interview situation, because many of your interviewees will have a limited knowledge about the topic, and the interviewer will have to stay within certain boundaries. Admittedly, you and your guest will be operating from a small database, but this exercise will prove helpful if you try to maintain a rhythm and a level of interest, regardless of the rough spots.

2. Prepare a list of the five most immediate and pressing questions you would want to ask in the following circumstances. Assume that you will have a limited amount of time, so make the questions brief and to the point. List them in descending order of importance.

   a. You have arrived at the scene of an explosion and have cornered the police chief. Your questions, for example, might be "Is anyone hurt or dead? Are people still in danger? How did the explosion happen? How will the investigation proceed? Is this incident related to a similar explosion last week?"

   b. You are interviewing an actress who will open tonight in a play she also wrote and directed.

   c. You are asking a person who has just been acquitted of a crime for his reaction.

   d. You are speaking with the head of a suicide hotline agency about how teenage suicide can be prevented.

   e. You are interviewing a college professor who says that the elderly in the United States are treated very shoddily and do not get the respect they deserve from the younger generations.

   Discuss your list of questions with classmates or co-workers.

3. Watch a television interview program and keep track of the questions asked by the host. Grade those questions on how interesting they were *to you*. In other words, how badly did you want to ask that question yourself?

   Keep track of issues you feel were left hanging, or weren't dealt with adequately. Also, write down questions you feel the guest evaded or did not answer completely.

   By taking careful notes, you will wind up with a virtual flow sheet of the interview program, and you should have a much better idea of how such programs progress when they are done well, and even when they are not.

Television and Radio Specialties

You can explore a number of specialty areas as a professional on-air broadcast performer. Sports reporting and play-by-play announcing, weather reporting, hosting radio talk shows, and narration are some common examples.

Some broadcasters move into one of these areas by chance. For others, a career as a sportscaster or weather reporter is a lifelong goal, attained after years of preparation for that big break that brings success.

Every area of on-air endeavor has its own special requirements. The special talents and skills needed for success in any given area are developed with experience. No one can prepare to be a great play-by-play announcer without on-air experience. Certainly practice off the air can help, but the actual pressure of being live and on the air provides the special incentive that lets you exceed even your own expectations.

Despite the fact that you can only hone your skills and develop the specialized knowledge you need through practice, the main requirement for proficiency in any specialty assignment is the same as for any on-air assignment. You need to start out as an effective broadcast communicator.

This chapter discusses some specialty assignments in broadcasting and gives a broad overview of the techniques used. The basic principles are refinements of the broader elements of good communication presented throughout this text and are applicable to other areas of electronic media such as podcasting. Broadcasting specialists use many of the specific techniques covered here.

- A sportscaster often must conduct an extensive interview (Chapter 8) and, during play-by-play, must do a good job on commercials (Chapter 10).
- A weathercaster, especially in times of weather emergency, must gather and present facts lucidly and responsibly in the news function (Chapters 6 and 7).
- A narrator must have an effective voice (Chapter 2) and must be able to grasp the essentials of the copy (Chapter 3).

There is really no way to explain how to become a sportscaster or a weather reporter. A few lessons and drills will never come close to providing the specialized knowledge required. That's why this chapter is brief and primarily introductory, touching on sports, weather, narration, and acting as host of special types of programming such as children's shows and movie presentations.

SPORTS

Knowledge of sports cannot be faked. Sports fans are often experts themselves, and this means that an aspiring sportscaster must have a strong interest in, and knowledge of, the games to be reported. A sports anchor must be well informed about all sports, even activities he or she may not find personally appealing. In many cities, for example, competitive bowling or curling is extremely popular. Hence, the sports reporter must project knowledge and enthusiasm, qualities that come about only by painstaking homework, in a sport that may be unfamiliar.

In addition, a wide personal database is important because opportunities for sports coverage open very quickly. Should a major fight be booked for your city, someone will have to handle the story, and if you work in the sports department, that someone is likely to be you. It is worthwhile to be aware of and interested in all the various types of sports work.

Types of Sports Assignments

Sports work generally falls into four categories: anchor work, sports reporting, play-by-play, and color. Anchor work in sports parallels that of news. Sports reporting also translates the role of radio or TV reporter from news to sports and increasingly the business of sports has become an added dimension in sports reporting.

Play-by-play is unique and requires a specialized set of abilities, discussed later in this section. Color work, dealt with in the section on play-by-play, provides commentary and insight.

Personality in Sports

It has been said that the sports reporter provides as much entertainment as the sport being covered. Personality and entertainment value play a much stronger role in sports than in news. In one market, for example, a popular feature of the top-rated sports reporter is a weekly recap of all the blunders that occurred in various sporting events, complete with musical background.

Such an approach obviously could not be used with news. Neither would the remark of a reporter that he had egg on his face (after an inaccurate prediction) be followed by the cracking of an egg on the reporter's forehead, as once happened in sports. Although this example is extreme, be aware that sports does allow for more expression of personality and entertainment values and, therefore, places an additional demand on the sports announcer.

Issues in Sports Coverage

Sports certainly is not all fun and games. News of FBI investigations and corruption in Division I basketball, doping in professional cycling, and sexual impropriety in the US gymnastics show that sports have a far-too-serious side. So although an element of entertainment is part of the sports broadcaster's repertoire, he or she must also function as a reporter, sometimes asking hard questions. Sensitive information must be dealt with responsibly. Also, anyone who has ever mixed up a score on the air knows that there is no room for error in the recital of who beat whom. Fans find such mistakes virtually unforgivable.

Sports Anchor Work

Typically, many games are still running or just ending as the TV sportscaster is about to go on the air. Network sports feeds, showing highlights of games and events, are fed at 5:10 p.m., 7:35 p.m., and 11:10 p.m. EST. In many cases, this means that some segments for the 11 o'clock news are recorded and put on air by a production person. The sports anchor, who has not seen the material, knows, from a printed rundown fed in advance, only that there is a 20-second piece on the Boston–New York game.

To further complicate matters, the sports anchor must keep track of games in progress. Some stations have courtesy arrangements with broadcast and cable networks that televise certain teams. These arrangements allow sportscasters to air clips of the contests, but in many cases *after each game has ended*. Imagine the rush to get a clip on the air when a home run in the bottom of the ninth inning breaks a tie game at 11:15!

The sports reporter, who often is an alternate anchor on weekends, helps out with production in stations large enough to support more than one sports person and also files local packages to be integrated into the sports segment.

Sports anchoring, then, requires the on-air enthusiasm of a die-hard sports fan combined with the pressure-handling ability of a breaking news editor. Sports reporting calls for the ability to assemble a news package and an eye and ear for stories that will interest fans. Some suggestions for effective anchoring and reporting are given in Box 9.1.

As more women become sports anchors, the profession has needed to reflect on the language and culture surrounding sports.

Sports Play-by-Play

A talented play-by-play announcer can generally find abundant work in local markets, although this work will usually be on a part-time basis. In small and medium markets, newspeople, staff announcers, and even sales personnel add to their income by broadcasting local sports. This is a difficult assignment, however, requiring good on-air skills and an extensive knowledge of the sport.

One important aspect of play-by-play is the differing nature of individual events. Think of the different approaches and knowledge bases required for hockey and for football. To illustrate, we contrast the attributes of play-by-play announcers for baseball, football, basketball, hockey, soccer, and boxing.

BOX 9.1 Tips for Sports Anchors and Reporters

1. *Stress stories that interest your local audience.* Remember, taking a new job and moving to a new area involves learning what makes headlines in local sports. In parts of Texas, for example, high school football often creates more excitement than the pro sport does. Other cities in various parts of the nation have strong passions for greyhound racing, candlepin bowling, or lacrosse.
2. *Prewrite as much as possible, and overplan for the sports segment.* Because of the last-minute nature of TV sports, expected segments do not always materialize and you must have material to fill.
3. *Write your copy as close to the visual as possible.* Unlike news, where it is considered undesirable to point copy to the video, in sports you must do so. Copy has to coordinate precisely with what appears on the screen at any given moment: "and he whacked this pitch . . ."
4. *Pay particular attention to variety in reading scores.* In radio especially, the sportscaster must invent many verbs to take the place of "defeated" or "beat." A long list of scores requires some imagination.

    A phrase such as "Boston overpowered New York, 9–3," adds color. Other useful verbs include, "squeaked past," "downed," and "hammered." Avoid stretching too far, though. "Obliterated" and "decimated" get a bit tedious. In fact, some local sportscasters can become rather comic in their attempts to hype the delivery of scores.

    If you do not feel comfortable using this type of device, it is better to avoid it. If possible, write the verbs right into the copy.
5. *Always keep your energy level high. Speak with intensity.* Enjoy what you are doing, and let it show.
6. *Remember that the personalities of the athletes are as important as the outcome of the games.* Listeners and viewers are interested in personal items relating to the players, too.

Baseball games have many periods of little or no activity, so the play-by-play person must be able to fill with talk of interest to the audience. This ability will become particularly apparent in rain-delay situations.

Baseball play-by-play also entails the ability to follow action quite a distance away. Good vision, or the ability to compensate for poor vision by an in-depth knowledge of the game, is essential.

Football is a technically oriented game, and the play-by-play announcer has to be up on the plays and able to follow them. A color commentator often provides in-depth analysis. Many statistics must be followed, including downs, yardage on previous carries, and so on. Things happen fast in football, and it takes great skill by the announcer to convey the action accurately and add an element of excitement.

Basketball, from the announcer's standpoint, can become almost nightmarish in its complexity. Listeners want the announcer to keep track of how many fouls a player has, how many rebounds, and how many points each player has scored in the game so far. There are fewer players than in football, however, and the announcer usually is stationed in a press box close to the action or on the floor next to the playing area.

Hockey is challenging. By the time the announcer has told the audience who is in possession of the puck, the game has moved to the other end of the rink. Hockey play-by-play announcers must be able to paint vivid word pictures on radio and keep up with the action on television.

Soccer, while a fairly simple game is fast. Its popularity is growing in the US. The ball can travel great distances across the field quickly and because there are few breaks in the action, the announcer needs to be able to translate this quick movement between players. There are 22 players on the field so a spotter may be useful to help with names and positions.

Boxing entails the ability to speculate and analyze. Almost all boxing broadcast today is televised, so the play-by-play commentator must be able to do much more than relay reports of who hit whom. The broadcaster must analyze the bout to determine why one fighter's style makes him vulnerable to the punches of the other or whether one fighter is being tired by body blows. It is also necessary to speculate, for example, whether a contestant's jabs are piling up points with the judges.

There are occasional opportunities to cover sports such as golf, where an announcer must constantly fill time, and track and field, where the play-by-play person must keep close track of the shifting positions of runners.

Although the requirements for individual sports differ widely, some of the basic skills and procedures remain constant. No game coverage procedure is more important than preparation. Rosters must be obtained, along with as much factual information about the team and its players as possible.

In most colleges and all professional organizations, sports information directors prepare kits of information especially for the play-by-play and color commentators.

Pay close attention to special rules, such as a three-knockdown rule in boxing or a sudden-death play-off in football. Learn the positions of the players, and check for hard-to-pronounce names.

Circumstances will dictate how much help you will have in preparation and actual coverage of the game. In football, spotters may be provided. For baseball, you will want access to the official scorer, who can inform you of rulings. Baseball fans have a particular interest in rulings, wanting to know, for example, if the player will be credited with an RBI (run batted in) or if the run resulted from a fielder's error.

Mike Tirico (see Figure 9.1), whose 10-year run doing play-by-play announcing of NFL football broadcasts for ESPN has made him one of the most popular personalities in sports broadcasting. Tirico has also covered the US Open (tennis) and the 2014 FIFA World Cup. In 2016 he joined NBC Sports and became studio host for the 2016 and 2018 Olympics. Tirico stresses the importance of preparation. He's said, "You can't just look at the back section of the newspaper or the sports section by itself. You need to understand everything that's going on."

Often play-by-play announcers are mated with a color commentator. Jesse Dorsey, from the "bleacherreport.com" writes "the color man is there for the same reason every time . . . They are there to give deeper insight into what has just happened on the floor. It is an interesting relationship (with the play-by-play announcer) that's difficult to balance at times, but when it works, it works miraculously."[1]

FIGURE 9.1 Sportscaster Mike Tirico, one of the best-prepared announcers in the business.

The popular combination of play-by-play announcer and color commentator allows for a logical division of duties and enables each sportscaster to concentrate more fully on the game. Although in many cases the color and play-by-play roles are integrated into one announcer's duties, when a separate color announcer is employed, he or she is expected to provide highly informative insights into the sport, including:

1. Details the casual fan might miss.
2. Anecdotes about the game and the players.
3. A personalized "feel" for what it is like to play the game—for example, how it feels to be checked into the boards or caught for a safety in the end zone.

The chemistry that makes certain announcing teams successful is an elusive concept. Among the more easily spelled out play-by-play and color principles are the following:

1. Let yourself become excited by the sport. Many former players are successful sportscasters because they love the game and are thrilled by a fine play, not merely because of their technical knowledge.

   Steve Levy, ESPN's legendary hockey sportscaster, brings an easygoing manner to his work. His love of sports shows in his entertaining and engaging style whether doing play-by-play or hosting ESPN's SportsCenter.
2. Don't repeat yourself. Listeners do not need to be told "It's a beautiful day here in Cleveland" more than once or twice. Reacting to the pressure of the need to fill time, announcers often become repetitious, and the only cure is awareness of this pitfall and an adequate supply of material to fill time.

   However, audience members do appreciate frequent repetition of the score. When in doubt and desperate for something to say, the score is as good as anything. Time can also be filled by reading scores of other games.
3. When in doubt about a play, wait until you know for sure to make the call. Identifying football players can become difficult, especially on a muddy field when uniform numbers become obscured.

However, a delay in calling a play sounds much better than having to backtrack and figure out who really did take the handoff.

4. When using statistics, communicate with those numbers rather than repeating them. The audience may or may not be interested to learn that the man at the plate is a .310 hitter. To be compelling, the announcer might say, "The pitcher is left-handed and the batter is a .400 hitter against lefties. He's also known as a good man in the clutch, and this is really one of the clutch situations of the season, with the Sox down by one run in the bottom of the ninth with a runner on second . . ." Such fluency of content and style requires a thorough knowledge of the sport and the players.

5. Never let up on energy or enthusiasm during the commercials. Play-by-play announcers are often called on to do commercials and should keep in mind that those commercials help pay their salaries.

6. Be sure to keep up with rule changes and ground rules. Getting acquainted with an official who can fill you in on changes is an excellent idea. Similarly, learn officials' hand signals.

7. It is better to give the score and time remaining too often than not often enough. This is particularly true for radio where the listener does not have the ability to view the graphics that would accompany the game's video.

8. Practice and develop your own methods of quickly spotting players and plays. Many knowledgeable sportscasters maintain that a sportscaster who lags behind the public address announcer is not doing his or her job.

9. Pronunciation of names is often a problem. In college and high school games, one of the best ways to check on pronunciation is to ask the cheerleaders, who often know the athletes personally. Use this option if you don't have time to track down coaches, players, or sports information people.

10. In play-by-play, avoid using numbers to designate people. Each player has a name, and it should be used.

In Focus on Technique, we outline some strategies for improving your presentation.

Focus on Technique

Improving Play-By-Play and Color

Sportscasting is highly competitive but appears to be a growing field. The proliferation of super-segmented sports cable channels has opened new opportunities for broadcast communicators conversant with the nuances of describing a game.

Almost anyone who has some knowledge of how a game is played can do play-by-play or color; unfortunately, very few of these people can do it well.

Many sports announcers note that practice is the key element in separating lackluster and incompetent sports calling from quality work. By and large they contend that if you work on *better preparation, on-air organization,* and *verbal skills,* you will consistently improve.

Here are some suggestions for improving in those three categories.

Preparation

• When you know you are going to be calling a game, work closely with the sports information director (usually called an SID) for both teams. The SID is the person who will be providing you with rosters and statistics. Call the SID early. Hone a good working relationship with the SID: a thank-you note is unexpected but quite welcome. If you want to thank the visiting team's SID in person, do so before the game because he or she will be too busy after.

Focus on Technique *(continued)*

- Make up detailed charts. Most sports announcers have their own system for their charts (which are often called "boards"). For football, as an example, many draw rectangular blocks to represent the various positions and fill in the starter and the backup. Whatever system you use, it is important that you can look down and perceive the names and numbers at a glance.

- Drill yourself on names and numbers. When you get the starting lineup from the other team's SID, make up a set of flashcards with the numbers. Pretty soon, you'll be able to recall all the names. (For example, shuffle the cards and pull out 22: it will be Rodriguez. 43 will be Martin. You may have to check the first few times, but you'll get it soon. It goes without saying that you will have learned all your team's numbers and names early in the season.)

  Don't bother learning first names unless there are two or more players on the team with the same last name.

- On your charts, or on index cards, or in whatever system you favor, keep lists of factors such as:—Personal anecdotes. ("LaRue's father was a halfback for the Cleveland Browns in the 1960s.")—Any records that might be broken during game day.—Stats from last year.

- As part of your preparation, listen to a tape of your previous week's show. If you're working on radio, get the game videotape and run it at the same time to see how well your play-by-play and color matched up.

- As you near show time, let the color commentator do the pregame show, if possible, and allow the play-by-play announcer time to go over the names and numbers. This is particularly important in hockey; hockey personnel change so quickly and the game is so fluid that the play-by-play announcer must be completely conversant with the names. (Note how much better a third period often is in terms of play calling than the first period; you can guess the reason.)

- When the opposing team takes the field or court, take note of any physical characteristics that stand out and write them down on your boards: Number 22=Mike Cowphin RED HAIR AND GLASSES. You'll find this particularly useful in basketball because in basketball it is difficult or impossible to see numbers during much of the play.

On-Air Organization

- Make sure that the play-by-play, color, and statistician/spotter stay in rhythm. One of the problems you are going to encounter is listening to directions from the control room (usually in a remote truck).

  A good technique is for only the play-by-play to listen to the truck when color is talking and vice-versa. Have the statistician/spotter take care of reminding the on-air people of duties they might forget, such as giving the legal ID at the top of the hour.

- Use some consistent method to remind yourself to give the score.

  Research shows that failure to give the score is the most frequently cited irritant among listeners and viewers. Some announcers use an egg timer. Others always give the score during a line change in hockey (which averages perhaps 70 seconds between changes) or after two outs in baseball.

- Make sure your statistician and everybody else who is going to be on air has a consistent formula for giving statistics. The hallmark of a novice is to give every statistic on the boards before the end of the first inning. Know in advance when the stats are going to be parceled out. Do not, for example, say, "Willis has stolen 30 bases this season" when he steps up to bat. Wait until and if he is on base.

Focus on Technique (continued)

"That's Morris's third three-pointer in the game . . . he averages five per game this season!" is an example of how to work in statistics.

Verbal Skills

- When calling a game, be sure to rid your verbiage of clichés. Don't ape the routines of famous announcers. No one is going to be impressed by your impression of Marv Albert—"Yes!"
- Try never to use the word "we." Once you start saying, "We need to stop them on this drive," people will start asking, "What number are you?" Don't become what's known in the industry as a "homer"—someone who roots for the home team. It is increasingly considered unprofessional.
- Remember that many color commentators are noted players and, as WBSU-FM General Manager Warren Kosierski notes, if you are not a noted player you cannot speak with the same authority as they can.

  So, instead of saying, "I predict they're going to run to the right," say, "They've run to the right in eight of their last ten running plays . . . let's see if they do it again."
- Keep in mind that verbal skills for radio and TV are different. With radio, you must carry more of the action. This becomes a problem when someone brought up on watching TV sportscasts gets on radio and doesn't describe the action properly. ("Yes!" will not help a radio listener much.) Remember, too, that play-by-play will dominate radio coverage while color will dominate TV.
- Use different approaches to giving the score. Although listeners and viewers complain that the score is not given often enough, they will also complain if it becomes repetitious. So instead of always saying, "Bulldogs 14, Pirates 7," try: "The Bulldogs are up by a touchdown. . . ."

A final note: remember that sports coverage, like the sporting event itself, is a team event. Big egos are seldom if ever appreciated. On-air people should take note that dozens of dedicated folks are working as hard as they are. Theresa Schindler, head of the Big East Sports Network, requires announcers to sit in the production truck before the game. "We want them to realize," she says, "how many people work hard to make the program a success."[2]

WEATHER

Today's weather forecast has evolved into a high-tech, graphically stunning presentation. In addition, weather forecasters are called on to make highly localized predictions that will affect hundreds or thousands of audience members in a particular region. Weather reporting has taken on greater importance in national news coverage as large hurricanes, tornadoes, flooding and fires have increased in frequency in recent years. Additionally, new software allows weather reporters to indicate localized conditions with pinpoint accuracy for local audiences.

The Weathercaster's Role

The modern weather reporter is often both a meteorologist and an entertainer.

The American Meteorological Society has established qualifications for meteorologists, and this professional organization issues a seal that is displayed on approved weather forecasters' programs.

For all practical purposes, a meteorologist entering today's world of broadcasting needs a four-year degree in that field. Although it is perfectly legal to be employed as a weather forecaster without a degree, meteorologist John Flanders notes that the competition for jobs is stiff and a degree in meteorology may be a decided advantage.

Why is it advantageous for a local weathercaster to be a trained meteorologist? Advancing technology has made weather forecasting a more exact science, and the process of giving a detailed weather forecast now involves fairly complex software packages and databases from the National Weather Service and other software providers.

Listeners and viewers now expect specific and more localized forecasts, and someone with this training is better able to predict such events as the likely path of a snowfall and ice storm or a thunderstorm. Remember, a small variation in the path of a snow storm can make an enormous difference to the city that is either hit or missed.

Note, too, that all forecasts are not the same. In periods of good weather, forecasters may not have much weather change to discuss but frequently discuss interesting weather patterns that may approach or that are impacting different parts of the country. In times of bad weather, the forecaster introduces the important factors providing detailed analysis and interpretation. The modern meteorologist-entertainer provides this type of information, and does so in a way that holds the interest of the audience.

The Image of the Weathercaster

The image of the TV weathercaster has gradually changed over the years. At one time it was common for the weather segment to be treated as comic relief for the local news block. The weathercaster was often cast in the role of buffoon, partly because we did not have adequate technology to really forecast weather. It seemed that he or she always got the forecast wrong, but went on day after day. News anchors would make funny remarks about the previous days' forecast. In the 1950s, 60s and 70s weathercasters stood in front of crude maps on which they drew crude lines with a marker. If the weather person was a woman, she was often chosen for her good looks as opposed to her forecasting ability. The change started in the 1980s as advances in local Doppler radar, satellite imagery and graphic capability allowed weathercasters to indicate daily forecasts with greater accuracy and visual interest. Later the Internet gave meteorologists access to weather and climate databases.

Today's advanced computer systems and the Internet have led to enormous improvements in satellite imagery, climate databases and software technology. These improvements have revolutionized weather prediction and the ability to visualize the weather forecast for viewers. Many television stations have specific weather apps that can be downloaded on smartphones and tablets, so the role of the weathercaster has become increasingly more important as viewers tune in to check the updates.

Weathercasting in general is given the status of a scientific endeavor that can affect the safety and well-being of viewers as well as their lifestyles. The weather person, as a result, is treated with the respect appropriate for a knowledgeable expert in a complex field.

Advanced Weather Graphic Systems

The image of competence in weather people is enhanced by the high-tech surroundings that now make up the typical weather segment. Sophisticated computerized graphic systems, like the one in Figure 9.2, make complex weather patterns and principles easy to understand for even the most unscientific of viewers.

Accu-Weather's Joel Myers, whose Pennsylvania-based weather service is used by CNN, MSNBC, and some 200 television stations in the United States and Canada, says that the sophisticated weather graphics came into their own during the 1980s. It was a time of "dramatic transition from hand-drawn weather maps and magnetic boards to sophisticated, attractive graphics prepared on microcomputer graphic systems," says Myers. A staff of 100 meteorologists and artists create the graphics and are available to speak with on-air talent, according to Myers. Alternative software systems from The Weather Company, Baron

FIGURE 9.2a Here's NBC's Al Roker in front of a large map showing weather across the entire U.S.

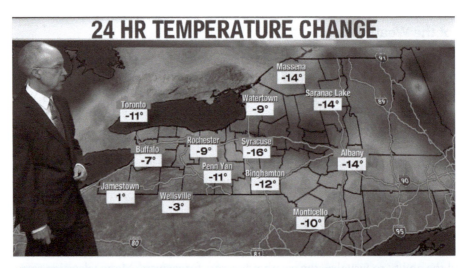

FIGURE 9.2b Jim Teske, WSYR-TV's chief meteorologist, provides viewers with an update on temperature changes for the Syracuse viewing area. Computer graphics aid meteorologists in explaining the many variables in weather reporting.

and others also provide the ability to create regional maps, logos, thunderstorm alerts and traffic alerts along with many other graphics capabilities.

The NOAA Weather Service (www.NOAA.gov) is another primary source available to weather forecasters. This government agency combines many different advanced systems to enable meteorologists to make accurate predictions. Television stations use the service to access tools such as Doppler radar which can detect all types of precipitation, wind strength and other information. Severe weather advisories that are broadcast using a crawl across the television screen while regular programming continues occurs when the service issues alerts for specific geographical areas.

The extensive use of TV graphics means that weather people often work closely with station art departments to create tailor-made computer graphics that combine the capabilities of more than one system.

Moreover, the graphics can create a visual impact that is part of the network's or station's visual signature. Note the effective graphics used by NBC's Al Roker (Figure 9.2a) and by WSYR, Syracuse, meteorologist Jim Teske (Figure 9.2b).

For the aspiring weather person, all this technology means that to prepare for a job in TV weather, you need enough computer literacy to let you learn how to operate computerized graphic systems that use the latest innovations in software. Systems vary widely from station to station and they change continually. Your best bet is to become generally knowledgeable with computer graphics, so you'll be able to apply your skills to whatever system you may encounter.

In small-market operations, the weather person often uses graphic templates that form the centerpiece of weather segments. In some markets art departments may provide assistance, but the weather person still does much of the hands-on work of preparing the graphics. Most veteran weather reporters say that the best way to get this experience is by interning at a local TV station.

Although difficult to come by, weather internships will give you a substantial advantage in learning what's currently available in weather graphics and how they can be used to create an authoritative on-air weather segment.

In radio, weather is seldom a specialty for on-air talent, although some stations use reports by area meteorologists to lend authority to forecasts and to tailor them specifically to the listening area. For most stations, weather information is supplied by the National Weather Service or news services like the Associated Press. The sheer volume of weather information on the AP network seems out of proportion to its presence on the air. The reason for the high volume of weather information, of course, is that stations have little need for old weather information. Timely forecasts are essential, as are accurate data on current conditions. Broadcast clients receive forecasts for a number of regions. They then select the data that fit their particular needs at the time.

FIGURE 9.3 Will Lyman is the voice behind some impactful documentaries.

Reporting on traffic and related weather hazards have added to the type of information broadcast stations carry regularly today. National weather services have added these additional services to the offer. Frequently this added information supplements the forecast when it's appropriate for the viewing audience.

Weather, then, has become a broadcast specialty that requires some highly specific skills by the on-air talent. In television and to an extent in radio, those reporting weather need more than an ability to perform well on the air. They also need a good basic knowledge of meteorology, and the computer skills necessary to effectively use the sophisticated computerized graphic and information systems that have become major components of modern broadcast weather reporting. Making the forecast understandable and meaningful to the audience is the hallmark of a successful communicator.

Meteorologists working exclusively in radio often are employed by one of a number of forecasting firms that provide local feeds to radio stations.

A Typical Workday for a Weathercaster

In television, the weathercaster for the 6 and 11 o'clock news might arrive at the station at 3:30 and begin to extract weather information from one or more computerized databases. Several different weather maps are fed via the Web or from the service provider, and the information on those maps must be studied and digested. Such information includes patterns of upper air movement, temperature, and wind direction.

Preparation for the Show

For some weathercasts, as many as 15 or 20 different maps will be prepared. Data are updated constantly and stored on computers for recall during airing of the weather. Before the weather segment airs, the forecaster will have prepared the maps and determined their order. He or she does a quick rehearsal of the patter that accompanies each graphic.

Some late night newscasts are featuring an abbreviated weather summary at the top of the show, followed by the longer weather forecast later in the program. As our weather patterns seem to be changing and getting more turbulent, weather is taking on greater importance in both local and national newscasts.

Graphic	Audio
Large satellite projection	A nice day in the Northeast today, with only a bit of light cloud cover from Pennsylvania . . .
Closer projection	The only trouble spot is this warm front, which will move . . .
Fronts illustrated on colored map	into our area by tomorrow morning.

Good weathercasting requires poise before the camera, a confident delivery, ability to ad-lib, and careful attention to posture and gestures. Many beginning weathercasters have a tendency to speak too quickly. Slowing down and delivering the forecast with greater interest and intensity can almost always improve the effort. As noted in the script above, try to match audio with the visual on the weather map.

Remember that during most weather presentations you'll be standing in front of a green screen with the weather map images electronically keyed behind you. Some stations have specific sets for their weather segments reflecting the growing importance of weather forecasting in those markets. New technology allows some weathercasters to use new, large touch displays that change the various map and weather displays with a touch of the finger.

The first rule is to keep a close eye on the camera that shows the map (and you) on the prompting device. Many studio cameras are robotically controlled today so you should arrange the proper camera placement before the segment starts. If your station uses a camera operator, ask to position the camera as close to you as possible so you can clearly perceive the relationship of you to the map, which is electronically keyed in behind you.

Second, don't be too quick to point to a particular area on the map, unless you're using a touchscreen system. Pointing in an imaginary dimension (at a green screen while you are coordinating your hand motion with the image you see on the prompter) takes practice. While you're picking up the skill, try to confine your gestures to general regions—or else you may wind up talking about tornadoes in Kansas when you are pointing to Illinois.

Weather Emergencies

In times of potentially unpleasant or violent weather, the weather forecaster's job becomes pressured. Weather reporting is particularly intense with spring floods, during the thunderstorm season in midsummer, and in periods of heavy winter snowfall. Probably the most white-knuckled of all forecasting is done in the Midwest, where tornadoes are a major threat, or along the East Coast and Gulf Coast during hurricane season. Weather forecasters may be called on to do extensive explanations of weather phenomena and must be prepared to respond to audience questions during weather emergencies.

If you plan a career in weather, be aware that there is more involved than designing maps and developing an on-air style. In times of weather emergency, you will have the heaviest responsibilities in the news report. More and more weathercasters are seen out in the storms providing live coverage.

NARRATION

The art and science of reading audio to juxtapose with video is rapidly developing into a distinct specialty. One reason for this is that firms and organizations increasingly use videotapes and PowerPoint presentations.

Documentaries also frequently use an off-camera narrator. Some narration is done on camera, but most is done voice over video. However, the term *voice-over* has acquired a separate meaning in relation to commercials and news, so the word *narration* more accurately describes the process of reading a script off the camera.

Purpose of a Narration

A narration must reinforce the program, providing an ebb and flow that matches with the video image on the screen. The voice must communicate effectively without being intrusive. Box 9.2 highlights some effective narration techniques.

Synchronizing Narration with Video or Stills

Narration can be recorded with the performer looking at a monitor, or simply taped and edited in later. Many producers favor narration working to picture because it saves them additional work in the editing process. Many announcers, though, favor recording the narration straight, without the distraction of a monitor. Some narrators will choose to work one way or the other, depending on the situation. Will Lyman (Figure 9.3), narrator of the PBS series *Frontline* and *Vietnam: A Television History*, notes that his technique varies.

"*Frontline* is occasionally done without seeing the video. But for the Vietnam series, I requested to work to picture so I would know what kind of scene I was speaking over. I didn't want to blast through some shocking picture."

BOX 9.2 Effective Narration Techniques

Industrial narrations, news narrations, and documentary work require some specialized skills. The vocal approach to a narration is not the same as for commercials or news. Among the techniques useful for this task are the following:

1. Strive to develop an open easiness, a personality behind the voice that communicates but does not dominate.
2. If working to a picture, position the screen and your script where both can be seen easily, so that you don't have to strain and adopt an unnatural posture. The problem of awkward posture, with its negative effects on voice and delivery, is common in narration situations but not often recognized.
3. Pay close attention to the projection of mood, a major requirement in narration. Project what you feel is the appropriate mood, along with the appropriate measure of personal involvement with the copy.
4. Avoid a hard-sell delivery. Narration, for the most part, requires more subtlety than do other assignments.
5. If long segments must be delivered strictly to time, use the mark-ups shown in Chapter 3 to indicate time cues. The right reading, for example, might have the second paragraph begin 2.5 seconds into the manufacturing scene. A note of this on your copy can indicate whether an adjustment is in order to hit the next scene properly.

HOSTING SPECIAL PROGRAMMING

Many of the more interesting assignments in broadcast work, such as acting as host of a children's show, are mostly extinct on the local level. However, many local stations have weekend or morning shows that feature events and happenings in the local community. The host needs to be able to interview and chat with guests in a way that informs and entertains the audience. The role of host in any presentation can be an interesting one. Many of the specialty assignments described in this chapter are good part-time options for a broadcaster.

Play-by-play, for instance, is an interesting way to supplement your income in a small market. Rare assignments such as game shows or movie programs will be part-time by their very natures.

If you have an opportunity to try a specialty assignment, take the job if at all possible and if the job will not sidetrack you from your ultimate career goal. Exposure to the demands of these jobs will help you improve as an all-around broadcast professional.

Master of Ceremonies

An infrequent but challenging assignment involves MCing such events as telethons or on-air fund-raisers. Here, the performer must have the ability to ad-lib virtually indefinitely. Also, he or she has to keep track of various and sundry schedules and activities.

The MC job, as those who have tried it know, entails a huge amount of physical and mental strain. Humor, intelligence, and good interviewing skills are essential. The primary responsibility is the ability to inject excitement into what may be intrinsically dull. Being an MC requires you to weigh the needs of the program against the sensibilities of your audience.

Radio Talk Show Host

As discussed earlier, the role of talk show host is demanding. It primarily demands interviewing skills but also requires good to excellent ad-libbing ability and strong projection of a personality.

Because radio talk is an entertainment medium, a host's career will be short-lived if he or she cannot captivate an audience. Political callers often try to project their agenda or beliefs on the air so it is important for the host to be able to steer the conversation when necessary. Another useful attribute is a sense of humor because callers can be rude or abusive. Helpful, too, is a good sense of when the talk is bordering on the slanderous.

A broad base of knowledge is essential to the talk show host's job. You simply cannot do without it.

Movie Host

The "sprocket jockey" still flourishes in some markets. The setting is usually a simulated screening room, but some presentations involve the host in costume, particularly the shows that feature horror movies. Specialized movie channels such as American Movie Classics have brought a resurgence of this job.

Few announcers make their living from hosting movie presentations, but it is an interesting assignment. The prime requirement is the ability to act relaxed and natural in an unnatural situation. Knowledge is important, too. Movie buffs can be more fanatical about trivia than even sports fans.

Children's Show Host

It is probably impossible to manufacture an on-screen liking for children if you prefer to avoid them in real life. Hosting a children's show involves understanding youngsters and being able to talk with them, not at them or down to them. Many elementary school teachers have become successful hosts in this sort of programming.

On the local level, children's shows are largely a thing of the past. Cable television networks such as Nickelodeon and Disney have taken over that role. At the local level many stations still do annual telethons to raise money for children's hospitals and similar causes. This opens the opportunity to work with community groups on live television.

Game Show Host

Although rare, local game shows still exist, often in the form of quiz programs that pit one school against another. On the national level, only a handful of personalities make a living at game shows.

The requirements for hosting programming of this type include the ability to handle figures easily because almost any game requires tallying points. You'll have to think quickly if something goes wrong, and above all you must be able to instill excitement and enthusiasm in each contestant's performance.

Health and Medicine Reporting

As a significant portion of the population ages, an increasing number of local television stations employ on-air talent who cover, either as their entire beat or as parts of their jobs, issues related to health. In some areas, especially large markets, those reporters are often physicians. General-assignment reporters, though, can and do take on these assignments.

Often the health and medicine report is mated with material fed from various satellite news services. The national reporter, who may be a physician, will feed material that can be localized and integrated with material gathered locally.

Although physicians and other health professionals have a natural "in" for such coverage, it's probably safe to say that any reporter can cover the medical beat as long as he or she knows how to talk with medical professionals, gather information, and relate it to viewers' and listeners' everyday lives. In fact, an experienced journalist has an advantage over the health professional in some respects, in that the journalist generally has few preconceived notions or biases and is likely to have a keen insight into what topics interest the average citizen.

Consumer Reporting

Just as physicians have worked their way onto the air as health reporters, many attorneys find themselves employed as consumer reporters. But being a lawyer is certainly not a requirement for this job; tenacity is. You generally cover stories of long duration; investigating a complaint may take weeks or months of waiting for responses by mail or telephone. Some stations specialize in "Your Stories" segments that originate out of complaints called in from viewers.

The role of the consumer reporter is sometimes broadened to that of something like a freewheeling social critic. For example, a very successful series that ran in the New York area recently dealt with drivers' increasing propensity not to yield the right of way to ambulances and fire trucks. This is an example of "consumer" reporting, because taxpayers are paying for services slowed down by inconsiderate drivers, and it also touches on some deep and important social issues.

SUMMARY

Specialty assignments in broadcasting can be challenging. Although they call for special skills, the basic requirements of broadcast communication still form the underpinning of the announcer's abilities. To specialize successfully, one often needs a specific academic or practical background.

Sports requires a great deal of knowledge and a willingness by the announcer to learn about sports new to him or her. Many sportscasters make their reputations as "personalities," but there are serious issues in sports coverage, and journalistic skills are necessary.

Sports anchoring is stressful because it involves a great deal of last minute checking before going on the air. Sports anchors must appeal to local audience interests, and they must be energetic and versatile in their on-air approach. Play-by-play announcers must have an in-depth knowledge of the sport. Each sport presents its own particular set of problems. Football, for example, is hard to follow because it involves so many players, rules, and technically oriented plays.

Play-by-play announcers must be excited by the games they cover. They must avoid repetition, and they must not call plays before they have verified the information. Also, announcers must do a good job on commercials.

Weather reporters are often certified meteorologists. They work with computerized databases and, for television, create attractive graphic presentations. Weather segments are complex and require someone who can discuss weather conditions in a clear, informative manner.

In addition, the weather anchor must present the information succinctly and with poise. The job of a weather forecaster can become very tense during weather emergencies.

Narration is a specialized skill. Good narrators do not intrude on program content. Narration must be relatively low key, and the projection of the proper mood is imperative.

Broadcasters occasionally have the opportunity to act as hosts of special types of programming. Except for radio talk show hosts, most of these assignments, such as telethon MC and host of movie presentations or children's shows, are not full-time jobs but, rather, offer supplemental income and interesting opportunities to expand skills.

EXERCISES

1. Use a portable digital recorder or a smartphone to record a play-by-play segment for a televised basketball, football, baseball, or hockey game. Do your preparation by compiling information from

prewrites in the newspaper. If there is not enough information in the local paper, pick up a relevant copy of a sporting magazine. With the TV audio down, of course, record your own version of the play-by-play, and review the tape.

2. Watch three weather forecasters on the three major network affiliates in your area. Take comprehensive notes on program elements. In a few paragraphs, compare and contrast the weathercasters for the following:

a. Level of interest they show
b. Level of interest they instill in you
c. Energy conveyed
d. Credibility
e. Use of graphics

NOTES

1 Dorsey, Jesse "Power Ranking the Best Commentator Combinations in the NBA". April 23, 2012. http://bleacherreport.com/articles/1155919-power-ranking-the-best-commentator-combinations-in-the-nba

2 Remarks made November 12, 1994, at National Association of College Broadcasters panel "Sports Production," presented with Len Clark, general manager of WJEV-FM, and Warren Kozierski, WBSU-FM; several of the suggestions provided here were discussed at that panel.

10 Commercials and Acting

Combining commercials and acting in one chapter may seem odd at first glance. Acting is usually considered to be an artistic endeavor. And critics of broadcasting often give us the impression that commercials could never be an art form.

In fact, however, broadcast commercials are done with the highest production standards, using the best talent available. The people you see and hear in broadcast commercials have usually had years of classical training and considerable experience in drama. The competition is fierce, the rewards great, and the work exacting.

This chapter discusses the basics of commercials and the performer's role in them. The techniques of acting are presented and discussed, with a focus on how they apply to radio and television commercials. The chapter closes with an exploration of freelance commercial roles.

BASICS OF COMMERCIAL ANNOUNCING

During the past half-century, broadcast advertising has come into its own as a separate discipline. Production capabilities are part of the reason. In the early days of television, for example, a standard commercial might involve nothing more than one camera pointing at an announcer pouring a glass of beer and giving his pitch. Only occasionally did any sort of drama come into play.

Modern commercials, though, run the gamut from 30-second mini-dramas, to collages of action scenes, to the mundane hidden-camera testimonial.

Radio commercials have evolved, too. In the early days of radio, many advertisements featured grand-sounding speeches describing the high quality of a particular product. Today the emphasis has shifted to shorter phrases that usually do not so much describe the attributes of the product as portray its benefits (how it will make you feel better, look better, and so on). Radio advertising now also makes much greater use of the dramatic scene, the minidrama.

The biggest difference in modern radio advertising is the focus on communicating with a *particular* audience. Commercial producers often fashion several versions of an ad: one for hit radio, one for country, one for easy listening, and one for adult contemporary formats. Hitting a specific target audience is what modern radio is all about. A really good performer can gear his or her reading to a specific audience.

Types of Commercials

Commercials come in several shapes and sizes, and a familiarity with them is helpful to a performer. Although there is some overlap, we discuss radio and television commercials separately.

Radio Commercials. Most ads fall into these categories: a straight reading of a *script,* a *donut,* an *ad-lib,* an *acted scene,* a *man-in-the-street,* or a heavily produced *montage.* Many spots contain elements from several of these categories. The following descriptions summarize the particular demands the respective categories place on a performer.

Straight reading: All you have to work with are the words in the copy. A straight reading demands careful attention to variations of pitch and pace. The performer must also be aware of the need for proper emphasis on words. Vocal quality is important, as is a good level of energy in the voice. The straight reading sometimes has music underneath the voice, called a music "bed."

Donut: Usually furnished by an advertising agency, a donut has copy already recorded on the beginning and end. The commercial is called a donut because it has a "hole" in the middle, which a local performer is called on to fill. For example, a typical donut may open with 10 seconds of a jingle for shock absorbers, then 10 seconds of musical bed, followed by another 10 seconds of jingle and copy. The 10 seconds of musical bed in the middle—the hole—allows the local franchiser of the shock absorbers to give his (or her) message. From the performer's standpoint, a donut requires particular attention to timing; the copy must be read in the time allotted. Also, the performer needs to match the style projected by the prerecorded elements. Reading over a bed requires timing and attention to the flow of the music.

Ad-lib: "Ad-lib" means improvised, done extemporaneously. An ad-lib commercial is usually done from a fact sheet. Sometimes, skilled broadcast performers can construct a convincing ad-lib by playing around with the wording of a set script. Ad-lib spots are quite popular at radio stations that employ one particularly good, well-known announcer. The ad-lib commercial is usually done live, although sometimes it is recorded for later airplay. Some buyers of airtime are fond of the ad-lib commercial because they feel that their product or service will benefit from identification with the air personality. In fact, the ad-lib commercial gives the appearance of a personal endorsement of the product.

The ad-lib is probably the most difficult type of radio commercial to do well. Rather than simply reading a phrase, you have to think of that phrase at the exact second you need it and deliver that line convincingly. The only way to train for this skill is constant practice. Bill St. James, one of the top freelance announcers in New York, recalls that he developed ad-lib ability by inventing descriptive copy for magazine photos. This is a good practice, and one of the exercises in this chapter focuses on it.

Incidentally, an announcer who can ad-lib convincingly has an eye and ear for detail, which also is developed only by practice. Keep alert for the inspiration you can draw from the sleek lines of a car or the condensation on a bottle of beer. Good ad-lib skills are extremely valuable to an air personality.

Acted scene: Normally, two voices are used in this kind of commercial, often a male and female. Because radio spots are short and lacking visual cues, every effort is made to avoid distraction, hence the variation between voices and the limited number.

The dialogue is usually informal, uncomplicated, and often humorous. At best it is the beautifully timed exchanges of the legendary Bob and Ray or Dick and Bert. (You can find them on YouTube.) At worst, an acted scene is a local "husband and wife" enactment, something to the effect of "My, dear, have you seen the prices at . . ." The acted scene demands a skill often overlooked in typical broadcast training: the ability to assume a character and sound natural while doing it.

Acting skills are essential for performers who want to pursue commercial work, and we address those skills later in this chapter.

Man-in-the-street: The man (or woman) interviewed about a product or caught unaware in the act of choosing the sponsor's detergent is not always a professional performer, although professionals do appear in such ads. Aspiring actors and actresses have been known to write companies praising a product in hopes of securing a man-in-the-street role. When a professional performer does assume such a role, a natural and unaffected manner is an absolute must.

Heavily produced montage: In the fast-moving genre of hit radio, some commercials contain many production elements and brief snippets of copy. This category can entail a combination of almost all the others: a sound effect, a quick dramatic scene, several pieces of music, and so forth.

This type of commercial requires the ability to put a great deal of meaning and excitement into a few words. You do not have time to develop thoughts or characterizations, so those words must be precisely right. "Stock car racing at the fairground—the time of your life!" is an example. That one line has to convey all the excitement and allure of the event.

During production of these montage commercials, a good sense of timing is also required because a phrase might have to fit precisely between two sound effects or other production elements.

Television Commercials. Many of the structures common in radio are adapted to television, although the TV ads have their own particular set of nuances. The basic categories of TV commercials are *mini-dramas, spokesperson presentations, pitch presentations,* and *voice-overs.*

Mini-drama: In TV, this kind of commercial is usually more than just an acted scene. It is a full-range 30- or 60-second drama that presents characters, conflict, and resolution at breakneck speed. When done for national agencies, these commercials are at the very top level of production lavishness and can be incredibly expensive. They involve the top competitive actors and actresses in the field, often chosen because they have the right smiles or interesting, arresting faces.

Although some of these mini-dramas appear downright hokey, keep in mind that they generally do the job they're constructed to do. Do you remember a series of cell-phone commercials where there is an interpersonal problem created in each situation as a result of cellular static? Even though these commercials are attempts to make us laugh at a ridiculous situation, they do deliver the message that the advertiser's service is better than the competitor's.

If you think about it, you'll be able to recall dozens of mini-dramas where some soap, food or household product has helped resolve conflict in a situation. Effective performance in a mini-drama requires excellent acting skills and a high level of energy.

Spokesperson presentation: This type of commercial often involves a celebrity using his or her actual identity, or it can be an *implied identity*, using someone who is recognizable as a character, but not necessarily as himself or herself. Jerry Seinfeld (Figure 10.1), for example, has done a series of commercials as a comedian in a variety of comedic situations for a credit card company.

A spokesperson like Flo does not have to be a celebrity, but he or she must have some sort of implied identity. In other words, an unknown performer can give a very convincing spokesperson presentation for a product or service. In this case, the performer's implied identity is reinforced with her white uniform used throughout the commercial series. Though the series is rather humorous, the character is always serious about the fact that her product can save you money.

What does this require of a performer? Basically, a self-effacing presence and an honest, convincing delivery.

Pitch presentation: This harkens back to the old days of television, when the "pitchman" would deliver a sales message about a product. The difference between a pitchman and a spokesperson is that the former is identified neither as a celebrity nor as a particular kind of individual. The product is of prime importance; the pitchman purely a conduit of information.

For example, consider the late Ed McMahon, a well-known celebrity who sold life insurance and dog food (not at the same time, of course). When he sold life insurance, he acted as a trusted spokesperson, implying that he, as an intelligent and trustworthy person, endorsed the insurance. When he gave a stand-up dog food commercial on the set of a variety show, he was not claiming any expertise but only touting the product's benefits, acting as a conveyor of information. The dog food was the star, rather than the performer.

A performer in a pitch presentation must have a very high energy level and must move well and handle props with ease.

Voice-over: The performer who reads the copy is not seen in a voice-over commercial. Rather, the performer's voice is heard as a major component of the sound track. The voice-over format is an extremely popular way of constructing commercials. It has the advantage of giving top billing to the product, not to an on-camera performer. A variant of voice-over work is dubbing in the voice of an actor who looks but does not sound the part in a commercial.

FIGURE 10.1 Jerry Seinfeld, a master of the scene, has used his unique comic perspectives for acted commercials in a variety of settings.

What we usually refer to as voice-over requires an excellent sense of timing, the ability to read voice to picture, and the skill to communicate vocally without distracting from the visual elements of the presentation. In many cases, the voice-over announcer is virtually anonymous, in the sense that a trumpet player is anonymous in an orchestral setting. After all, no one listening to a musical bed in a commercial stands up and says, "Listen to that trumpet!" If that were the case, the trumpet player, regardless of his or her skill, would have detracted from the message. This is a rather roundabout way of making the point that the viewer is not supposed to be astounded by the voice-over announcer's fine delivery. In fact, much of the general public probably is not aware that there is such a category as voice-over announcers.

Voice-over work is quite challenging and, under the right set of circumstances, very profitable.

Radio and television commercials take a variety of incarnations. Keep in mind that many hybrid forms use several elements of the foregoing categories.

Now that we've defined the *whats,* let's examine some of the *whys.*

Goals of a Commercial

It is often assumed that the goal of a commercial is simply "to sell a product." In the long run that may be true, but there are many intermediate steps in the process. Is the purpose of a line to "sell" a bank or to make the listener believe that the bank is staffed by knowledgeable and helpful people who take an individual interest in their clients? More often, the latter statement is the immediate goal, with selling the bank a broader objective.

A performer really has to understand the goal of a commercial before he or she can come up with a decent delivery. Dig a little deeper into the copy. Find out what the copywriter is trying to get across in each word and phrase.

For example, do not assume that the only goal of a travel agent's commercial is to sell vacations. In the long run, that may be true, but the immediate goals for a broadcast communicator might be to:

- Make the listener aware of how absolutely miserable this winter weather is
- Convey a sense of excitement concerning the possibility of visiting a Caribbean resort
- Communicate the idea that this vacation is a real possibility, an affordable option

Being fully aware of the goals of a commercial will give you valuable cues to the points that ought to be stressed and to the proper inflections and rate of reading. This applies to any line you're delivering as an "announcer" or to any copy being delivered in the character of someone else, an "acted" part.

Straight versus Acted Delivery

One common fault of commercial performers is the inability to assume a role, the tendency to take the guise of an announcer when the performer should be donning the persona of a character in a play. There is a very fine line between a **straight delivery**, as in the delivery used by a radio personality reading a script, and an **acted delivery**. The importance of understanding acted deliveries lies not in differentiating but in being able to play a role convincingly.

For example, the producer of a college promotional film looking for a narrator auditioned a number of announcers who made their livings in broadcasting, and actors who made their livings on stage and in film. An actor won hands down. "I wanted someone who could convince the audience that he was an alumnus of our college," the producer said, "and who could assume that role. The fellow we chose had only an average voice, but he really slipped into that identity. Most of the announcers would have been inappropriate." Do not assume, however, that a broadcast communicator is always required to take on an identity. Whereas an identity was indicated for the college film, the narrator of a *National Geographic* documentary would appropriately use a straight delivery, almost a news style. The narrator, in that case, is not taking on a role.

In most cases, the producer of a commercial or other work will give you guidance about which type of delivery to give. The crucial thing from your standpoint is the ability to summon acting skills when you are called on to play a part.

Acting

Although this book cannot present an acting course per se, acting skills are essential to a performer and are often overlooked in broadcast curricula.

Many professionals in the commercial field recommend that students take as many drama courses as possible, and that's good advice. You cannot be trained as an actor in one chapter, but some exposure to the principles of acting is valuable, both for picking up practical skills and as a jumping-off point to further instruction.

In this overview we discuss the methods of *assuming a role, giving a natural delivery,* and using actors' *techniques.*

Assuming a Role. Many jokes have been made about the actor who stops in mid-scene and asks the director, "But what's my motivation?" That is often a legitimate question because motivation is the key to assuming a role and carrying it through a situation described in a plot.

Why does a character say a line? Why does he or she say it in a particular manner? Why does the character look, talk, walk a certain way? All those aspects should reflect motivation, and being able to convey motivation is what spells the difference between an actor and a mere reader of lines.

An actor playing a southern gentleman type will have to do more than work up a drawl. If the character is indeed a southern gentleman, he will undoubtedly have a certain way of moving: courtly and gentle gestures, perhaps. A southern gentleman is likely to have a proud bearing. If he is older, he will undoubtedly move differently from another southerner, 20 years younger.

A wide array of physical traits make up a character. As the great acting teacher Konstantin Stanislavski noted, small physical actions "and the moments of belief in them" acquire a great deal of significance on stage.

Other traits will play a role in the actor's rendition of a character. Do highly educated people speak in a different way than people with little education do? In most cases, they do, of course. And these traits must be *consistent* within the portrayal of a character. That is why television and screen writers often work up a complete biography of a character, including education, military service, political affiliations, and family history. Most of this information is never used directly, but it is important to the actors for the sake of character development and consistency. Novelists often undertake much the same process, drawing up an extensive biography of each character before the book is started.

You must do the same as an actor in a commercial. If background information is not presented to you, invent some. Make the character a *real* person.

Assume you have been assigned to do the voice of a banker in a commercial.

What kind of neighborhood does she live in? What does her family mean to her? What political party does she belong to? How much education has she had? Many of the questions may seem irrelevant. Indeed, for the immediate needs of the role, they very well may be, but filling in the details that make a character human can help you bring that character to life.

Let's look at another example. You have been cast in the role of a tough cop in a TV commercial for cold medicine. The advertiser, who wants to overcome the "macho" male's disdain for taking medicine for the sniffles, has constructed a commercial featuring a big-city patrol officer walking down the street, saying, "You know, when people are depending on me, I have to be at my best. I can't let a cold get me down. So when I feel the first signs of a cold coming on, I take Coldex. It's tougher than even *my* cold." The lines have all been written, the camera angles all blocked out, but it is your job to do the most important part. You must bring this character to life. How do you do it? By creating a personality sketch and relating those traits to your character's traits. Here is a possible—but not definitive—point-by-point analysis.

- *Voice quality.* Do big-city cops talk softly? Hardly. A gritty, rough voice is a possibility, as is a faint hint of an Irish brogue.
- *Posture and movement.* Most likely this character would have a purposeful stride, with a great deal of confidence in his step. One realistic gesture quite in keeping with this character is to point to the camera (the viewer) when he says, "You know, when people. . . ." When he finishes the line ". . . tougher than even *my* cold," this character just might point to himself with his thumb. Gestures would typically be heavy and broad.

     Assuming this manner of posture and movement would be helpful even if the characterization were for radio. Many radio performers use posture, gestures, and facial expression as a way of reinforcing the character.
- *Facial expression.* In the movies, police officers run the gamut from social smiles to angry insolence.

    Specific Character Traits of a Tough Street Cop. Talking slightly out of the corner of the mouth would be appropriate for this character. (Remember, *appropriateness* is the key. Talking from the side of the mouth would not be appropriate for the character of a librarian.) Another appropriate trait would be a squinty expression, common among patrol officers who walk dusty, windy city streets.

Other facial expressions? Try a knitted brow for the line ". . . when people are depending on me" and a slight jut of the jaw for the line ". . .tougher than even *my* cold." Note that the goal is not to assemble a mechanical grab-bag of expressions, but rather to decide what expressions and mannerisms would be believable in this character and would accentuate the message.

- *General character traits.* We want the character to be likable, so let's invent some likable points. He is easygoing but tough. Our cop has a lot of street smarts, but probably not an extensive formal education. He likes making small talk with the merchants on his route and has a real fondness for kids, but he won't take any guff from them.

A little personal history: he is the father of six, his brother is a priest, and he gets misty-eyed at Irish ballads.

Obviously, all these details will not be reflected point by point in the commercial, but the traits will build a persona for the character you invent. The personality traits add up to a satisfying whole, rather than a cardboard cutout.

Think of those four categories—voice quality, posture and movement, facial expression, and character traits—for any character you portray in a radio or television commercial. And although acting in a dramatic series is beyond the scope of this book, keep in mind that the process of defining characters applies to all types of drama.

Traits for Some Other Characters. Now let's apply those four categories to two different characters.

PERSONALITY SKETCH #1

Character: A young male homeowner telling us why he got his mortgage at a particular bank.

Voice Quality: You would not expect a gravelly voice or a deep bass from a younger man. However, the voice should transmit the qualities of confidence and responsibility. After all, he is trying to convince you of the right way to make an important decision.

Posture and Movement: Youth is important here, to show that young people can get mortgages, so the character's posture and movement must reflect health and vigor. He probably exercises regularly, perhaps playing basketball.

His body language would surely be open and direct. He would not sit hunched over with hands crossed over his chest. And although his posture reflects confidence, he doesn't have a cocky swagger, and he projects a certain vulnerability.

Facial Expressions: Smiles easily, but definitely is not the giggly type. Sincere, he has a level, but not challenging, gaze. By contrast, our policeman friend probably had eyes that drilled right through you.

Other Traits: Probably well educated, an engineer perhaps. He is organized, neat, owns an SUV, and is a member of his local church group.

PERSONALITY SKETCH #2

Character: A 25-year-old career woman searching for a new car. The commercial copy is intended to show that she knows what she wants, and knows that the people at Smith Dodge can give it to her with a minimum of fuss.

Voice Quality: Bright and energetic, but certainly not sultry and definitely not dumb-blonde breathless. There's no aggressive quality in her voice, just a confident assertiveness.

Posture and Movement: She walks purposefully, and her posture is straight. She does not make unnecessary movements.

Facial Expressions: Intelligent expression, level gaze, smiles easily but is not a jovial type.

Character Traits: Well-educated person with strongly shaped goals. She probably works very hard at her job. She is physically active and has a variety of hobbies and interests, such as skiing and jogging.

Employing character sketches has the advantage of helping you determine whether an action will be in character or out of character. Basing the personality on character sketches allows the actor to assume a role and deliver the lines with naturalness.

A "Natural" Delivery

Aim at giving a "natural" delivery. The word "natural" is somewhat deceptive because a radio or TV commercial is not a natural situation. Instead, the important element is the *appearance* of naturalness. In real life, people mumble, have speech impediments, and exhibit other characteristics we generally do not want to reproduce in a performance. "Naturalness" boils down to an unaffected performance, a projection of a recognizable character to the audience.

When assuming a role, the broadcast communicator must make every effort to avoid a cloud of artificiality.

Here is where *motivation* comes into play once again. There's nothing more to motivation than understanding something about the character and understanding why he or she is delivering the line. Is the character surprised? Angry? Patiently trying to convince us of something? For instance, expand on the character of the career woman looking for a car. To give some additional insight into the character, here are some invented lines of dialogue: "I want a car that fits my lifestyle—practical, but not *too* practical. After all, what's life without a little excitement?" These lines reveal a little more of the character's personality. She is a bit adventuresome and wants a car that does something besides transport her from place to place. However, she's a hard-working career woman, not an heiress, and probably would not opt for an exotic, expensive auto. So the lines assume a new meaning, and the actress would be wise to add just a touch of mischief to her voice and expression, some hint of the thirst for excitement that dwells beneath a staid exterior.

Another example concerns a different motivation. It is a scene in a shabby auto repair shop where the mechanic tells a young man he needs a new exhaust system. "A whole new exhaust system?" the young man replies. "But you put in a new system just a month ago!" What is the motivation for this line? Frustration, anger, disgust with the whole operation. The character will, of course, go to the sponsor's shop next time. His reaction is pretty obvious. Other reactions and motivations might require more thought, especially in a voice-over, where there are no visual cues to reinforce the message. In most cases, the voice-over calls for a straight delivery, not assuming a role, but there is no reason not to assume certain personality traits if they are appropriate. Here are some possible ways to analyze the motivation behind voice-over copy.

Copy: Voice-over for special airline fare to California.
What the performer wants to communicate: A sense of excitement, almost incredulity, at these extremely low fares. The voice-over performer is a bearer of good news.

Copy: Voice-over to convince small investors to deal with a certain brokerage house.
What the performer wants to communicate: The voice-over performer's vocal qualities and delivery must imply that he or she is a sincere person who really wants to tell others about the good service at this particular brokerage house. The voice-over announcer might think in terms of playing the role of an intelligent neighbor.

The point is that unless these lines are delivered with motivation in mind, some artificiality will be projected into the delivery, regardless of whether the performer assumes a believable character. The voice-over for the airline fares, as a case in point, would not be very effective if the delivery were somber. The investment brokerage spot would be very ineffective with a singsong, top-40 disc jockey delivery. Would you invest with a brokerage house represented by an announcer who sounds as if he or she is about to say, "Hey there, girls and guys"?

One other point: it is entirely possible to assume a character and understand the meaning and motivation of the copy and still appear artificial. If character and motivation are in order, the causes of artificiality can include the following:

1. *Unnatural pronunciation.* Be wary of saying "thee" for *the* or "ay" as in *skate* for the article *a,* which is usually pronounced "uh." Don't overenunciate.

    If the script calls for a dialect, make sure you can speak it convincingly.

    Critical listening with a tape recorder is the only reliable guide.

    Most acting textbooks contain phoneticized dialect guides, and it would be very helpful to study them. Dialect work is extraordinarily difficult, so there's no disgrace in not being able to master it. Many broadcasters don't; just turn on your radio anywhere in the country on St. Patrick's Day.

2. *Stilted dialogue.* Sometimes artificiality is the copywriter's fault. However, the performer usually can't change dialogue. If you are having trouble with a line such as "My, this certainly is a wonderful product, Joyce; we must order it right away," walk away from the line for a few minutes. Try to say the line in your own words, paying attention to believable phrasing. Now, give the stilted line with the same type of delivery you used when in your own paraphrase. Some pieces of dialogue will never sound right, but this method can sometimes help.

3. *Overacting.* Putting too much into a performance is just as bad as injecting too little. The most effective way to catch overacting, or "a stench of ham," as it is sometimes called, is to have a knowledgeable teacher or colleague critique your performance. Video and audio recording help, too, of course.

4. *Inappropriate movement.* A gesture that is completely in character with the part you're playing may appear totally inappropriate on television.

On TV, you are working in a confined space and must often create the illusion of movement rather than executing the movement itself.

For example, a commercial that calls for you to walk across a used car lot requires compact and controlled movement because the distortion of the TV lens would make a normal gait appear as though you were bounding across a basketball court. Walking and moving on television is a skill in itself, which can be developed only by practice and viewing tapes.

Factors that add artificiality to an otherwise well-constructed performance can be eliminated only by awareness and constant practice. There are very few "naturals" who can stroll onto a site and walk and talk well, because appearing on television is, as mentioned, an "unnatural" situation. The same principle applies to radio, perhaps more strongly because a performance relying entirely on voice can be difficult to pull off well.

Techniques

In addition to the abilities required to assume a role and to bring about a natural delivery, television and radio commercials, whether acted or with a straight delivery, require mastery of certain specialized techniques. A technique is loosely defined as a method whereby a performer treats certain details of his or her craft. Techniques unique to television and radio are considered in the sections on those topics, but we'll close this acting session by discussing techniques for improving any type of broadcast performance.

Of primary importance is the ability to *animate your delivery.* Animation literally means "putting life into," and that's exactly what you'll be called on to do when reading copy.

Veteran New York voice-over commercial actor Nick Schatzki, who has voiced commercials for clients such as Eastman Kodak Company and *Newsday,* notes that one way to bring copy to life is to visualize someone to whom you are speaking. Picture a single individual, he advises, and talk directly to that person. If necessary, form a mental image of that person sitting, in miniature, on top of your microphone.

Breathing life into copy is not accomplished purely by voice quality.

Remember, communication is the goal. You have undoubtedly heard many voice-overs by acclaimed actor Morgan Freeman (Figure 10.2) without realizing it was Freeman.

FIGURE 10.2 Morgan Freeman is a premier voice-over artist who communicates on a seeming one-to-one basis with the audience.

Freeman has the ability to "lose" himself in a role; by that, we mean to become such a genuine communicator that the audience forgets that he is a performer. Google on "Morgan Freeman voice-overs", watch the video results that are returned, you will see what we mean.

Understanding Copy

Understanding copy is largely a function of the methods of analysis discussed in Chapter 3. If you combine that analysis with the techniques of identifying motivation and determining the goals of a particular commercial, you can attack the job with a thorough comprehension. The following pointers are important to developing commercial technique.

1. Good acting skills will always increase your ability to communicate and animate copy. Acting training usually focuses heavily on methods of infusing life into a character. Many pros, including Lester Lewis, recommend that you take a variety of drama courses and get some stage experience, if you can.
2. Working before a live audience is a helpful experience for any broadcast communicator because it gives a sense of how things play. Broadcasters trained only in broadcasting sometimes lack a sense of comedic timing, for example, a skill best honed in front of living, laughing people.

The ability to animate copy is a technique useful in both radio and television commercials, and for all practical purposes, in any other form of broadcasting, too. Techniques specific to each medium are discussed next in the sections summarizing radio commercials and television commercials.

Radio Commercials

Earlier, the basic types and structures of radio commercials were described.

Radio spots rely entirely on sound, so the broadcast communicator must be particularly sensitive to what sound can do and must be adept at maximizing the impact of the sound elements. This means that you will be concerned with more than just the vocal delivery. Also important is the ability to play off other elements, such as music and sound effects. In addition, special talents are required of a radio commercial performer, talents unique to the field.

> **Unique Aspects of Radio Commercials.** In a sense, the producer of a radio commercial has a more difficult task than does someone constructing an ad for television. Why? Because the radio copy must be aimed with pinpoint precision at a target audience. In another sense, this factor can be regarded as making the job easier because the TV producer is in the position of having to please almost everyone.

The essence of the discussion is that radio is a one-to-one medium. The successful performer on radio is the performer who can put across a message on a personal basis. You will be called on to do some tasks unique to the medium. Of primary importance is ad-libbing from a **fact sheet.**

The ability to do a credible job ad-libbing from a fact sheet, and the related ability to please sponsors, can take you very far in modern radio. The effectiveness of an ad-lib commercial lies in the injection of the performer's personality into the spot. In radio, personality is still very much alive. In earlier times, personalities such as the late Dick Clark could maintain that kind of role on television. Clark was the acknowledged master of the ad-lib commercial, both on radio and television. His absolutely natural delivery was stunningly effective in pleasing sponsors and motivating buyers.

BOX 10.1 Ad-Libbing from a Fact Sheet: An Example

Build an effective ad-lib around this fact sheet.

- The Charter House Restaurant, 411 Grand Avenue, serves the widest array of seafood dishes in the city.
- Seafood is caught fresh every day and brought right from the boat to the kitchen.
- Specialties include lobster for two, a complete dinner with wine, Caesar salad prepared at the table, and baked potato. All for $27.95.
- Colorful atmosphere, including the Clipper Ship Lounge where fishnets line the walls. There are brass nautical decorations. One-ton anchor outside entrance.
- Owners Joey and Paul Italiano provide first-class hospitality at bargain prices.

Here is one way, but not the only way, a radio air personality might do the ad-lib.

When you dine at the Charter House Restaurant, you get a great bargain, and you can choose from the widest array of fine seafood dishes served anywhere in the city. Do you know where the Charter House is? Well, it's up on 411 Grand Avenue, right off the Seashore

BOX 10.1 *(continued)*

Expressway, and that's important because if you know that section of the city you also know that the Charter House sits right on the water, next to where the fishing boats dock. The seafood comes right off the boats and into the Charter House kitchen, so whenever you eat at the Charter House you're getting today's catch.

Right now you can enjoy the "Lobster for Two" special, a complete dinner that comes with a Caesar salad prepared at your table—hey, that's a show in itself—and you also get wine and baked potato. All for $27.95. . . remember, that's for two people, $27.95 for a complete dinner.

By the way, the food at the Charter House is only part of the experience.

If you've never been there, make it a point to stop in and have a drink at the Clipper Ship Lounge. . . that's the place where they have fishnets on the walls and all those brass nautical gizmos.

And you'll know you're in the right place when you see the one-ton anchor outside the door.

We were there last week and had a great meal and great service, too. The owners, Joey and Paul Italiano, make sure you get first-class hospitality at bargain prices. That's the Charter House Restaurant, 411 Grand Avenue.

Production Basics. In radio, the performer often does the production work as well. This requires basic skills such as using an audio console, mixing sources, and operating a variety of equipment. The skills are essentially the same as those outlined in Chapter 5. In a commercial, the goal is to use these skills to enhance the commercial message.

The performer must be sensitive to production details, such as relative levels of sound from different sources. For example, reading over a music bed requires a delicate balance. The music can't be loud enough to drown out the voice, but the music must not be so soft as to be imperceptible.

Extensive instruction in production is beyond the scope of this text. Note that knowledge of production can always be helpful to a performer, so even if your ambitions lie in on-air work, taking as many production courses as possible will be extremely worthwhile. Why? Notice how a good grounding in production techniques can help you enhance a message in a radio commercial in the following examples.

- You are reading a piece that is set outdoors, but you're in the studio and picking up a lot of echo and reverberation from the walls. A basic knowledge of acoustics would let you make your spot more believable by setting up a simple baffle to block sound reflection and eliminate the echo and reverberation.
- Knowing the characteristics of different mics can enable you to choose a mic with a great deal of "presence" for an intimate feel in a perfume commercial.
- A knowledge of special effects and how to produce them can add to the message. Use of filters, for example, can cut down on the frequencies passed through the console and can produce a weird, unearthly effect, useful for attracting attention if used appropriately.

Delivery Techniques. Two more specialized techniques are indispensable in radio and also have some specific applications in television, especially in voice-over work. The techniques are *reading to time* and **compressing copy**. They are two of the most useful skills you can develop, and frequently are the talents that separate a good description from one recognized as being top drawer.

Reading to time. Some professionals maintain that reading to time calls for an ability you are, or are not, born with. Others contend that constant practice can develop this skill, and we're inclined to agree with the latter view. The bottom line in this dispute is that no one can teach you how to read copy in exactly 30 seconds. It is a talent that can be achieved only by experience. The goal is to develop an internal clock that lets you know when the pace has to be picked up or slowed down.

Why read to time? Well, many commercials have a certain time slot allotted for copy, and if it is 19 seconds the copy *has* to be 19 seconds, no more and no less. In most radio stations, 30-second spots must last precisely 30 seconds because they may be used in a "hole" provided in a network newscast and therefore can't fall short or run long.

Although there is no magic formula for developing this skill, incorporating the following suggestions into your practice can help speed the process of learning.

1. *Develop a familiarity with music and music phrasing.* Listen critically to music and learn to identify key changes, or the distinction between a trumpet solo and a clarinet solo. This is helpful because music beds can be used as cues. If, after a couple of rehearsals, you find that you should be giving the prices of the products when the musical key changes from C to G, you can use the key change as a landmark from which to adjust the rate at which you read the rest of your copy. In the long run, this will be easier and less distracting than trying to keep one eye glued to a timer or stopwatch. Knowing the background music also helps you to match your delivery more naturally to the music bed.
2. *When you start practicing development of a time sense, shoot for hitting 10 seconds, not 30, on the dot.* Once you have mastered 10 seconds, try reading 30-second spots exactly to time, thinking in terms of three 10-second segments. Another way to practice is to read a 30-second spot and then cut it down to 25 seconds. Do it again, aiming for 35 seconds.
3. *Mark your copy with time cues, as shown in Chapter 3.*

   Compressing copy. Successful performers frequently point out that one of the most valuable skills in their arsenals is the ability to put a lot of words into a short time.

The reason is simple. Time is money, and the more commercial words a sponsor gets for his or her time allotment, the happier the sponsor will be. As a result, copy is often written very tightly, and frequently there are more words in a 30-second spot than could normally be read comfortably in 30 seconds.

This requirement may get out of hand. A merchant once presented one of the authors with a page and a half of single-spaced typewritten copy and requested that it be "squeezed into" a 60-second spot.

Compressing copy, reading rapidly without a rushed, chatterbox delivery, is a valuable skill that can be enhanced by practice and the following specialized techniques.

First, *use a musical analogy.* When an orchestra speeds up a piece of music, the relationship among the notes and rests remains the same: a quarternote is still one-fourth as long in duration as a whole note, but both will be shorter in duration when the tempo is picked up. The same is true of rests between notes. They remain proportional.

The biggest fault of the performer who produces a rushed, hurry-up sound is reading the elements of the copy out of proportion. The result is a change in the phrasing, sometimes eliminating all natural pauses between words or phrases. Another symptom of the hurry-up syndrome is a monotone, where the "melody" of the copy is altered.

When you have to speed up your delivery, remember not to change the *relative* rate of delivery, and don't alter the melody of your voice. Speed up everything, but do not change the relationship among words.

Second, *read ahead in your script.* Reading ahead allows you to speed up the copy and retain its naturalness. Typically, in a hurry-up delivery, the performer forms a direct connection between eye and mouth, becoming less a communicator and more a reading machine, concentrating on speed and losing meaning and flow. Stay a sentence ahead in the copy, and you will phrase the words in a more natural way because you will be saying a sentence, not reading words.

Television Commercials

Earlier, we examined some types of television commercials and discussed what they demand of a performer, as well as how to create a character for television or radio. This section explores some specific techniques of making television commercials.

It is important to understand that the television commercial industry is, in most cases, not a part of the television broadcast industry. Many commercials are produced by independent production houses, and the performers generally are trained as actors, not as broadcasters. Television voice-over work has a greater percentage of broadcasters.

Local TV stations do produce commercials, but the broadcaster in these markets usually doesn't do a lot of on-camera work. Voice-over work is, however, typically assigned to the broadcaster in local markets.

On the national level, commercial production is a highly specialized business, with spots written by ad agencies and produced by independent houses.

In this environment, performers typically work on a freelance basis.

Regardless of whether the assignment is on a local or on a nationally syndicated TV spot, the importance of properly creating a character and giving a genuine delivery cannot be overstated. In addition, TV has some very stringent technical requirements that, if not adhered to, can put performers out of the running before they get a chance to show their talents. These techniques are unique to on-camera acting.

On-Camera Acting

A television camera is a merciless instrument, capable of picking up every detail of a performance, good and bad. An actor or performer must constantly be aware of the power of this unblinking eye and must develop the following specialized skills.

Ability to Control Movement. Turning to face someone, a simple act in everyday life, can be horrendously complicated in a television studio.

The performer must be able to turn without causing the studio lighting to cast uncomplimentary shadows. Too large a movement will pull the performer from his or her mark, usually a piece of tape on the floor, thus throwing off all the camera angles.

Performers frequently must be able to talk with another on-air person without looking directly at him or her. In the theater, actors typically direct their gazes downstage, toward the audience, so that more of their faces are visible to the audience. In some circumstances, you must do the same on TV: look in an unnatural direction during dialogue so that the camera sees more of your face.

Television, like football, is a game of inches. The performer must develop the necessary skills to stay on a mark, move the same way in subsequent takes, and remember his or her body positions at the end of a take so that they can be matched up with the beginning of the next take.

Ability to Control Mannerisms. "You wouldn't believe some of the faces people make when they're on camera," said the late Vangie Hayes, casting director for the J. Walter Thompson advertising agency in New York. She noted, "Some performers feel that they have a talent for punctuating everything they say with a raised eyebrow. But that mannerism becomes very distracting."

Ability to Project a Type. Time in a television commercial is limited, so there is little opportunity to build a character by dialogue or exposition.

Much of the character's personality must be readily apparent, which is why the woman who plays a young mother has to be a young mother "type." Her identity must virtually leap from the screen.

Types in commercial acting include the young mother, the young father, the distinguished spokesperson, the sexy leading-lady type, the macho male, and the "character" part. Cultivating your particular type, whether you are destined to play college professors or cab drivers, is important. Obviously, you must be believable within your type, meeting age and physical requirements.

A strong Brooklyn accent may work to your advantage in seeking cab driver parts, although you would be well advised to lose it for any other type of mass media work.

Type casting is very important in commercial work, and specialists often put "young father" or "character type" right on their résumés. Identify your strengths, especially your ability to play a type, and exploit them.

> **Handling Props.** The days of the stand-up commercial with prop in hand are pretty well past, although some local stations still use this structure and on occasion a national spot will do it for novelty. When a product is held, the close-up often features a professional hand model.

For simply handling a prop, the rule of thumb is not to let it glare on the camera lens. A book, for example, must be tipped at the proper angle to keep the reflection from the lights from making the cover glare badly. A second, but just as important, rule is never cover the product with hand or fingers.

Props in modern commercials are more likely to serve as items to be consumed.

Commercial performers frequently are called on to ingest a product, and they must do so with as much satisfied, ecstatic zeal as can be summoned within the bounds of common sense. If you are eating a slice of pizza, the director will expect you to be capable of reacting to the taste of the pizza. If you are drinking milk, be prepared to communicate enjoyment.

You will be expected to portray an enormous amount of delight in the consumption of a product. Remember, if you ever are lucky enough to secure a part in a commercial such as this, you will be operating in a big business and will be expected to perform on cue, as a professional.

> **Freelance Assignments.** National commercial work is mostly done on a freelance basis. Many of the performers are actors, and some, especially in voice-over work, are broadcasters.

On a local level, more professional broadcasters participate.

Freelance assignments are available on the national and local levels, although an employee of a particular station may frequently find restrictions placed on the types of outside work in which he or she may engage. Parts in commercials are obtained through:

- Ad agencies, which handle advertising accounts for clients and often do the scripting and casting for the commercial
- Model and talent agencies, which supply talent and take a cut of the talent's compensation
- Production houses, the firms that actually film or tape the commercial
- Broadcast stations, which assign commercials to in-house talent and sometimes hire freelancers

The competition for parts in commercials, especially TV commercials on the national level, is intense. Before you even enter the ring, you should have examples (audio, video, or both, depending on your interest) of your best work to present to the casting director of the organization you approach, or to an agent. You will also need a résumé summarizing your previous commercial experience, if any, along with your training. An 8-by-10-inch black-and-white portrait photo is often required. It is essential to have a web-based portfolio.

In some cases, a commercial performer must belong to a union, such as the Screen Actors Guild (SAG) or the American Federation of Television and Radio Artists (AFTRA). Unions are examined more closely in the final chapter of this book.

What are the qualifications for picking up a commercial role? The late casting director and author Vangie Hayes once said she looked for "the ability to talk to someone. There was a time when most announcers were the 'deep, disembodied voice,' but today the emphasis is on communication." One attribute of a performer's voice, Hayes noted, was the level of interest it carries. "I think a good voice is a voice that you would hear on a TV in another room, and walk into that room just to see what's going on.

A good voice is also an interesting voice . . . perhaps even a voice with a little rasp in it." Hayes agreed with those who advise that practice is the only way to improve.

Compare your performance to those of professionals, and always be aware of areas in which you can polish your skills.

A Final Note

Commercial performance can be extremely lucrative, a comforting thought when you consider that broadcasting on-air work as a whole does not pay very well. Yes, top performers do make a great deal of money. But at the local level, especially in small markets, on-air talent generally makes less than salespeople or management and in very small stations, than secretarial help. Remember that those at the top *are* at the top, the very top, of a fiercely competitive pyramid. The top news anchor jobs, for example, are not easily obtained.

Securing commercial roles is never easy, but the field does offer quite a bit of opportunity. And for staff radio personalities and certain television staff on-air performers, the ability to deliver a commercial convincingly is a sure step to career advancement. *Never* underestimate the role of commercials and the value of developing the talent to do them well. As long as there is broadcast advertising, the performer who can convince us to use a product or service will be in demand.

SUMMARY

Broadcast advertising has emerged as a separate discipline. Modern commercials take many forms. Among those forms in radio are straight reading, donut, ad-lib from a fact sheet, acted scene, man-in-the-street, and heavily produced montage. Forms in television include mini-drama, spokesperson presentation, pitch presentation, and voice-over.

The long-range goal of a commercial is to sell a product or service, but there are many intermediate steps. The commercial, for example, might seek to create a sense of excitement in the listener and then communicate that the product or service offered is affordable and a realistic option. This is much more sophisticated than simply saying, "Buy this product." A commercial performer must be able to do a straight delivery (announcing) and an acted delivery (assuming a role).

Acting is a discipline within itself, and proficiency can require years of study. However, familiarity with some basic principles is helpful for any broadcaster interested in commercial performance. The primary consideration in acting a role is determining the motivation, the complex of factors that cause a character to say a line in a particular manner.

The actor must do an analysis of a character and determine that character's physical traits, level of education, voice quality, posture and movement, facial expression, and other traits. It is vital that the actor's delivery be consistent with the overall personality sketch of the character.

Commercial actors must particularly avoid unnatural-sounding speech, stilted dialogue, overacting, and inappropriate movement.

The way a performer treats his or her craft is often defined as technique. In very basic terms, applying to both television and radio, technique is the means of animating copy, bringing it to life.

Radio and television commercials have unique aspects to which special techniques must be applied. Radio commercials involve polishing the technique of reading from a fact sheet, being able to integrate production basics into the overall effort, and such specialized delivery techniques as reading to time and compressing copy. Television commercials call for the specialized techniques of on-camera acting and handling props.

Most performers in commercials that are broadcast nationwide work on a freelance basis. Parts for commercials are subject to stiff competition, but the financial rewards are great. In fact, the entire broadcast commercial industry offers handsome rewards to performers at many levels.

EXERCISES

1. Write a 30-second television commercial for a raincoat. The commercial must contain a dramatic scene, with one actor talking about why his or her raincoat is a great piece of apparel. Here's an example.

   Video: Salesman gets off airplane with a coat slung over his shoulder
   Video: Puts coat on
   Audio: My St. Cloud raincoat has put up with downpours in New Orleans, snow in Buffalo, wind in Chicago.
   Video: Salesman sees distinguished client walk up to him.
   Audio: And in my business, you can't afford to look sloppy. I've got to look sharp.

   In addition to writing a commercial, prepare a personality sketch of the main figure. Decide on voice quality, posture and movement, facial expressions, and general character traits. For example, traits for our salesman would probably include a hard-driving personality and a lack of tolerance for poor products. Because he is demanding, he picks a good coat, which is the point of the commercial.

   Do this for the following four characters. The characters can be male or female, and you can vary the characteristics of the coat (it does not have to be a dress topcoat). Write a script and a personality sketch for a. a fisherman; b. a rich, dashing man or woman about town; c. an international reporter; d. a detective on a long outdoor stakeout.

   After you have written the commercials and character sketches, perform the scene. Do it from the standpoint of each of your four characters.

2. Record three versions of a standard 30-second radio script, using an existing script or one you write.

   Do one version in exactly 25 seconds, one version in exactly 30 seconds, and another in exactly 35 seconds.

3. Ad-lib a 60-second (approximately) commercial from a magazine ad.

   Use as little of the ad's direct wording as possible. Try to draw inspiration from the photo, rather than the text.

11 Polishing Your Skills

What separates those few broadcast performers who reach the top from those who seem to get stalled down below? The answer is complicated; it has to do partly with native skill, luck, and ambition. But beyond those factors, what most characterizes people who get to the top and stay there is the ability and the determination to improve. Those are the people who learn from their mistakes and benefit from self-critiques and critiques by others.

This chapter, though brief, is very important. It tells you how to use self-evaluation to improve your skills. These are the methods used by top professionals. If you regard self-improvement as a lifelong discipline, you'll be less likely to stagnate in your career and more likely to rise to the heights of this very competitive field.

EVALUATION

You can improve on-air delivery in three ways:

1. Listening to or viewing a recording of yourself and doing a self-critique
2. Having a teacher, supervisor, or co-worker critique your performance
3. Ask a local professional to review your recording

The third option is often more productive, but sometimes more difficult to come by. In small markets, for example, few people may be willing or able to offer a worthwhile critique and suggestions for improvement.

When an external critique is available, it frequently comes as part of the process of grading in an educational setting or standard performance evaluation in an employment situation. Such advice is valuable, and although it may not always be correct, it is wise to listen, file the information away mentally, and use it for reference whenever you engage in self-criticism.

Evaluating your own performance may lack objectivity, but it can provide an irreplaceable insight into performance. Viewing or listening to your own tapes, at regular intervals, during all stages of your professional advancement, is invaluable.

What to Look for in Audio and Video Recordings. Be as objective as you can, and don't make excuses. Don't think, "Well, I really meant to say something else, but I understood what came out." Evaluation must be done from outside your own head, so to speak, from the standpoint of the listener or viewer. *Evaluate in terms of pure communication.*

Be sure that ideas and moods are communicated in such a way that the audience will perceive them immediately. Ask yourself if the communication elements are clear.

Next, break down the *whys*. Why was a commercial not as good as it could have been? Where were the mistakes, and how could weak areas be improved? Do not settle for a general overall negative feeling: *break down problem areas into specifics*.

Be vigilant in hunting for mistakes in pace, a lack of variety in the reading.

Is the pitch right? Does the delivery sound phony? Isolating any and all of these factors can help in your quest for self-improvement. If the pace is inappropriate, for example, experiment until you arrive at a pace that reinforces the message, rather than detracting from it.

As noted in Chapter 3, any interference in communication detracts from the impact. In addition to the problem areas just specified, distractions such as poor diction, regionalism, unusual voice patterns, or oddities in appearance divert the audience's attention from the message. When viewing or listening to recordings, *identify distractions*.

For example, do you constantly raise one eyebrow during a newscast?

Make a consistent effort to keep that eyebrow down from now on. If your pitch drops repeatedly at the end of each and every sentence, work on vocal variety.

You can evaluate pure communication, breaking down problems into specifics and identifying distractions for airchecks or in practice sessions.

Practice sessions are a must for improving on-air ability and provide a low-pressure environment for ironing out the problems uncovered during self-critique.

Additional applications for practice sessions are listed in the following section on improvement.

Self-evaluation can be painful but extraordinarily productive. Use recordings as much as possible; even your smartphone can be a valuable tool. Look and listen objectively. One excellent prescription for self-evaluation is to have someone record you when you are not aware it is being done. This way, you will be natural and won't be *trying* to do an exceptional job.

This strategy works well with critiquing sports play-by-play. Have your play-by-play recorded and set the file aside for a few days. Then listen to your description; if you can follow the game by what you've said, you probably did a good job. It is important not to play the recording for two or three days because if you listen right after the game, you will be filling in from memory many details that should be clear from your description alone.

Remember that self-evaluation can be positive as well as negative. Note what you do well, in addition to finding fault. This will identify strengths and head off discouragement. *Do not give up. Keep working.*

A Complete Self-Evaluation. When listening to or viewing a performance keep the checklist shown in Box 11.1 before you. The section titled "Voice and Diction" applies to both television and radio; "Visual Presentation" contains items specific to television.

BOX 11.1 Self-Evaluation Checklist

• •

Voice and Diction

Pitch

Does my voice rise and fall naturally, without any artificial patterns? Yes ___ No ___

Voice Quality

Is there resonance in my voice? Yes ___ No ___
Is it free of a tight, pinched quality? Yes ___ No ___
Is it free from hoarseness or a guttural quality? Yes ___ No ___

BOX 11.1 *(continued)*

Diction

Do I clearly separate words? Do I say "it was," rather than "ih twas"? Yes ___ No ___
Is my delivery free from regionalism? Yes ___ No ___
Is my diction free of clipped, too-precise quality? Yes ___ No ___
Is my diction free of other distractions? Do I say "bottle," rather than "bah-ull"? Yes ___ No ___

Breath Control

Is my voice free from breathiness? Yes ___ No ___
Do I sound as though I have an adequate air support and supply? Yes ___ No ___
Do I avoid running low on breath during reading? Yes ___ No ___
Do I have adequate diaphragmatic support during the reading (check this during the on-air session)? Yes ___ No ___

Interpretation

Do I understand the basic ideas of the copy? Yes ___ No ___
Do I *appear* to understand the basic ideas of the copy? Yes ___ No ___
Can I now, after listening to the recording, immediately repeat the flow of ideas in the copy? Yes ___ No ___
If the piece is a commercial or public service announcement, can I now summarize the thrust of the copy in a single sentence? Yes ___ No ___
Checking the reading against the script, do the key words I had marked still appear to be the correct words? Yes ___ No ___

Expression

Did I give proper stress to the key words? Yes ___ No ___
Does the reading make sense and lead to a compelling point? Yes ___ No ___

Mood

Do I project a proper and appropriate mood for the copy? Yes ___ No ___
Is the reading devoid of overplaying, overacting, or a maudlin quality? Yes ___ No ___
Are transitions clear? Is it perfectly evident where one piece of copy stops and another begins? Yes ___ No ___
Does mood change during transitions? Yes ___ No ___

Pace

Is the pace appropriate to the piece? Yes ___ No ___
Does it reinforce the message? Yes ___ No ___
Does the pace sound natural? Yes ___ No ___
Does the pace vary within copy? Are the variations appropriate? Yes ___ No ___

Naturalness

Does delivery sound conversational? Yes ___ No ___
Does it sound like speech, and not like reading? Yes ___ No ___

BOX 11.1 *(continued)*

Is my reading believable? Yes ___ No ___
Is my reading sincere? Yes ___ No ___
Is my reading free of elements of obvious and outright imitation? Yes ___ No ___

Phrasing

Are words naturally delivered in phrases? Yes ___ No ___
Is the reading free of any unclear phrasing (an adjective that "dangles," for example, leaving the listener unsure of exactly what is being described)? Yes ___ No ___
Are pauses used properly and effectively? Yes ___ No ___
Are only necessary pauses added to the copy? Yes ___No ___

Energy and Interest Level

Does the delivery interest you, and would it interest members of the audience? Yes ___ No ___
Is energy level appropriate to the copy, not too hyper or too laid-back? Yes ___ No ___
Do I appear to care about what I am reading? Yes ___ No ___

Visual Presentation

Appearance

Is my on-camera presentation free of visual distractions such as unruly hair or poorly fitting clothes? Yes ___ No ___
Are gestures natural, instead of movement seeming stiff or forced? Yes ___ No ___
Is eye contact direct and level, while still seeming natural and comfortable to the viewer? Yes ___ No ___

Facial Expression

Is my expression appropriate for the copy? Yes ___ No ___
Do my expressions change during reading? Yes ___ No ___
Is head movement natural and not distracting, free of bobbing, and always within the frame? Yes ___ No ___

Posture and Body Language

Does my posture express interest and energy? Yes ___ No ___
Is my body position natural and not rigid or stiff? Yes ___ No ___

Take your self-evaluation seriously, and be critical. If you are fortunate enough to have a colleague willing to provide an honest critique, share this checklist with him or her.

As you evaluate your performance, jot down the "no"s on a separate sheet of paper and, if possible, index counter numbers of the audio- or videotape machine at the point where you noticed the particular problem. This will give you the opportunity to go back and review the negative aspects of your performance. You should note the positive aspects of your work, too.

Also write down some coherent notes (notes you will understand next week or next year) to yourself on your separate sheet of paper.

Performance can be evaluated many ways. Sometimes you may want only a quick review, at other times an in-depth study. This list is kept flexible so that you can tailor it to your individual needs. Exercise 1 at the end of this chapter provides a possible framework for complete self-evaluation. Keep your notes and your recordings *forever*. This way, you can establish a lifelong baseline from which to judge your improvement. A checklist for long-term plans is shown in Box 11.2.

BOX 11.2 A Checklist for Long-Term Plans

Evaluation does not end with an examination of the mechanics of an aircheck. There is also a strong need for lifelong, career-wide checks and plans. Ask yourself the following questions.

Do I have a daily regimen of vocal and breathing exercises, such as those described in Chapter 2? Yes ___ No ___

Do I have a target body weight, and do I maintain that weight? Yes ___ No ___

Do I take advantage of any opportunity to ad-lib (sports coverage, acting as host of telethon, etc.)? Yes ___ No ___

Do I constantly develop my vocabulary by reading widely and looking up unfamiliar words? Yes ___ No ___

Do I read a variety of material, including news magazines, trade journals, and literature? Yes ___ No ___

Do I observe and learn from others? Yes ___ No ___

Do I have long-term goals? Yes ___ No ___

Improvement

Once problems have been identified, you can practice to eliminate the distracting or inappropriate elements. You need a low-pressure environment in which to practice the following skills:

1. *Hone your ability to read a sentence or more ahead in copy.* This is valuable for radio as well as television. To repeat an important point made earlier, radio announcers must be able to glance up from copy to read clocks, find carts, or look for other pieces of copy. Reading ahead helps you think in terms of communicating phrases and thoughts, rather than just reading words.
2. *Ad-lib.* You can't be embarrassed by clumsy ad-libs made during practice, and practicing extemporaneous skills can prevent those ad-libs from being clumsy in the future. Ad-lib anything during practice: humorous patter, music intros, news reports based on notes. Ad-libbing is largely an acquired skill.
3. *Fine-tune your sense of timing.* Practice condensing 30 seconds worth of copy into 15 seconds. This skill will be a lifesaver when you are trying to hit a network newscast "on the money." Also practice reading copy strictly to time, developing the accuracy of your internal clock.

When you are practicing, force yourself to keep your eyes moving ahead in the copy. Aim for staying a full sentence ahead, but experiment by going as far ahead as possible.

Accentuating Your Strengths

Improvement is more than eliminating the negative. The positive points in your delivery, and your particular strengths and abilities, deserve to be accentuated, too.

The first goal of a broadcast communicator should be to correct deficiencies.

But once those problem areas are uncovered and corrective work is under way, start thinking about exploiting those strong points.

- Do you have a strong sense of logic and analytical thinking? You may be able to develop world-class interview skills.
- Do you have an engaging personality? Perhaps a career as a radio personality, specializing in strong personality identification, is for you.
- Do you have a strong interest in people and their ideas? Then you may have a valuable advantage in the radio or television talk-show field.
- Do you have an interest in, and understanding of, business and finance? Business and consumer reporting is an extremely robust and durable specialty. Consider combining some studies in business or economics with journalism if this field interests you. Maria Bartiromo (Figure 11.1), for example, majored in journalism and economics at New York University. Try your hand at some business-related news reporting, and you may find yourself in demand.

FIGURE 11.1 Maria Bartiromo has become one of the most recognizable business reporters due to her understanding of economics and her excellent reporting skills.

- Are you a good writer? Think about strengthening that skill and applying it to radio or television news. Good writing, to a newsperson, is *always* an asset.
- Are you a hustler and self-promoter, always making calls, meeting people, and making deals? Think about possibilities in freelance commercial or voice-over work, where talent and the ability to promote yourself can lead to high financial rewards.

The list is just about endless. Look within yourself and your background for special qualities that can be polished and strengthened. Adapting your special talents to meet specific broadcast requirements can be vital for getting that specific job.

A Word about Health and Fitness

Physical vigor, a key to success in broadcasting, is often overlooked as a factor in skill building and career advancement. Realistically, you need not be a bodybuilder or marathon runner to compete in on-air broadcasting. You must, however, have the stamina to work long hours and still appear bright and energetic on mic or camera.

Remember, too, that taking time off from work due to illness is very much frowned on in the broadcast industry.

Although broadcasting is a demanding job, both physically and mentally, those demands won't contribute to your level of physical fitness. A mail carrier benefits from walking and a warehouse worker from lifting, but you'll spend most of your working hours sitting in a studio or driving from appointment to appointment. That is why a personal fitness program is beneficial and just as important as any skill-building program. There is no shortage of good physical fitness advice today, so take the responsibility for researching the issue and finding what's right for you.

A special note for TV performers: weight will always be a concern to you, so consider diet strongly when planning a fitness program. It may be an unfair prejudice but it exists nonetheless.

Case Histories

The material presented in this chapter is not isolated theory passed down from an ivory tower. Almost any successful professional has a history of career experimentation and broadening professional horizons, combined with a calculated plan of personal improvement. Various career paths might be taken. Consider, for example, the case of a salesman for a large manufacturing firm. This man was extremely successful but not very happy. He had a background in amateur theatricals and decided to audition for some part-time television and radio work.

His audition showed promise, and he was signed on to do some general-purpose freelance announcing, and began to supplement his income with commercials.

What a natural career extension for a salesman! His contacts and knowledge of advertising helped him to become highly successful.

Success in commercials brought him to New York City, where a role in a soap opera was added to his résumé. Quality of life in New York was not up to his expectations though, so he applied for, and got, a weathercaster job in his hometown, a smaller market. The weather job evolved into a host position on a magazine-type show.

The career path did not stop there, however. His knowledge of advertising eventually led him to establish an advertising and public relations agency, which provides artistic and financial rewards, combined with the challenge of running a small business.

Although this broadcaster tried a number of career paths, none were false starts and none of the effort was wasted. All this experience and all the skills acquired add up to a whole in his present job.

Persistence and a constant drive for self-improvement pay off. Take the case of an announcer who worked weekends while in college. He was a DJ at a CHR (contemporary hit radio) station, but that job soon became unsatisfying and the pay was poor. He was offered work at a station doing album-oriented rock, and it proved to be an excellent slot. But the station's format was changed to nostalgia, which he did not particularly like. He did a competent job, though, studying the music and making a tremendous effort to fit within the format.

Eventually, a sales position opened at a country station, and he took it, wanting to discover whether sales was really the part of broadcasting that would make him happy.

That did not turn out to be the case. Air work was his goal, and he started sending out tapes and extending feelers through friends in the business. He did not regret having tried sales, because the question of whether sales was his natural spot always would have been a haunting one if the effort had not been made.

The result of his career search? The morning drive job in an AOR (adult oriented radio) station in one of the nation's largest markets. The program director who hired him was impressed not only with his radio background but also with his demonstrated willingness to work hard and adapt.

The ability to recognize and correct deficiencies is crucial. Note the case of a young woman, a recent college graduate. Rather stocky and having a coarse-sounding voice, she lacked at first some of the physical attributes expected of a news reporter. Her main attribute was her skill as an on-air newsperson, cultivated by endless, backbreaking experience. Eventually, she also made some improvements in appearance and vocal ability.

After college, she returned to her hometown and became a volunteer at the cable station, doing anything and everything she was asked. On-air work didn't come until a year later, when she convinced the cable system director to let her produce and host a 15-minute weekly feature. The feature enjoyed moderate success, and after another year she asked the director of the cable station to help her find a job in news. The director made some calls and secured an interview for her at a small station.

The woman advanced to a larger station. It happened to be in the same market as her college, so she could ask her former performance professor to watch her newscasts and critique them. Eventually, she moved on to a good job in one of the larger medium markets.

Although she did not have a large amount of natural talent, her constant efforts to improve, and her willingness to seek and accept criticism, *made* her a good on-the-air communicator.

SUMMARY

The ability and determination to improve is as important to the on-air broadcaster as raw talent. Evaluation is vital to improvement; you can listen to or view a tape of yourself, or have an instructor or colleague monitor the tape and offer criticism. When reviewing your own tapes, be as objective as possible.

Evaluate in terms of pure communication. Break down problem areas into specifics. Identify distracting elements, such as poor speech habits. Use the self-evaluation checklist presented in this chapter, as well as the checklist for long-term planning.

Once problems have been identified, you can begin the process of improvement.

In addition to working on problems uncovered in critique, an improvement program centers on enhancing strong points. Discover your special abilities and capitalize on them.

Many pros project the image of smooth success. Often, however, it took struggle, failure, and more struggle to get where they are today. And it took determination, careful attention to make improvements, and the willingness to adapt and to sample opportunities.

EXERCISES

1. Evaluate one of your recordings using the checklist provided in this chapter.

    Prepare an audio or video in a field you particularly enjoy and hold as a career goal, such as rock music air personality work or television news.

Make an effort to check yes or no in every category. If the answer to a question is yes, grade your performance on that particular attribute—excellent, good, or fair. For example, after answering this question

Does the pace sound natural? Yes ___ No ___

Try to quantify the naturalness of the sound on a scale of 1 to 5. Was the level of naturalness good (4) or excellent (5)? In the margin of the checklist, make notes on these and other items.

2. Use the same method for evaluating the performance of an on-air professional in your selected field. Choose someone whose work you particularly admire.
3. Design a series of five exercises to deal with the particular problems you encounter in your on-air delivery.

One announcer who had problems with ending patterns, for example, read 10 minutes' worth of copy and played back the tape, carefully scrutinizing the ending patterns. The tape confirmed that every sentence ending went down in pitch, over and over and over. Then the announcer wrote notes in her copy to help overcome the problem. Her notes represented changes in pitch and looked like this: "(maintain pitch) After an investigation we found that the records would still be unavailable to the public. (raise pitch slightly) Back to you in the studio Sandy."

These notations, and constant repetition, helped the situation significantly.

Remember that the point of self-evaluation and self-improvement is that no standard set of exercises will help everyone in every situation. As a professional, you must take responsibility for isolating problem areas and working toward their resolution. The five exercises you develop can be a good start toward this goal.

12 The New Media Frontier and the Independent Performer

Evolving digital technologies have changed the power structure in modern media. Where at one time gate-keepers guarded what were phenomenally expensive outposts of broadcast technology and only admitted a few people who they deemed qualified to participate, today many performers and creators start on their own terms—as entrepreneurs.

Sometimes the roles of creator and gatekeeper actually change polarity, with existing media seeking out those who have already made their mark with independent Internet publishing, video, audio, or a combination of other media. In such cases, the independent creators find themselves in the driver's seat, setting the terms for how mainstream media can access their product. Many, in fact, choose to remain independent, keep nearly all their profits, and rely on their own marketing skills to reach what may be a small but ultimately profitable audience niche.

This chapter will provide a brief introduction to the tectonic changes in the media landscape, offer a snapshot of how the new media economy works, and explain how media innovators use a portfolio of media platforms to produce a system that makes, figuratively, *one plus one equal three*—in other words, the platforms combine to synergistically cross-pollinate and cross-promote.

HOW TECHNOLOGY HAS CREATED A NEW UNIVERSE OF OPPORTUNITY FOR MEDIA INNOVATORS

About 20 years ago one of this book's authors freelanced narrations at a studio that found itself confronting a crippling problem. A new building next door had installed a freight elevator that produced a low-pitched rumble that was plainly audible in any recording made in the studio. While we were able to spasmodically record in the interim when the elevator was not in operation, that work-around obviously ate into the studio's productivity. The owners swallowed hard and invested many thousands of dollars into electronic filters to block out low frequencies. The filters had to be wired into a huge mixing console, a difficult and ungainly task that occupied an engineer for several days.

Today, the same author records audio at home in a small studio in a converted closet. Recently, he confronted a similar problem when a detour sent many heavy trucks by his house, producing a low-pitched rumble that, as before, was plainly audible in the final product. So he had no alternative but to invest in a filter that removed it.

The filter was a plug-in to his audio production software. It was downloaded *for free,* as was the production software. The total "investment" was the ten minutes it took to download and install the plug-in. Moreover, the overall quality of the audio from the home-brew studio easily surpasses what was produced in the $150,000-plus studio of two decades ago, with none of the expense and vexations of elaborate mixing boards, patch-bays of wires, and the astonishingly complex tape machines that were necessary to record and mix multiple tracks.

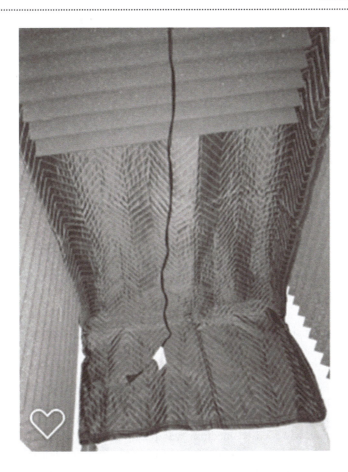

FIGURE 12.1 Shots showing how a small studio was put together.

All that hardware has been replaced by a standard computer, free software downloaded from the Internet, some inexpensive sound treatment panels tacked to the wall of a closet, a small audio interface, and an excellent microphone that cost less than $400 (Figure 12.1).

The point: An announcer who absorbs some basics of technology and business is now equipped to enter media on his or her own terms, and the outlook for the entrepreneur becomes more promising each day. To understand why the future holds such opportunity, though, it's necessary to glance briefly into the past.

WHAT HAPPENED TO LEGACY MEDIA?

"Legacy media," as we use the term, refers to technologies and methods of distribution and monetization that exclusively fueled the media from, let's say, the mid 20th century until a decade or so ago.

The most salient factor of this era is that most media organizations were breathtakingly capital-intensive businesses. It cost millions of dollars to start a TV station, for example, not to mention the fact that you needed a federal license to do so. While the cost of printing presses was lower (but still staggering), the costs of production and distribution assured that for the most part only players with a substantial fortune could take a place at the media table.

Monopolies and Oligopolies

The investment often resulted in what was figuratively referred to as a license to print money. A car dealer, for instance, pretty much had to advertise in the local paper, as did many large retailers in the area, ensuring a steady stream of profits. While television and radio stations had to compete for a more divided pie than print media, they still held an "oligopoly" (control by a limited number) in their markets.

National media, broadcast and print, held a similar oligopoly. Almost any type of national medium was, by definition, a major business, and barriers to entry were steep. Major corporations were the only entities that could reach broad, undifferentiated audiences (in other words, a general audience without many shared characteristics among audience members), but also fairly narrow demographics of targeted markets. (A "demographic" is a statistical representation of a population.) Narrow demographics, such as people of a certain age and income interested in a particular lifestyle, were smaller in number but harder to identify and reach, so even a highly targeted medium still faced formidable obstacles to entry.

At the same time, a narrowly focused medium was potentially very profitable because businesses that needed to reach a certain market—say, a manufacturer advertising high-tech skis used by experts on the slopes—would virtually have no other choice but to advertise in the handful of media reaching the target audience.

How the Internet Changed the Process of Reaching Narrow Audiences

The old type of legacy media described above was based on what media economists call a "scarcity" model. Because only a few entities could provide the service, they could command a steep price for it—in the case of media, the cost of advertising.

But in the new media model, the impact of scarcity is sharply diminished. While only a handful of people will ever own a national television network or metropolitan newspaper, *anyone* can have a YouTube channel or a website dealing with some aspect of a profession, hobby, or lifestyle. While it is unlikely that such an entrepreneurial channel or blog would reach massive numbers, it is possible that the venture could reach a small number of people who are very interested in the subject matter and are therefore a desirable and profitable audience for an advertiser or for the media entrepreneur looking to sell his or her products and services.

An important point worth repeating: such a hyper-narrow audience—the kind that realistically can be reached by an entrepreneur—can produce a profit by *sale of advertising* that appeals to the audience or by *synergistic cross-pollination that drives an audience to buy goods* or services also sold by the entrepreneurial proprietor of the site.

Sources of Revenue

The legacy media method of obtaining advertising was expensive: You had to hire salespeople to contact clients. Sometimes the clients would come to you, as you were one of the only games in town, but even then the process involved personnel designing the ad, supervising layout or production, scheduling the ad, and collecting the payment.

The new media method is simple, and if you have a blog or a website you can start in an hour. If you don't have a blog or a website, you can start in two hours if you don't waste any time visiting Blogger.com or Wordpress.com and setting one up.

Adsense and Adwords

Google allows the entrepreneur to carry advertising through two programs, Adsense and Adwords, which are really opposite ends of the same transaction.[1]

Adwords is the service that allows those who want to sell ads to "buy" a keyword or phrase. An example might be "microphones." Search on the word in Google and a series of hyperlinked ads will appear on the right-hand column and a few at the top of the left-hand column. Manufacturers have paid for placement in the ad columns (the search results themselves are not ranked by payment), indicating how much they will pay for each click-through on the ad. Essentially, the key words and phrases have been auctioned off to the highest bidder. While there are other factors that relate to how the results are ordered, the bid on the word or phrase is the primary determinant.

Adsense is the flip side of the mechanism. Google pays proprietors of Internet sites to let Google ads appear on those sites, and funnels what Google's analytics consider relevant ads to those sites. Sites then receive a cut of revenues from the clicks on the ads Google placed on their digital territory. Sites that have large numbers of visitors and specific, attractive content are typically the venues that make the most income from the Adsense program. Revenue generated by sale of the keywords on Adwords is used to buy advertising on Adsense.

How Profit is Generated by Automated Advertising

You can see the benefits that accrue to both sides in the equation. Someone who makes, let's say, beekeeping equipment can buy the word "beekeeping" or some similar word known to people in the trade and have his or her ad appear as a sponsored link whenever anyone searches on the word. To make things even better, the sponsor doesn't even pay for the ad until the viewer clicks through to the website.

If you run a website about beekeeping and want to carry advertising, you can simply cut and paste the code that Google provides to you to enable the advertising program. Google uses sophisticated algorithms (sets of equations that in effect think for themselves) to analyze the traffic on your site and insert the ad most likely to be successful; if you get a lot of beekeeping traffic it's a safe bet that Google's algorithms will figure it out.

Affiliate Programs

Another way to include advertising on your site is through what is called "affiliate" marketing, meaning that you provide a link to a product sold by another vendor on your page and you receive a small commission from the sale. Amazon.com is probably the most accessible affiliate program to join as the company has, obviously, a huge selection of merchandise and a well-established mechanism to link to the Amazon site. All you have to do is copy some code, paste it into your site, and collect commissions when your readers click through. The process to apply is simple: https://affiliate-program.amazon.com/

There are many other affiliate programs, and an Internet search will turn up dozens or, depending on your diligence, hundreds. The authors cannot endorse programs nor warn you away from some, so we strongly advise doing extensive research and checking online references.

Affiliate programs do work, but be aware that the income you receive can be miniscule, a clutter of ads on your site can actually drive people away, and there are ethical issues involved in joining an affiliate network. (See this chapter's *Think About It*.)

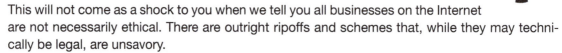

Think About It

The Ethics of Affiliate Marketing

This will not come as a shock to you when we tell you all businesses on the Internet are not necessarily ethical. There are outright ripoffs and schemes that, while they may technically be legal, are unsavory.

All this becomes *your* problem if someone clicks through from a link on your site or an ad on your podcast and gets scammed. You also need to think about whether the product you are selling reflects favorably on your brand.

There is another problem with affiliate marketing that is troubling ethically and legally. If you recommend a product, and receive a commission on that product, should you inform your readers, viewers, or listeners? It's considered good form and in some cases a matter of law to do so (more on that in a second), and most high-profile digital personalities are scrupulous about informing their audience that, for example, they receive a commission if you join a web hosting service that you access by clicking a link on their site. Some have "disclosure pages" on their sites.

A related issue: If you review a product that you receive for free you must also disclose the financial arrangement.

The Federal Trade Commission provides guidance for proper disclosure. You can find out more at https://www.ftc.gov/news-events/press-releases/2017/04/ftc-staff-reminds-influencers-brands-clearly-disclose. The rules are not always clearly defined and there is a lot of gray area, but reading through this set of guidelines can help you navigate these increasingly treacherous waters.

SYNERGISTIC CROSS-PROMOTION

The material presented so far in this chapter is not specific to "announcing," but nonetheless is important to understanding the fundamental way in which the type of media we are concerned with has become democratized and thus has the potential to become a profitable venue for performers with an entrepreneurial bent.

The lesson to take away from the previous few pages is that digital media allows an entrepreneur to engage in the process of sales without great investments in facilities or personnel. Your audiobook or e-book requires no physical trucking across the country or loading onto store shelves, for example. Anyone with a computer or smartphone can buy your creation from anywhere with a cell or Wi-Fi connection.

Making money from your skills and talents might not be your ultimate goal—you may simply want to communicate your message, and that is fine. However, there is an undeniable appeal to being able to buy food and pay rent, and as such the remainder of this chapter will demonstrate in broad strokes how many media entrepreneurs turn their passion for performance into a part- or full-time living.

The three chapters that follow get into specifics of technical and performance considerations for media performers.

The New Media Economy and the Digital Performer

Even though online media ventures can be profitable the vast majority are not. This is not to say that people don't make money on the Web; they do, but often not with one product. While as far as the authors know there are no statistics to back this up, it seems apparent that most who make a sizable digital footprint use a media ecosystem of related sites and products, a network of different offerings designed to cross-promote and drive eyeballs and dollars (either from advertising or direct sales of some product) to the parts of the network that produce those sales.

For example, there is no way of which we are aware to make money directly from a Twitter feed. However, Twitter is an excellent mechanism for driving customers to a location where something *is* for sale. For example, an author might gain thousands of Twitter followers by dispensing useful information or links and occasionally post a tweet that sends clicks to a site where the author's e-book or audiobook is sold. Blogs sometimes do attract enough readers to profit directly from advertising, but you'll notice that even on blogs from very successful media personalities there is often a link for "speaking" or "consulting." Giving speeches can be quite profitable, in part because event planners are accustomed to spending money to hire speakers and typically have funds available in their budgets.

Podcasts (syndicated audio programs that we will define more closely in Chapter 13) sometimes attract sponsors. You can solicit sponsors directly or, through some podcast syndication firms, allow various vendors to place ads in your podcast. However, if you listen to podcasts regularly you will certainly observe that many contain announcements calculated to drive listeners to related products put out by the podcast producer: perhaps the website, where downloadable PDFs are for sale, or where memberships are sold, or any of dozens of other e-commerce scenarios.

YouTube performers can make substantial advertising profits if they have huge audiences, and the mechanism is simple and similar to Google's (it actually is a Google program because Google bought YouTube in 2006). However, many YouTubers use the ecosystem principle to lead prospects to other products—such as video instructional courses or tutorials, which can sometimes be quite lucrative.

The arrangements described above are often described as a "hub and spoke" media marketing model, where various media are the "spokes" and serve to drive viewers and listeners to the central "hub," usually an owned website where the media entrepreneur makes available the profitable wares.

An illustration of the hub-and-spoke model employed by one of this book's authors is shown in Figure 12.2.

The products at the center—the hub—are accessed through an owned website. (By that we mean that the proprietor of the website owns the name of the domain and has full control of the domain. This is important because while you can obtain a free website from a company that includes its name in the web address, changes can occur and you may have less control over your digital destiny than you think; also, having a complex web name with the provider's name a part of your identity muddies your brand.)

The items at the center of the hub are the only ones designed to make a profit. Books (in this case, books on improving communication skills) are sold through the website via a link to Amazon.com. Audiobooks are sold via a link to the audiobook site Audible.com. Arrangements for booking voice-overs and speaking appearances are detailed on the website.

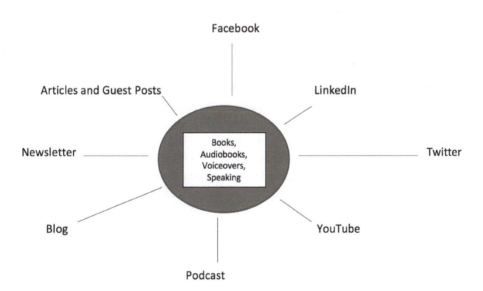

FIGURE 12.2 The hub and spoke is a visual representation of how a new media synergy can be accomplished.

The spokes are designed to feed traffic to the hub. Here's how:

Facebook is used to post occasional excerpts from the author's blog or books, along with other information readers might find useful, and each post carries a link to the hub where the books are sold.

LinkedIn is used to post the author's advice on business communication, again pointing to the hub where the books on communication skills are available.

Twitter is used for short informational pieces about 90 percent of the time, with roughly one in ten tweets used to promote a book, often an audiobook. The author specializes in narrating westerns and has cultivated some followers who like that genre and occasionally re-tweet his announcements about recent audio releases.

YouTube is employed as a host for clips of the author's speeches and media appearances, and is used as a tool to book appearances.

The author's **podcast** is a light-hearted look at odd words, and contains a plug for one of the author's communication books at the end of the performance.

The **blog** contains advice primarily on giving presentations, and not surprisingly feeds audience to the link to buy the author's book on business presentations.

An **email newsletter** distributes a monthly collection of tips for business writing, and—again, not surprisingly—feeds back to a link to the author's book on business writing. Also, the email list of subscribers is used judiciously to promote seminars given by the author.

Finally, **guest posts and freelance articles** point readers to any and all of the spoke and hub locations described above.

CONCLUSION

Very few performers or media professionals of any stripe thrive in a one-dimensional cocoon any longer. While you may be focused on announcing for broadcasting and the Internet, and those may be your hub products, it's to your advantage to become competent in other spoke media that will drive your core activities.

Note that this admonition applies to legacy broadcast media as well. On-air personnel are generally expected to maintain an aggressive social media presence and be skilled in the use of those tools.

The next three chapters will examine, respectively, three areas in which a voice performer can independently market his or her skills: podcasting, Internet video, and home-based narration of audiobooks and voice-overs.

SUMMARY

The evolution of digital media has dropped the cost of production and distribution to the point where almost anyone can enter the game. Having said that, it is a game with a great deal of competition.

Still, the mechanisms to potential profit are not terribly complex; at the most basic level they involve placing code on a website and receiving fractional payments from advertisers. More elaborate profit venues for independently produced media are often created via a "hub and spoke" model, in which different media are used to synergistically cross-promote and earn audience by providing some useful or appealing content that is interspersed with content designed to drive audience to buy designated products.

A good understanding of social media and other media venues is becoming essential for a performer in any aspect the business.

EXERCISES

1. One of the most widely read experts on the new media is Michael Hyatt, who wrote the best-selling book *Platform: Getting Noticed in a Noisy World*. While the authors are not necessarily endorsing

Hyatt's products or services, please do the following for this exercise: Visit his website (MichaelHyatt. com) and note all the cross-pollination. In other words, make a list of products and services that you are driven to by the content of the blog and the website. (Hint: Start by looking at the "speaking" tab on his website.) Find at least three instances *where a spoke drives you to a hub product.*

2. Visit YouTube and search for advice on any subject about which you'd like to learn more—whether it be salsa dancing or changing spark plugs. Note any instances in which you are referred to some other related product, such as an online tutorial. List three direct linkages from those providing advice on YouTube for free to a product that is paid for. (Note that some of those products that are paid for may earn money through affiliate links.)

3. Pick a topic that interests you and find three podcasts dealing with it. Listen to the podcasts and chart ways in which they drive you to other spokes or hubs in the host's media ecosystem.

NOTE

1 This section on Google adapted from work by Carl Hausman published on his blog and distributed to his classes.

13 Podcasting

Any broadcast communicator can, within a matter of a few days, start production of a regular program that has the potential to reach millions of listeners anywhere on the planet. Virtually any topic or format is on the table, including commentary, interviews, expert advice, humor, memoir, or documentary.

In the interest of full disclosure and common sense we have to add a couple of disclaimers. While you have the potential to reach millions, podcasting (which we will define more closely in a minute) is a cluttered and competitive arena, and gathering an audience is no simple matter. Also, podcasting is a content-intensive endeavor, so coming up with an angle that appeals to an identifiable and reachable audience is not easy, either.

Having qualified that, there is no more "democratic" medium in the world: You can produce your program with modestly priced equipment, syndicate it (distribute it in a way to make it available) for free or for a few dollars a month, and utilize your podcast as a springboard for exploiting your skills in the new media frontier.

THE BASICS OF A PODCAST

In general terms, a podcast is an audio program that is produced on some sort of schedule and is downloaded by the listener. It is generally heard on a portable device that plays MP3 files, but many people listen to podcasts on computers.

Development of the Genre

"Podcast" originated as an amalgam of "iPod" and "broadcast." You might not be aware that when the iPod was introduced in 2001 it was truly a revolution in the technology of audio; major news magazines put the device and its primary developer, Apple founder Steve Jobs, on their covers. The small device could hold hundreds of files, usually songs, and as it contained no moving parts it was easily transportable. As such, it was an improvement in light-years over portable (some said "luggable') cassette machines and a later generation of portable CD players, which were still bulky and somewhat delicate.

As a point of interest, the iPod and iTunes were both introduced at about the same time and were a revolution not only in consumer technology but also in media economy. See **Tech Talk,** below.

Tech Talk

As you may remember from earlier histories recounted in this book, development of media technology is often hindered by a chicken-and-egg dilemma. Such was the case in the early days of radio when manufacturers wanted to sell radios but potential consumers were reluctant because there was little programming. The entertainment industry was reluctant to produce programming because there were very few sets that could receive the programs. But after mutually beneficial business arrangements were put in place, both sides prospered.

Apple founder Steve Jobs was a believer in seamless integration and developed the chicken and egg at the same time: iTunes, an online storage area that was referred to as an "online jukebox," and the iPod, a portable device that allowed users to store hundreds of songs they purchased online—an astonishing technological achievement at the time. A couple of years after its introduction iTunes became a full-fledged online store. While many in the music industry were skeptical, it soon became apparent that millions of consumers made iTunes their source for music, and in the late 2000s, for video.

A factor sometimes overlooked in the history of both radio and the iPod is the role that law and regulation played in overcoming stalemates that held up media revolutions. In the early days of radio, there was no clear-cut way for broadcasters to legally use songs on air. The invention of a system to reimburse composers and artists with royalties for each song played, based on sampling, overcame that stumbling block. In 2003, Steve Jobs almost singlehandedly engineered a similar coup when he convinced recording artists and industry executives to allow individual songs to be downloaded from the iTunes store (a practice prohibited by many of the contracts that were designed to protect artists from having their albums sold piecemeal).

iPods are still sold but their audio functions have largely been subsumed by the increased capabilities of smartphones. Video today is commonly consumed on smartphones, tablets, and large video screens.

Moral of the story: when, and only when, you combine a new technology with a way for consumers to use that technology, the change in media consumption habits can be astonishing. The virtual marketplace that was created by iTunes, in fact, served as a model for the Internet media system that supports podcasting today.

What Are Podcasts, Exactly?

While podcasting carries the inherited name of the iPod, it is of course no longer restricted to one device. However, the definition of a podcast does become complicated when factoring in its method of distribution, which is actually essential to the understanding of the term. Some argue that the appellation "podcast" only applies to an audio program that is stored on a dedicated directory and delivered to those who request it through a syndication service, something we will define in a moment. Others use the term to indicate any audio program that is downloadable from any Internet site. Another variation on the term is "video podcast," which refers to video distributed on a regular basis.

Where Are Podcasts, Exactly?

The explanation is complicated, but bear with us because it not only helps clarify the definition started above but also provides an insight into how the industry is structured. Note that what follows is general in nature and that some may quibble with the parts that qualify what a podcast is, exactly, but in broad terms, a podcast:

- Exists **on a server,** a high-powered computer that answers requests for access and download. Often, but not always, those servers are owned and maintained by firms that specialize in podcasting. Some of the more well-known firms include Libsyn, Podbean, SoundCloud, and Podomatic. (More on podcast hosts later in this chapter.)
- Is **syndicated,** meaning distributed to those who subscribe to it. The most commonly referred-to method of syndication is RSS. (Now, remember, we said this was complicated, and we will now live up to our promise.) Even the meaning of RSS is open to interpretation: Some industry observers say RSS stands for *Really Simple Syndication,* although many claim it stands for *Rich Site Summary.* In any event, the RSS feed is what notifies types of computer programs called "readers," "catchers," "aggregators," or "directories" (defined in the next bullet-point) that a new episode of a podcast is available for download. The RSS feed uses a language called XML that is designed to communicate with "readers," "catchers," "aggregators," or "directories" and is used to syndicate blogs as well as podcasts. There are other syndication systems beside RSS but RSS is the most widely supported. **Bottom line:** RSS is a syndication system and it means sending out a piece of computer code enabling another program to automatically download a feed of material that is "broadcast" on the Web.
- As mentioned, the programs that automatically find the feed are called "catchers," "readers," "aggregators," or "directories." There are differences among the terms but dissecting the fine points is beyond the scope of this chapter; for the sake of broad understanding, just remember that they *are the equivalent of your digital video recorder.* You use them to monitor the myriad feeds out there and capture only what you want. If you want to listen to a podcast about cars, for example, you would set your reader accordingly, perhaps to NPR's "Car Talk."
- One of the most popular venues for catching podcasts is iTunes. iTunes combines the ability to catch the podcasts you want with an app (small computer program) that makes it easy to see which episodes have been captured and allows you to easily play them on a portable device or computer.

PODCASTS IN THE MEDIA MARKETPLACE

Podcasts have surreptitiously become an important part of the media landscape. Data from the Pew Research Center show that about one in five Americans age 12 and over say they have listened to a podcast in the past month. While the podcast economy is small, the latest figures from Pew indicate that about $34 million was spent in podcast advertising in 2015.[1] It should be noted, though, that it is difficult to measure any circumstance involving podcasts because there are few standard procedures or methods of operation.

Podcast Formats

You can find a vast array of subject matter. As this was written, the most frequently downloaded podcasts in the US included:

- "Revisionist History," in which author Malcolm Gladwell looks at an historical event that he believes may have been misinterpreted or misunderstood.
- "The Joe Rogan Experience," in which comedian, actor, and martial arts commentator Joe Rogan conducts interviews. It's both an audio and video podcast.

- "Planet Money," which features interviews about economic issues.
- "30 for 30" Podcasts from ESPN, original audio documentaries with similar content to the popular TV series.

Most of the very popular podcasts are issued once a week, but some, such as "Planet Money," come out twice a week.

Having said that, many podcasts come out on different schedules or no preset schedule, although it is generally ceded that regular publication on a fairly reliable schedule boosts listenership.

Appeal of Podcasts

Podcasting was typically viewed as a medium on the far periphery of the mainstream until, perhaps, 2014, when a news/documentary podcast titled *Serial* started racking up massive downloads and won a Peabody award for journalism excellence.

It became apparent that for an increasingly mobile society a medium that played in autos and portable MP3 devices—and could be stopped or started at will—could be as engaging and addictive as a television series. Eventually, many more news organizations, businesses, and entrepreneurs are embracing the format because, as Internet business guru Pat Flynn notes, podcasting "fits into people's lives."[2]

Flynn also maintains that podcasting is one of the best ways to "scale intimacy," meaning that you can build a strong personal-seeming relationship with a listener even if you grow the program to tens of thousands of listeners. "When you think about it," Flynn writes. "when a person is listening to you, your voice is in their ear (literally if they are listening with earbuds). It's intimate. They can pick up on your intonation, the emotion in your voice. I find, as a podcast listener myself, that it's easier to empathize with a story if I'm able to listen to the storyteller. If done right, they can transport listeners to a particular moment in time that may be relatable to you in some way. Finding common ground with your listeners is an amazing way to build relationships."[3]

HOW TO DO A PODCAST IN TEN STEPS

Equipment, abilities, and budgets will of course vary, and you will need to develop skills in audio editing, but in general terms here are the sequential steps you can follow to get started.

Step One: Decide on a Format

Chances are, you have an area in which you have a strong interest or expertise, or both. If you can find an angle to your subject that might interest listeners, determine how best to package that idea. For example, your podcast can be you providing a direct narration, editing together a documentary, or conducting an interview. (The interview format is extremely popular but requires some special accommodations, which we will discuss below.) It's your program and you don't have to entomb your format in cement, but it's safe to assume that most media consumers are comforted by and attracted to consistent formats, so some planning at the beginning stage will pay dividends. Conducting research is simple; just do an Internet search on "podcasts about sports" or "music podcasts" and you'll see what your competition is. Note that just because a podcast exists on a similar subject it does not mean that there is no room for your unique angle on the topic. Lack of competition, in fact, might signal an overall dearth of interest in the topic.

You aren't bound to a specific length, either, although we feel safe in generalizing that it is most comfortable for regular listeners if you maintain more or less a uniform standard. The typical length is up to you. Again, this is clearly a generalization but podcast listeners seem to gravitate toward fairly long programs, perhaps averaging about a half hour, because they often use podcast listening time to fill existing slots while commuting or at the gym; consumers poised at a computer are likely to seek shorter programming.

Step Two: Get the Appropriate Microphone (or as Many Mics as You Will Need)

We are not advising that you sacrifice quality for economy or simplicity, but it is clearly the case that pod-cast listeners are much more forgiving of lower-quality audio than, say, consumers of audiobooks. From a practical standpoint, this means that you can often get away with a good-quality headset mic or a fairly inexpensive USB-connected mic. (These low-end options would not be good alternatives for voice-over commercial work, independent narration, or, as mentioned, audiobooks.)

By USB-connected mic, we mean a microphone that has as its output the same type of connector that links printers and other devices to your computer, a "universal serial bus." This is very convenient, but while USB mics are making great improvements, microphones that output to an XLR connector are generally of higher quality—not necessarily because of the connector but because the XLR is the standard used in cabling and mixing boards in professional studios.

If you opt for a high-quality XLR mic, you will need an "interface" (Figure 13.1) to translate the signal from an analog to a digital format. Interfaces range from simple one-input-one-output arrangements to complex mixers that can handle several mics. Be aware that if you use a dynamic or a ribbon XLR mic, your output may be low and a consumer-grade interface may not provide enough amplification to produce a robust signal. If that is the case, an inline pre-amplifier will be needed; the authors use, with satisfaction, a model trade-named "Cloudlifter" (Figure 13.2).

If you plan to make interviews a part of your podcast, there are several microphone options available.

- You can use one mic to record one or more interviewees. As described in this book's various entries on microphones, you'll usually want an omnidirectional mic; be aware, though, that in non-studio environments you can run into problems with background noise if using an omnidirectional mic.
- You can gang-connect the mics. You can use different USB inputs on a computer and can use adapters to plug multiple USB sources into one input. Be aware, though, that ganging mics doesn't allow you much control over different volume levels from speakers. You can adapt to different loudnesses of guests and co-hosts by positioning them closer and farther away from the mic, or mixing their mics into separate channels, or editing the levels after the recording. If you are using XLR mics you'll be

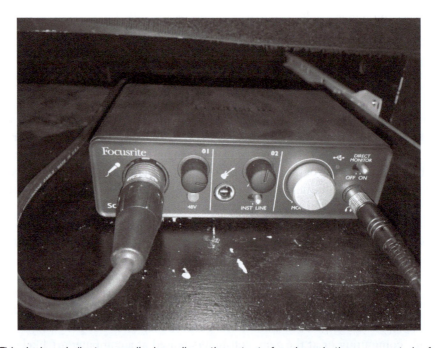

FIGURE 13.1 This device, similar to a small mixer, allows the output of a mic and other sources to be fed into the computer.

FIGURE 13.2 If you use some dynamic mics, you'll need this device to boost the signal. The Cloudlifter, basically a pre-amp, significantly enhances both the volume and quality of the sound.

using some sort of interface or mixer anyway (more on this to follow) and you can set each mic with a physical or virtual dial.

- You can import your guest or co-host over a cell, landline, or Internet connection. One of your best alternatives is to use Skype or Google Hangouts to record the input. You don't have to plug anything in: The software pipes the audio directly into your computer.
- If quality is of utmost concern, you can have your guest or co-host record the audio on a high-quality mic at a different location. For example, if you are recording in your home in New York and your co-host is at her home in Los Angeles, you can converse by standard telephone fed into your headphones but record the audio separately on a high-quality mic. Following the recording, your co-host can email you her voice recording and you edit it together with yours. While this produces excellent quality, be forewarned that it is a *lot* of work to edit two ends of a conversation together.

Step Three: Obtain a Recording Device (or Use the Hard Drive of Your Computer)

You can record directly onto your computer hard disc or use a separate recording device hooked into your computer. Advocates of separate devices argue that you're asking for trouble if you overburden the computer with essentially two tasks: processing the incoming audio and running the software that records it—along with all the other functions that may be occurring at the same time.

For newcomers to the podcast process, we see nothing wrong with recording directly on the computer hard drive, though. Should you wish the convenience and stability of a separate recorder at a later time, it is a simple matter to add it into the chain later.

Step Four: Download and Learn How to Use Audio Editing Software

Earlier chapters of this book provide a well-rounded summary of digital audio editing. In terms of podcasting, we note that there are few "advanced" applications that would require complex software solutions, except of course in cases where your podcast required recording and editing of elaborate music sessions.

As the premise of this chapter was that podcasting can be inexpensive, we suggest at least for the beginning of your podcast career you begin scaling the learning curve with the free software Audacity. There are occasional functions that require separate, free, third-part plug-ins, but the community of Audacity users provides many online tutorials and discussion boards.

Step Five: Prepare a Recording Area

While podcasts don't always require studio-quality sound, studio-quality sound is a nice attribute and you would be surprised how some inventive improvisation can produce excellent audio.

While we will address this issue more fully in the upcoming chapter on audiobooks, it is important to point out that there are two attributes involved in finding and fine-tuning a recording space: **sound isolation** and **acoustic treatment**. They are different!

Sound isolation means keeping unwanted external sound out. Sometimes we call this "sound proofing" but because no material can really be impervious to sound it's more accurate to recognize that the goal is to limit sound infiltration that interferes with your recording. Building sound-isolating barriers is beyond the scope of this chapter other than to note that you can reduce vibration a great deal by using good-quality shock-mounts for your microphone stands. If vibration from the floor is an issue, four old tires upon which you place a piece of plywood can be a quick-and-dirty fix that works surprisingly well.

By far the most productive way to achieve a measure of sound isolation is simply to find a quiet place to locate your recording. Usually higher rooms in a house or apartment or office building are quieter as they are more removed from traffic; however, the higher you go the more peril you face from airplane noise, which, incidentally, is a problem in many of the most acoustically advanced professional studios. Try moving your microphone to different spots in your residence. If you can tolerate it, record in the middle of the night when people around you are quiet. And if you really need quiet and have highly portable equipment, drive your car to a remote location. Modern cars have excellent sound isolation: Remember, they are engineered to attenuate the noise from trucks and 70-mile-per-hour winds.

Acoustic treatment means keeping echoes and other distortion from marring the quality of your recording. Basically, the goal is that you do not want to record in a room with hard surfaces because the resulting echoes will make your work sound tinny and harsh. Commercially available acoustical treatment panels (Figure 13.3) are designed to absorb and diffuse sound that originates within the studio and thus preserve an intimate, rich sound.

Many podcasters are not in a position, financial or logistically, to provide full acoustical treatment to the area in which they record their podcasts, but some simple measures can improve conditions dramatically:

- Put down a throw rug if you have a hard floor.
- Put up and draw curtains.
- Use sound-deadening material in back of the microphone. Any sort of foam rubber or mattress topper can help.
- Put towels or thick tablecloths over desks and tables.
- Consider recording in closets . . . seriously. Closets make excellent echo-absorbers.

FIGURE 13.3 These panels are very useful in deadening room echo and add a professional quality to the sound.

Step Six: Prepare your Album Cover and, If You Want to Use Music, Your Theme

Attractive artwork for a podcast is as important as a cover for a book. You can make your own artwork if you have some graphic design experience and flair. Some sites, such as Canva.com, make it relatively simple for someone with no design skills to produce various graphic works, including the "covers" that will serve as your branding for your podcast.

There are other affordable alternatives. You are probably familiar with Fiverr.com, a site where free-lancers bid on various jobs and the prices are usually quite economical (though not always five dollars, as various services are added on to the base price). One of the authors' podcast cover was designed by a freelancer from Fiverr for a grand total of $15 (Figure 13.4).

Should you go that route, be sure to specify that your freelancer be conversant with the standards for iPod album covers. iTunes, in particular, is rigidly strict about proportions and pixel size and will reject artwork that does not meet specifications. More on iTunes in Step Eight.

Many podcasts use an opening or closing theme. Be aware that you *cannot* simply appropriate a piece of music you hear on the Internet; you will likely be violating copyright law. You will need royalty-free music for which you are granted the rights to use repeatedly. This does not necessarily translate to a big expense. Check out www.melodyloops.com, which offers a huge variety of royalty-free music specifically for podcasters and other producers.

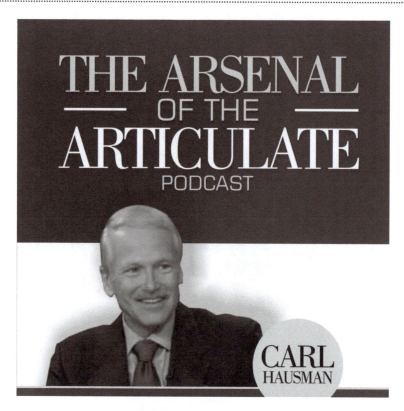

FIGURE 13.4 Podcast covers are tricky to make, but you can find many freelancers who know the technique.

Step Seven: Mount Your Completed Podcast on a Hosting Service

There are various services that, for free or for a very modest fee, will host your podcast. What this means is that the audio file is uploaded to the host's server and the host sends out the RSS feed.

You may ask why you can't simply upload your podcast to your own website and have listeners download it from there. You can—but that means that good luck can turn into bad luck if your suddenly overburdened site crashes or your Internet service provider hits you with overage fees for excessive use of bandwidth. Plus, setting up feeds is more complex and thus having your podcast mounted on your own site could inhibit what is certainly your goal—to have listeners subscribe.

For five dollars a month, one of the authors hosts his podcast on Libsyn, one of the largest commercial podcasting sites, and has enjoyed flawless service, seamless listing on iTunes, and access to extensive downloading statistics. There are many such services available, some with free options. You can do your own research: Do web searches on Libsyn, SoundCloud, Podbean, Podomatic, Ourmedia, Buzzspout, and Archive.org. And this is not a definitive list. There are many other services that provide various tiers of service.

Step Eight: Get Your Podcast Listed on Directories

A directory is a listing of podcasts and will typically be the destination where people go to subscribe. There are dozens of podcast directories (a good list can be perused at https://www.buzzsprout.com/learn/podcast-directory and at www.podcastplaces.com), but iTunes is the most popular and certainly the place to start. Commercial hosting services such as Libsyn provide you with guidance on how to accomplish this, and iTunes offers instructions as well. You will need an iTiunes account to list your podcast there.

Step Nine: Strive for Continual Improvement

Remember that you are only as good as your latest episode. If you are looking to add new listeners, the audio in their ears at this moment is what produces loyal listeners or drives them away.

Podcasting is an excellent venue for developing your skills. You get to do it all: narrate, ad-lib, interview, whatever you want to pursue, and in a fairly low-risk environment if it is your podcast and you are not relying on it for rent money.

Many podcasters note that they have made dramatic improvements in their on-air delivery simply by experience and repetition. Always focus on improving your skills. This chapter's Focus on Technique provides some examples germane to podcasting.

Focus on Technique

Announcing Tips for Podcast Hosts

While broadcast communication is an easily transportable skill, adaptable to almost any type of technology, here are some suggestions particularly useful for the new podcaster.

- Be wary of in-jokes and laughing excessively at things you find funny that the listener might not understand or appreciate. This is a common problem in podcasts, especially those involving multiple hosts and guests.
- Don't be afraid to re-introduce co-hosts or guests, especially if there are several of them on the podcast. If the listener gets lost, you may lose him or her for good.
- Do background research on the subject and the guest. Guests may tolerate an unprepared host in a broadcast setting where there is presumably something to be gained from widespread exposure, but in a podcast you are often asking the guest to take a chance on you and your program. As the guest will be well aware that it is not a live program and probably will not be reaching an extensive audience, he or she may not be particularly willing to walk you through the points you should have researched before starting the program.
- If you are interviewing, keep the focus on the guest. Vague, rambling questions are irritating and don't produce good answers.
- Keep mistakes to a minimum. Yes, this sounds like obvious advice, but the very nature of a podcast is that it is recorded, edited, and then uploaded. The editing gives you a valuable opportunity to smooth out flubs in the show. However, and this is a major caveat, fixing mistakes is enormously time-consuming and saps energy that could be more wisely invested in the next program. So don't nurture the attitude that, "we can fix it later." Yes, fix what you have to fix, but don't make your performance a sloppy first draft.

Step Ten: Cross-Pollinate and Promote

Be sure you integrate your podcast with other media you produce. For example, you will certainly want to promote your podcast through your Twitter feed and your blog posts.

At some point you may consider "monetizing" your podcast. There are services that will place ads in podcasts and pay you a fee, or, should you be clued into the economic ecosystem of your particular subject, you can certainly approach potential sponsors yourself and negotiate placement of a commercial within your podcast.

SUMMARY

Podcasting is one of the unexpected success stories of the audio world. Despite early uncertainly as to whether an audience would really listen to a product that had to be downloaded and stored, the convenience of a podcast has proved to be irresistible to a public often on the move and hooked up to an electronic device.

EXERCISES

1. Pick a topic of interest to you and create a half-hour podcast. At this point, don't worry about the niceties of recording and uploading. Simply do it in one take, from start to finish, and record on what is available, even on your smartphone. The main goal is to plan what you are going to do and do it. If you plan a five-minute introduction, a 15-minute interview, and a five-minute closing, stick to that plan as closely as you can.
2. Set up an interview with a friend or classmate through Skype or Google Hangouts or both. Remember that your interviewee can be in the other room or in a different hemisphere. It actually doesn't matter, given the technology available to you.
3. Listen to three podcast episodes that cover a topic that interests you. In about 400 words, describe their similarities and differences, and explain what you liked about each and did not like.

NOTES

1 http://www.journalism.org/2016/06/15/podcasting-fact-sheet;/
2 https://www.smartpassiveincome.com/10-reasons-why-podcasting-is-the-1-content-platform/
3 https://www.smartpassiveincome.com/10-reasons-why-podcasting-is-the-1-content-platform/

14 Internet Video

A communicator working with a modest setup can reach many thousands—even millions—of viewers on readily accessible video platforms. If you have an entrepreneurial bent, are not allergic to experimenting with various technologies, and have the patience to continually fine-tune your product and monitor your statistics, you may find that Internet video can become a showcase for your talents and even a lucrative career in itself.

THE RISE OF INTERNET VIDEO

YouTube, the largest video-sharing platform, was created little more than a decade ago but has already become the most prolific source for video: In a 60-day period, more video is uploaded to YouTube than was created by the three major television networks in 60 years.[1]

The existence of video on the Internet was made possible by computer programs that compressed the massive amounts of data eaten up by moving pictures and refinements in the video camera itself.

The ability for the home user to create a product for Internet video stems from galloping advances in video editing software—programs that allow the user to move, process, and manipulate the files. Although it's been stated before in different contexts, it's astonishing to observers who began in the business a couple decades ago to witness how capabilities that a short time ago were only accessible to highly trained producers with breathtakingly expensive equipment and software have now become accessible via a standard computer and programs selling for a few hundred dollars, or, in some cases, downloadable for free.

HOW ANNOUNCERS AND PRODUCERS USE INTERNET VIDEO

Internet video offers a wide landscape of opportunities for on-air performers. Among them are the following.

YouTube Channels

All YouTube users have the option of creating a channel, which at its most basic level is not much more complicated than logging in and clicking on a command titled "create a channel." Having a channel allows you to post a piece of artwork that represents your brand, gives you some space on your display to describe your content, enables you to be located by searches both within YouTube and search engines such as Google, and allows your viewers to be notified when you have new content, thus bringing them back repeatedly.

Some channels, notably those offering humor or gaming commentary, have millions of subscribers, and the web of connections spans the globe. For example, at the time this was written in late 2017, a comedian and commentator going by the name Jenna Marbles, who muses about life as a millennial, broadcast to almost 17 million subscribers. A young woman from Mexico named Yuya dispensed beauty tips to almost 18 million. And a Swede who calls himself PewDiePie railed about video games and other topics to an audience of more than 54 million.[2]

And yes, as you are probably aware, it is possible to make money from YouTube, though no one claims it's easy. Your channel needs to have a sizable audience (at last check, 10,000 lifetime views) and pass scrutiny by the YouTube Partner Program before being hooked into the Google-powered automatic ad placement program. While YouTube rates are based on a variety of calculations, and all the methods of calculation are not published, an accepted rule of thumb is that a producer earns about $2,000 per million views.

Embedded Videos

Communicators who use their blogs or websites as their primary mode of interacting with their audience can also exploit the embedding capability of YouTube to add a video presence. Embedding is a process whereby a link to a YouTube video is placed on a web page and the video plays on that page when clicked. The ability to embed videos is often not fully understood or appreciated by many web producers or bloggers. It's a simple operation involving little more that copying and pasting some YouTube-generated code; the huge advantage here is that the bandwidth eaten up by the video (which can be considerable) is supplied by YouTube and not by you and your Internet service provider.

While not a direct money-maker, the ability to embed videos has profound implications for anyone with an Internet presence. You can include videos from other sources simply by providing a link on your own web page, meaning that you can, in effect, make your website a portal to all sorts of interesting video.

Online Training

Learning new skills is a long-standing human impulse, and as such has propelled the growth of many different types of media. As one example, note that the "self-help" book was instrumental in expanding the reach of traditional print publishing.

Video is a natural medium for teaching because it not only shows processes in action but can be stopped and started at will. Video is used as the basis for many online courses, even when it is as simple as an instructor talking over a series of slides.

Production and narration of online training is not limited to college courses; it's an opportunity open to anyone. If you have any skill that someone might want to learn—playing the ukulele or proficiency in page-layout software—you may have the basis for a training video. You can produce it and place it on your own website, or visit the many e-learning sites open to the general public. Udemy, for example, says it hosts over 45,000 courses; it actively seeks people to create courses and offers tutorials in how to produce a course for the site. Udemy offers the platform and the basic shell for the course, you create the content, Udemy takes care of mounting it on its server and collecting the fees paid by viewers, takes a percentage of the profit and forwards the profit to you. Udemy also offers online tutorials for prospective producers.

Documentaries

Independent documentary producers can find small but enthusiastic audiences and in some cases sell their work. There are various platforms that make this possible, including Vimeo, which for a modest monthly membership fee offers a mechanism for displaying their video on a pay-per-view basis (see: https://vimeo.com/ondemand/startselling).

You can also make your documentaries available on iTunes, Amazon, and YouTube, all of which have varying royalty percentages and mechanisms for distribution and licensing. Each venue also has different strengths. For example, Griffin Hammond, who produced a 33-minute independent documentary about a hot sauce called Sriracha, writes in a post on Medium.com that Vimeo offers the best profit margin, taking a 10 percent cut of income, compared to the average 22 percent he pays in commissions to other sites. When he sells a download of Sriracha for $2.99, Vimeo keeps $.30.

Hulu and Amazon Prime license the work and present it free to subscribers and provide a small fee to Hammond per view. While the per-unit profit is much smaller than on Vimeo, though, the raw numbers are bigger. While Hammond may earn only pennies per view on Amazon Prime and Hulu, one-twentieth of Vimeo's rate, he has received more than half a million views on those platforms. When his post was written in early 2017, Hammond had earned $136,813 in revenue from 720,858 views. Ad-based You-Tube revenue was the poorest performer, he reports.[3]

Video Podcasting and Vlogging

You can syndicate a video podcast using many of the same services described in the previous chapter. Also, you can use embedded video or a YouTube channel (or some other video services) to put your blog—sometimes called a "vlog" meaning "video blog"—in video form.

What You'll Need for Internet Video

You can spend a lot of money in a hurry when buying video equipment, but you don't have to. Some fairly low-cost options and imaginative improvisation can get you up and running.

For the most basic home video setup, you'll need *a camera*, a *microphone,* a *backdrop,* and *video editing software.*

Cameras

There are four basic types: a *webcam*, a *smartphone*, a *stand-alone video camera*, and a *digital SLR.*

Webcam. Webcams (Figure 14.1) plug into your computer and send video directly to the computer, usually using some proprietary software designed for the camera. The advantage of a webcam is that you can control everything through the computer, although you can edit the video with third-party software. Webcams are not very portable though, unless you hook them to a laptop and move the computer, which can be exceedingly awkward. Your range of motion for the camera is generally dictated by the length of the USB cord that plugs the webcam in. A webcam does not have the video range of a stand-alone video camera (more on this follows) and thus it's not the right tool for, as an example, recording an outdoor scene where there is a lot of movement. Having said that, good-quality webcams can produce a surprisingly good picture under static conditions and are simple to use and relatively inexpensive.

Smartphone. There's an old saying that the best camera is the one that you have with you. As most of us have access to a smartphone (Figure 14.2) at all hours of the day and night, it is a logical choice for Internet video. In actuality, smartphone video is actually of pretty good quality, and you can buy attachments for your phone that will improve resolution. The problem is that there is no physical zoom on a smartphone (unless you buy a separate lens attachment). The zoom on your phone simply magnifies the picture, giving the appearance of moving closer, but the magnification will result in a significant loss of resolution. Getting the video from the phone to the computer for editing usually involves an intermediate step such as emailing it or saving it to a cloud file, and because the phone is recording to its own memory, storage space will be limited.

Stand-Alone Video Camera. These devices can be expensive as you escalate in quality—pro-quality units can cost thousands of dollars—but even consumer-grade cameras provide a great advantage in flexibility of use (Figure 14.3). They also can present a challenging learning curve and there are sometimes a couple of steps involved in getting the video from the camera to the computer, either

FIGURE 14.1 The newest generation of webcams can produce surprisingly good video.

FIGURE 14.2 Today, the smartphone can be used not only to capture video but control it. Here it is being used to control a prompting device for the announcer.

FIGURE 14.3 Stand-alone video cameras are extremely versatile.

FIGURE 14.4 Single lens camera used for video; the camera is at the far lower right.

through a wire or exchanging a chip. Video quality for a stand-alone camera is typically high and in expensive models can be excellent, and you will have more options in terms of zooming and following action. Focusing and following moving objects while staying in focus is much easier with a stand-alone camera than with other devices, and many units have built-in image stabilization, meaning that the internal electronics smooth out the bumps from small jarring and shaking.

SLR stands for "single lens reflex." What this means is that one lens is used to focus the image for recording and for visualization of the image—in other words, what you see is what you get (Figure 14.4).

The SLR has long been the staple of high-quality photography because it allows precise framing and focus of the shot as well as producing a very high-quality image through the sophisticated lenses associated with still cameras.

These attributes had no bearing on video until still photography converted to digital formats and the media for recording the images evolved to the point where there was adequate storage for video. Now, a digital SLR with a healthy memory capacity can hold several minutes of video and the lens system produces amazing quality—not only rivalling professional broadcast cameras but even the resolution seen in a major motion picture. Unsurprisingly, the digital SLR has become a favorite of independent video producers, especially documentarians. However, note that these cameras typically don't have much storage capacity—you'll have to change chips or export the video after a few minutes—and they don't follow-focus as well as a video camera, making them less suitable for movement and action.

Microphones

It may seem counterintuitive, but good-quality audio is probably more important to most video on-air presentations than the picture. Viewers will tolerate amateurish video; in fact, some anecdotal reports we have read suggest that people who seek out material on YouTube are turned off by professional appearing or cinematic video. But poor audio will send your audience packing.

You have three options for audio in the home-based studio: the *microphone that comes with your camera*, a *shotgun*, a *lavalier*, or a *hand-held*.

Camera Mics. These are truly a last resort as they are not generally of very high quality and will by their nature be at some distance from the subject. Most video cameras and video-capable SLRs come with a receptacle for plugging in an external mic (Figure 14.5). If they don't, they won't be of much help to you.

Shotgun Mics. Named became they are long and bear a passing resemblance to a rifle or shotgun (Figure 14.6), these instruments focus on a narrow cone of sound directly in front of them, meaning that they can reject noise from other directions and amplify the sound from the speaker

FIGURE 14.5 Before you buy any video camera or SLR, be sure it has the option for an external mic.

FIGURE 14.6 A shotgun is a good choice for a home producer because it filters out a great deal of background noise.

FIGURE 14.7 A good-quality lav can make a home studio sound terrific. While they don't typically reject a lot of noise, they are so close to the talent that the talent's body blocks external sound.

or other sources of sound. Shotguns can be pricy, but medium-range models can do a good job, and the capability of a shotgun makes it a versatile part of your toolkit. Note, though, that they are still susceptible to background noise, especially noise coming from behind the speaker, and to poor sound acoustics.

Lavalier Mics. Named after a piece of jewelry hung around the neck (as these mics originally were), lavaliers (Figure 14.7) now come with a clip to attach to clothing. For miking people talking they are unsurpassed because they hug the sound contour of the body, producing an intimate, clear audio. The drawbacks include the fact that if you have more than one speaker you'll need more than one lavalier and the attendant machinery to gang them, and the fact that you'll have to cope with a wire. Many lavaliers are wireless but still need a wire to get from the part of the mic that is clipped on to a transmitter usually worn on the speaker's belt. Lavaliers, then, are best suited, and perform very well, in static, studio-type setups.

Hand-held Mics or Mounted Mics. If you don't mind the mic showing or are in a situation where the instrument will be mounted on a desk or a boom near the mouth of the person speaking, a hand-held will suffice, although you will have the issues of wires and occasionally noise. But for a two-person interview conducted news-style, hand-helds are a perfect choice.

Backgrounds

Some major YouTube stars use *no specially constructed backgrounds* at all: Their video is sometimes shot in bedrooms or basements. Others have *sets ranging from simple to elaborate*. Some choose to record in front of a *greenscreen* and edit the background in later. There are pluses and minuses to each approach.

> **No Background Other than the Immediate Environment.** Recording in a normal environment adds realism and immediacy to the recording, and is often part of the atmosphere viewers seek out. But while such a natural approach may work for comedy or beauty tips, it might lack the panache you would need for a training video where you are marketing your expertise. Also, casual environments are also prone to vagaries in lighting, noise, and visitors.
>
> **A Constructed Set.** This doesn't have to be complex like a television station's news set. A simple brick wall is the favorite of many video performers, and if you don't have a brick wall you can always purchase a sheet of imitation plastic brick veneer at your local home-improvement store. Bookshelves are popular backgrounds and add some depth and warmth to the shot. Sometimes a "branding element" (an identifying logo or other device) can be introduced into the background. For example, one of the authors uses his web address (pasted to a wall with vinyl lettering) as part of the set (Figure 14.8).

Some web-based programs use a combination of sets and location action. The very popular fitness program Ric's Corner (ricdrasin.com) features interviews with fitness experts recorded in a small set, but often ventures out to the gym or, in an engaging discussion of diet, to one of the host's favorite restaurants. While his guests and locales vary, Drasin sticks to themes that endear him to his audience and makes it a point to release new programs frequently and regularly. "I think being consistent is the key to success and good content," he says.

A great advantage of the constructed set is the ability to control for external factors. In the set shown in Figure 14.9), lighting is provided by two instruments up front and lighting coming from the rear. This is known as three-point lighting (Figure 14.10), the scheme used in most professional TV; three-point lighting models the subject's features and keeps the subject from fading into the background. You can achieve three-point lighting with some surprisingly inexpensive lighting instruments available online and in some photo supply shops. For home video, you don't need to spend a lot of money on lighting gear because you won't be moving the stuff around very much. Enhanced durability is much of what causes the price to rise for high-quality equipment.

FIGURE 14.8 With just a little planning, you can create a good background for your videos.

FIGURE 14.9 The lighting instruments in this photo cost less than $100 and produce very good results.

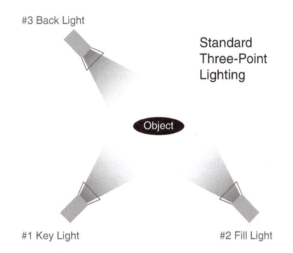

FIGURE 14.10 A key light, a fill light, and a back light provide both modeling and separation from background.

Green Screen. Green screens are curtains or panels that are of a color easily filtered out of video with an editing program and replaced with whatever image you choose—meaning that you can paste in an elaborate news set or make it appear as though you are standing in front of the Kremlin.

The specialized backgrounds are usually green but blue is often used as well. The particular shade is called "chroma-key" green after a process developed to remove a background color. You can even buy chroma-key green paint if you want to make a permanent set.

Choma-key effects take some time and tinkering and wrinkles and shadows on the background can cause issues with the picture that is superimposed over it. Some of the most practical and affordable options to reduce winkling are backgrounds that are stretched on a hoop. The hoop folds in on itself and makes a three-foot circle that is easy to pack up and carry. When you loosen the hoop, it expands to a rectangle, in the case of the device shown in Figure 14.11), four-by-six feet.

Video Editing Software. These programs allow you to cut, paste, and enhance video and also add special effects and graphics. You can spend a lot of money on such programs; high-end software

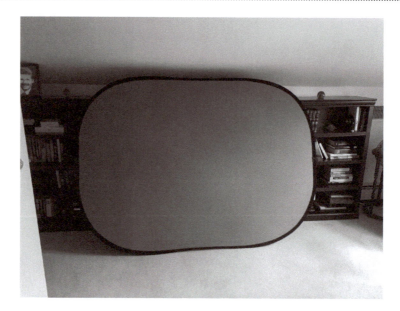

FIGURE 14.11 A simple wire frame expands and keeps the green material smooth.

also will provide you with many editing options (some of which you'll probably not use) and can be very complex.

You may already have had training in certain video programs, and that may help make your decision easier. If you are on a budget, you will be wise to start with free or low-cost programs and upgrade later. Free programs that are perfectly workable for most home video applications include iMovie and Windows Movie Maker. A step up in price, from about $50 to $200, are AVS Video Editor, Adobe Premiere Elements, and Corel VideoStudio Pro, all quite workable. Camtasia, near the high end of this price category, has some excellent video editing capabilities even though many users primarily purchase it for its screen recording capabilities (for example, recording voice-over-PowerPoint or Skype calls). High-end programs, about $300 and up, include Final Cut Pro, Adobe Premier Pro (now sold by yearly subscription) and Avid Media Composer (a very powerful program used for, among other applications, Hollywood movies).

The above list is certainly not definitive and is meant only to serve as an example of the range of programs available. Note that you should check features carefully to make sure the program, regardless of its processing power, meets your needs. Do you do a lot of sharing or uploading to YouTube, for example? If so, a program with such capabilities built in can save you some time and effort.

PERFORMING TIPS FOR ENTEPRENEURIAL VIDEO

Announcing to a camera in a professional studio shares much of the same skill-set as performing in a vlog produced in your basement. But then again, there are differences and special skills you'll need to bring into focus.

Here are ten performance tips for appearing in and producing your own video.

1. **Keep Your Energy Level High**
    Working in a bustling studio often infuses you with energy, but being alone in your room with a camera won't have the same effect. As noted elsewhere in this book, video is by nature an enervating medium, meaning that it appears to rob people of energy. If this happens to you in a studio, it will have double the draining effect at home. Don't become manic, but never let yourself lean to listlessness.

2. **Be Careful of Appropriateness of Content**

The Internet is a mirror with a memory, and while you may be in a room in your house your performance is NOT private. Jokes you tell to your friends may not cause a stir but if inappropriate can be offensive and damaging to your reputation and the video may never go away even if you take it down. Once it is copied and shared you have no control. There's an old saying in comedy: "Will it play in Peoria?" The precise history of the phrase is uncertain, but it basically means, "will this material work in a traditional, mainstream town? [such as Peoria, Illinois]." So exercise judgment about what you put on the Web. Be sure it's funny and be sure—if you care, and you probably should—that it's in good taste. Poorly conceived humor has come back to bite even the biggest YouTube stars, people known for their outrageousness. See this chapter's *Think About It* box.

Think About It

A Youtube Star and an Anti-Semitic Joke

YouTube star PewDiePie, otherwise known as Felix Kjellberg, lost big contracts with Walt Disney Corporation and Google after the *Wall Street Journal* reported that he had posted a video in which two men held a sign saying "Death to All Jews."[4] Although Kjellberg initially apologized, he struck back later in an angry post claiming that the *Journal* had taken his words out of context—that what he had intended a joke was portrayed as his true feelings. "I am sorry for the words I used as I know that offended people, and I admit that the joke itself went too far. I like to push boundaries, but I would consider myself a rookie comedian," he said, according to the *Guardian* newspaper.[5]

What's your view? We all know that the nature of humor is to tread in areas that may make some uncomfortable. But where does an Internet performer draw boundaries? Does the nature of the Internet—a vast array of offerings where people can easily opt in or opt out—make highly controversial material more acceptable? Should we have a different standard of acceptability for YouTube than for mainstream media?

---

3. **Start with Content Quickly**

In traditional television, audiences are accustomed to prolonged openings and introductions, but Internet audiences are far less tolerant. Get right to the point, show passion, and give the backstory later in the presentation.

4. **Maintain Eye Contact**

Internet video is a more intimate medium that broadcast television, and viewers will be unsettled by a speaker who does not look into the camera. This poses problems because unlike television studios, small home-based setups are typically not equipped with prompting devices. You can overcome this problem to some degree by doing multiple takes and editing them together; jump-cuts are a distraction but are becoming accepted in Internet video. But if you have trouble remembering your lines consider a small-scale prompting device (Figure 14.12). These devices typically work with a tablet or smartphone and are affordable.

5. **Pay Attention to Your Appearance**

Even if you are not on broadcast television, appearance matters. Video magnifies oddities of appearance—meaning that a clump of hair sticking up that might not even be noticed by an observer in person can make you appear positively bizarre on screen. Check yourself in a mirror and don't be shy about applying a little powder to cut down the shine on your face.

FIGURE 14.12 Here you see a small-scale prompting device located over the computer monitor. To the right is an LED flat-panel light. While you can't see it in the shot, there is an iPad flat under the prompting device and the script reflects on the mirror that covers the lens. The lens doesn't see the reflected script, but the announcer does. This is an ideal setup for a home or small office because you can be on-camera and control everything yourself, using a smartphone to control the prompting device (as shown in Figure 14.2) and having the video image captured by the camera displayed on the computer screen.

6. **Keep Mannerisms in Check**

   If it just you and the camera there is no one to warn you if your habits are becoming distracting. One of the authors recently watched an Internet video performed by a speaker experienced before live in-person audiences but not so much in front of the lens. The speaker repeatedly employed an up-and-down gesture with his arm that was not only meaningless but brought to mind a traffic cop on a busy intersection. Moral: Don't cause people to laugh at you unless you are doing comedy and want them to laugh—and then, make sure they laugh for the right reasons.

7. **Keep Your Volume Up**

   There is a tendency, when it is just you and a little camera in a small room, to drop volume way down. This produces a lackluster effect. Don't shout—but be sure you project; it pumps up your energy level and makes your voice sound more pleasing as well.

8. **When On-Camera, Err on the Short Side**

   Less is often more when it comes to Internet video. Don't stretch. Make your point, project your personality, keep your energy up, and quit while you're ahead. While there are advantages to longer videos—because the algorithms that determine the ability of a video to go viral tend to favor time watched, which is obviously titled in favor of a video that spans more time—your first few offerings should be compact.

9. **Be Clear About Your Topic**

   If you are doing a five-minute segment about tuning a guitar be sure you stick to the subject and be doubly sure that when you are adding descriptions of and keywords for the video you are clear and straightforward about the content. Many Internet video users are searching for a solution to their problems, so don't let them down.

10. **Consider Your Audience**

    In the point above, we referenced the fact that viewers often come to Internet video in search of a solution. You are offering solutions in search of an audience. The point is that if you key into the needs and desires of your audience you stand a better chance of making that audience grow. There's an adage in Internet marketing that says "hot traffic" is worth much more than "cold traffic." Hot traffic is when someone comes across your Internet presence by seeking you out. Cold is where they stumble upon you. Producing a consistent product that brings your viewers back is one key to heating up that traffic flow.

SUMMARY

Establishing a video presence on the Internet involves projecting your personality in an intimate way and giving your audience what they want. This does not mean that your performance should be predicated merely on what you think will gain audience; such an approach, in fact, can be counter-productive. As automotive pioneer Henry Ford purportedly said, if he had, at the beginning of his career, asked his potential buyers what they wanted, they would have said, "faster horses."

In other words, the Internet communicator's role straddles a fine line of audience cultivation and individual creativity.

EXERCISES

1. Assume you are going to create a series of "how-to" YouTube videos giving your audience advice in an area about which you are knowledgeable. This may have nothing to do with your goal as an Internet broadcaster but for the sake of this exercise assume that role. Come up with ten ideas for five-minute episodes. Keep the ideas focused on the broad context. For example, earlier in this chapter we used "tuning a guitar" as an example of something a novice might seek out on video. If tuning is one of your ten episodes, what might the overall theme be? Guitar for novices? If so, might not some of the other episodes in your series be, "Choosing the Right Guitar for You," "Understanding Chords," and "Strumming with a Pick vs. Using Your Fingers?" Try that same organizational pattern in picking your theme and ten episodes. You only need to write a sentence for each.

2. Conduct an Internet search of highly viewed YouTube channels and pick one that has a million or more subscribers. Then view five of the videos, or five five-minute segments if they are very long. In about 200 words, describe what the episodes had in common and how they were different—in other words, what was the over-arching theme and how did the individual episodes avoid repetition and keep the audience's interest.

3. Using a smartphone or a video camera (if you have one) conduct an experiment with three-point lighting. You don't need professional equipment. Just moving a few lamps around will suffice. Record yourself or someone else in front of a background when there is no lighting other than the standard room light. Now, position a light so it illuminates the background or the head and shoulders of the speaker. Put another light in front of and slightly to the left of the speaker, and another slightly to the right. Compare the final results and show them to classmates. Don't be afraid to experiment. Subtle changes can make a big difference in the quality of the picture. Your goal, remember, is to make the image have some depth and liveliness.

NOTES

1 http://mashable.com/2011/02/19/youtube-facts/#1iKQcYzkvGqt

2 http://www.businessinsider.com/most-popular-youtuber-stars-salaries-2017/#no-1-pewdiepie-541-million-subscribers-18

3 https://medium.com/@GriffinHammond/5-lessons-learned-from-my-profitable-indie-documentary-2017-update-fd8ded8be493

4 https://www.wsj.com/articles/disney-severs-ties-with-youtube-star-pewdiepie-after-anti-semitic-posts-1487034533

5 https://www.theguardian.com/technology/2017/feb/16/pewdiepie-antisemitic-video-media-wall-street-journal

15 Home-Based Narration and Voice-Over

Perhaps no other field in the new media landscape is so immediately hospitable to entrepreneurs as the fields of voice-overs and narrations. This is not to say, by any means, that it's an easy path to success, only that the technical barriers are fairly low and there are certain well-blazed paths to participation that are at least accessible to almost everyone.

THE OPPORTUNITIES IN VOICE-OVER AND NARRATION

First, a definition: When we say "voice-over," we are usually referring to radio commercials and spoken audio for television commercials. The terminology is not precise in that "voice over" technically means (in most applications) that the announcer's voice is laid over some other source of audio or video, but this general description is accurate enough for our purposes. We will use "narration" to indicate such tasks as performance in documentaries (which, of course, also involves voice over video), training productions, and audiobooks. There are many other applications for which we could use either word, including providing the voice for telephone hold systems or acting in commercials or as a voice for animation.

Some of those tasks are beyond the scope of this text, but the general principles we set forth here will apply to just about any type of voice application, and will be specifically germane to commercials and audiobooks.

WHAT YOU WILL NEED

In order to produce professional-quality audio—a product that is a notch above the good-quality product that will suffice in podcasts and most video—you need a *sound-isolated-and-treated space*, a *high-quality mic*, and reasonably powerful *audio editing software*.

Spaces that Produce High-Quality Audio

To review, there is a difference between "sound proofing" and "sound treating." What we call sound proofing is something of a misnomer because very few structures can be impervious to sound, and the best we can hope for is sound reduction (of unwanted noise) but the point is that for high-end audio applications the background must be reasonably free of intrusive outside noise.

By sound treating, we are referring to isolating the recording area to ensure that the studio does not produce echoes or inject some other unwanted acoustic characteristics, such as a hollow reverberation or a muffled, claustrophobic sound.

Sound Reduction and Isolation for High-Quality Audio. Keeping unwanted sound out is harder than you might suspect. Here are some options, presented with the most difficult and elaborate first, and easier options further down the list.

- **Build a recording studio.** This involves using materials with low sound transmission factors, insulation with materials that block sound (oddly enough, shreds of old denim work very well), constructing a "room within a room" with floors mounted on rubber spacers, and double-windows that are constructed with the glass at an angle so as not to encourage vibration. As if this weren't difficult enough, remember that you will have to breathe inside and thus will have to pay special attention to installing a low-noise ventilation system.
- **Buy a pre-manufactured sound-isolating room.** These go by various trade names; "Whisper Rooms" are among the most well-known. Pre-manufactured rooms (Figure 15.1) are generally shipped in sections and assembled on the location where they will be used. Most include some provision for ventilation, and low-noise fans are often part of the package. Some do not have rigid walls and others are constructed from blankets. In such cases, while there may be some significant sound attenuation, the purpose of the room is usually more geared toward sound treatment than isolation (more on this in the section below).
- **Adapt an existing room to keep out as much noise as possible.** Finding the quietest part of a home or other building in which to locate the space is more than half the battle. In general, the higher you are in a building the quieter it will be because you are more isolated from noise from traffic

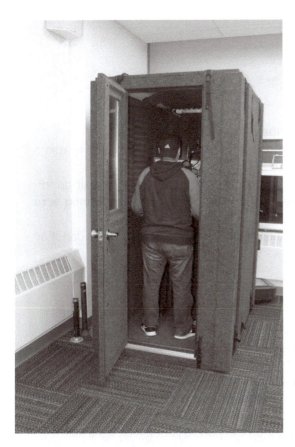 

FIGURE 15.1 There are many different trade names for sound isolation booths, with Whisper Room being one. Here is an outside view of a sound booth and an inside shot.

and passersby. However, being higher—especially on the top floor—makes you more vulnerable to airplane noise. Other noise sources you need to avoid are heating and cooling systems and the sounds of toilets flushing and other plumbing noises. Heavy curtains over windows help keep out some noise, as do rugs on the floors upstairs if you own or occupy that part of the building. While an inconvenience, sometimes the best way to mitigate the types of noises that ruin recordings, such as airplanes or garbage trucks or barking dogs, is to work around them. Just stop, re-record, and edit. This is a more common situation than you might expect; the authors have been in more than one professional recording studio where we had to kill time while waiting for a low-flying plane to leave the overhead airspace. And if all else fails, try recording late at night. The world is a surprisingly quiet place at 2 a.m.

- **Rent a professional studio.** Rates vary widely, but if you know how to run the equipment and don't need engineering assistance (in other words, you don't need an engineer employed by the studio to help you out), you can sometimes negotiate a good rate for a production studio that won't be used at a certain time. There are drawbacks to this arrangement (aside from the price) in that if it's a long project, such as an audiobook, you'll need access to the same studio during the duration of the project. Changing of recording venue produces a different ambient sound, which will be awkward halfway through your audiobook.
- **Finally, keep your computer at a distance.** Probably the number one culprit in external noise is the computer fan. Place your computer in back of a directional mic if possible. Other sound-reducing hacks are described in this chapter's *Tuning into Technology*.

Tuning into Technology

Keeping Cool

Ventilation is a challenge in a home studio because the movement of air is noisy.
Cooling of air is noisier still, and an air conditioning unit can produce enough noise to ruin a recording.

You may have no choice but to cool the room first and then shut off fans and air conditioners and record until you can't take it anymore and run the cooling devices during your break.

But doing this will inevitably cause your computer to become hot and turn on its fan. Fan noise is the bane of home recording.

There are a couple of work-arounds:

- You can actually put the computer in a separate room (or at least many feet away from the mic) if you run an external monitor and long USB cords for the mouse and keyboard.
- You can attempt to keep the computer cool by keeping open space for ventilation around it. In the case of a laptop, this means putting it on some sort of mesh riser than allows the bottom to stay cool. One of the authors uses a mesh monitor stand with a drawer into which he inserts the type of ice block you use in a cooler (Figure 15.2). They are cheap and you can easily keep several in rotation throughout a recording session. If you don't have any sort of riser you can always set the laptop right on the plastic ice blocks; it's a little tippy, but it works.

Tuning into Technology *(continued)*

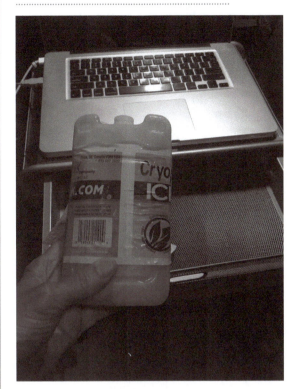 

FIGURE 15.2 Necessity is the mother of invention. This is a monitor riser, but works beautifully to cool the laptop in order to keep the fan from coming on and making noise.

Sound Treatment for High-Quality Audio. Not to belabor the point, remember that sound treatment means taking steps to ensure the sound in the studio has a pleasing quality, and is a separate issue from sound isolation. We repeat that because the concepts are constantly confused and a clear comprehension is important to the understanding of the suggestions below.

In order to "treat" audio to produce a good sound:

- Find a fairly small room with a rug. If you don't have a carpet, you can always lay down a throw rug. If you have no choice other than to work in a large room, you can partition a part of the room off. More on this will come in a following bullet point.
- Related to the point above, note that closets often make good areas for recording. For one thing, they are typically small and more often than not are rectangular. Without getting into the acoustic weeds, remember that it's generally advantageous to record in a room where one side is wider than the other; this prevents certain types of sound reverberation. If your closet is full of clothes, don't despair: hanging clothes are good at blocking reverb.
- Place some sound absorption material on the walls. As mentioned in the Podcasting chapter, a firm called Auralex makes a popular tile which is light and easily attached to the wall. You can fasten them with adhesive and easily remove them, so your installation need not be permanent. It is also simple to hang them with a small nail, the hole from which can easily be repaired at a later date. You can also cut the tiles to seamlessly cover the walls of your studio area, as in Figure 15.3.

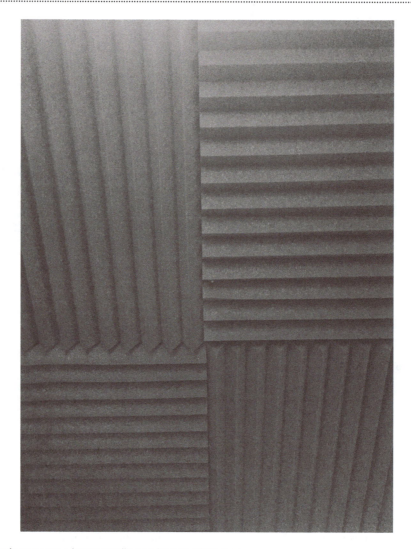

FIGURE 15.3 Here's one way a home studio can be sound treated.

- You can improvise with the sound treatment. After all, the goal is to improve the sound, not to look pretty. Some producers have used egg cartons (which have projections similar to the Auralex tile) attached to the wall to disrupt reverberation and soften the sound reaching the mic. Moving blankets (thick, padded blankets used to cushion furniture in a truck) are cheap and available at home improvement stores. You can hang them from walls or use them as an easily constructed sound containment booth.
- Figures 15.4–15.6 show a sound treatment room constructed by one of the authors. The frame is made of PVC pipe, which is inexpensive and available at any home improvement store. PVC is very easy to work with because it is light and you can cut it with a hand saw and the parts can be fitted together with connectors sold at the same store where you obtain the PVC. Moving blankets can be hung from the pipes with clamps or by other connectors placed through a small hole in the blanket.
- Place some sound-absorbing padding above the microphone. This absorbs a great deal of reverb and warms up the sound considerably. You will have to do some improvising here, but an inexpensive mattress topper, the type sold in virtually every department store, is light and can be suspended or folded over the mic area.
- Put a towel or blanket below the microphone. Sound waves bouncing from below can make the recording sound tinny; also, having a towel on the surface of the desk helps prevent friction noises from, say, your shirt cuffs scraping on the surface.

FIGURE 15.4 Here's how Phil Benoit built a sound-treated studio at home.

FIGURE 15.5 Phil Benoit hung thick moving blankets from the frame and positioned a table inside the booth.

FIGURE 15.6 Here's a no-frills way to prevent reverb.

Be sure to put some sound-absorbing material behind the mic. Reverb from the rear is common and deleterious to the warm, "studio-quality" sound you are seeking. One way to accomplish this is with a manufactured device that sits behind the mic and wraps part-way around it.

You can also improvise your own device or make or buy a padded box that surrounds the mic. Some voice artists use these box arrangements when travelling.

High-Quality Mics for Home Audio

You can find extensive guidance on microphone use and selection elsewhere in this book, but there are some special considerations that a home-based voice-over or audiobook artist must take into consideration.

Cost. More than likely you will be footing the bill for your mic, so an extremely high-quality studio mic of the type used to record professional musicians may simply be out of the question. Don't despair: You don't need a $2,000, super-sensitive mic, and for the type of work you'll be doing that type of instrument could be counterproductive (for reasons explained below). You certainly do want a mic that produces high-quality sound, and because requirements for most voice-over and narration work are higher than for podcasting you'll need to step up to a higher-level than, say, a headset mic. While it is beyond the scope of this book to make brand-specific recommendations, we can point out that a great deal of professional voice-over and narration has been recorded with the Rode NT1A (Figure 15.7), a condenser mic that sells for about $230, including an excellent shock mount.

Two of the authors use the Shure SM7B (Figure 15.8), a dynamic mic selling in the $400 range, for audiobook recording. Widely used in broadcasting and in music recording, the SM7B has a very warm sound and is good at rejecting background noise.

The arbiter of how a mic will function is how it sounds in your studio with you speaking into it. A good-quality audio store will generally let you exchange a mic within a few days if it doesn't work well for you; check with the salesperson in advance. If necessary, try several mics until you find the one that fits you.

We are going to offer a suggestion that runs counter to the advice you will see on various sites about home recording and suggest that you give serious thought to a dynamic mic versus a condenser. Large-diaphragm condensers are frequently recommended by audio engineers and many can certainly offer good value and a robust signal. They also typically don't need any pre-amping to feed into your digital conversion unit. However, by their nature condensers pick up a wide range of sound, including a lot you don't

FIGURE 15.7 A Rode NT1A, a high-quality condenser mic that sells at a very reasonable price.

FIGURE 15.8 The Shure SM7B, a dynamic mic that produces an extraordinarily warm and rich sound.

want to pick up, including ambient studio noise, plosives, and mouth noise—not to mention stomach rumbles. Dynamic mics by and large are less sensitive to these unwanted sounds. Some dynamics, such as the SM7B, are very good at rejecting noise from the rear. The SM7B also has a built-in pop filter.

Audio-Editing Software for Home Use

Most facets of audio editing have been covered earlier in this text, and there are only a couple of small points specific to home voice-over and narration.

- **First,** whatever program you use be sure you learn about the processing capabilities because you may have to equalize and limit. For example, the Audiobook production company ACX, the production arm of the Amazon audiobook firm Audible, sets specific parameters for the work you submit. Your final recordings must be within specified ratios for loudness, noise reduction, and audio peaks. Without a good understanding of how to process to meet these standards, you will clearly be at a disadvantage.

- **Second,** make sure that you learn techniques that will enable you to stop and start during a long session. As an example, in the free program Audacity, there is a pause command that, coupled with another command, lets you pick up recording instantly in the same track, allows you to position your cursor at the point where you finished or edited out a mistake and start in again, often without any discernable editing noise. Other programs have a feature called "punch and roll," which plays back a couple seconds of the audio then automatically opens the mic for you to continue at the new entry point. Many narrators like this feature because it allows them to keep their rhythm of the sentence. Regardless of the particular software, in long-form narration you will be doing a lot of stopping and starting and it's crucial from an artistic and time-saving standpoint to master the commands that will make this as easy as possible.

FINDING FREELANCE BUSINESS

Because audio files can be easily exchanged over the Internet, and as for reasons explained above home production is readily achievable, there is now a brisk commerce in narration. While it is not always particularly profitable from the announcer's point of view, opportunity abounds.

For voice-over work, there are many sites that connect clients with voice artists. This list is not definitive nor does it imply endorsement, but we do note that sites such as voices.com, upwork.com, and freelancer.com list a variety of assignments. Such postings often include:

- Commercials for radio stations
- Narrations for videos
- Narrations for documentaries
- Narrations for instructional videos
- Recorded messages for phone systems (there is much more of this work than you might suspect)

Some of the work advertised is to be performed in-studio at various locations but most, according to what we have seen, is meant to be recorded in the announcer's facility.

Sites offering to connect producers and voice performers have various structures and fee systems, so be sure to do your homework.

There are also several sites geared toward narrators of audiobooks. Two of particular interest are librivox.com and acx.com.

Librivox is a repository of public domain (not carrying a copyright) audiobooks that are read by volunteers. You can get started easily at this site because there is a forum of volunteers in which veterans help newcomers.

ACX is the production arm of Audible, the Amazon-owned audiobook publisher. ACX (which stands for Audiobook Creation Exchange) acts as a clearinghouse, matching authors with narrators. Authors of existing print books either hire narrators at an agreed price or split royalties with the narrators.

Authors post on the site and provide audition material for prospective narrators. You can peruse the site and sort the prospective projects by genre before you audition (Figure 15.9).

Another good reason to visit the ACX site is to read and view the many excellent tutorials the company offers to people who want to enter the home narration business. Visit the site and click on the link "What you need to get started" to access the free instructional material.

acx

Philip Benoit

Specializing in westerns, I bring a compelling storytelling style and vocal characterization to fiction and make the abstract concrete in philosophy/religion books.

Gender: Male
Location: PA,United States
Website: www.philipbenoit.com/

Available for: Royalty Share or $100-$200 PFH

Audiobook Samples | About | Credits | Awards and Recognition

▶ **The Mountain of Slow Madness**

Category : Fiction
Language : English
Gender : Male

Accent : American–Western
Vocal Style : Range: low to mid range

Performance Notes
This short story is part of a series of works of Western fiction by Carl Dane featuring Marshal Josiah Hawke and his deputy, Tom Carmody. In this story the pair set out to find out why a young girl has wandered into town alone in a severe state of shock. Characters include a saloon maven who is romantically involved with Hawke, and a fanatical pastor whose mesmerized parishioners carry out his violent plots against local citizens. Carmody, a mountain man of humble origin, deploys a surprisingly deep knowledge of the Bible to debate the reverend who seeks to use scripture to justify the deputy's impending demise. The story is told by the marshal, and the narrator must create vocal renditions of male and female characters, two of which are children.

▶ **Another Song within Dialogue**

Category : Fiction
Language : English
Gender : Male

Accent : American–Western
Vocal Style : Storyteller

Performance Notes
This one of several samples from a book about a young man from Oklahoma who comes of age during the period leading up to and including World War II. It illustrates how I handle the need to sing a song passage woven into dialogue among male and female characters.

▶ **I sing the Oklahoma Alma Mater**

Category : Fiction
Language : English
Gender : Male

Accent : American–Western
Vocal Style : Storyteller

Performance Notes
From a novel about an Oklahoma youth coming of age during World War II, this is a scene from a football game during his college years at Oklahoma. As narrator, I have to sing the OU alma mater to represent the crowd at the game chanting it together. There is also a brief rendition of the voice of Walter Cronkite as the Sooners' public address announcer.

▶ **Shortgrass: Mennonite Hymn**

Category : Fiction
Language : English
Gender : Male

Accent : American–Mid-West
Vocal Style : Storyteller

Performance Notes
From a novel about the life of a young Oklahoma Mennonite caught up in events leading up to and including World War II, this clip of the young man in a church service includes a passage in which I sing a portion of a classic Mennonite hymn.

▶ **North Side Hellion**

Category : Fiction
Language : English
Gender : Male

Accent : American–General American
Vocal Style : Engaging

Performance Notes
Excerpt from a historical fiction novel about Chicago gangsters during the Prohibition era. Narration intersperses with vocal characterizations of fictional and historic figures of the period.

▶ **Betty Zane**

Category : Fiction
Language : English
Gender : Male

Accent : American–Western
Vocal Style : Storyteller

Performance Notes
This excerpt from a Zane Grey novel that I narrated as part of a four-book boxed set demonstrates a story telling style that uses narration in action combined with vocal characterizations of male and female characters in dialogue with one another.

FIGURE 15.9 A screenshot of Phil Benoit's narrator page on ACX.

PERFORMANCE TIPS FOR VOICE-OVERS, NARRATIONS, AND AUDIOBOOKS

Previous chapters have covered many of the basics you'll need to know to compete in this area, but here are ten pointers unique to working in an entrepreneurial environment.

1. **Accustom yourself to listening critically to your own material.** You'll usually receive feedback only after something is submitted, and without a director and/or engineer participating in the process as you record, the onus is largely on you to monitor pronunciations, technical quality, and expressiveness of the read. (Some experienced home-based announcers have high-quality phone lines installed in their home studios and can record and communicate live via another phone line with a producer in a distant location, but such a scenario is several years down the road for someone just entering the business.) So in essence, you must be your own editor. Give your client as clean a recording as possible. Audio that requires many changes and edits not only wastes time on both ends but can give you a reputation as a someone who is sloppy.

2. **Edit with "room tone."** Room tone is simply the ambient sound in your studio. One of the most common mistakes made by beginners in long-form narration is to leave edits exposed (hearing the click where you have taken something out or stopped and started) and/or pasting in pure silence to cover it up. The pure silence generated by a computer program will be jarring—it will obviously be an edited section. When you start your recording session, sit quietly and record about ten seconds of nothing. Pick a quiet second or so of that and use that to edit. If you need to take out a pop, delete the pop and paste in room tone. Remember, don't just paste in silence; it will sound like the recording has shut off because the normal sound of the background will suddenly drop out. Our advice is to record room tone for each session because, believe it or not, the ambience in your studio will vary subtly from day to day and you want to completely sonically disguise any of your edits.

3. **Mark up your copy.** In addition to the markup techniques discussed in Chapter 3 on Understanding the Message, you'll face an additional challenge when reading an audiobook: Different characters. How do you remember who is who, and how do you keep the voices straight? Co-author Phil Benoit faced this challenge in narrating a recent multi-volume audiobook with more than eighty characters. In this chapter's Focus on Technique, he explains how he did it.

Focus on Technique

A Rainbow of Audiobook Characters

In narrating a work of fiction, to a certain extent you are an actor who gets to play all the parts. That is a common observation by experienced audiobook narrators who have developed a style that allows the listener's attention to drift away from the narrator and focus on the story itself as conveyed by the words of the characters in the work.

Of course with the fulfilling task of "playing all the parts" comes the challenge of distinguishing characters one from another, and offering credible performances that successfully depict a variety of character types, personalities, and genders.

I have written before about some of the techniques that work for me when trying to interpret various types of characters, but in some works, simple tricks of the trade like lightening the force of delivery for female characters while slightly raising the pitch, are not sufficient to address the situations depicted in the narrative.

Focus on Technique *(continued)*

I am currently producing a boxed set of four different books—classic westerns by the likes of Zane Grey—which were originally published more than 100 years ago. In one of the works in that collection, there are numerous characters, and a number of passages in which those characters engage in good-natured banter about the goings on that take place on a cattle ranch. In several such passages that take place in a bunkhouse, seven or more characters trade rapid-fire wisecracks about other characters and situations in the story. The characters have names like Shorty, Slim, Weary, Cal, Chip, Happy Jack, and Jack, and their lines are intermingled in a snappy repartee that reflects the quirks of each character's personality.

The obvious challenge for the narrator is to represent each character's persona succinctly and accurately while clearly differentiating the characters from one another as the dialogue unfolds.

In my previous outings narrating western fiction, characters have most often interacted in short scenes involving at most two or three characters at a time. And those characters appeared off and on throughout the book. It was not difficult to differentiate them when they had conversations.

A multifaceted dialogue, though, is considerably more challenging for a number of reasons. How do you establish a presence for the individual characters? How do you make it clear, using only your voice, who is speaking when, while keeping in mind that you are not performing a drama, but reading fiction from a book?

Here's what I came up with to address this challenge.

First, I decided I had to read well ahead of where I was in my recording process to get as detailed sense of who these characters are as I could. Do they have any distinct physical characteristics? What are they wearing? Do they possess any special skills or abilities that might help me get to know them? In the bunkhouse scene, for example, the character called Slim was so named because he was quite the opposite of what the name implied; he was portly and short of stature. But he was also a good horseman, and highly respected as such by his fellow cowhands.

Once I got a sense of who the characters were, I had to decide what they sounded like, and how I could render their unique voices in my performance.

I did this by thinking of classic characters that I am familiar with. For example, I decided that the owner of the ranch should sound something like Ben Cartwright of the classic TV western, *Bonanza*. The protagonist and title character, Chip, would have a John Wayne quality because he was often engaged in taunting exchanges with the lead female character, Della, reminiscent of films featuring "The Duke" and Maureen O'Sullivan. If the voice of an actual person did not come to mind, I characterized a person as a "Granny, well-met," or simply as "morose."

I made a sheet of notes using a kind of shorthand to describe my assessment of the key traits and voice types I had decided on for each character. It is posted in front of my mic in my announce booth (Figure 15.10).

Characters are listed with brief notes on their quirks and personalities. They are assigned colors to link them to their lines in the manuscript.

On the sheet I also assigned a color to each character, and beside each character's name, I drew in a small box using a colored pencil. So, for instance, next to the minor character, Mr. Denson, who sounds like Strother Martin (*Cool Hand Luke*) is an orange box, while James G. Whitmore, the ranch owner, gets a green box.

Next I went through a printout of the script and marked each character's "lines" with the corresponding color for his or her character. This is helpful because passages often just begin with a line of dialogue and don't identify the speaker until the end of a lengthy speech. So, when I see a passage underlined in blue, I know that the character is Chip, and I know to affect that voice. If Della speaks next, I can see that coming when I note the red colored lines beneath her words, and I switch to the modified Maureen O'Sullivan that I've chosen for her voice.

Focus on Technique *(continued)*

- Janie C Whitmore authoritative BnCartwright

  Shorty formal material fact midrange to oritone

- Jack Bates baritone cowboy

- Cal Emmett Little Joe

- Chip Cake Splinter Caka Claude Burnett: JohaWayne

- Happy Jack moore

- Weary Gabby Hayes

  Slim docp but pinched

- Della Whitmore raise pitch slightly; soften

- Mr Denison strother Martin

- Mrs Denson Granny Wollmet

- Louise Cake the Countess

FIGURE 15.10 Phil Benoit, who has narrated many audiobooks, keeps character sketches so he knows the characteristics of each voice. It's handy, because in audiobooks you have to switch back and forth many times and you don't want to trust your memory. Here are quick notes he made color coding the dialog to the appropriate voice styles. We reproduced them typos and all for the sake of authenticity.

Next I had to rehearse. I read the script aloud until I felt comfortable that I had the voices down. (I don't do impressions, so my Ben Cartwright will never be confused with the real Lorne Green; the best I can manage is to "suggest" his intonations, pitch, and force when he created Ben's character in the classic western series.)

When I've gone over the dialogue enough to acquire a good sense of who's speaking and how they all sound together, I record. There is a lot of starting and stopping, but with skillful audio editing, the finished product sounds reasonably credible. I backstop my own opinion about this by asking (coercing?) my wife Candy to listen to the book, chapter by chapter. So far I'm meeting the "Candy Standard," so I have reasonable confidence in the outcome of my process.

My background as the narrator with a resonant authoritative baritone is of little use in these heavy dialogue situations. That's a hurdle to overcome, but it's also rewarding to learn new skills and approaches and produce something fresh. The chapters in this book are relatively short, so I get a frequent sense of accomplishment as I finish one little melodrama at a time in the march toward a believable and, I hope, entertaining completed audiobook.

4. **Aim for consistency.** In long-form narration, such as audiobooks, audiences are keenly aware when your approach or mic position is different. Be sure you're in the same physical position when you stop, take a break, and re-start. If at all possible, avoid repositioning anything in the studio or changing settings in programs. Also, be aware of the fact that after you take a break you'll typically be louder

when you start up. That's only natural after you've been refreshed by some time away, but it's much more jarring from a listener's perspective than you might expect. Be sure to keep your energy up when you are finishing a session so that you don't figuratively limp toward the end, and monitor your volume when you start fresh.

5. **Differentiate between speakers and narrators.** Here's a seemingly simple sentence: "'I don't have any idea how to get there,' Frank said." To an audio narrator, though, it presents a problem. If you are using a special voice for Frank, perhaps if he is a gangster in a novel, the attribution ("he said") should not be in Frank's voice. Even if you are not using a voice characterization, you need a difference in tone between the conversational part of the sentence and the "he said." It helps if you inject a pause before the attribution. Almost all experienced audiobook narrators do this; just insert an extra beat and you'll get the sonic separation necessary to differentiate between your role in re-creating the speaker and serving as the narrator.

6. **If you have to use an accent, be sure it is correct and doesn't "wander."** If you have acting ambitions, doing multiple parts that require accents can be rewarding but it also is extremely challenging. To be frank, nothing sounds as amateurish and comical as a poorly done accent. Use the accent guide in the Appendix of this book as a starter, and then check out the many websites that will provide you with guidance. One that we can recommend is www.dialectarchive.com. Some narrators find it easier to mimic an actor who is doing the accent in question. Feel free to hunt up characters in movies on YouTube clips and use them for inspiration. Regardless of your choice of instruction, though, remember that it is critical that you keep the accent in question consistent. Listeners will, without question, notice if your inflections vary from chapter to chapter. It is very easy for this to happen, so make sure you listen to your previous rendition when beginning that character anew.

7. **Don't sound like an announcer, unless the assignment calls for someone who sounds like an announcer.** This admonition applies to both straight narration and acted parts. If you view various posting sites for auditions for voice artists, you will frequently see the admonition, "No Announcers!" You have been warned.

8. **In general, slow down.** A rushed read is distracting and does not impart the personal, story-telling nature invoked in narration. If you are doing voice-over for a commercial, you may be asked to speed up, but for the wrong reasons: the producer wants more words crammed into the spot and feels he or she wants to get the most words for the buck. Audio is about communication, and a natural pace simply communicates in a more genuine manner.

9. **In general, don't speak too loudly.** You might want to up the volume on a commercial; for most narrations you are, as mentioned in the point above, seeking a level of intimacy. This is not accomplished by booming, "HELLO ALL OF YOU OUT THERE IN AUDIO-LAND." Be careful of mouth and breath noises, but in general you will be better off working a little closer to the mic than you are used to and speaking a little more softly when doing a narration.

10. **Remember at all times that you are acting a role, even if your piece is nonfiction.** You may have noticed that up until this point we have avoided discussing any demarcations between "announcing" and "acting." There is a reason for that: Even if you are doing a "straight read," you are assuming a guise; perhaps you are a trusted advisor, an educated consumer, or a teacher leading someone through the points illustrated in the documentary. Granted, you may not be emoting in an English accent, but you are still taking on the role of a character. Always begin your planning for any audio work with an evaluation of what persona you will be adopting, put some thought into a delivery that reinforces that role, and stay consistent.

SUMMARY

Having a computer, an Internet hook-up, and a good-quality audio setup allows you entrée to a world of freelance announcing and acting assignments. You will need technical as well as verbal skills, and need to approach the process of finding gigs in a careful, methodical way.

EXERCISES

1. Record a couple of minutes of audio of a character with a foreign accent. It doesn't really matter what material you choose. Use the chart in the Appendix to come up with the approximate sounds both in terms of vowel and consonant sounds and listen to native speakers on the Internet to help approximate the rhythm. You might also check out good actors experienced in accents; for a tour de force, see this montage of Meryl Streep: https://www.youtube.com/watch?v=aPUedwHP_Ro

2. Visit ACX.com and pick out five jobs you believe you would be qualified to audition for. Explain, in a paragraph for each, why you think you would be a good choice.

3. Visit Audible.com and search on a book that will have several different versions. Anything by Dickens will suffice. You can listen to fairly long samples for free, so compare the approaches of three different actors. (You won't be hearing the same parts of the book, but you'll get the general idea.) In about 200 words, explain which performer you believe did the best job, and why.

16 Career Advancement

Talent, skill, hard work, and a desire to improve are useless if you can't get a job. On-air broadcast work is difficult to break into. Competition is tough even for low-paying, entry-level jobs. And if your career pattern is typical, once you have broken into broadcasting, you will change jobs several times.

Your first job will probably be the toughest to get. The pay will be low and the work demanding. But you'll probably learn more about the business of broadcasting in your first job than in any course you take. Professionalism in on-air work comes only through experience. Broadcasting is a business you learn in the business.

In this chapter, we focus on what you need to do to get and hold a job.

We discuss opportunities available to broadcasters and pass on hints from professionals about what techniques are most likely to help you get started in the field. We also discuss the tools of getting hired—résumés, audition material, and developing contacts. And finally we look at salaries and contracts.

ON-AIR OPPORTUNITIES FOR BROADCASTERS

With the understanding that a beginner will be paid as a beginner, even with a college degree, you are ready to start your search for a broadcast on-air position.

That first job will almost certainly involve duties you will not like or want to do, but versatility is essential. Although your goal may be TV news anchoring, you may have to pull many radio music show shifts. Aspiring radio personalities must do news. Sportscasters may have to produce commercials. All duties you will be asked to perform must be done with a smile, for realists understand that there are dozens of applicants for even the most humble positions, and hundreds for the desirable jobs.

You must be in good physical condition because your career will frequently involve terrible hours. A shift may start at 5 a.m., continue until 2 p.m., and then begin again with the evening newscast at 5 p.m. In radio, shifts of six days per week are common. And don't expect holidays off. The show, so to speak, must go on. Colds and the flu won't automatically qualify you for a day off, either. If you are expected to sign on the station at 6 a.m., you *must* be there unless you can rouse the manager out of bed to take over your shift.

After a year or so of successful and dedicated work in a small market, you might, we repeat *might,* be able to move on to a better small market or a medium market. Never take such advancement for granted because the competition is stiff. A modest broadcast job, which does not pay more than that of a kitchen helper in a good restaurant, can easily attract dozens of applicants.

If these prospects do not discourage you, if you are so set on on-air work that you can ignore the odds, and if you realistically think you possess the talent to overcome the challenge of hundreds of other applicants, you may have a future as on-air talent.

On-Air Jobs

An important consideration in the life of an on-air performer, in news or radio personality work or any other part of the industry, is that your career path is likely to resemble that of a gypsy. Your résumé will look like it was written by Rand-McNally, as some broadcasters say.

There is no reason why a broadcaster must move from market to market if he or she is content to work in a small town. Broadcasting from small towns often is of high quality, and the small-market environment offers safety and ease of existence unknown in major cities. Small-market broadcasters do not become rich and famous, but they enjoy a fine quality of life and a great deal of influence.

Medium-market on-air people also can enjoy good-quality lifestyle, and cities considered to be medium markets—such as Syracuse, New York, or Austin, Texas—offer, in smaller doses, every advantage of a major city.

Medium markets frequently have professional sports teams, symphony orchestras, and major universities. They also are more likely to have affordable housing than major markets do.

The big money, however, comes in the major markets, like Boston and Philadelphia. Radio personalities make generous salaries, and the salaries of TV news anchors are in the six-figure range. The majors are difficult to crack, however, and there is no accompanying rise in job security.

Sometimes newcomers to broadcasting elect to settle in major markets and work their way up through low-level jobs, such as mailroom or even janitorial duties. This approach has pluses and minuses, which we discuss shortly.

As we mentioned, the beginner will have to do many jobs not directly related to what he or she perceives as an ultimate career goal. Such exposure is beneficial for two reasons:

1. Trying a wide variety of jobs gives you exposure that will be valuable later on in your career. The value might not be apparent immediately, but any experience in the business usually is an asset regardless of your career path. If, for example, you wind up in some form of management, that period in sales or production will certainly enhance your knowledge of the business overall and make you a better manager.
2. You may not have enough ability to pursue the career path you think you want to follow. Or, you may want to do well as a disc jockey but find that you hate the job. Many an aspiring disc jockey has found more satisfaction in news, and vice versa.

People in a position to hire you will appreciate—even demand—versatility and a willingness to work in a variety of assignments. Virtually without exception, they will place a higher premium on demonstrable professional experience than on a professor's statement that you were a fine student. And you may be required to start in an off-air job and earn the chance to go before the camera or microphone.

Humility is important, not so much as a rite of initiation but as a realistic approach to the task of finding a broadcast job. Your realistic self-assessment and willingness to work will translate into what broadcast executives think of as a good attitude.

The inboxes of broadcast executives are cluttered with applications, and many of them echo the contention that the chances of a newcomer, slim to begin with, are often made worse by a somewhat arrogant approach to the application process. Many neophytes refuse to hear of anything other than on-air work, even though production or writing or other duties might be the only available avenue toward their goals. Other applicants destroy their credibility by overstating their résumé qualifications, for example, by listing "extensive experience in documentaries" to describe participation in two college projects.

Moving into Management or Related Duties

A realistic assessment of on-air work shows that it is difficult to obtain, and advancement involves tooth-and-nail competition among a veritable army of dedicated, talented people. But even though on-air work does not become a lifelong career for many, it does provide an excellent springboard into other occupations. Some on-air talent moves into management, especially in radio.

Program directors often started as announcers. Today's radio program director has a job that is often a cross between chief announcer and executive in charge of the music, programming legalities, and overall station sound. News on-air people can move into news management. Most news directors have some on-air background, which contributes to their understanding of the overall news effort. The top levels of station management are generally drawn from the ranks of sales. But there is nothing to prevent a radio staff announcer from combining his or her early career with experience in time sales.

In some markets, selling is part of the job. In most radio markets, good salespeople out-earn on-air talent.

The entire chain of human communication is interrelated at almost all levels. On-air performers frequently elect to move into positions in advertising and public relations. Contacts made during and after working hours facilitate this kind of change, and the insights picked up during years of on-air work will help in this or any other career.

PREPARING FOR YOUR FIRST JOB

Your first job in broadcasting will probably be the most difficult to get. There is intense competition. If you have talent, though, and are willing to take a job that may be less than ideal, eventually you will get hired. Once your foot is in the door, you have a chance to compile a record of performance. Then you will be better able to select the kinds of situations that let you advance in the career direction that suits you best.

Preparation for a career in broadcasting involves two major components: academics and practical experience. For on-air work, a third ingredient is a certain amount of native talent. You can't do much about your degree of innate talent, so let's look at the things you can do something about.

Academics

It is difficult to recommend a precise academic program without knowing exactly what career path you will follow. You will probably explore several areas before settling into your major career focus. Let's look at some academic preparation that can be helpful in on-air work.

You're reading this textbook, so you are probably taking at least one academic course in broadcasting or communications. Preparation in this area can be a focused program given in professional training schools, a slightly longer preparation in two-year schools, or a four-year program that adds other courses and awards a bachelor's degree. More advanced work at the master's degree level and beyond is usually designed to prepare people for broader professional responsibilities in the communications field.

Whether you're aiming for on-air work in radio or TV, in news or entertainment, one overall guideline applies: *Learn as much as you can about as many things as you can.* You're looking for depth *and* breadth.

If you're a communications major in a four-year program, take as many courses outside that major as you can. Try for a good mixture of such areas as political science, history, economics, and literature. Earlier we recommended that you consider a double major. If you do, select your second major in one of the areas just mentioned.

In Focus on Technique, Dan Rather reinforces the notion that good writing skills and hard work are essential if you aspire to succeed in this field.

Focus on Technique

The Most Valuable Attributes in a Broadcast Career

Those who have successfully navigated the career path that puts them in front of cameras and microphones are almost unanimous in identifying two off-camera attributes that propelled them in their careers.

1. The ability to write well
2. The willingness to work very, very hard

Focus on Technique *(continued)*

A connection between writing well and working in news is reasonably apparent to even the most casual observer, but many students enter the field expecting to survive solely on their presentation skills. Even though a small number do, most find that the ability to put thoughts on paper is critical.

Dan Rather (see Figure 16.1), the former anchor of *The CBS Evening News*, offered his thoughts during an interview relating to the points presented in this chapter. He notes that writing skills are among the first attributes looked for in the arduous process of getting and keeping a job at CBS News.

But the value of writing extends beyond news jobs. Radio staff announcers often write and read their own copy. Sportscasters must be lucid writers, and even sports personnel who do play-by-play and color must compose clear descriptive copy for such program parts as the pregame show.

Don't forget that the *process of job hunting* requires extensive written communication. Broadcast executives are virtually unanimous in their contention that a well-written cover letter is the essential part of the application package. And once you get a job, you must *keep* it.

Hard work and long hours are the coin of the realm in broadcasting.

Students often harbor the misconception that once you've made it on-air, the ride is downhill. Actually, though, the path becomes steeper.

As Rather puts it: "Some people think this is a glamorous business. And in a way, it is. But don't be seduced by that. It doesn't come without a price . . . this line of work requires extraordinary commitment."

Those who succeed, he notes, are the people "who burn with a bright flame."

FIGURE 16.1 Dan Rather, veteran broadcast journalist, notes that those who succeed in broadcasting "burn with a bright flame."

In modern "personality" radio formats, on-air DJs need to be extremely creative. They need to know how to write and produce material quickly and professionally. To prepare for that kind of work, courses in creative writing and drama are very helpful.

Courses that help you with technical aspects of broadcasting will be an asset. Particularly at the entry level, knowledge of camera operation and editing in television news, and of audio production in radio, is usually necessary. Formal training in performance skills is also valuable, of course.

Preparing yourself academically is easier to do *before* you get a job. If you find out later that you should have taken more history courses while you were in college or that advanced TV production would have been helpful, it can be difficult to correct the deficiencies. Get as much academic preparation as you can while you are still in school and you'll improve your immediate employment prospects as well as your ability to advance.

Practical Experience

In broadcasting, a vital ingredient in preparing for a career is getting practical experience. Get all the practical experience you can while you're in school. People who do the hiring in broadcasting will invariably ask you what you did as a student to develop your skills in a practical setting.

You can get a certain amount of useful practical experience by working at the campus radio station. If you're interested in broadcast journalism, you can also gain useful experience by writing for the student newspaper or literary publications. If you're fortunate enough to have radio or television facilities on your campus, take advantage of any opportunities to work on production crews or in other assignments related to the media. Remember that these experiences will look good on your résumé, so you'll want to keep track of exactly what you did for these productions. Don't overstate what you did, but give yourself credit where appropriate.

Give yourself an advantage when you get involved in these on-campus "laboratory"-type experiences: take them seriously. The more disciplined you are in such situations, the better you will be prepared to work in a professional setting.

This is the place to make mistakes. And, like everyone else, you'll make plenty of them. The difference between your on-campus job and the professional setting is that in the campus setting there usually is life after mistakes.

Try not to write off mistakes by assuming they don't matter because "it is just the college station." Instead, find out what you need to do to correct the problems. Don't let yourself develop a careless attitude about your performance.

Strive to be as good as a paid professional broadcaster.

All the campus media experience you can get will not take the place of work in an actual professional setting. Internships and summer work offer you the best chances to get real professional experience while you are still a student.

Landing an entry-level position in broadcasting is tough enough. If you have not had an internship, it's even tougher. Most people who hire broadcasters say they consider internships more valuable than a heavy concentration of academic work in broadcasting.

Learn as much as you can early in your college career about how to get the internships that will give you the kinds of experience you need. Most internship programs have good and bad jobs. Try to find out which internships provide solid experience. Don't be afraid to branch out from on-air work.

The fact is that there simply aren't many opportunities for on-air work in most internship programs. Do try, however, to aim for the general area you want to work in. If you're interested in radio, don't jump at the first internship that comes along in a TV promotions department.

And when it comes to internships, you don't necessarily gain an advantage by looking for the biggest market. You may be relegated to running for coffee—although, to be honest, there is something to be said for the educational value of even the most prosaic tasks in a major news organization.

On the other hand, if the market is too small, you may find it difficult to get any feedback.

Often in such operations interns get shunted into an area that is not covered by other staff people. In such situations, you can get tied down to performing a single task throughout your internship. As a result, you have less chance to gain experience and knowledge outside of that single area.

Regardless of operation size, it is of primary importance to get at least one internship. If you have the opportunity to do more than one internship, take it. The experience you get from internships is worth sacrifice and hard work. Remember there are many more applicants than entry-level jobs in the broadcasting profession, and the vast majority of those you'll be competing with will have either professional experience or internships on their résumés.

To compete effectively, you'll need the edge that internships can provide.

JOB HUNTING

Once you have finished your academic and practical preparation, you begin making your bid to enter the broadcasting field. Getting your first job is extremely difficult. Many more people are looking for on-air work than there are good jobs. People with talent who really want a job badly will find opportunities, and eventually there may even be well-paying, prestigious positions.

The key is to persevere long enough to get your foot in the door.

Television

You will find it particularly difficult to start out in commercial TV on the air. You will be competing for jobs with experienced people with tapes that show actual news-reporting assignments. Those who manage to land on-air TV jobs usually start out as news reporters.

In a small market, the job of reporter can include camera operation and video editing. The hours can be long and the work exhausting. When your contemporaries work 9 to 5 and earn much better money, it can be difficult to hang on long enough to turn the corner in your career.

A good point of entry is involvement with the television station's web feeds and social media. Television stations covet younger viewers—after all, any media operation needs to replace aging audiences over time—and frequently turn to social media as the proper venue for reaching this audience segment.

Younger applicants who are tech-savvy thus stand a very good chance of getting a foot in the door.

Radio

Brad Murray, former general manager of WQSR-FM in Baltimore, says that getting started in an on-air career in radio is a matter, for most, of learning the ropes in small markets and shooting for the larger markets when you have made your mistakes and learned how to handle yourself in a variety of situations. Murray says that there are virtually no opportunities on the air for entry-level on-air people in the large markets.

Hiring in major markets is very precise. WQSR-FM tries to hire on-air people who fit the demographics of the listeners. The station appeals primarily to people ages 35 to 44. On-air people in that age range are far more likely to understand what the music means to listeners than is someone who doesn't have the same associations between life experiences and particular record cuts.

Breaking into radio at the small-market level is a matter of being willing to take jobs that may not offer much pay and benefits. Be willing to take almost any on-air opening you can get as a first job. Your objectives are to start building a résumé, get as much experience as possible, and perfect your skills as an on-air performer. Once you've gotten some practical experience, you can begin to look at opportunities that more precisely fit your requirements for salary and career advancement.

Whether you're looking for your first job or shooting for that major-market anchor position, though, you need to develop some specific tools and techniques to present yourself effectively to whoever is doing the hiring.

SELF-MARKETING TECHNIQUES

Now that the groundwork has been established, let's consider the nuts-and-bolts business of getting hired and, once you're hired, furthering your career.

Your college experience and academic preparation will serve as a good foundation.

To properly showcase your academic preparation and practical experience, you'll need to put together an effective résumé and a showcase tape, two of the tools commonly used in self-marketing.

Résumés and Portfolios

Although a good **résumé** and portfolios are important for a beginning broadcaster, they are not the be-all and end-all of a job search. A beginner's résumé rarely if ever contains elements evocative enough to urge a program director, news director, or station manager to hire that person based on the résumé alone. An audio or video sample is obviously important, and must demonstrate raw talent, but in the absence of good, solid, professional on-air work, an audio or video is not in itself a very powerful marketing tool for the beginner.

Remember that your material will commonly be in direct competition with those of experienced professionals, and experience is usually the deciding factor.

Samples are only tools in the marketing effort. By themselves, they will not get you hired. Being hired requires interviewing, following up on leads, and making contacts. With the understanding that a résumé and portfolio are the first steps in job hunting and career development, let's examine each tool.

Résumé

A good résumé will stress experience. Recognizing that experience for a recent graduate will be sparse, stress whatever coursework or internships you have had that are particularly relevant.

Candace Kelley, a journalism professor at Rowan University and an experienced anchor (Figure 16.2), producer, and writer, recommends that your résumé be available as a PDF from your online portfolio site (more on that below) and contain the following.

Fairly minimal contact information—just your name, email, and phone number. You don't want to post your address online and don't want to limit yourself geographically if a potential employer's first impression is that you live too far away.

A listing of your technical skills and proficiencies; it is important to stress your social media competence as well as programs in which you are competent, especially those involving production and media metrics.

FIGURE 16.2 Candace Kelley, veteran television anchor and reporter.

Work experience separated out between journalism work and non-journalism employment. Experience in retail, for example, that demonstrates an increasing level of responsibility is important, but not as important as professional experience. So don't make the reader hunt: clearly separate both categories.

Don't be reluctant to mention experience gained in the classroom. If you took a class that involved anchoring a live newscast, for example, be sure to include it. It is relevant.

Your Online Portfolio

The most common method of self-marketing is to construct a comprehensive online portfolio.

You can set up a good website for free; some of the more common venues (but certainly not all) are WordPress.com, About.me, and Wix.com.

Instruction in setting up a web home is beyond the scope of this text but if you are unfamiliar with the process you are, frankly, unemployable in commercial journalism and incapable of mounting an independent, entrepreneurial venture, so it is essential that you catch up in any way you can.

What goes online?

Here are some suggestions:

- An anchor segment. Get the best-quality video or audio segment you can, both in terms of performance and technical quality. Nothing says "amateur" like bad audio. Also, remember, that whatever piece you position as your lead might be the only thing the viewer watches, so if it's not impressive potential employers may not be inclined to move past the first 30 seconds of your online reel.
- Two or more packages; try for 1:30 each. Coverage of a great story is an advantage, remember that it is your skills that you are packaging, not the story itself. Make sure that the stand-ups in the packages are filled with action and movement. News directors like to see you do more than stand in one place holding a mic.
- Feature pieces, segments demonstrating your interview skills, and something that shows that you can use a camera.
- Some writing samples. Show employers that you know how to write VOs, VO/SOTs, and packages.
- A live-shot. Professor Kelley recommends you use live-shots from class, or record something with Facebook live to demonstrate not only how well you handle a live-shot but also your proficiency with social media.
- Other relevant work, such as newspaper articles and blogs.
- A link to your résumé.

If you are seeking a job in radio staff announcing, you will want to post:

- Some music intros.
- A brief newscast. Even if you are not applying for a news position, you want to demonstrate versatility.
- One or two commercials, one of which shows your acting ability.
- An ad-lib.

Job Leads and Sources of Leads

It is not unheard of for broadcast executives to respond to an unsolicited email, letter, or phone call, but more often than not available jobs are posted on the Web or someone in search of talent does his or her own searching.

You can scope out the market by doing your own searches for on-air jobs, using descriptors for the market where you want to work and/or the type of work you want to pursue. Also, you can mine opportunities in sites such as Indeed.com, journalismjobs.com, and TVjobs.com.

Some sites allow you to sign up to receive emails when positions matching your criteria are posted.

Don't forget LinkedIn.com. Often prospective employers will search out candidates through this site.

Networking

While online networking is important, don't underestimate the power of old-fashioned in-person contact.

Join as many professional organizations as you can and attend meetings and conferences.

If you have an ideal geographical target, you might consider a trip to that area, and can email or mail in advance, saying you are going to be in the region anyway.

Broadcast executives are more likely to agree to talk to you if you will be in the area anyway because they are very reluctant to invite anyone to travel a long distance to discuss a job that may not exist. Say that you want to discuss the station and the business in general, not a particular job.

Contacts

Every contact you make, every interview you arrange, is a factor in your favor. Do not look on "contacts" as a dirty word because in the business of broadcasting it is not.

Broadcasting is a business of contacts. Here are suggestions for developing your own set of contacts:

1. *Stay in touch with your college communications department and with the alumni association.*
2. *Keep in touch with alumni.* Write down the names and addresses of alums and keep track of their progress. College and university "old boy" networks can be extremely valuable.
3. *If you are turned down for a job, try to keep the person who turned you down as a contact.* Never, never burn your bridges with an executive who does not hire you. You may have been a close second choice, but if you express anger and outrage at not getting the job, you'll never be in contention again. Instead, contact the person who did not hire you and find out, in a nonconfrontational way, why you didn't get the job. Say that you are concerned with self-improvement and would like to know how to better yourself. Perhaps it was a simple matter of needing more experience, and the job could be yours next time.

THE BUSINESS END

Broadcasting is a business run by businesspeople. Some of these people may have been performers at one time, but they are not generally motivated by artistic goals. Quite properly, they are concerned with turning a profit. The fact that broadcasting is a business means that we must discuss pay and general working conditions.

Salaries

Salaries in the broadcast field, particularly for on-air performers, are generally far lower than most members of the general public might expect. This is particularly true in small markets, where even well-known local broadcasters may be making close to minimum wage.

At the entry level in broadcasting, pay is very low. Along with print journalism, broadcasting ranks among the lowest professions in salaries paid to beginners.

Until you have established a track record, there isn't really much to be done about the poor pay level. This situation holds generally true whether you're looking at television or radio. Expect to be offered as little as between $15,000 and $23,000 per year in most small- and medium-market stations if you're looking at news jobs.

Especially disheartening is the fact that many in the business report that salaries are actually going *down*, particularly in medium markets where populations are stable or decreasing and economies stagnant.

A beginner generally does not have a good chance of cracking the top 60 or so markets. That means, for a while at least, working in a smaller market and accepting a small salary. Your starting salary will reflect the size of the market, the health of the station, and the worth of your position. Every station manager has a good idea of the maximum value of a particular job. The morning drive announcer at a local radio station, for example, will never be paid more than the position generates in advertising revenue. The station owner and/or manager, obviously, will also have to deduct overhead and allow for a fair profit.

Therefore, the person controlling the purse strings will know that no morning announcer, no matter how good, is worth more than $400 a week for this particular position. The market reaches a point of diminishing returns.

The particular economic conditions in a market, such as the popularity of the station and the amount of competing signals from major stations, will determine the maximum value of that position.

Yes, major-market air professionals make a great deal of money, but that is a long trip down a difficult road. And even a moderate salary in a larger market can leave you devastatingly poor because the cost of living in a big city is so high. When considering jobs, check the cost of apartment rentals before committing yourself.

Contracts

You may be asked to sign a one- to three-year contract after being hired by a broadcast station. This is not likely for a beginner, however, because most small markets do not have contracts.

Contracts specify many different things but always put salary figures in black and white, often with built-in escalator clauses. Sometimes the salary is renegotiated yearly.

A contract entails an obligation on your part and on the station's part. It will state a specific period of time in which you agree to stay in the station's employ, but in *most* cases stations will not hold you strictly to this clause. You can typically escape a contract as long as you are not going to a directly competitive station within the market. If you want to move to a competitor before your contract has expired, however, you may have a fight on your hands.

Contracts also work for you, specifying some of your working conditions and hours. Most contracts say that you can be discharged only for "good cause." That vague term is not ironclad protection, but it is better than none at all.

CONCLUSION

Your study of broadcasting in college and your early work experiences do not lock you into an announcing career. If your career does not develop as you want, your broad education and communication skills will serve you well in any type of job.

Many interesting alternatives are related to announcing. The authors of this book, for example, have intertwined years of work as air talent with jobs in teaching, journalism, advertising, writing, public relations, civilian and military broadcast management, and acting.

Yes, it is a tough business. But do not be unnecessarily discouraged, because although many who study broadcast announcing do not make it, thousands DO! If you honestly believe you have the talent, motivation, and drive, *go for it.*

And if you want inspiration, think about the rewards reaped by Don Alhart, the man with the world's longest career as a television journalist.

A Final Note

Commit and Communicate:

Rochester, NY Anchor Don Alhart—Guinness World Record Holder for Longest Career as a Television Journalist—Offers Advice to Aspiring TV Anchors

Don Alhart, who turns 75 in May 2019 (Figure 16.3), isn't the type of veteran journalist who coasts toward a comfortable retirement while reliving the glories of the good old days. After, at the time

A Final Note *(continued)*

FIGURE 16.3 Don Alhart is the Guinness World Record holder for the longest career as a television journalist.

of this writing, almost 53 years on air in Rochester, NY, he still maintains a full schedule of two newscasts a day—having never taken a sick day in all those years—and is currently, according to co-workers, the newsroom's go-to guy for advice about the latest apps.[1]

His obsession with technology has roots in his childhood: He grew up helping out at his father's appliance store, and after school he would pursue such projects as wiring the house for his own makeshift radio station.

Technical versatility proved an asset when he began pursuing a career in broadcasting. Alhart worked in various capacities—engineer, camera operator, and film lab assistant—before landing a news job with WOKR-TV, Channel 13 in Rochester (now WHAM-TV), after graduating from Ithaca College.

Alhart, now the station's associate news director and principal anchor, a five-time winner of the Edward R. Murrow Award for excellence in television news, and a member of the New York State Broadcasters Association Hall of Fame, says that willingness to evolve with new techniques and technologies is one of the characteristics he observes in young co-workers who navigate to higher plateaus in their careers.

Among the career suggestions he offers to aspiring news anchors:

Adapt. "Yes, I use Twitter and Facebook," Alhart says. "But adapting to changes in the news business is more than just about technology. For example, I use a much more casual on-air style today, something I picked up from the younger people in the newsroom."[2]

A Final Note *(continued)*

Become part of the community and commit to it. "Find a reason to be where you are, get involved, and put down roots," Alhart advises, noting that once your heart is in the community, viewers will be able to sense your commitment and you, in return, will be able to grow in your relationship with the audience. Alhart, who has won many local-service awards and has been actively involved with the Rotary Club, a service organization, since the 1970s, says he applied for only one other job since starting his career at Channel 13. He auditioned for an anchor position at WJLA-TV in Washington, DC. He didn't get it. "I found out later that the reason they didn't hire me was that even though the interview had gone well, they could tell my heart wasn't really in it. My roots were here."

Put yourself in the place of the viewer. "I advise new reporters at the station to go to the local shopping mall and just listen to people. Find out what people are talking about, what their concerns are." You are the ears, the eyes, and the voice of your audience, he adds.

Tell creative stories. Alhart counsels young reporters to craft fresh and inventive ways to communicate the facts. "Build your stories," he says. "Make them move toward a strong conclusion, just as you would if you were giving a speech. Also, look for different angles: Instead of interviewing people at their offices, for example, go to their houses. And remember to help the story unfold by asking good follow-up questions. Yes, you want a list of a few questions to start with, but don't blindly stick to it. Pay attention and follow up on what's really interesting."

Be positive. Alhart, renowned for his equanimity, has in his office a framed historical photo of two uniformed men, sanitation workers, posing for the camera, beaming. He saw an article about the men in the local paper and paid five dollars to the paper for a 5-by-7 glossy. "The job of these two guys was primarily picking up dead animals off the street. But look at their expressions! I keep this as a reminder that if they can enjoy their jobs, you can too, no matter what kind of day you've had."

Don Alhart is recognized by Guinness World Records as having the longest career as a television broadcaster: 50 years and 179 days—a landmark he set on December 2, 2016. As of this writing (August, 2017) he continues to extend his run.

NOTES

1 Jeff DiVeronica, "Don Alhart: 50 Years on the Air," *Rochester Democrat and Chronicle*, August 2, 2017.
2 All Don Alhart quotes from personal interview, June 23, 2017.

Appendix
Foreign Pronunciations

No portion of a textbook can provide you with anything approaching a complete guide to foreign pronunciation. We have, however, condensed two valuable tools in this section; although they are not the answer to all pronunciation problems, they can lead you to the answers.

First, we provide some useful web resources.

Next, we include a simplified guide to the International Phonetic Alphabet (IPA). The IPA reproduces most sounds found in human speech.

Third, we provide an all-purpose chart outlining the fundamentals of foreign pronunciation. This chart, which we have developed over a period of years, will serve as a quick reference: find the letter, read across the chart to the appropriate language, and you'll see the most common pronunciation.

WEB RESOURCES

Note that in practical terms it is impossible for Americans to mimic sounds native to other languages from a printed reference; also, it is extremely difficult for Americans to make sounds found, say, in Arabic or Chinese without special training.

Web-based dictionaries often not only transcribe the pronunciation but provide an audio file as well; you can click and listen.

Among the resources with audio pronunciation samples that the authors use are:

https://www.dictionary.com/

https://www.merriam-webster.com

There are many sites that offer audiofiles of pronunciation of obscure placenames and the like. As a blanket statement let us note that many of these sites rely on user contributions and you will find conflicting entries. It is important to listen to several entries and use your best judgment.

Among the most reliable used by the authors are:

https://forvo.com/

https://pronounce.voanews.com/

YouTube is also useful. Use your judgment, but if you do some research you may find pronunciations there that would be difficult to find on other sites.

THE INTERNATIONAL PHONETIC ALPHABET

The IPA was developed by the International Phonetic Association, which is headquartered in London. Originally, the alphabet was created by a small group of teachers in France interested in transcription of language sounds, and in the 1880s a journal was published using only phonetic transcription.

Soon, the idea of an alphabet that would apply to all languages became a reality; it has proven useful to linguists, speech scientists, and others.

However, the IPA has never achieved the widespread acceptance its developers had hoped for. It is more complex than traditional phonetic transcription (such as wire-service transcription used in this book) and is still rather limited in its accuracy.

So while the IPA's use in the newsroom and air studio is limited, it can be handy for those looking to develop fluency in native or near-native pronunciation.

Also, if you use Wikipedia, you will find pronunciations given in IPA.

This IPA table provides all the English sounds. (If you want to pursue study of non-native speech sounds, we second the advice given above and suggest you contact a native speaker, or an infinitely more patient CDROM and foreign-language dictionary, which will tutor you on the special IPA characters used for native sounds.)

In the meantime, though, you may find IPA transcription handy for certain applications. We have attempted to remove one obstacle often encountered in learning the IPA: the fact that the sounds are presented out of any typical order and you must memorize the whole system before it makes sense. Instead, we present the IPA by listing the native American English sounds in the order we learn them: by alphabetized consonants, by alphabetized consonant pairs, by alphabetized vowels, and then by alphabetized vowel pairs.

You can now learn the rudiments of the IPA in less than an hour.

The IPA: Single Consonants

Common consonant sounds listed by the English letter usually associated with that sound. This table lists single consonants.

B	/b/	boy
C	/k/	cat
	/s/	cell
D	/d/	dog
F	/f/	fan
G	/g/	gone
H	/h/	hot
J	/dʒ/	judge
K	/k/	kill
L	/l/	low
M	/m/	man
N	/n/	night
P	/p/	pig
Qu (kw)	/kw/	queen
R	/r/	rain
S	/s/	stop
T	/t/	toy
V	/v/	vest
W	/w/	want
X (ks)	/ks/	box
Y	/j/	young
Z	/z/	zebra

The IPA: Paired Consonants

Paired consonants, listed by the English letters usually associated with their sounds.

CH	/tʃ/	chew
NG	/ŋ/	sing

SH	/ʃ/	<u>sh</u>oe
TH (unvoiced)	/θ/	<u>th</u>in
TH (voiced)	/ð/	<u>th</u>en
WH	/HW/	<u>wh</u>en
ZH (voiced SH)	/ʒ/	plea<u>s</u>ure

The IPA: Single Vowels

Common single vowel sounds. The long *a* in "ate" and the *i* in "ice" are actually combinations of two vowels sounds.

These sounds are listed by the English letter usually associated with that sound.

A (long)	/ei/	<u>a</u>te (diphthong)
A (long)	/e/	<u>a</u>ge
A (short)	/ae/	b<u>a</u>ck
E (long)	/i/	m<u>ee</u>t
E (short)	/ɛ/	b<u>e</u>d
I (long)	/ai/	<u>i</u>ce (diphthong)
I (short)	/I/	h<u>i</u>t
O (long)	/o/	<u>o</u>pen
O (short)	/a/	h<u>o</u>t
U (long)	/u/	t<u>u</u>be
U (short)	/ʌ/	<u>u</u>p

The IPA: Complex Vowels

Common complex vowels and diphthongs (vowel combinations) listed by the English letter(s) usually associated with the sound.

AW	/ɔ/	th<u>aw</u>
er	/ɚ/	winn<u>er</u>
ir	/ɛ˞/	th<u>ir</u>d
OO (long)	/u/	b<u>oo</u>m (same as t<u>u</u>be)
OO (short)	/ʊ/	l<u>oo</u>k
OW	/aʊ/	n<u>ow</u>
OY	/ɔi/	b<u>oy</u>
uh	/ə/	<u>a</u>bout, b<u>a</u>nan<u>a</u>
yu	/Iu/	acc<u>u</u>se (within word)
yu	/ju/	<u>u</u>se (at start of word)

Transcribing words with the IPA

Now, you can simply choose the sounds and place them together within slashes //—which signify IPA transcription.

For example:

effort = /ɛfɚt/

think = /θeIŋk/

come = /kʌm/

For multisyllable words, place an accent (′) before the stressed syllable:

above = /ə′bʌv/

A secondary stress is indicated by an accent (′) on the lower part of the letter before the syllable that receives secondary stress:

renewing = /ˌri′nuiŋ/

Foreign Language Pronunciation Chart

Vowels	FRENCH	GERMAN	ITALIAN	SPANISH
a	as in: "f<u>a</u>ther"	as in: "f<u>a</u>ther"	as in: "f<u>a</u>ther"	as in: "f<u>a</u>ther"
aa		"g<u>a</u>te"		
ae, ai	"ai," "b<u>e</u>t," or "g<u>a</u>te"	"ai," "r<u>i</u>de"		"ae," "ai," "r<u>i</u>de"
au	"s<u>o</u>"		"c<u>ow</u>"	"c<u>ow</u>"
e	"b<u>e</u>t" or "<u>u</u>p"	"g<u>a</u>te" or "b<u>e</u>t"	"g<u>a</u>te" or "b<u>e</u>t"	"g<u>a</u>te"
é	"g<u>a</u>te"		"g<u>a</u>te"	
ê	"b<u>e</u>t"			
è	"b<u>e</u>t"		"b<u>e</u>t"	
eau	"s<u>o</u>"			
ei	"b<u>e</u>t"	"r<u>i</u>de"		"g<u>a</u>te"
eu	"b<u>u</u>rn"	"s<u>oi</u>l"		
ey	"y<u>e</u>t"	"r<u>i</u>de"		
i	"gr<u>ee</u>t"	"gr<u>ee</u>t" or "k<u>i</u>ss"	"gr<u>ee</u>t" or "<u>y</u>" (before or after vowels)	"gr<u>ee</u>t"
ie		"gr<u>ee</u>t"		"y<u>ea</u>"
o	"sh<u>o</u>re" or "<u>u</u>p"	"s<u>o</u>" or "s<u>a</u>w"	"s<u>o</u>" or "s<u>a</u>w"	"s<u>o</u>"
ô	"s<u>o</u>"			
ö, oe		"t<u>u</u>rn," "s<u>a</u>y" (pursed lips)		
oi	"w<u>a</u>ft"		"b<u>oy</u>"	"b<u>oy</u>"
ou	"st<u>oo</u>l"			

Consonants*	FRENCH	GERMAN	ITALIAN	SPANISH
b		sounded as "p" when at the end of a word		
c	as "k" when final sound in word; "s" before <u>e</u>, <u>i</u>, <u>y</u>; "k" elsewhere	"kh" before <u>a</u>, <u>o</u>, <u>u</u>	"ch" before <u>e</u>, <u>i</u>, <u>y</u>; "k" before <u>a</u>, <u>o</u>, <u>u</u>	"s" before <u>e</u>, <u>i</u>, <u>y</u>; "k" otherwise
ch	"sh" "ck"	(aspirated)	"k"	
ck			"kk"	
d		"t" when at the end of a word		"th" within or at the end of a word
dt		"t"		
f	as in English	as in English	as in English	as in English
g	"zh" before <u>e</u>, <u>i</u>, <u>y</u>; elsewhere as in "get"	as in "get" when first sound in word; sometimes guttural "ch"	"j" before <u>e</u>, <u>i</u>, <u>y</u>; as in "get" before <u>a</u>, <u>o</u>, <u>u</u>	"h" before <u>e</u>, <u>i</u>, <u>y</u>; as in "get"
gh			as in "get" before <u>i</u>, similar to "bi<u>lli</u>ards"	
gl				
gn	"ny" as in "onion"		"ny" as in "onion"	
h	silent	as in English	silent	silent
j	"zh"	"y"	often as "i"	"h"
ll				"y"
m, n, ng	when preceded by vowel, in the same syllable, the vowel is nasalized			

Consonants*	FRENCH	GERMAN	ITALIAN	SPANISH
ñ				"y" added before following vowel sound
q	"k"			
qu	"k"	"kv"	"qw"	"k" before e̱, i̱
r	guttural rolled, or trilled	guttural or trilled		
s	as in "see"; "z" between vowels	"z" when beginning word or before vowel; as in "see"	as in "see"	
sc	"sk" before a̱, o̱, u̱; "s" before e̱, i̱		"sk" before a̱, o̱, u̱; "sh" before e̱, i̱	
sch		"sh"	"sk"	
sp		"shp" at beginning of a word		
st		"sht" at beginning of word	"t"	
t	as in English	as in English	as in English	as in English
th	"t"	"t"		
v		"f"		"b"
w	"v"	"v"	rare, like "v"	
x				"s" when preceded by consonant
z		"ts"	"ts" as in "cats" or "dz" as in "fin-d-s"	

*Pronounced very much as they are in English; exceptions are noted here.

SOME GENERAL PROBLEMS AND RECOMMENDATIONS INVOLVING FOREIGN PRONUNCIATION

PROBLEM: Assuming you know the convention to use, is the word or phrase (not a proper name or place name) pronounced with foreign inflection?

If so, how much?

RECOMMENDATION: Attempting to pronounce foreign words and phrases with the inflection used by a native speaker of that country can sound affected in many circumstances. For example, an announcer reading a commercial for a Mexican fast-food restaurant would appear affected if he or she trilled the *r*s in burrito, unless that announcer were adopting a character role. On the other side of the issue, American announcers do not have the flexibility to anglicize pronunciations as severely as the British, who pronounce Quixote as Kwiks'-oht. The American announcer must come up with compromises depending on the situation.

1. Most foreign pronunciations sound natural, unaffected, and acceptable when rules of foreign pronunciation are followed. However, the word is pronounced as an educated native English speaker would say it, not as a native would say the word. An American speaker, for example, knows that the *au* configuration in German is pronounced *ow*, and would use that pronunciation. The speaker would not, though, try to reproduce a German accent precisely. Likewise, the speaker following this rule would not trill *r*s in Spanish words and would not make the *n*s in French words too nasal.

2.   The most notable exception is announcing for classical music programs, for here the announcer is expected to be an expert. Typically, the classical music announcer should give full inflection to the words, using native pronunciation.

PROBLEM: What about proper names and place names?

RECOMMENDATION: Follow convention; use American pronunciations for names of well-known people or places according to these guidelines:

1.   The names of major cities and countries are spoken according to American convention (for example, Munich, not München). In most cases, an American-flavored pronunciation, rather than an imitation of native inflection, is best. The final *ch* in Munich, then, would be pronounced like an American *k*, not gutturalized, as in German.
2.   Proper names of newsmakers are usually pronounced without foreign inflection. However, it is always correct to pronounce a person's name the way he or she says it, whether that person is foreign or American. Many names in classical music are by custom pronounced with foreign pronunciation and full inflection.
3.   It is good form to pronounce names of people and places with foreign inflection if those people or places are not famous. A story about a small wine-producing town in France, for example, could be read with native French inflections given to the words.

It is difficult to decipher foreign pronunciations from tables of vowels and consonants. Moreover, a table is not always available, so it is worthwhile to memorize the general characteristics of the major languages. It is also worthwhile to listen to recordings of foreign speakers.

FRENCH

At the end of a French word, the letter *e*, without an accent, is not pronounced (étoile). This is also the case for final *es* (étoiles) and for the *ent* ending on verbs (ils parlent).

Most final consonants are not pronounced. A phonetic approximation of "Parlez-vous français?" ("Do you speak French?"), for example, is "Pahr-lay voo frahn-say?" Most of the consonants are pronounced like English consonants. Some vowels before *n* and *m* are nasalized (enfant, sont, fin, enchanter, un americain).

In short, a vowel or diphthong is nasalized when it is followed by *n* or *m* in the same syllable; en/fant, em/ployer, am/bu/lance.

J is pronounced *zh*, like the sound in beige. Accents usually fall on the last syllable: bataille, terminée. Otherwise syllables receive about equal stress: in-té-res-sant, Mon-a-co.

GERMAN

There are few if any silent letters in German. Some sounds are not approximated in English, such as the ö (the mark above the letter is an umlaut). This vowel can be either short or long, in the same sense that the English a is long in "lake" but short in "bat." The long ö can be approximated by rounding the lips as though you were going to say "oh" but saying "ay" as in "say" instead. To shorten the vowel, don't say "ay" as in "say" but rather "eh" as in "bed." Two main indicators of a long vowel are that it is before only one consonant (much the same as in English) or that it is at the end of a word.

Other major facets of German vowel pronunciation are that *au* is pronounced *ow*; *eu* is pronounced *oy*; *ei* is pronounced like the word "eye"; and *ie* is pronounced *ee*.

Common consonant pronunciations: *d* is pronounced as *t* when occurring at the end of a word. Another common word ending substitution is *p* for *b*. The letter *j* is pronounced as a *y*; *s* is pronounced as *z*; *w* is pronounced as *f*.

Native German speakers will pronounce a beginning *s* as *sh* when words start with an *st* or *sp* cluster; *ch* is pronounced as *kh*, a guttural *k*.

"Sprechen Sie Deutsch?" ("Do you speak German?") would be approximated as "Shprek´h-en zee Doytch?"

Accents in German are most commonly on the first syllable. It is also helpful to know that all nouns are capitalized in written German.

SPANISH

Spanish is very regular in its pronunciations, and you can figure out many Spanish words and names by remembering that *i* is pronounced *ee*, and *e* is pronounced *ay*. Typically, *a* is pronounced *ah* as in "father" rather than *a* as in "apple" (a convention that applies to many languages).

For consonants, remember that *ll* is pronounced as a *y*.

Caballero ("gentleman") is pronounced cahb-ah-yay´-row.

In Spanish, the *r* is trilled, but in most cases you will not try to approximate this in English pronunciation. *J* is pronounced like an English *h*. Accents usually fall on the last or next-to-last syllable; occasionally accent marks tell you what syllable to stress.

ITALIAN

Italian words are pronounced much as they are spelled. Unlike English, double consonants are pronounced as in cappello (hat) and carro (cart) in contrast to capello (hair) and caro (dear).

Be aware that Italian *ci* and *ce* take on a *ch* sound, as in cibo (food) and cena (supper).

Also, as often in English, Italian *gi* and *ge* take on a *j* sound (Giovanni, gelato). The letter *h* is silent and is mainly used to change *ci*, *ce*, *gi*, *ge* sequences from *ch* and *j* sounds to *k* and *g* sounds (Cecchetti, Ghia).

The letter combinations *gn* and *gl* are pronounced something like the first *n* in onion (ogni, meaning "every") and the *ll* in billiards (figlio, meaning "son").

Keep in mind that *i* is pronounced *ee* but that *e* can be *ay* (meno) or *e* (Elena) and that *o* can be *oh* (sole) or *aw* as in English law (forte).

The letters *i* and *u* before and after another vowel (with the exception of the *ci*, *ce*, *gi*, *ge* sequences) are generally pronounced *y*, as in yes (chiamo), and *w*, as in wet (buono).

Next-to-last syllables frequently receive stress in Italian words, but there are many words with stress on other syllables.

RUSSIAN

Russian language copy written in the Cyrillic alphabet is transliterated for English speakers. This means that in broadcasting, the words have been converted to English equivalents, although the pronunciations still are somewhat irregular. The *ev* in Gorbachev, for example, is usually pronounced *off* by American speakers who transliterate.

Index